Ritual Poetry and the Politics of Death
in Early Japan

GARY L. EBERSOLE

Ritual Poetry and the Politics of Death in Early Japan

PRINCETON UNIVERSITY PRESS
PRINCETON, NEW JERSEY

Copyright © 1989 by Princeton University Press

Published by Princeton University Press, 41 William Street, Princeton, New Jersey 08540

In the United Kingdom: Princeton University Press, Oxford

Library of Congress Cataloging-in-Publication Data

Ebersole, Gary L., 1950–

Ritual poetry, and the politics of death in early Japan / by Gary L. Ebersole.

p.   cm.

Bibliography: p.

Includes index.

ISBN 0–691–07338–4

ISBN 0–691–01929–0 (pbk.)

1. Death—Political aspects—Japan. 2. Japan—Court and courtiers. 3. Funeral rites and
ceremonies—Japan. 4. Japan—Politics and government—To 794. 5. Japanese poetry—To 794—
History and criticism. 6. Mythology, Japanese. I. Title.

DS827.D4E24 1989 393'.0952—dc19

88–29325 CIP

First Princeton Paperback printing, 1992

Publication of this book has been aided by the Japan Foundation

This book has been composed in Linotron Perpetua

Princeton University Press books are printed on acid-free paper,
and meet the guidelines for permanence and durability of the
Committee on Production Guidelines for Book Longevity of the
Council on Library Resources

Printed in the United States of America

8   7   6   5   4   3   2

to Noriko

Contents

Acknowledgments

This study would never have been possible without the training and support of my teachers—Ralph Slotten, Joseph M. Kitagawa, and Frank Reynolds. Richard Pilgrim and Richard Gardner read very rough drafts of early chapters and provided important critiques and encouragement. Some acute comments by Harry Harootunian in a later stage were important in framing part of my argument. Cathie Brettschneider has followed this study from its earliest stages through final production, adding the skill of a professional editor. Finally, my colleagues in The Center for Comparative Studies in the Humanities have provided a rare intellectual and professional environment. Their enthusiasm and intellectual diversity have been a source of constant stimulus in my work.

The completion of this study was facilitated by my having been awarded several academic quarters solely for the pursuit of research and writing. For this I am thankful to the Dean of the College of Humanities, G. Micheal Riley, and my department Chairs. I have also benefited from several small research grants from the College and The Graduate School of the Ohio State University, as well as an NEH visit-to-collection grant. I want to express my gratitude for this assistance. The tables and charts were prepared by Tad Lamb of the College of Humanities Computing Center.

The following publishers kindly gave permission to quote from the standard English translations of the *Kojiki*, *Nihonshoki*, and *Man'yōshū*: University of Tokyo Press for Donald L. Philippi, trans., *Kojiki* (Tokyo, 1968); Charles E. Tuttle Co. for W. G. Aston, trans., *Nihongi: Chronicles of Japan from the Earliest Times to A.D. 697*, 2 vols. in one (Rutland, Vt., and Tokyo, 1972); and Princeton University Press for Ian Hideo Levy, *The Ten Thousand Leaves*, vol. 1 (Princeton, 1981).

Finally, two persons deserve special mention. Marilyn Robinson Waldman has been the ideal colleague for the past six years. With that rare combination of an extraordinary intellect of great breadth and acuteness and a talented administrator of vision, she is also a true friend whom I look forward to working with for many years to come.

Noriko Yamazaki Ebersole has been my biggest supporter for the last seventeen years. This book is dedicated to her in love.

Notes on Transliteration and Abbreviations

The primary texts used in this study survive in a number of different manuscript versions, and one must decide which of the available modern annotated texts to use. Throughout this work I have relied upon the following volumes from the *Nihon koten bungaku taikei* (hereafter NKBT), published by Iwanami Shoten, one of the most popular and readily available collections:

Kurano Kenji and Takeda Yūkichi, eds. *Kojiki/Norito* (NKBT 1). Tokyo: Iwanami Shoten, 1958.

Takagi Ichinosuke, Gomi Tomohide, and Ōno Susumu, eds. *Man'yōshū* (NKBT 4–7). Tokyo: Iwanami Shoten, 1957–1965.

Sakamoto Tarō, Ienaga Saburō, Inoue Mitsusada, and Ōno Susumu, eds. *Nihonshoki* (NKBT 67–68). Tokyo: Iwanami Shoten, 1967, 1965.

The NKBT readings (*yomikudashi*) have been followed in the transliteration of Chinese characters and names. There is something of a problem with consistency in these matters among the most popular English translations of these texts—Donald Philippi, trans., *Kojiki* (Tokyo: University of Tokyo Press, 1968); Donald Philippi, trans., *This Wine of Peace, This Wine of Laughter* (New York: Mushina Books, Grossman Publishers, 1968), a translation of the verses in the *Kojiki* and the *Nihonshoki*; W. G. Aston, trans., *Nihongi: Chronicles of Japan from the Earliest Times to A.D. 697*, 2 vols. in one (Rutland, Vt., and Tokyo: Charles E. Tuttle Co., 1972); and Ian Hideo Levy, trans., *The Ten Thousand Leaves*, vol. 1 (Princeton: Princeton University Press, 1981), a translation of Books 1–5 of the *Man'yōshū*. I have used these translations whenever possible for the reader's convenience, but for the sake of consistency and clarity I have silently altered those names and other terms that are of importance when not doing so might have caused the reader some confusion. In every case I have provided the relevant pages in the NKBT and the English translations. When I have altered a translation in any substantial way, this fact is duly indicated in the notes. Unattributed translations are my own. In such cases I have again cited the relevant pages in the NKBT as well as the source of other relevant translations.

In citing poems from the *Man'yōshū*, I have adopted the following form: MYS 1: 5–6 for *Man'yōshū*, vol. (*maki*) 1, verses 5–6. Finally, I have reluctantly adopted a simple form of giving dates, using the style 2/15/646 to indicate the fifteenth day of the second lunar month of the second year of the reign of the Emperor Kōtoku. The calendrical system used in the *Nihonshoki* and the *Man'yōshū* is too cumbersome for the purposes of this study. Although in some ways it might have been preferable to follow the original entries faithfully, this format would frequently have detracted from the point being made. The reader should understand, though, that the lunar months given do not coincide with the months of the Western calendar. For an introduction to the Japanese calendrical system and related matters, please consult Earl Miner, Hiroko Odagiri, and Robert E. Morrell, *The Princeton Companion to Classical Japanese Literature* (Princeton: Princeton University Press, 1985), pp. 399–414.

In quotations from the primary texts, I have used parentheses to indicate editorial notes found in the Japanese manuscript and square brackets to indicate explanatory material that I have added. In the text I have used "Court" with a capital "C" to indicate the reigning sovereign and his or her faction; "court" with a small "c" refers to all the members of the hierarchical society of the capital.

Ritual Poetry and the Politics of Death
in Early Japan

Mythistory, Ritual, and Poetry in Early Japan

> [586] Summer, 5th month. The Imperial Prince Anahobe tried to force his way into the Palace of temporary interment in order to ravish the Empress Consort Kashikiya-hime.
>
> *Nihonshoki*

The period 645–710 C.E. in Japan is often referred to as the Taika Era, "the Era of Great Change," a name borrowed from the first regnal period (645–650) of the Emperor Kōtoku (r. 645–654). The seventh and early eighth centuries indeed saw tremendous changes in Japan. Among others, the presence of Buddhism increased significantly, the nation moved rapidly into a stage of secondary orality with the rise of literacy among the elite as the Chinese script was adopted and adapted, and a Chinese-style imperial system and bureaucracy were introduced. In 646 the famous four-article *Kaishin no chō* or Reform Edict was promulgated and the doctrine of absolute sovereignty proclaimed. A wide array of imperial edicts were issued and other steps taken in an effort to consolidate power in the hands of the imperial family and, it was hoped, to forestall debilitating succession disputes that had long plagued the country. A crucial part of the concerted effort of the Court to consolidate its power was the creation and dissemination of a "mythistory," a religio-political ideology that sought to legitimate the new order, most especially the position and power of the imperial family and other major clans.

This mythistory asserted that the imperial family was descended directly from Amaterasu, the Sun Goddess; that its members were living *kami*; and that the imperial rule had been unbroken from the beginning of time. Through the rhetorical strategy of proclaiming the timeless nature of the socio-political order, this mythistory sought to obscure its recent origins; by linking the this-worldly order to the sacred order of the High Heavens, it sought a higher legitimation. Yet this "timeless order" was repeatedly subjected to severe challenges occasioned by the vicissitudes of history, the obtrusive biological "fact" of death, and frequent succession disputes. This situation was, of course, not unique to Japan. As Peter Berger and Thomas Luckmann have noted in their study of the dynamic nature of the process of the social construction and maintenance of a cultural world of meaning or a symbolic universe:

the symbolic universe [of a given society] provides a comprehensive integration of *all* discrete institutional processes. The entire society now makes sense. Particular institutions and roles are legitimated by locating them in a comprehensively meaningful world. For example, the

3

political order is legitimated by reference to a cosmic order of power and justice, and political roles are legitimated as representations of these cosmic principles. The institution of divine kingship in archaic civilizations is an excellent illustration of the manner in which this kind of ultimate legitimation operates. It is important, however, to understand that the institutional order . . . is continually threatened by the presence of realities that are meaningless in *its* terms. The legitimation of the institutional order is also faced with the ongoing necessity of keeping chaos at bay. *All* social reality is precarious. *All* societies are constructions in the face of chaos. The constant possibility of anomic terror is actualized whenever the legitimations that obscure the precariousness are threatened or collapse. The dread that accompanies the death of a king, especially if it occurs with sudden violence, expresses this terror.[1]

Death is always a central element of a culture's understanding of the world and humankind's place in it. Each death inevitably alters the social relations that obtain among the living, but this social disjunction takes on heightened importance when death removes an influential political figure from the world. In a hierarchical court society, such as that in early Japan, the death of a high-ranking member affects the relative status of large numbers of contiguous others within the web of relations and interdependencies that constitute that society. The death of the sovereign, for instance, generates a major redistribution of power, position, and prestige within the court. This redistribution is not easily or "naturally" achieved, however, since most of the members of the court are in one way or another in competition with each other as they jockey for position. This social process of the redistribution of power, position, and prestige will be referred to below as "the politics of death."

The politics of death finds historical expression in different forms in different cultures, societies, and ages. The choice of this topic as a central focus on early Japan is not arbitrary; it will enable us to disclose important aspects of the symbolic center of the early Japanese world of meaning that might otherwise remain obscure. In a recent comparative study of mortuary rituals, Richard Huntington and Peter Metcalf have rightly noted that

The study of death rituals is a positive endeavor. In all societies, regardless of whether their customs call for festive or restrained behavior, the issue of death throws into relief the most important cultural values by which people live their lives and evaluate their experiences. Life becomes transparent against the background of death, and fundamental social and cultural issues are revealed. . . . In centralized kingdoms everywhere—Africa, Europe, Asia—events surrounding the death of the king reveal most strikingly the nature of each polity and the structure of its political competition.[2]

The perspicacity of this statement will become evident in the course of this work. Yet, somewhat surprisingly perhaps, there has been no serious or sustained study of the death rituals of early Japan in any Western language.[3] Among the reform edicts of 646 one finds a number of edicts that sought to regulate funeral practices down to the minutest details of coffin construction, the relative sizes and elevations of tombs for persons of different ranks, the respective offerings for each rank, and so on. The implication that the regulation of death rituals was considered an integral part of the Court's sweeping program to "reform" the government and to consolidate its power and authority is unmistakable.[4] Included among the prohibitions was the following:

When ordinary people die, let them be buried in the ground, and let the hangings be of coarse cloth. Let the interment not be delayed for a single day.

The construction of palaces of temporary interment is prohibited in every case, from Princes down to common people [*ōyoso ōkimi yori shimotsukata, ōmitara ni itaru made ni, mogariya tsukuru koto izare*].[5]

This and other passages in the edict refer to the practice of double burial in early Japan. Although study of this practice has remained outside the ken of most Western scholars, together with the associated ritual and symbolic complex surrounding the period of temporary interment, it is a key to unlocking the world of meaning of the early Japanese court. It is impossible, for instance, to appreciate properly the political machinations in the court following the death of a sovereign without taking the early Japanese understanding of death into full account or recognizing the importance of the death rituals as a venue for court members to position themselves in the succession process. Only by recovering the larger symbolic world of meaning that informed the politics of death will we be able to make sense of a series of otherwise enigmatic details in myths, or in entries like that cited at the head of this chapter in the *Nihonshoki*, the earliest extant imperial chronicle. There one finds a report of seemingly bizarre or irrational behavior by an imperial prince, Anahobe. Shortly after the death of the Emperor Bidatsu, he is said to have attempted to break into the temporary enshrinement palace housing the sovereign's corpse in order to possess sexually the widowed empress secluded therein. In the following pages I will demonstrate that such behavior reported to have occurred in the court during the period of the temporary interment of a sovereign was in fact perfectly rational and meaningful within the operative symbol system. We will find, for instance, that Anahobe was a historical agent whose relative position within the socio-political matrix of the court led him to attempt to manipulate a culturally available ritual complex and to act in a symbolically charged manner in an effort to appropriate the imperial charisma unto himself.

The study of a ritual complex such as that surrounding the practice of double burial requires more than the delineation of a timeless symbolic structure or mythic archetype and a simple description of its processional unfolding. What is essential, insofar as it is possible, is to understand the socio-political status and the relative positions of historical (or narrative) actors within the court society and the constraints their positions would have placed on their actions and public expressions during the ritual period of temporary interment. As Pierre Bourdieu has written:

Understanding ritual practice is not a question of decoding the internal logic of a symbolism but of restoring its practical necessity by relating it to the real conditions of its genesis, that is, to the conditions in which its functions, and the means it uses to attain them, are defined. It means, for example, reconstituting—by an operation of logical reconstruction which has nothing to do with an act of empathic projection—the significance and functions that agents in a determinate social formation can (and must) confer on a determinate practice or experience, given the practical taxonomies which organize their perception.[6]

Many earlier studies of myth and ritual, including those by historians of religions and symbolic anthropologists such as Victor Turner and Clifford Geertz, have contributed to our understanding of the symbolic complexes informing a wide variety of myths and rites. Mircea Eliade, for instance, sought in his many works to disclose the specifically religious or existential meaning of the symbolism. Without impugning the value of such studies, it must be said that they sometimes seem to suggest that myth and ritual exercise an intrinsic power over human beings while they ignore the conditions of the production of specific myths and rituals. The "deep meaning" and efficacy of myths and rituals are presented as almost timeless and inherent in the symbolic complexes themselves. Moreover, the claim is often made that even if the spiritual meaning is no longer recognized at a conscious level, it nevertheless operates at a subconscious level or is preserved as esoteric knowledge by specialists of the sacred.

In this work, however, the focus will be on the public rituals of the imperial court, including the death rituals, whose meaning and efficacy came from a broadly shared symbolic universe. This universe, though, was not simply "a given" with a unitary meaning for everyone; rather, it was a cultural resource that could be exploited by different individuals and groups to different ends for their own immediate purposes. This study, then, is concerned not so much with the universal matter of death as with the specific ways in which the early Japanese dealt with death in the court. Every effort will be made to disclose the *history* of specific myths and rituals, that is, the conditions of their genesis, performance, reception, and textualization.

Myth and ritual are two forms of symbolic expression that mediate and are mediated by other cultural discourses—genealogical, legal, economic, literary, and so forth. They are not, as we will see, timeless and static structures but dynamic agents in the ongoing process of the creation and maintenance of a symbolic world of meaning. Rather than being essentially conservative forces of social cohesion, as many students have held, they are cultural resources, which can be appropriated (adopted and adapted) and used for specific individual and/or factional purposes.[7] The study of myth and ritual must capture the complex dialectical nature of their cultural-historical expression and reception and engage the modalities of change.[8] Myth and ritual can indeed be used to maintain or legitimate a social order, but they can also be used to challenge and contest it.

The practice of double burial in early Japan and the associated myth and ritual complex will be reconstructed in the following chapters. This reconstruction, however, is a "reading" of these practices rather than an "authentic" reconstruction. This reading is dictated by the fact that virtually our only access to the myths and rituals of early Japan is through texts. Systematic information on the double burial practices and the politics of death must be gathered in scattered sources, most especially in the *Kojiki* (712), the *Nihonshoki* (720), and the *Man'yōshū* (late eighth century). Consequently, the site of the double burial practices is found in the scene of writing itself.

The status of these texts as historical documents needs to be addressed at the start. These three texts loom large as literary sources for the study of almost any topic concerning early Japan, including the practice of double burial. There are others, of course, most notably the *fudoki* or provincial records,[9] the *norito* or Shinto prayers and ritual invocations,[10] and the *Engi-shiki*, a Heian period ritual text,[11] but they are later sources. The *Kojiki* represents the oldest extant literary work in Japan. Although it is generally thought of as a mythological text, it presents itself as a historical chronicle. The *Nihonshoki*, on the other hand, is usually referred to as a historical chronicle structured along the lines of Chinese dynastic histories, although the "*Kami no yo*" or "Age of the Gods" section consists of myths. Finally, the *Man'yōshū*, an anthology of Japanese poetry, is often cited as the earliest extant work of Japanese literature.

The preface to the *Kojiki* is our best source of information on the genesis of this text and the intention behind its production. It begins by briefly rehearsing the cosmogonic myth and the divine descent of the imperial line down to the Emperor Temmu (r. 673–686). Then, after recalling the Jinshin War in which Temmu gained power, the work's editor, the Asomi Ō no Yasumaro, continues in praise of this emperor:

his wisdom was vast as the sea, searching out antiquity; his mind was bright as a mirror, clearly beholding former ages.

Whereupon, the Emperor said:

"I hear that the *Teiki* and *Honji* handed down by the various houses have come to differ from the truth and that many falsehoods have been added to them.

"If these errors are not remedied at this time, their meaning will be lost before many years have passed.

"This is the framework of the state, the great foundation of the imperial influence.

"Therefore, recording the *Teiki* and examining the *Kuji*, discarding the mistaken and establishing the true, I desire to hand them on to later generations."

At that time there was a court attendant [*toneri*] whose surname was Hieda and his given name Are. He was twenty-eight years old.

He possessed such great native intelligence that he could repeat orally whatever met his eye, and whatever struck his ears was indelibly impressed in his heart.

Then an imperial command was given to Are to learn the *Sumeramikoto no hitsugi* and the *Saki no yo no furugoto*.

However, the times went on and the reign changed before this project was accomplished.[12]

It is clear that the *toneri* Hieda no Are was an accomplished oral reciter, yet it is a matter of great dispute in Japanese scholarship as to whether the *Kojiki* was recited completely from oral memory or whether Hieda no Are memorized written texts and then recited it.[13] Whatever the case, the preface indicates that oral recitation still retained a high degree of prestige in the late seventh century, for although written histories and genealogies existed, oral recitation and the *kataribe*'s (reciter's) memory were considered more authoritative than written texts. Although literacy was not unknown in the court, it was still limited and a living oral tradition continued to be prominent. Consequently, many of the poems (*uta*) and narrative tales preserved in these written texts must be understood as having originally been oral performative pieces, either sung or recited. Such poetry and narrative were publicly performed, giving them a collective status that written texts did not have. Oral performance of myths, clan genealogies, popular narratives and legends, poems of praise, and eulogies were expressions of the all-encompassing ritual nature of the court. The oral performative contexts of many pieces preserved in the three texts can be imaginatively restored and the pieces can then be studied in the same way anthropologists and historians of religions study other forms of symbolic activity.

As the preface to the *Kojiki* indicates, the imperial order to record the *Kojiki* was an effort to "rewrite" history. This project was presented by the emperor as a necessary corrective designed to expunge errors and "falsehoods" in other existent clan histories, oral and written. These "falsehoods" probably refer to histories and genealogies that differed from the imperial family's version of Japanese history. As part of its rhetorical strategy, the *Kojiki* presents itself as the only true and authentic history, which it claims is "the framework of the state" and "the great foundation of the imperial influence." Scholars in various fields have long recognized that the control of the past, whether in terms of the sacred myths and rites, of clan genealogies, or of the ability to write history, is an expression of power and one that functions to consolidate such power. "Who controls the present controls the past. Who controls the past controls the future," reads the motto of George Orwell's

1984. This political dictum would seem to have been understood by the Emperor Temmu in the seventh century.

The *Kojiki* was not committed to its final written form during Temmu's lifetime, and indeed it was not picked up again until 711 in the reign of the Empress Gemmei, Temmu's niece and daughter-in-law. Thus, it represents an eighth-century version of this mythistory. It is not a timeless sacred narrative but a factional account of the past, which was no doubt contested for some time.

The textual history of the *Nihonshoki* remains a source of scholarly debate. It may have resulted from an imperial order issued in 714, two years after the *Kojiki* was finished, by the Empress Gemmei (r. 707–715) calling for a national history to be compiled that would carry the chronicle down to (then) modern times. The *Nihonshoki* as we know it was delivered to the Empress Genshō in 720. Its main compiler seems to have been Prince Toneri (676–735), the fifth son of the Emperor Temmu. The two empresses here and Prince Toneri are all directly related to the Tenji–Temmu–Jitō branch of the imperial family. Like the *Kojiki*, the *Nihonshoki* begins by recounting the myth of the creation of the world, but it extends its coverage down to the time of the abdication of the Empress Jitō, Temmu's widow, in 697. In the latter section dealing with "human" sovereigns, the entries are arranged by imperial reign and by month, day, and year following Chinese practice. This text is the single best source of information on the court in this period of history, although the early sections are less reliable as "hard" history than the chapters on more recent sovereigns. The *Nihonshoki*, too, is a product of the eighth-century Court's historiographic project and in many ways is a factional mythistory that seeks to legitimate the power, position, and prestige of the imperial family.

The *Man'yōshū* is more difficult to characterize in a few lines, and its textual history is equally obscure on many points. It consists of twenty books or *maki* (literally "scrolls") containing 4,516 verses (the number may differ slightly depending on how variants are counted). The earliest extant manuscript, the basis of the *Nihon koten bungaku taikei* (NKBT) annotated version used in this study, dates only from the thirteenth century. The first two books, and possibly the rest as well in a more general sense, were compiled under imperial command utilizing a number of different sources, including early poetry collections such as "The Kakinomoto Hitomaro Collection" and Yamanoue Okura's (660–c.733) "Forest of Classified Verse" (*Ruijū karin*). More than one committee seems to have been involved in the process of editing and compiling, whereas the guiding hand of Ōtomo Yakamochi (d. 785) is evident in the later books.[14]

No single principle of classification of the poems characterizes the *Man'yōshū* as a whole, although three classificatory terms—*sōmon*, *banka*, and *zōka*—are prominent. *Sōmon* or *sōmonka* may be translated as "dialogue poems" or "relationship poems."[15]

Such verses always concern the relationship of two persons and are frequently love poems, although there are also verses on children, parents, friends, and so on. Frequently there are poems in response to earlier poems, prompting the designation "dialogue poems." *Banka* are funeral laments, and the term seems originally to have meant "coffin-pulling songs." Finally, *zōka*, literally "miscellaneous verses," is a catch-all classification used for the majority of verses included in the anthology.

No single principle of editing or compilation characterizes the *Man'yōshū* as a whole, either.[16] The poems in the first two books, collectively known as the *Shoki-Man'yōshū*, however, are arranged chronologically by imperial reign and then within each reign. This fact is crucial for our purposes in using the *Man'yōshū* to inquire into the politics of death and the eighth-century Court's historiographic project. Prose headnotes provide the purported generative context of the poems and "authorship." ("Authorship" must be put in quotation marks since some of the verses were originally oral pieces, and the term is inappropriate if used in its modern and graphic sense.)

The great majority of the verses in the first two books are from the reigns of the Emperor Tenji (r. [662]–671), the Emperor Temmu (r. [673]–686), and the Empress Jitō (r. [686]–697). This span seems to indicate that the original intention behind the anthology was to have it serve as a historical record in its own right. The Temmu and Jitō chapters of the *Nihonshoki* are the only ones that do not contain any poems. This fact has led many Japanese scholars to suggest that the poems in the first two books of the *Man'yōshū* are those that might have been included in the imperial chronicle. The prose headnotes and editorial endnotes attached to many poems reflect a heightened concern to document the historical "facts" related to any given poem. One of the most striking elements of this historical consciousness is its graphic nature; that is, the editors rely on *written* texts whenever possible, including the *Kojiki* and the *Nihonshoki*, to confirm purported authorship, performative locus, and dating. The memory of oral reciters is never appealed to as a source of authority concerning a claim. If these notes are from the eighth century, they indicate the extent to which literacy prevailed in the court in the years since the *Kojiki* had been committed to writing.

The *Kojiki*, the *Nihonshoki*, and the *Man'yōshū* are all part of the Court's larger historiographic project. This assertion is based on the following related considerations. The *Kojiki* (712) and the *Nihonshoki* (720) were produced within a decade of each other, whereas the *Man'yōshū* dates from a generation or two later. Their temporal proximity would in itself suggest that it might be useful to read them as a set rather than as three isolated texts; but there are other compelling reasons for doing so. A central intention informing the production of each of these texts was to order and structure specific past occurrences in such a manner that the existent socio-political order was identified with a higher sacred order. Thus, they were part of the concerted effort to create and promulgate a mythistory that would legitimate the relative distribution of power, position, and prestige in early Japan.

In addition to their temporal proximity, the texts were produced within the imperial court. Consequently, they share the same "horizon of expectation." In addition to a shared intertextuality, they assume the same audience and, thus, were given narrative form (or in the case of the *Man'yōshū*, anthologized) based upon an understanding of audience expectations. When shared with an audience, orally or in writing, narratives help to construct a common world as they cognitively and emotionally involve the audience with the author, singer, reciter, or editor in the act of reception. This social dimension of narrative generally has been ignored by both literary critics and historians of religions who have studied the texts of early Japan. Yet anyone making a serious historical inquiry must study both the generative occasions and conditions of production of the literary artifacts *and* their affective and effective dimensions in history (i.e., original intention and reception, later recontextualization and reception).

No single text presents the entire worldview of a culture or reveals the totality of the symbolic universe at the time of the text's genesis. Indeed, texts often obscure certain aspects even as they reveal others. Yet, those elements that have been obscured or repressed often reveal through their absence important information concerning the intention(s) informing the texts and the conditions of their production. For this reason I adopt a reading strategy employing each of the three texts in turn to understand the others in a ceaseless dialectic—a strategy that I call "triangulation." If Huntington and Metcalf are correct, by focusing on the double burial practices of the imperial court, and specifically the period of temporary interment, we should be able to "reveal most strikingly the nature of [the early Japanese] polity and the structure of its political competition."

Ian Levy has argued that "The history of Japanese poetry offers us an opportunity, unusual in world literature, to discern, from extant texts, the process by which a lyric voice is born from an archaic ritual verbal art."[17] He assumes, along with many others, that prior to the later half of the seventh century, Japan was a "primitive" or archaic culture with timeless myths that were unquestioningly accepted by all. This assumption is, however, untenable. Far from being timeless, the myths of the *Kojiki* and the *Nihonshoki* represent the eighth-century Court's recension of certain available paradigmatic narratives that are made to serve as interpretive frames in its historiographic project. The myths are textually employed to legitimate certain clan genealogies, hereditary roles, titles, land holdings, complex economic arrangements, and rituals. It is only because the *Kojiki*, the *Nihonshoki*, and the *Man'yōshū* represent the earliest *written* texts that over the centuries they have come to assume the importance they have in Japanese cultural history. Yet, it must be recognized that this importance and valuation are retrospectively ascribed. As Byron Earhart has noted, the *Kojiki* and the *Nihonshoki* were never that popular or widely circulated in early Japan.[18] To say this is not to minimize the centrality of these texts to any study of early Japan, but rather to underscore the point that they represent a historically conditioned factional mythistory, not a universally recognized one.

Nevertheless, these three texts provide an excellent opportunity to discern some of the implications of the increasing literacy of the imperial court and the ways in which the Court retrospectively gave narrative form to the past in order to legitimate its present and to guarantee its future. The *Kojiki*, the *Nihonshoki*, and the *Man'yōshū*—and the constituent narratives that make up these texts—were not merely a passive mirror of the culture in which they were produced; they were dynamic cultural agents in its creation. Robert Weimann has argued that all works of literature have two basic functions: "on the one hand, the work of art [is] a product of its time, a mirror of its age, a historical reflection of the society to which both the author and the original audience belonged. On the other hand . . . the work of art is not merely a product, but a 'producer' of its age; not merely a mirror of the past, but a lamp to the future."[19] In considering these three texts in the following pages as narrative structures that sought to order events according to a meaningful sequential pattern, that is, as products of historiographic activity, I will borrow a leaf from Hayden White in his well-known work, *Metahistory*, where he wrote: "I will consider the historical work as what it most manifestly is—that is to say, a verbal structure in the form of a narrative prose discourse that purports to be a model, or icon, of past structures and processes in the interest of *explaining what they were by representing* them."[20]

Insofar as a narrative, in whatever form, presents itself as relating actual events in the past, it will be considered as a product and producer of historiographic activity. Only by accepting the texts on their own terms and as they present themselves to the reader can one gain any understanding of the strategies and intentions of the creators of these texts. The only difference in the use of the texts below from that proposed by White is that insofar as the early Japanese did not privilege prose as the preferred vehicle for "historical" discourse, neither will we. Thus, *uta monogatari* or poetic and prose tales found in the texts will be considered as the products of historiographic activity, as will myths, legends, and so on.

In the study of historiography, the texts themselves are the primary objects precisely because one wants to know how the author(s) or editor(s) gave significant narrative form to certain happenings, real or purported, transforming them into "events" that were held to be important. Each of the three texts is "situated at the confluence of documentary evidence and ideological prescription."[21] They all simultaneously provide information about the culture at the time of their genesis and represent a retrospective ordering and narrative framing of happenings for the purposes of legitimating the socio-political order. The status of the *Man'yōshū* in this regard has been succinctly captured by Yoshinaga Noboru in the title of his study, *Man'yō—bungaku to rekishi no aida* (*The* Man'yōshū—*Between Literature and History*), although one must understand this history to be a mythistory.[22]

Every instance of historiographic activity involves human agents with specific goals that inform the resultant narrative product. Thus, no narrative, including myths, is ever a "pure" document or a passive mirror of the age of its genesis free of individual, factional, or other socially determinate elements that help to inform it. At the same time, no individual or group is free to generate a "historical" narrative at random or from scratch. There are always preexistent, culturally available, and validated verbal forms, structures, and strategies for constructing convincing narratives or narratives that would be judged relevant and meaningful in specific contexts. Since the creators of such narratives desire them to be accepted as factual accounts, they must of necessity draw on the culturally available verbal and rhetorical resources in order to realize this goal. Marshall Sahlins's characterization of the dialectical relationship of history and structure is apposite here:

History is culturally ordered, differently so in different societies, according to meaningful schemes of things. The converse is also true: cultural schemes are historically ordered, since to a greater or lesser extent the meanings are revalued as they are practically enacted. The synthesis of these contraries unfolds in the creative action of the historic subjects, the people concerned. For on the one hand, people organize their projects and give significance to their objects from the existing understandings of the cultural order. To that extent, the culture is historically reproduced in action. . . . On the other hand . . . as the contingent circumstances of action need not conform to the significance some group might assign them, people are known to creatively reconsider their conventional schemes. And to that extent, the culture is historically altered in action.[23]

It is precisely for the reasons Sahlins mentions that in all cultures change is not only possible, it is inevitable and continual. Various strategies, however, are often adopted in different cultural discourses—rhetorical, ritual, legal—precisely in order to deny that such change has occurred. The politics of death as expressed in the myth and ritual complex surrounding the practice of double burial in the court represents an important instance of this denial for, as we shall see, the mythistory rehearsed and reenacted during the period of the temporary interment of the corpse sought to deny that the sovereign's death was "really" final or constituted a radical break in the socio-political order. It is precisely the strategies adopted in retrospectively seeking to legitimate the succession that will be the object of study below.

The Structure of the Study

Chapter One, "Ritual Poetry in the Court," introduces a variety of types of oral performative poetry from the imperial court. The focus is twofold: (1) on the ways such poetry functioned in performance in the daily ceremonial nature of the court, marking out social distance and intimacy, difference and identity; and (2) on some of the ways these verses were retrospectively textualized and anthologized in order to contribute to the Court's larger historiographic project. After a cursory look at the prestige of poetry in early Japan and the operative belief in *kotodama*, the magical spirit power of special words, the following types of ritual poetry are explicated: *kunimi* or land-viewing poems, poems on imperial excursions, poems of praise of specific places and sites, poems of love and longing, poems of pacification of the spirits of the dead and of places, and two different types of *banka* or funeral laments. This chapter provides essential background information on the pervasive ceremonial nature of the court where a special rationality structured the actions of the individuals who found themselves enmeshed in the complex web of socio-political interdependencies that constituted this society. The extant poems prove to be revealing records of the constraints under which all public expression took place.

Chapter Two, "The Mythology of Death and the *Niiname-sai*," opens with a brief look at the early Japanese understanding and experience of death as evidenced in the poetry of the *Man'yōshū*. The focus then shifts to the religio-political complex surrounding the death and burial of the sovereign or a would-be ruler and the *niiname-sai*, the First Fruits or Harvest Festival. This chapter should be of special interest to historians of religions, for it offers a new religio-political reading of a number of major mythic sequences concerning Izanagi and Izanami, Amaterasu and Susano-o, Ninigi and Ko-no-hana-sakuya-hime, and others. I argue that the Izanagi–Izanami sequence not only provides an ideal model of the imperial double burial rituals but also reflects the historical "reality" of the politics of death in the court. I also suggest that the Amaterasu–Susano-o sequence links the celebration of the *niiname-sai* with the full exercise of the power and privileges of the sovereign, as well as reflects the existence of the *mogari no miya*, the temporary interment palace, as a strategic locus of symbolically meaningful historical action in the succession process. Similarly, the Ninigi–Ko-no-hana-sakuya-hime sequence will be shown to provide the mythic paradigm for the *niiname-sai* while it also narratively links this ritual with the problem of the succession and legitimacy. This chapter provides the necessary understanding of the symbolic complex found in the myths involving death, the *niiname-sai*, and the succession, for a fuller appreciation of the records of the double burial practices in the court.

Chapter Three, "The Liminal Period of Temporary Enshrinement," reconstructs, insofar as it is possible, the ritual practices surrounding double burial. It begins with the mythic narrative of Ame-no-waka-hiko, who was sent down from the High Heavens to pacify the land but instead sought to usurp power himself, and the better-known tale of Yamato-takeru. Kikuchi Takeo's thesis that there was a relation between the timing of the final burial of a deceased sovereign and his/her successor's celebration of the *niiname-sai* is explored and found to be probable. Then the focus shifts to the *Nihonshoki* records of political maneuvering during the period of temporary interment of a sovereign, demonstrating that the *mogari no miya* rituals provided an important locus and vehicle for such maneuvering in patterned and predictable ways. The tale of Prince Anahobe, who reportedly tried to break into the temporary enshrinement palace in order to possess the widowed empress, is shown to have significant parallels to the Amaterasu–Susano-o myth.

The period of temporary enshrinement of the sovereign's corpse is demonstrated to have been a liminal period par excellence. In the double burial ritual complex the ontological status of the recently deceased sovereign betwixt-and-between life and death precipitated the same liminal state in the court. Two heretofore ignored loci of religio-political power in the succession process during this period are disclosed in this chapter, both of them female—the interior of the *mogari no miya* and the Ise Shrine, where the Ise Priestess was a locus of the imperial charisma. Finally, the extensive *Nihonshoki* records of events preceding and following the death of the Emperor Temmu in 686 are introduced as important documents in the study of the politics of death in the court.

Chapter Four, "The Poetry of the *Mogari no Miya*," continues the focus on the rituals of the period of temporary enshrinement, but now through the extant poems from within the *mogari no miya* and others performed publicly outside. Using the Greek oral lament tradition for comparative purposes, the performative context and "voice" of a number of *banka* are imaginatively restored. Because double burial continues to be performed in rural Greece even today, a number of recent anthropological fieldwork studies have provided immediate insight into a living oral funeral lament tradition. Evidence is elicited to suggest, among other things, that (1) *banka* were often given multiple performances; (2) *banka* were orally generated and circulated by poet-reciters; (3) they could be adapted for specific conditions and needs; (4) the deceased was sometimes given a "voice" in laments; (5) there were performative loci that were gender-defined, with the interior of the *mogari no miya* an exclusively female and private ritual space, whereas the area surrounding this structure was a mixed-gender space for public rituals; and (6) *banka* were employed not only in rituals but in oral and written historical narratives as well.

Chapter Five, "Mythistory, Rhetoric, and the Politics of Marriage," pulls back, as it were, from the tight focus on the *mogari no miya* ritual complex to gain a wider view of the various cultural discourses involved in the succession process and the Court's historiographic project. Specific attention is given to the significance of "marriage politics" in the succession from the mid-sixth through the end of the seventh century. Soga no Umako was one of the first to recognize the possibilities inherent in arranging strategic marriages of daughters to individuals holding critical positions in the court. Many passages in the *Nihonshoki* and extant poems in the *Man'yōshū* can be understood only by taking the relational positions in the socio-political configuration of the court into full account.

One vivid example of the interplay of genealogical and mythic factors that were skillfully employed in order to usurp power involves the figures of the Emperor Kōtoku (r. 645–654), the Empress-Consort Hashibito, and her brother, Prince Naka no Ōe or Nakatsu Ōe (later the Emperor Tenji). Through outmaneuvering Kōtoku in entering strategic marriages and a daring act of "symbolic incest," Naka no Ōe was able effectively to deprive his uncle of real power. This "event" is recorded not only in the *Nihonshoki* but also in the famous "Poem of the Three Mountains by Nakatsu Ōe" (MYS 1: 13–15), a striking instance of the use of a traditional narrative to comment allegorically on the socio-political situation in the court.

This chapter also explores the way in which the death of the sovereign could expose an individual to attack in the court because of a sudden positional vulnerability. By concentrating on the situation following the death of the Emperor Temmu in 686, the dangerous, liminal nature of the period of the *mogari no miya* is disclosed in sharp detail. Following the temporary interment of Temmu, Prince Ōtsu made (or is retrospectively portrayed as having made) a doomed attempt to appropriate the imperial charisma (*tama*) unto himself through an act that is comprehensible only by understanding the symbolic and ritual complex surrounding the practice of double burial and informing the politics of death. The case of the tragic Prince Ōtsu is further explored by reconstructing the skeletal outline of a popular "history" of the events surrounding his death, which I have labeled "The Ōtsu no miko uta monogatari." This outline provides the opportunity to consider again the interplay of structure and history and to consider the opportunities this cultural dialectic provided to historical agents in the court.

The "Conclusion" rehearses the major findings of this study, offers methodological comments on its larger implications for the history of religions and literary studies, and finally suggests possible directions for future research.

CHAPTER ONE

Ritual Poetry in the Court

Poetry in preliterate Japan was more than "just" literature. In fact, it is incorrect and misleading to speak of "literature" at all in a primary oral culture such as Japan was before the introduction of the Chinese script. All poetry was orally performed, either sung or recited, giving it an immediacy that a written text does not have. Poems were performances or acts, not artifacts. Thus it is no accident that the word for a Japanese poem (*uta*) is the same as that for song (*uta*), whereas Chinese poems (i.e., originally "written poems") are clearly distinguished and are called *shi*. The early Japanese did not distinguish religion, politics, and literature in the ways we do, for poetry/song participated immediately in these other dimensions of social life to a far greater extent than is now generally recognized. Verse forms were at once part of an intellectual discourse and a social practice. It will be one of the goals of this and later chapters to indicate some of the ways *uta* functioned in the life of the early Japanese in the stage of secondary orality, the transitional period in which oral performative forms survived alongside writing that was being introduced among the intelligentsia. It is this period from which the earliest extant texts discussed here date.

Not all poetry in early Japan was ritual poetry, of course, so the comments and generalizations below concern a selected group of poems, including examples of the major types of ritual poetry found in early Japan such as land-viewing and praise poems, dialogue poems, commemorative poems of imperial excursions, poems for the pacification of the spirit of a deceased individual, and funeral laments. Moreover, the primary focus will be on the functional aspects of this ritual poetry rather than on the specifically aesthetic dimensions.

Only by taking the immediate socio-political aspects of public performative poetry into full account can such poems serve as significant documents in historical studies. Without in any way seeking to ignore or play down the aspects of continuity that characterize religious ritual and ritual poetry, it is also important to consider whenever possible the intentions of the human agents engaged in the performance of public rituals and ceremonies. In doing so, we must pay careful attention to the occasion of a reported performance as well as the relative socio-political positions and relationships of the performer (or in the case of a surrogate performer, his patron) and his/her audience. The same verse can "mean" different things on different occasions, with different audiences. Viewed in isolation, or out of its performative context, ritual—and ritual poetry—too easily appears as a timeless and essentially "frozen" expression of human religiosity.

In attempting to deal with Japanese poetry of the primary oral stage or even the early secondary stage one immediately faces a difficult methodological problem: direct access to this oral performative poetry is impossible. Paradoxically, perhaps, the only access to the oral stage of early Japan is through written texts that have survived. These texts, however, were not intended to serve as ethnographic monographs, and the oral poems incorporated within them are frequently preserved out of their generative and performative loci and, moreover, sometimes in altered form. Nevertheless, because the earliest texts, including the *Kojiki*, the *Nihonshoki*, and the *Man'yōshū*, come out of Japan's transition from a primarily oral culture to a literate one, at least among the intelligentsia and in the court, they preserve enough evidence of the oral aspects of the culture to permit certain generalizations. The textual evidence, however, must be supplemented by and interpreted in light of what scholars have learned about orality since the pioneering work of Milman Parry in the 1920s.[1]

The work of historians of religions often involves the informed imaginative re-creation of earlier ritual performances based upon limited textual evidence. Any study, such as the present one, that seeks to relocate the (now) literary texts in their earlier performative contexts will have to use comparative data from other cultures in order to recreate these contexts imaginatively. Introducing comparable examples from other cultures and times where appropriate enables one not only to supplement the available textual data but also to avoid the myopic (and sometimes ideologically and ethnocentrically informed) assumption that early Japan represents a unique cultural and religious situation.

Japanese folklorists such as Tsuchihashi Yutaka[2] have produced an impressive number of studies on the *Kikikayō* and *Man'yōshū* poems in which they have attempted to reconstruct the rituals mentioned in the poetry by using contemporary Japanese agricultural festivals and planting songs, as well as ethnographic studies of other cultures, as comparable situations, and then extrapolating backward. Konishi Jin'ichi has also recently used comparative material in his study of early Japanese poetry.[3] Such developments in the field of Japanese studies must be acknowledged and applauded, even when one is unable to accept all the authors' suggestions and conclusions. The results of the research of these and other Japanese scholars deserve to be more widely known but also need to be supplemented and extended.

The Prestige of Poetry

Poetry or song (*uta*) figures prominently in the extant texts from early Japan, so by studying these texts one is able to gain some sense of the function of poetry in early Japan. Song was frequently used and experienced as a form of the exercise of power. It was a linguistic means of manipulating religio-political power in the human sphere as well as of manipulating the spiritual powers, including the *kami* and the spirits of the dead. Song was sung and poetry recited not only for aesthetic pleasure but as a means of ordering and controlling potentially dangerous aspects of the world. This sense of the efficacy of poetic language survived until much later in Japanese history and was prominent in the Heian and medieval periods. Indeed, it is still found in the present in attenuated form in certain rural areas and ritual practices.[4] Probably the best-known literary reference to the magical power of poetry, however, is found in Ki no Tsurayuki's Japanese preface to the *Kokinshū* (early tenth century) where he states: "It is poetry which, without effort, moves heaven and earth, stirs the feelings of the invisible gods and spirits, smooths the relations of men and women, and calms the hearts of fierce warriors."[5]

While commentators have at times suggested this statement is so much hyperbole on Tsurayuki's part, it represents the prevailing attitude in early Japan and much of the Heian period. Significantly, Tsurayuki, following tradition, locates the origin of poetry with the *kami*.[6] In this and other medieval texts, as had been the case earlier, poetry is intimately related to myth, and myth in turn blends with "history" in our modern sense. There were a variety of rituals in early Japan in which poetry played an important part, but all these rituals were based upon the more general belief in the magico-religious efficacy of special words. This belief is generally referred to in the Japanese scholarly literature as *kotodama shinkō*, the belief in the spirit power (*tama*) of words (*koto*); scholars continue to disagree on when this belief first came to be held by the Japanese.

Itō Haku, one of the foremost modern *Man'yōshū* scholars, has argued persuasively, I think, that although the word *kotodama* is not found prior to its appearance in that anthology, the belief in the magical efficacy of words existed before the eighth century.[7] More controversial is his suggestion that the very appearance of the term *kotodama* indicates that as foreign culture and foreign languages, especially Chinese and Korean, poured into early Japan, the Japanese looked back nostalgically to "the age of the *kami*" when "pure" Japanese was used in all rituals. Itō suggests that the early Japanese may have felt the need to proclaim their own language superior to the foreign ones.[8] Whether his position is correct on all points or not, there can be no doubt that the rapid introduction of Chinese culture, and most especially the Chinese script, provoked a far-reaching transformation of Japanese culture. In the face of the introduction of writing in the court and the probable prestige associated with it, some oral ritual functionaries and *kami*-serving ritual clans may have felt both a socio-economic and religio-political need to proclaim the superior efficacy of the oral over the written word.[9] Only by recognizing the socio-political and economic dimensions of "religious" rhetoric can we (1) understand why the concept of *kotodama* appears so late in the texts and (2) avoid murky evolutionary claims that the Japanese of the Man'yō age "were capable of objectifying processes entailing language because their mind functioned somewhat more subtly than did those of their ancestors."[10]

The poem MYS 11: 2506 alludes to a certain divinatory practice in early Japan in which an individual hid himself near a crossroads and sought to overhear the conversation of the first passersby. This conversation overheard by chance provided the material for the diviner's analysis. That poem reads:

kototama no	Through the *kotodama*
yaso no chimata ni	in an evening divination performed
yūke tō	at a multiple crossroads
ura masani noru	the prediction was clear:
imo wa aiyoramu	my love will return to me.[11]

Here the term *kotodama* clearly refers to the magical efficacy of the words in the divination ritual. It is found in other poems as well, such as the following (MYS 5: 894), by Yamanoue Okura from 734 C.E.:

kōkyo kōrai no uta isshu	Poem wishing Godspeed to the Ambassador to China
kamiyo yori	It has been recounted
iitsute kuraku	down through time
soramitsu	since the age of the gods:
Yamato no kuni wa	that this land of Yamato
sumekami no	is a land of imperial deities'
itsukushiki kuni	stern majesty,
kotodama no	a land blessed by the spirit of words.
sakihō kuni to	Every man of the present
kataritsugi	sees it before his eyes
iitsugaikeri	and knows it to be true.
ima no yo no	
hito mo kotogoto	Men fill this land
me no mae ni	with their numbers,
mitari shiritari	but among them our Emperor
hito sawa ni	sovereign of the high-shining sun,
michite wa aredomo	a very god,

takahikaru
hi no mikado
kamunagara
mede no sakari ni
ame no shita
mōshitamaishi
ie no ko to
erabitamaite
ōmikoto
(kaeshite, taimei to iu)
itadaki mochite
morokoshi no
tōki sakai ni
tsukawasare
makari imase
unahara no
he ni mo oki ni mo
kamuzumari
ushiwaki imasu
moromoro no
ōmikami-tachi
funa no he ni
(kaeshite, funa no he
ni to iu)[12]
michibiki mōshi
amatsuchi no
ōmikami-tachi
Yamato no
ōkuni mi-tama
hisakata no
ama no mi-sora yu
amagakeri
miwatashi tamai
koto owari
kaeramu hi wa
mata sara ni
ōmikami-tachi
funa no he ni
mi-te uchikakete
suminawa o
waetaru gotoku
achikaoshi
Chika no saki yori
Ōtomo no
mi-tsu no hama bi ni
tada hate ni

in the fullness of his love,
chose for this mission
you, the son of a house
that governs the realm under heaven.
And with the favor
of his great command,
you have been sent
to the distant borders of China.
(another version has "by imperial
command")
As you set out,
all the mighty deities
that, in their godliness, abide
by the shore and by the offing,
there to rule the plain of waters,
lead you by the prow of your ship.
And the mighty gods
    of heaven and earth,
first among them
the Supreme Spirit of the Land
    of Yamato,
soar from the distant heavenly skies
to watch over you.

And on the day when,
your mission accomplished,
    you return,
again the mighty gods
shall take the prow of your ship
    in their noble hands
and bring you straight
as a black rope stretched
from Chika Cape
to your berth by Ōtomo's noble beach.
Go without hindrance,
go with good fortune,
and quickly return!

mi-fune wa hatemu
tsutsumi naku
sakiku imashite
hayakaerimase

hanka   Envoys

Ōtomo no   I shall sweep the beach clean
mi-tsu no matsubara   by the field of pines
kakihakite   at Ōtomo's noble cove,
ware tachimatamu   and stand there waiting for you.
hayakaerimase   Quickly return!

Naniwa tsu ni   When I hear the news
mi-fune hatenu to   that the imperial craft
kikoekoba   has berthed in Naniwa Cove,
himotoki sakete   I shall run to greet you,
tachibashirisemu   my waistcord trailing loose.[13]

This is a very late poem from the *Man'yōshū*, but because of that fact several points deserve notice. Though a highly Sinified poet, Yamanoue Okura here employs the *chōka*, a public form used for official and ritual occasions, with accompanying *hanka* or "envoys" ("repeating poems"). When the poet refers to the marvelous power of *kotodama*, he specifically notes that this power has been *orally* passed down (*kataritsugi*) from generation to generation. That is, although he lived in large measure in a literate world, he also knew and recognized the efficacy of oral performative poetry and did not disparage it as quaint or as a belief of the ignorant masses.

In this verse, poetry functions as a prayer for the safe journey and return of a departing ambassador. Such verses were recited in order to activate or harness the power of *kotodama*. The poet repeatedly employs the honorific *mi-*, which was believed to be of help releasing the *kotodama*. The *chōka* also includes direct praise of the land ("this land of Yamato/ is a land of imperial deities' stern majesty/ a land blessed by *kotodama*"), an element apparently felt to be necessary for the gain of the blessings mentioned.[14] The *uta* also proclaims that the results of the efficacy of *kotodama*, the magical power of words, are already visible in the present human sociopolitical realm. Praise is additionally directed toward the imperial family and the politically well-connected ambassador. Moreover, the *chōka* and the first envoy both end in the imperative *-mase*. This is consonant with a belief that asserting something in a ritual language and context would help to bring about its realization.

The act of invoking the power of *kotodama* was known as *kotoage*. This term is found in all three of the texts. In the *Nihonshoki*, for example, the *kami* Okuninushi's pacification of the land of Izumo is accomplished by his uttering *kotoage*.[15] After

Izanagi flees the netherworld where he was polluted by contact with death, he utters special *kotoage* at a stream, an act that either gives it purifying power or enables him to use this power.[16] In the well-known tale of Yamato-takeru, the tragic hero suffers a fatal blow after he inappropriately performs *kotoage*.[17] Other examples, including references to *kotoage* in *Man'yōshū* poems and in the "historical" sections of the *Nihonshoki*, could be cited,[18] but these few examples suffice to suggest that *kotoage* was a fairly common practice in early Japan.

The ritual use of poetry in early Japan participated in the more general complex of beliefs and practices involving the magico-religious power of special words. There were, among others, blessings, curses, and spells that almost anyone could use, but there also seem to have been special groups associated with these practices, including the *hokaibito*, apparently wandering minstrels, referred to in MYS 16: 3885–3886.[19] These itinerants are said to have performed songs as they wandered from village to village invoking good fortune. Later one finds mention of the *kataribe* and *asobibe*, guild-like associations of special ritual reciters and functionaries. Late in the seventh century the Court established a special governmental bureau for the regulation of *yokikoto* or *yogoto*, special forms of address and praise used in relation to the imperial family.[20]

Kunimi *or Land-Viewing Poems*

The land-viewing poem (*kunimi uta*) has been widely recognized as a distinct type of ritual poetry, although it is closely related to other forms of praise poems.[21] In the simplest structural terms, the land-viewing ritual in early Japan involved three important ordered parts: the sovereign or some other ritual functionary (1) climbed a hill, (2) then visually surveyed the countryside below, and (3) recited words of praise of the specific site. These three elements are not unique to the *kunimi* ritual, however, for this ritual participated in a larger, more general religio-political complex. It is this larger world of meaning that informed the structure of the *kunimi* ritual. The performance of this ritual, on the other hand, constituted the enactment or realization of specific parts of the larger complex in history.

Textual references to the *kunimi* ritual must be looked at in two ways—first, for the general morphology of the ritual, and second, for specific instances of its realization in time. But in addition to the structural sequence of the performance of the *kunimi* ritual and its possible significance, we must also search for the specific meanings and intentions behind individual performances of it. The following (MYS 1: 2) is an excellent example of a land-viewing poem.

Sumeramikoto Kagu-yama ni noborite ku- nimishi tamau toki no ōmi-uta	Poem by the Sovereign when he climbed Kagu Hill to view the land
Yamato ni wa	Many are the mountains of Yamato,
murayama aredo	but I climb heavenly Kagu Hill
toriyorou	that is cloaked in foliage,
ama no Kagu-yama	and stand on the summit
noboritachi	to view the land.
kunimi o sureba	On the plain of land,
kunihara wa	smoke from the hearths rises, rises
keburi tachitatsu	On the plain of waters,
unahara wa	gulls rise, rise.
kamame tachitatsu	A splendid land
umashi kuni so	is the dragonfly island,
akizushima	the land of Yamato.[22]
Yamato no kuni wa	

This verse has been treated in English by Alicia Matsunaga and Ian Levy.[23] Levy rightly notes that the poem participates in the tradition of ritual affirmation of the phenomenal world.[24] He errs, however, in implying that prior to the 640s, ritual poetry was static and its performance egoless, presenting the clan's collective vision of the world without any individual motives or intentions involved in either the poetry's genesis or its performance.[25] Such a view of the function of ritual poetry is based on the false assumption, implicit in the term "prehistorical," which is frequently used for preliterate societies, that the primary oral stage of culture had no "history" per se. "Naive" readings take rhetorical mythistories as presenting historical fact, but neither myth nor ritual simply mirrors the existent religious worldview in a passive manner; both are important and dynamic elements in its creation.[26]

Kunimi was a part of an annual agricultural ritual, imported from China. The public ritual was a stage on which in each specific performance of the *kunimi* ritual the emperor represented himself to the people as precisely the sacred king who, as the premier ritual intermediary between the realm of the *kami* and the human sphere, alone had the power to assure peace, prosperity, and fertility in the land. Through the ritual act of viewing the land and reciting words of praise, he sought to pacify and move the *kami* to grant a bountiful harvest. At the same time the words of praise of the beauty and prosperity of the land reflected back on the emperor himself, serving as an immediate demonstration of his power and position.

The sovereign was simultaneously the ritual and political head of the nation. In early Japan the legitimacy of the ruler's exercising sovereignty over various local clans and their leaders was maintained on genealogical grounds by positioning the ruler in the direct line of descent from Amaterasu, the Sun Goddess. Her own sovereign position in the divine hierarchy was similarly explained in myths that, while they claimed to disclose an eternal order, also served to justify the existing or emerging historical—that is, changing—status quo. Although each *kunimi uta* was consciously patterned both rhetorically and ritually *as if* an unchanging eternal order were merely being reaffirmed, in an important and undeniable sense each performance of a *kunimi* ritual sought to create and sustain a historically specific sociopolitical order precisely by creating the illusion of permanence and unbroken continuity. By simultaneously presenting the new human order and aligning it with the divine order, each ritual performance sought to win the public's acceptance of the legitimacy of the socio-political order.

Every new sovereign redistributed power, wealth, and status in order to demonstrate his own power, wealth, and status and to maintain and supplement them. The hierarchical nature of society was never unchanging but rather was in constant flux, with annual and semiannual promotions and demotions a regular part of the ritual calendar in the court. Moreover, the divine hierarchy among the *kami* in the High Heavens was itself subject to frequent turmoil and change, as the extant myths clearly attest, for they frequently deal with matters of legitimacy involving genealogy, succession disputes, attempted coups d'état, and so on. The factional mythistory preserved in the *Kojiki* and the *Nihonshoki* has a history of its own. The cult of Amaterasu, for instance, developed in a specific time period in early Japan, and this divinity emerged as preeminent among the *kami* only as the imperial clan emerged as such in the human realm. Thus, in studying early Japan we must not be lulled into adopting a romantic vision of this time. The myths and rituals preserved in our texts present the ideological ideal that those in power hoped to use to justify the distribution of privilege and wealth within the newly constituted social hierarchy. This worldview was hardly "an unchanging and essentially religious truth" but rather a precarious human "myth" that was to be played out in history. At the same time, in seeking to appreciate the function(s) of ritual poetry such as MYS 1: 2, we must not stop at the semantic content of the verse or at reconstructing its patterned performance. We must also explore its use in the larger historiographic project of the imperial family by asking other questions, such as why was the ritual poetry (rather than other readily available *uta*) preserved in written form and anthologized as it is at the beginning of the *Man'yōshū*? Why does the prose headnote attribute the poem to Jomei when every sovereign presumably performed the *kunimi* ritual each year? These and related questions will be considered later.

The texts from early Japan clearly witness to the important political dimensions of the *kunimi* ritual and the performative recitation of poems praising the land within this context. The earliest references to *kunimi* found in the *Nihonshoki* may be found in two entries under the reign of Jimmu, the first "human" emperor. The first entry, located before Jimmu's formal installation as emperor, refers to the existence of a hill called Kunimi no oka but does not mention the ritual itself: "[663 B.C.E.] 9th month, 5th day. The Emperor ascended to the peak of Mount Takakura in Uda, whence he had a proper prospect over the land. On Kunimi Hill there were descried eighty bandits."[27] Following this, Jimmu is told by the heavenly *kami* to gather clay from Kagu-yama (the hill found in MYS 1: 2 above) and to make eighty sacred platters and sacred jars for use in sacrificing to the deities of heaven and earth (*amatsu yashiro kunitsu yashiro*). He is promised that if he does this while pronouncing a sacred formula, his enemies will quickly yield to him.

In this first entry, *kunimi* is narratively associated with Kagu-yama, sacrifice, and sacral kingship. Throughout the early centuries, Kagu-yama would continue to play a central role in the imperial cult. It is interesting to note that in this first entry it is others, described as "bandits" (*takeru*), and not Jimmu who occupy Kunimi no oka. It is unclear whether their having positioned themselves on the summit of this hill was intended as a provocation, although if the narrative reflects resistance to the attempt by the imperial family to appropriate the right to perform the land-viewing ritual exclusively onto itself, this may well have been the case. Most scholars are in agreement, however, that when in MYS 1: 2 the Emperor Jomei is reported to have climbed Kagu-yama to perform the *kunimi* ritual, he thereby symbolically identified himself with Jimmu, the paradigmatic first sovereign, by occupying the same place.

The next entry in which *kunimi* is mentioned portrays Jimmu actually performing the ritual:

31st year [630 B.C.E.], Summer, 4th month, 1st day. The Imperial palanquin made a circuit, in the course of which the Emperor ascended the Hill of Wakigami no Hohoma no Oka. Here, having viewed the shape of the land on all sides, he said:—"Oh! what a beautiful country we have become possessed of! Though a blessed land of inner-tree-fibre, yet it resembles a dragon-fly licking its hinder parts." From this it first received the name of Akizu-shima.[28]

The three essential ritual actions mentioned earlier are evident here: the emperor ascends a hill, views the land, and offers words of praise. The words of praise, *ananiya*, are virtually identical to those spoken by Izanagi and Izanami in the cosmogonic myth when they see each other's naked body after circumambulating the heavenly pillar.[29] Thus, in this entry in the *Nihonshoki* there is an obvious attempt to identify the ritual action of viewing the land with the cosmogony. In an important sense, the *kunimi* ritual is presented as the equivalent of the re-creation of the land. The annual renewal of the world in spring is, of course, recognized and celebrated in agricultural societies around the world,[30] and the cosmogonic myth is often re-cited in these and associated fertility rites. The *kunimi* ritual participated in this worldview. Whereas Izanagi and Izanami had *descended* from the High Heaven to create the land, however, the emperor *ascends* the hill to view the land and to proclaim it good. From the summit, like the heavenly *kami* in Takamagahara, he views the land below. Indeed, in the operative religio-political ideology of early Japan, the sovereign performed these and other ritual actions as a *kami* (*kamunagara*).

Another *uta* from an apparent *kunimi* ritual is preserved in both the *Kojiki* and the *Nihonshoki*. The *Nihonshoki* locates the song in the spring, as one would expect.

6th year [275 C.E.], Spring, 2nd month. The Emperor [Ōjin] made a progress to the province of Ōmi. When he arrived near the Moor of Uji, he made a song, saying:—

When I view
The Kazu plain
Of the myriad leaves,
The prospering villages are visible;
The highest part of the land is visible.[31]

The next clear reference in the *Nihonshoki* to the *kunimi* ritual is not found until the following entry in the Yūryaku Chapter:

6th year [462 C.E.], Spring, 2nd month, 4th day. The Emperor made an excursion to the small moor of Hatsuse. There, viewing the aspect of the hills and moors, in an outburst of feeling, he made a song, saying [*mi-uta yomishite no tamawaku*]:—

komoriku no	The mountain of Hatsuse
Hatsuse no yama wa	Of the hidden country
idetachi no	Is a mountain
yoroshiki yama	Standing beautifully,
washiride no	Is a mountain
yoroshiki yama no	Projecting beautifully.
komoriku no	The mountain of Hatsuse
Hatsuse no yama wa	Of the hidden country
aya ni uraguwashi	Is truly lovely,
aya ni uraguwashi	Is truly lovely.

Hereupon he gave a name to the small moor, and called it Michi no Ono.[32]

The incantational nature of this verse, with its repeated words of praise of the site, should be obvious. The praise was designed to win over the local *kami* and to ensure the fertility of the land and a bountiful harvest. Although it is difficult to accept these entries as historically reliable, they are nevertheless important to note. The very fact that the performance of the *kunimi* ritual is projected back into the reigns of these sovereigns indicates that the compilation of these texts was considered an act supremely identified with the exercise of sovereignty.

Other references to *kunimi* rituals might be cited, but they are not sufficient in number to permit one to speak with any certainty about the historical origins of this ritual practice in Japan. Similar rituals were practiced earlier in China, leading some Japanese scholars to suggest that *kunimi* was a continental import. This may well be true, but it is extremely difficult to pinpoint when the ritual was introduced to Japan or to say that other similar rituals may not have predated the Chinese land-viewing ritual. A related scholarly debate has continued as to whether the ritual originally was confined to the court or was once practiced by many local clan chieftains (*uji-gami*). The evidence is again inconclusive, but Tsuchihashi and others have presented suggestive evidence that the ritual was once widespread. Tsuchihashi notes, for example, the existence of place names like Kunimi-yama, Kunimi-dake, Kunimi-toge, and so on throughout Japan from present-day Kagoshima-ken in the south to Akita-ken in the north. He suggests that *kunimi* was originally a folk practice.[33] The poem MYS 3: 382 is often cited in support of this position:

Tsukuba no Take ni noborite Tajihi no ma-hito Kunihito no tsukuru uta isshu, narabe ni tanka

Poem by Tajihi Kunihito upon climbing Tsukuba Mountain, with tanka

tori ga naku
Azuma no kuni ni
takayama wa
sawa ni aredomo
futakami no
tōtokiyama no
nami tachi no
mi ga hoshi yama to
kamiyo yori
hito no ii tsugi
kunimi suru
Tsukuha no yama o
fuyugomori
tokijiki toki to
mizute ikaba
mashite kōshimi
yukige suru
yamamichi sura o
nazumi zo waga keru

Many are the lofty mountains
in the eastern country,
where the cock cries,
but since the age of the gods
men have told of Tsukuba Mountain,
the one beautiful to look upon
with its noble peaks
rising side by side—
a pair of gods—
and climbed to the summit
to view the land.
It is still shackled in winter's
      bonds,
not yet time for climbing,
but if I passed by
without seeing its view,
it would make me yearn even more.
And so I have come,
struggling up the mountain path
through the melting snow.

hanka

Envoy

Tsukuha ne o
yoso nomi mitsutsu
ari kanete
yukige no michi o

I could not merely glance
casually from afar
at Tsukuba's peak
but came up to the summit

nazumi keru kamo   struggling up the path.
                                                    through the melting snow.[34]

This poem probably dates from around 757, making it a very late poem in the
Man'yōshū, and clearly suggests that by that time at least, others besides the emperor
performed *kunimi*. It is uncertain, though, whether Tajihi performed this ritual as a
private individual or in an official capacity. The former seems to me unlikely. The
poem MYS 3: 324–325 is another example of *kunimi* performed by someone other
than the emperor, in this case by the poet Yamabe Akahito (fl. early eighth century).[35] Although the evidence is insufficient to make any strong claims one way or
the other, with the centralization of power in the hands of the imperial clan and
certainly after the Ritsuryō period,[36] the performance of the ritual probably became
the imperial prerogative, in which case its performance by others would have been
restricted.[37]

The Meaning of Miru: The Ritual Act of Gazing on Something

The ritual activity of viewing in the *kunimi* was not a passive visual reception of the
landscape but rather an intentional ordered act, which in turn ordered the spatial
area encompassed within this vision. The religio-political significance attached to the
verb *miru*, "to see" or "to view," in early Japan has been insufficiently appreciated
by Western scholars. The special significance attached to the verb *miru* or its stem
form *mi*, found in various compounds, was not confined to the *kunimi* ritual. This
fact is clearly confirmed in the poetry of Hitomaro and other court poets.

Morishige Satoshi has cogently argued that in the modern period we cannot simply assume that the early Japanese "saw" things the same way we do, or for that
matter that the same Chinese character in its verbal form or in some combination
necessarily meant the same thing over time. On the basis of an extended study of
mi in the *Man'yōshū*,[38] he suggests that in the Man'yō age when people heard (and
later with the introduction of writing "saw") the word *miru* or *mi*, a complex group
of related associations came into mental play, both consciously and unconsciously.
Most important, the *mi* in *kunimi* means to "possess" something exterior to oneself.
Morishige finds it significant that, although the written characters are different, an
inanimate "thing" or "object" (*mono*) is aurally the same as "living thing" (*mono*). To
"see" something/someone is to "know" it or her/him. Here the semantic—and
perhaps psychological—meaning is identical to the older English usage of "to know
a woman" for "to (sexually) possess a woman." The cosmogonic myth involving
Izanami and Izanagi is relevant for our understanding of the "deep meaning" of the
sexual connotations of viewing/pacifying/possessing the land: it is the fact that they

see each other and then offer words of praise that leads to their sexual union and the creation of the land out of chaos.[39]

Dozens of poems from the *Man'yōshū* could be cited to demonstrate the element of control over something or someone implicit in *mi*, but a few must suffice. For example, MYS 2: 91 reads:

Sumeramikoto, Kagami no Ōkimi ni tamau mi-uta isshu	Poem presented by the Sovereign [Tenji] to Princess Kagami
imo ga ie mo tsugite mimashi o Yamato naru Ōshima no ne ni ie mo aramashi o	Constantly would I gaze upon your house. Would that my house were on Ōshima Peak in Yamato.[40]

The implicit meaning of "constantly would I gaze/ upon your house" (*imo ga ie mo/ tsugite mimashi o*) can be grasped by recalling the many instances in the *Kojiki* and the *Nihonshoki* where a *kami*, an emperor, or a prince sees a beautiful woman and desires her. The following passage, for instance, turns on the sexual nuance of the phrase "to see someone." When Ōkuni-nushi went to the land where Susano-o was dwelling, "[Susano-o's] daughter Suseri-bime came forth and saw [*idemite*] him; they looked [at each other] lovingly and became man and wife."[41]

Poems of Praise and Imperial Excursions

Hitomaro and other poets exploited the traditional meaning of *mi* in their poetry, including that cast in the public ritual *chōka* form. A famous set of poems by Hitomaro (MYS 1: 36–39) celebrates an imperial excursion by the Empress Jitō (r. [686]–697) to the mountains of Yoshino outside the capital.[42] The poems both illustrate the ritual act of viewing the land and help to reveal other dimensions of public performative poetry.

Yoshino no miya ni idemashishi toki Kakinomoto no Asomi no Hitomaro no tsukuru uta	Poems by Kakinomoto Hitomaro at the time of the imperial procession to the palace at Yoshino
yasumishishi wago ōkimi no kikoshimesu ame no shita ni kuni wa shi mo sawa ni aredomo yama kawa no	Many are the lands under heaven and the sway of our Lord, sovereign of the earth's eight corners, but among them her heart finds Yoshino good for its crystal riverland

kiyoki kōchi to
mi-kokoro o
Yoshino no kuni no
hana chirau
Akizu no nobe ni
miyahashira
futoshikimaseba
momoshiki no
ōmiyahito wa
funa namete
asagawa watari
fune kiyoi
yūgawa watari
kono kawa no
tayuru koto naku
kono yama no
iya taka shirasu
mizu hashiru
taki no miyako wa
miredomo akanu kamo

hanka

miredo akanu
Yoshino no kawa no
tokoname no
tayuru koto naku
mata kaerimimu

yasumishishi
wago ōkimi
kamu nagara
kamusabisesu to
Yoshino gawa
tagitsu kōchi ni
takadono o
takashirimashite
noboritachi
kunimi o seseba
tatanazuku
aokaki yama
yamatsumi no
matsuru mi-tsuki to
harube wa
hana kazashimochi
aki tateba
momichi kazaseri

among the mountains,
and on the blossom-strewn
fields of Akitsu
she drives the firm pillars of
    her palace.
And so the courtiers of the great
    palace,
its ramparts thick with stone,
line their boats
to cross the morning river,
race their boats
across the evening river.
Like this river
never ending,
like these mountains
commanding ever greater heights,
the palace by the surging rapids—
though I gaze on it, I do not tire.

Envoy

Like the eternal moss
slick by the Yoshino River
on which I do not tire to gaze,
may I never cease to return
and gaze on it again.

Our Lord
who rules in peace,
a very god,
manifests her divine will
and raises towering halls
above the Yoshino riverland
where waters surge,
and climbs to the top
to view the land.
On the mountains
folding upward around her
like a sheer hedge of green,
the mountain gods present their offerings.

They bring her blossoms in springtime
to decorate her hair
and, when autumn comes,
they garland her with yellow leaves

(hitotsu ni iu, momichiba kazari)	(Another source says, "garland her with yellow leaves").
yukisou	And the gods of the river
kawa no kami mo	that runs alongside the mountains
ōmi-ke ni	make offerings for her imperial feast.
tsukaematsuru to	
kamitsu se ni	They send cormorants forth
ukawa o tachi	over the upper shoals,
shimotsu se ni	they cast dipper nets
sade sashiwatasu	across the lower shoals,
yamagawa mo	Mountain and river
yorite tsukauru	draw together to serve her—
kami no miyo kamo	a god's reign indeed!
yamagawa mo	A very god
yorite matsureru	whom mountain and river
kamu nagara	draw together to serve,
tagitsu kafuchi no	she sets her boat to sail
funade suru kamo	over pools where waters surge.[43]

Verse 36 includes the expected praise of the land, while the empress's control over the human realm is demonstrated as the courtiers' daily lives are ordered both spatially and temporally around her. Verse 38, the second *chōka*, presents the empress ascending the mountain and performing the *kunimi* ritual, but here she is explicitly referred to as a living *kami* (*kamu nagara/ kamusabisesu to*). The *kami* of the mountains and rivers are declared to be serving the empress; through the efficacy of the *kunimi* ritual, now not only human society but all of nature is under her sway. The ideological dimensions of public performative ritual are evident here. As Levy has noted, "There is a sense in all this rhetoric that it is because of her divinity and, again, as 'proof' of it, that the panorama of the land that follows spreads around her as it does."[44] The Empress Jitō establishes the Yoshino palace and performs the *kunimi* ritual, viewing the land and praising it, because she *is* the divine sovereign. She does these things "as a *kami*" (*kamu nagara*) "so that she might display her quality as a god" (*kamusabisesu to*). The ritual actions are at once a demonstration and a revelation of the identity of the divine order and the historical, social, and religio-political order.

Yoshino, the site chosen for the performance of these ritual actions, was not chosen arbitrarily. Yoshino had both important mythic and historical associations. Jitō's husband, the Emperor Temmu (r. [673]–686), had fled to Yoshino before the Jinshin War, a succession dispute, in which he gained power. The central importance of this site is clearly attested to by the fact that there are sixty poems in the *Man'yōshū* on Yoshino. Moreover, the *Kojiki*, the *Nihonshoki*, and the *Man'yōshū* collectively record at least forty-five imperial excursions there, of which thirty-one are from Jitō's reign.[45]

When Prince Ōama, later the Emperor Temmu, fled to Yoshino as his brother, the Emperor Tenji, lay critically ill, he feared for his life. The flight from the capital was undertaken in haste. The first night, Ōama stayed in the Soga Palace, the Shima no miya, arriving in Yoshino the next day. Within a matter of months it became clear that Prince Ōtomo intended to move against him militarily. This inaugurated the Jinshin War. Ōama was joined in Yoshino by his sons, Princes Takechi, Ōtsu, Kusakabe, Osakabe, and Ishikawa and eventually won a decisive victory, deposing and executing Ōtomo (now recognized as the Emperer Kōbun). The *Nihonshoki*, however, does not attribute Temmu's victory exclusively to the military prowess of his generals but to divine favor as well. One finds a report of one of his generals becoming possessed by two *kami* who directed that, to ensure victory, special offerings be made at the tomb of the Emperor Jimmu and that others be presented to the *kami* themselves.[46] Another *kami* reportedly possessed a priest in order to inform one of Prince Ōama's generals of the direction from which enemy troops were approaching, while Prince Ōama himself was reportedly successful in interceding with the *kami* of heaven and earth (*ametsuchi no kami*) to halt a violent thunderstorm.[47]

For Temmu and Jitō, Yoshino was an especially important and sacred site associated with their victory in the Jinshin War. It was identified in their minds as a place where other rituals had been especially effective in securing the succession.[48] It is significant that Temmu's first recorded imperial excursion to Yoshino after his formal accession was on 5/5–7/679 when he called together all the imperial princes and had them take a collective public vow that they would not engage in a bloody succession dispute following his death. In this regard we might pause to look at MYS 1: 25–27, attributed to Temmu. These verses read:

sumeramikoto no ōmi-uta	Poem by the Sovereign
mi-Yoshino no	On the peak of Mimiga
Mimiga no mine ni	in beautiful Yoshino
toki nakuso	without end
yuki wa furikeru	snow was ever falling,
ma nakuso	without any break
ame wa furikeru	rain was falling.
sono yuki no	Like that snow
toki naki ga goto	without end,
sono ame no	like that rain
ma naki ga goto	without any break,
kuma mo arazu	without any turns
omoitsutsu zo koshi	I have come deep in the memories
sono yamamichi o	of that mountain road!

aru hon no uta	The poem in another source
mi-Yoshino no Mimiga no yama ni toki jiku so yuki wa furu tō ma naku so ame wa furu tō sono yuki no toki jiki ga goto sono ame no ma naki ga goto kuma mo ochizu omoitsutsu zo koshi sono yamamichi o	On Mt. Mimiga in beautiful Yoshino outside the bounds of time the snow falls they say, without a break the rain falls they say. Like that snow outside the bounds of time, like that rain without a break without any turns I have come deep in the memories of that mountain road!
(migi kuku aikawareri yorite koko ni kasa- nete nosu)	(In the poems above several phrases differ from each other. Thus both are given here together.)
sumeramikoto, Yoshino no miya ni ide- mashishi toki no ōmi-uta	Poem by the Sovereign, at the time of his procession to the Yoshino Palace
yokihito no yoshi to yoku mite yoshi to iishi Yoshino yoku miyo yokihito yoku mi	The good people [of the past] found it good, looked well and pronounced it good. Look well on Yoshino, good people, look well.
(Ki ni iwaku, hachi-nen tsuchinoto-u no go-gatsu kanoe-tatsu no tsuitachi no kinoe- saru, Yoshino no miya ni idemasu to ieri.)	(The *Nihonshoki* says an imperial excursion to the Yoshino Palace was made on the fifth day of the fifth month of the 8th year of the reign.)[49]

If the last poem indeed comes from the occasion mentioned in the editorial end-note, then it alludes not only to the distant past but also to the Jinshin War, which was still within living memory. Yoshino had indeed been very good to Temmu, but it was also the site of painful memories of doubt, fear, and bloodshed. We can hear Temmu imploring his sons to remember well the lessons of the past lest they be cursed to repeat them. (And let us recall that the *Nihonshoki* reports that he extracted oaths from his sons to the effect that if any of them should raise a hand against another brother or shed any blood, that son's family should be cursed.) The repetition of the words *yoshi, yoki,* and *yoku,* all of which mean "good" or "well," coupled with the invocation of the place name Yoshino, gives this poem a strong incantatory nature. Perhaps through the recitation of this verse in Yoshino, Temmu hoped to bring good fortune upon his sons and to ensure a smooth transfer of power after his death.

In this light MYS 1: 25 can now be seen as an exhortation of a father to his sons to remember the long and arduous path he had followed to the pinnacle of power in Japan. Standing in Yoshino brought the memories of all the past struggles, waged ceaselessly over those years, back into the minds of Temmu's sons, who had fought alongside him or at least witnessed the Jinshin War. The variant is interesting in that it draws a sharper juxtaposition than does 1: 25 between a timeless natural cycle and the immediacy of human struggles in history.

There is some suggestion that Yoshino was also a sacred purification site associated with a belief in the restorative powers of the springs there that could keep one young.[50] Yamamoto Kenkichi points to MYS 1: 22 as an example of this belief. It reads:

To-ochi no himemiko, Ise no Jingu ni mairishi toki, Hata no yokoyama no iwa o mite Fufuki no Toji no tsukuru uta

During Princess To-ochi's pilgrimage to the Ise Shrine, Fufuki no Toji made this verse upon seeing the range of crags at Hata

kawa no e no
yutsu iwamura ni
kusa musazu
tsune ni mogamo na
toko otome ni te

As the grass
does not grow on the cliffs
over the river,
may you eternally be
a young maiden![51]

The *yu* in *yutsu* is pointed to by Japanese scholars as meaning the spirit power of growth and life.[52] Here the rocks or cliffs are considered unchanging. The purification rite involved here was known as *ochi-mizu*, literally "change-young-water." The identity of Fufuki (or Fubuki) no Toji is unclear, but she seems to have been a maid of some sort in the court. Another set of poems, MYS 3: 242–244, also seems to refer to the belief in the magical powers of the springs in Yoshino. It reads:

Yuge no miko, Yoshino ni idemashishi toki no mi-uta isshu

Poem by Prince Yuge at the time of his excursion to Yoshino

tagi no e no
Mifune no yama ni
iru kumo no
towa ni aramu to
waga omowanaku ni

I dare not think
I shall last eternally
like the clouds
on Mifune Mountain
above the rapids.

Kasuga no Ōkimi no kotae matsuru uta isshu

Poem presented by Princess Kasuga in response

Ōkimi wa
chitose ni masamu
shiragumo mo
Mifune no yama ni

Our Lord shall be
for a thousand years.
Will there ever come a day
when the white clouds vanish

tayuru hi arame ya	from Mifune Mountain?
aru hon no uta isshu	A poem from another source
mi-Yoshino no Mifune no yama ni tatsu kumo no towa ni aramu to waga omowanaku ni	I dare not think I shall last eternally like the clouds that rise on Mifune Mountain in splendid Yoshino.
(migi isshu, Kakinomoto no Asomi no Hi- tomaro no kashū ni dezu)	(The above poem is in the *Kakinomoto Hi- tomaro Collection*.)[53]

Not only is the belief in the *ochi-mizu* rhetorically incorporated in these poems, the editorial note to the variant suggests that ritual poets such as Hitomaro were involved in generating and circulating such verses. The attributions to Prince Yuge, Princess Kasuga, and even to Hitomaro do not necessarily indicate authorship. Rather, such attributions recall one of the occasions on which the *uta* were recited. Such ritual prayers and responses may well have been a kind of set form, widely recognized and used by any number of individuals journeying to Yoshino. In this regard, another set of poems also on Yoshino, MYS 3: 315–316, is of import. Those poems read:

boshun no tsuki, Yoshino no rikyū ni ide- mashishi toki, Chūnagon Ōtomo Kei mi- kotonori o uketamawarite tsukuru uta is- shu	Poem presented by the Chūnagon Lord Ōtomo in response to an imperial command during the imperial excursion to the detached palace at Yoshino in the late spring
(tsui ni tanka, imada tōjō o tazaru uta)	(with tanka, the verse[s] were not recited at the time)
mi-Yoshino no Yoshino no miya wa yama karashi tōtokarurashi kawa garashi sayakekarurashi amatsuchi to nagaku hisashiku yorozu yo ni kawarazu aramu idemashi no miya	It seems the mountains around the palace at splendid Yoshino make it noble, it seems the river makes it bright and clear. Let it endure, forever unchanging, as long as heaven and earth, for ten thousand years— the palace of our Lord's procession.
hanka	Envoy
mukashi mishi Kisa no ogawa o	Gazing now on the stream at Kisa

ima mireba
iyoyo sayakeku
nari ni keru kamo

that we gazed on in the past
ever clearer
it has become. [54]

This is a typical praise poem on an imperial palace. It contains an allusion to the rejuvenating powers of the waters of Yoshino, and it incorporates the ritual act of viewing in the envoy (*mukashi mishi . . . ima mireba*). The editorial note calls our attention to the fact that members of the imperial family often ordered poems recited for them and in their presence. The interlinear note, based on an unnamed source, observes that the poem was not recited during the procession, though we are not told why. Yet the very fact that this point is mentioned at all indicates that normally it would have been orally recited. In a still largely oral society, certain individuals were expected to generate such verses orally upon command. The existence of many variants of *uta* suggests that similar oral verses were generated on different occasions and by different individuals drawing upon the culturally available fund of patterned oral forms and formulae.

Another example of a ritual praise poem is MYS 1: 52–53, consisting of a *chōka* and an envoy. It celebrates the well of the imperial palace, and the surrounding land, at Fujiwara built by the Empress Jitō:

Fujiwara-miya no mi-i
no uta

Poem of the Imperial Well at the
Fujiwara Palace

yasumishishi
wago ōkimi
takaterasu
hi no mikoto
aratae no
Fujii ga hara ni
ōmi-kado
hajimetamaite
Haniyasu no
tsutsumi no ue ni
aritatashi
meshitamaeba
Yamato no
ao Kagu-yama wa
hi no tate no
ōmi-kado ni
haruyama to
shimisabi tateri
Unebi no
kono mizuyama wa
hi no yoko no

Our Lord, sovereign
of the earth's eight corners,
child of the high-shining sun,
founds her great palace
on the fields of Fujii,
of the rough wisteria cloth,[55]
stands
on the bank
of Haniyasu Pond.
When she casts her gaze
[she sees] Yamato's
lush Kagu-yama
beyond the Great Gate
of the Rising Sun,
a spring mountain
standing luxuriant,
and Unebi,
this abundant mountain,
beyond the Great Gate
of the Setting Sun,
standing an abundant mountain

ōmi-kado ni	in mountain-like youth,
mizuyama to	and Miminashi,
yamasabi imasu	a mountain of green sedge,
Miminashi no	beyond the Great Gate
ao sugayama wa	of the Rear,
sotomo no	handsome,
ōmi-kado ni	stands god-like,
yoroshinabe	and Yoshino Mountain—
kamisabi tateri	beautiful its name—
na kuwashi	beyond the Great Gate
Yoshino no yama wa	of the Falling Shadows,
kagetomo no	in the distance
ōmi-kado yu	in the clouds,
kumo iniso	standing tall!
tōku arikeru	Here in the divine shadows
takashiru ya	of high-ruling heaven,
ama no mi-kage	in the divine shadows
ame shiru ya	of heaven-ruling sun,
hi no mi-kage no	may these waters gush forever,
mizu koso ba	the clear waters of the imperial well!
tokoshie ni arame	
mi-i no mashimizu	

tanka	Tanka
Fujiwara no	Born into a line
Ōmiya tsukae	that serves the great palace
aretsugu ya	at Fujiwara,
otome ga tomo wa	Those maidens
tomoshikiro kamo	how we envy them!
(migi no uta, saka imada tsubairakanarazu)	(The name of the author of the above poems is yet unknown.)[56]

Though unattributed, these poems were no doubt created and performed by a professional court poet. They belong with others extolling the reign of Jitō, including MYS 1 :36–39, Hitomaro's poems on Jitō's imperial procession to Yoshino, and MYS 1: 50–51, on the Fujiwara Palace. One finds the standard epithets for the sovereign here as the *chōka* opens—"Our Lord, sovereign/ of the earth's eight quarters"— which serve immediately to link this sovereign with all the others before her. The *chōka* then goes on to conjure up a panorama of 360 degrees as the empress casts her gaze around her in the stylized ritual action of the sovereign-as-living-*kami*. As the sovereign, she is at the center of the land and the universe. The four gates of the palace open up on the four cardinal directions, each dominated by a mountain that is praised for its beauty and special quality. Kagu-yama to the East is the repository of the power of luxuriant growth or fertility; Unebi to the West is the repository of youthful male virility. To the North is Miminashi, handsome and god-like, and to the South is Yoshino, the locus of so many memories and another sacred site. Facing south, the typical position for the sovereign, Jitō commanded a view of the land filled with myth and history. This poem again has almost an incantatory quality to it, suggesting its oral nature and its intentional use as a ritual prayer seeking to activate and harness the spirit powers of the land through the workings of *kotodama*.

Jitō's many journeys to Yoshino were more than merely a nostalgic excursion into her personal past; they were part of a concerted effort to link (*musubu*) the past and the present and thus legitimate the political status quo. In MYS 1: 36–39 above, Hitomaro rhetorically incorporates other mythico-historical elements associated with Yoshino and the past in order to strengthen the identity of Jitō and the present socio-political hierarchy with this idealized past. The fields of Akitsu, for instance, refer back to the Dragonfly Island of Yamato, found in the *Kojiki* and in Jomei's land-viewing poem, MYS 1: 2. Morishige has suggested that here Hitomaro uses the place as a *katami*, a site or object associated with a deceased individual, to help recall the myth,[57] yet this need not be considered a new development as he suggests.[58] The "geographicization of space" or the emplotting of narratives in geographical sites is found everywhere and at all stages of cultural development;[59] it is not "new." In MYS 1: 36–39, though, we may be able to glimpse new narratives and recent memories being associated with the Yoshino area.

The geographicization of space (or the creation of a sense of place[60]) is an ongoing process involving an ordering of the site by giving a narrative form to the collective historical memory associated with it. This memory is, of course, a selective memory, and the process is subject to manipulation in various ways. Which tales and allusions are added, or alternatively which are played down or deleted—either to be forgotten or remembered in "peripheral" traditions and groups[61]—are determined by the specific needs of the individuals and groups who occupy positions of power. What is new in this set of poems is not the creation of a spatial *katami* in and of itself but only Hitomaro's specific reordering of the past and the present to enhance the status and prestige of this sovereign, Jitō. If we overemphasize the patterned nature of such poems (linguistically and in performance), our reading will present the false impression that the poems were static and timeless; on the other hand, if we over-emphasize the uniqueness of a given poem (or poet, for that matter), we may miss the ways in which it participated in the larger religio-aesthetic tradition.

The headnote to MYS 1: 36–39 introduces another major form of ritual poetry in early Japan—that commemorating excursions by members of the imperial family. This type figures prominently in the *Shoki-Man'yōshū*. Book 1, for example, is largely devoted to such poems. The following list consists of poems specifically related by the prose headnotes to a journey by a member of the imperial family: MYS 1: 3–4, 5–6, 9, 10–12, 17–19, 20, 22, 27, 34, 35, 36–39, 40–42, 45–49, 54–56, 57–60, 61, 64–65, 66–69, 70, 71–73, 74–75, 78, 79–80, and 81–83. This list indicates that nearly two-thirds of the poems from Book 1 (64.3 percent in my count; someone else might include yet other poems) concern imperial excursions.

Scholars have long recognized the ritual nature of the public procession, a cultural phenomenon found in many stratified societies. The public procession is, among other things, a demonstration of charisma, order, and status. As Clifford Geertz has noted, royal progresses "locate the society's center and affirm its connection with transcendent things by stamping a territory with ritual signs of dominance. When kings journey around the countryside, making appearances, attending fetes, conferring honors, exchanging gifts, or defying rivals, they mark it, like some wolf or tiger spreading his scent through his territory, as almost physically part of himself."[62]

Thus, any record, be it prose or verse, of an imperial excursion is also a political document, and any public recitation associated with it, either as part of such a progress or retrospectively recalling it and praising the imperial family member, is a political act. The poems on imperial excursions in early Japan, then, illustrate an important cultural dialectic: they at once had their genesis in the religio-political center of the society and participated in its re-creation and maintenance. This dynamic is part of the cultural-historical meaning of the poetry, a meaning that is not to be found only by looking at the surface of the semantic content of the poems. As with the *kunimi* poems, one must have binocular vision, as it were, keeping in view both the "timeless" patterned nature of the procession and the historically conditioned temporal and spatial loci of the specific excursions. Geertz (himself following Edward Shils, following Weber) has offered the following suggestive remarks on the cultural dynamics of charisma, order, and status:

if charisma is a sign of involvement with the animating centers of society, and if such centers are cultural phenomena and thus historically constructed, investigations into the symbolics of power and into its nature are very similar endeavors. The easy distinction between the trappings of rule and its substance becomes less sharp, even less real; what counts is the manner in which, a bit like mass and energy, they are transformed into each other.[63]

In this light, then, it is not unusual to find rulers undertaking ritual processions in early Japan, complete with the requisite fanfare and entourage of courtiers and servants. To be able to carry a large number of people and things in one's trail is a public expression of power and prestige. Thus, the prominence of poems from ritual processions in Book 1 of the *Man'yōshū* is not accidental; it represents one of the many editorial decisions informing the structure of the anthology that had a political motivation.

It should be noted, however, that the compilers of the *Man'yōshū* did not recognize poems on imperial excursions or even travel poetry as a distinct type. The editors themselves offered a simple typology consisting of only three types of poetry: *sōmon* or personal exchanges, *banka* or ritual funeral laments, and *zōka* or miscellaneous poems. Book 1 consists entirely of *zōka*, subsuming the poems on imperial excursions. Book 2, which contains a section of *sōmon* and a larger section of *banka*, has no poems on imperial excursions; whereas Book 3 does contain poems on imperial excursions, once again classified as *zōka*. The poems MYS 3: 242–244 are significant examples. The fact that they are classified as miscellaneous poems rather than as personal exchanges, even though 243 is clearly stated to be a response to 242, can best be understood by inferring that the public ritual occasion of the poems dictated this classification.[64]

Book 1 of the *Man'yōshū* contains poems located temporally under the reigns of seven sovereigns—Yūryaku (456–479), Jomei ([629]–642), Kōgyoku ([642]–644), Saimei ([655]–661), Tenji ([661]–671), Temmu ([673]–686), and Jitō ([686]–697)—but it is equally significant that the poems are spatially located as well. The editorial section headings give the location of the imperial palace of the period in question in the following form: "The reign of the Sovereign [Yūryaku], who ruled the realm under heaven from the Asakura Palace in Hatsuse" (*Hatsuse no Asakura no miya ni ame no shita shirashimeshishi sumeramikoto no yomi*), "The reign of the Sovereign [Kōgyoku], who ruled the realm under heaven from the Kawahara Palace in Asuka" (*Asuka no Kawahara no miya ni ame no shita shirashimeshishi sumeramikoto no yomi*), and so forth. The original Japanese does not identify the individual sovereign by his or her regnal name, or even by sex. Rather, the personal identity of the individual sovereign is subsumed under the collective identity of the line of sovereigns as *sumeramikoto* (modern reading *tennō*). This title is shared by male and female alike, rather like "the president" or "the prime minister," so that even the English translations of *sumeramikoto* as "the empress" or "the emperor" represent extrapolations from the information encoded in the place name. Note, too, that the verb here translated as "ruled" is literally "knew" (*shirashimeshishi*), again suggesting the associated meanings of "possessing" mentioned earlier and metaphorically invoked by Geertz.

In looking at MYS 1: 36–39 above, we noted the rhetorical assertion that the sovereign was able to establish the palace and capital precisely because she was a divinity, while the existence of the palace and a bustling capital under her gaze, with courtiers "racing" here and there in her service, was a demonstration of this "fact." One of the functions of such public spectacles, then, was to assert and affirm ritually that the socio-political structure was the natural expression of an ontological reality. In terms of the imperial ideology informing the *Kojiki*, the *Nihonshoki*, and the

Man'yōshū, the existing distribution of power and prestige was a direct consequence of the divinity of the imperial family.

For the early Japanese the capital existed wherever the sitting monarch (the English phrase is itself suggestive) was.[65] Put another way, the center of the universe for the early Japanese was wherever the imperial *tama*, usually translated as "spirit" or "soul," resided. There was only one imperial *tama* that passed from one sovereign to—or more properly "into"—the next. This belief led to, or at least supported, the assertion of the essential identity of all the sovereigns in an unbroken line of descent from Amaterasu, the Sun Goddess. In some respects one could think of *tama* in terms of Weber's "charisma"; to do so, however, would be to miss the essential point that for the early Japanese the *tama* was in some sense a thing. It was occasionally visible and, if not corporal, could reside in corporal bodies, although it was not permanently confined to any one body. It could leave the body at night during sleep, as evinced by dreams, or at other times, causing illness. The early Japanese experienced some anxiety over the *tama*'s departing the body, and they developed a variety of rituals to make sure it did not do so, or to recall it if it escaped. The former rituals were meant to "bind" (*musubu*) the spirit to the body or some object; the latter, called *tama-furi*, to recall it. That the *Man'yōshū* identifies specific sovereigns by the spatial locus of the imperial palace is comprehensible and logically consistent with the larger Japanese world of meaning and the prevailing understanding of *tama*.

In early Japan the imperial journeys commemorated in verse are almost inevitably journeys out from the imperial palace, whether the destination is a hot spring, a summer palace, or a hunting ground. Such poems, moreover, are of two distinct kinds, each with its own characteristic tone. First, there is the praise poem that lauds the divinity of the imperial family member, such as MYS 1: 36–39 above; second, there is the poem that expresses the pain of separation from loved ones occasioned by an imperial excursion. This latter type, however, is not so much an expression of individual feeling on the poet's part as it is a stylized expression of the power the imperial family exercises over others, for an imperial command takes precedence over personal desires. In this sense, the focus of the poem is not exclusively on the poet. At the same time, and perhaps more important, the pain and longing (*koi*) occasioned by the physical separation serve to express the essential hierarchical relationship between the sovereign and the poet (or his patron), a relationship characterized by a difference or distance in status. Poets, in fact, sometimes express this relationship in precisely these terms, calling the imperial family member "a distant *kami*" (*tosu kami*) as in MYS 1: 5. The greater the pain of separation expressed, the more exalted and powerful the imperial family is purported to be.

The first variety of poem of praise is found in MYS 3: 235, from the reign of Jitō, and a variant of the same:

sumeramikoto, Ikazuchi no oka ni idemashishi toki, Kakinomoto no Asomi no
Hitomaro no tsukuru uta isshu

Poem by Kakinomoto Hitomaro at the
time of the Sovereign's excursion to Ikazuchi Hill, "the hill of thunder"

ōkimi wa
kami ni shimaseba
amakumo no
ikazuchi no ue ni
ioraseru kamo

Our Lord,
a very god,
builds her lodge
above the thunder
by the heavenly clouds.

migi, aru hon in iwaku, Osakabe no miko
ni tatematsuru to ieri. sono uta ni iwaku,

A variant of the above poem has it dedicated to Prince Osakabe. The variant reads,

ōkimi wa
kami ni shimaseba
kumo gakuru
Ikazuchi-yama ni
miya shiki imasu

Our Lord,
a very god,
spreads his palace precincts
on the hill of thunder,
hidden in the clouds.[66]

The similarity of these two variants has led many scholars to suggest that this kind of poetry was largely set in style and content and was adapted by oral poets to the specific occasion at hand. This interpretation would be consonant with what we know of other oral traditions. Such poems are, like MYS 1: 36–39, essentially poems of praise that proclaim the divinity and exalted status of the imperial family member, whether that person be the empress or an imperial prince. A fuller example of this formal poetry is MYS 3: 239–240, consisting of a *chōka* and an envoy, along with a variant once again. It is also a skillful blend of direct declamatory praise and reflective praise, the latter achieved by focusing on the low status, relative to the imperial family, of the poet and others.

Naga no miko Kariji no ike ni idemashishi
toki, Kakinomoto no Asomi no Hitomaro
no tsukuru uta isshu

Poem by Kakinomoto Hitomaro at the
time of Prince Naga's excursion to Kariji
Pond

yasumishishi
wago ōkimi
takahikaru
waga hi no miko no
uma namete
mi-kari tataseru
wakakomo o
Kariji no ono ni
shishi koso ba

Our Lord, sovereign
of the earth's eight corners,
our child of the high-shining sun,
lines his steeds
and sets out on the royal hunt.
On the fields of Kariji,
on his hunting trail
among the slender rushes,
the boar and the deer

ihaiorogame	crawl prostrate to behold him,
uzura koso	the very quail
ihaimotohore	crawl on the ground around him.
shishi ji mono	Like the boar and the deer,
ihaiorogami	we crawl prostrate to behold him,
uzura nasu	like the quail,
ihaimotohori	we crawl on the ground around him.
kashikomi to	In awe, we serve him.
tsukaematsurite	However much we look upon him
hisakata no	as we would gaze on a true clear
ame miru gotoku	mirror
ma-so kagami	gaze with eyes that see
aogite miredo	the far firmament,
harukusa no	he is, like the spring grasses,
iya mezurashiki	ever more precious,
wago ōkimi kamo	our Lord.
hanka isshu	An envoy
hisakata no	Catching in a net
ame yuku tsuki o	the moon in its course
tsuna ni sashi	down the far firmament,
wago ōkimi wa	our Lord makes it the canopy
kinugasa ni seri	of his silk umbrella.
(aru hon no hanka isshu	(A variant from another book
ōkimi wa	Our Lord,
kami ni shi maseba	a very god,
ma-ki ni tatsu	constructs a sea
arayama naka ni	among the crags
umi o nasu kamo)	where tower thick black pines.)[67]

The element of relective or inverse praise, of raising the relative status of the prince by lowering oneself, is foregrounded here as Hitomaro compares himself and the other courtiers and functionaries to animals and birds crawling on the ground. There is clear evidence that such ritual prostrations, including crawling around on all fours and imitating animal noises, were practiced in the court. (See Chapter Four.) At the same time that he employs this device, Hitomaro also uses the declamatory voice—"Our Lord,/ a very god"—to assert the prince's divinity. The verse also displays fixed and stylized expressions that allude to mythic paradigms with which this prince, Prince Naga, is identified in order to demonstrate his divinity—"our child of the high-shining sun" and "However much we look upon him/ as we would gaze on a true clear mirror/ gaze with eyes that see/ the far firmament." The first standard epithet identifies the prince as a direct descendant of Amaterasu, and the second recalls the episode in the myth of the descent of Ninigi from Takamagahara ("the far firmament") where Amaterasu gives a sacred mirror (*ma-so kagami*), one of the three imperial regalia, to her grandson and says, "This mirror—have [it with you] as my spirit [*mi-tama*], and worship it as you would worship in my very presence."[68] The poet, thus, proclaims that looking upon the person of Prince Naga is the same as looking upon Amaterasu herself, while serving this prince is the same as worshiping the Sun Goddess.

Poems of Longing on Imperial Excursions

Poems of separation resulting from imperial excursions are also poems of ritual praise. They are often read as love poems, and their ritual nature is not immediately apparent. The poems MYS 1: 5–6 are the first examples of this type of poetry of separation and longing to appear in the anthology.

Sanuki no kuni Aya no kohori ni idemashi-shi toki, Ikusa no ōkimi no yama o mite tsukuru uta

Poem by Prince Ikusa as he looked at the mountains while on the imperial procession to Aya County in the land of Sanuki

kasumi tatsu
nagaki haruhi no
kure ni keru
wazuki mo shirazu
murakimo no
kokoro o itami
nuekotori
ura nakeoreba
tamatasuki
kake no yoroshiku
totsu kami
wago ōkimi no
idemashi no
yamakosu kaze no
hitori oru
waga koromode ni
asa yohi ni
kaerainureba
masurao to
omoeru ware mo
kusamakura
tabi ni shi areba
omoi yaru
tazuki o shira ni
Ami no ura no
amaotomera ga

Not even knowing
if the long spring day
has drawn through its mist
into evening,
my heart,
these twines of inner flesh,
in pain,
weeping,
like the tiger thrush,
inside my soul—
like a strand of jewels,
it's fit to set this into words:

My Lord,
that distant god
passes through the mountains
and the winds blow down
to furl back my sleeves
here where I sojourn alone,
grass for pillow.
Then even I
who thought I was a brave man
find my breast
like the salt
the fishergirls burn
on Ami Cove,

yaku shio no   afire with longing.
omoiso yakuru
waga shimogokoro

hanka   Envoy

yama koshi no   Winds out of season
kaze o toki jimi   blow from the mountain pass,
nuru yoru ochizu   and each night that I sleep
ie naru imo o   my heart is heavy with longing
kakete shinoitsu   for my wife back home.[69]

At first glance this might appear to be simply a love poem, yet one must not be overly hasty in determining the poem's "meaning." Origuchi Shinobu argued many years ago that it was inappropriate to carry modern understandings (one might add Western ones as well) of love into the *Man'yōshū*.[70] The early Japanese understanding of love ("the universal emotion") was not identical to our own but was predicated upon the related understanding of the *tama*. Moreover, we cannot assume that the emotions of love could be expressed in the same ways among different social classes in early Japan. More specifically, the court society and the social constraints placed upon its members generated specific kinds of poems of love and longing unique to that setting.

The public form of MYS 1: 5–6 and its significance has been insufficiently appreciated by Western scholars. The fact that the *chōka*, a public recitative form, is employed here should caution us against taking this set of poems as a private expression. If we assume for the moment that the headnote is reliable, this poem was recited by Prince Ikusa (or for him by a surrogate) during the imperial excursion mentioned.[71] It was not written to be sent back to his wife but would have been intended in performance for an audience from the entourage accompanying the emperor. The public nature of this poem would, in fact, have militated against Prince Ikusa's expressing a purely personal emotion. These observations suggest that we must look further and more specifically to the poem's social and performative contexts for its deeper meaning. Not all or even most of the poems of separation and longing preserved in the *Man'yōshū* are *chōka*, of course; but the existence of a significant number of these poems suggests that what we today might take as private personal emotions were at times in early Japan actually public rehearsals. It is this public presentation of the poetry and the intention behind it that require explication.

It is a serious error to take the *Man'yōshū* poems of longing as spontaneous expressions of private personal emotions because a hierarchical court society is so structured as to inhibit precisely such expressions. Norbert Elias has done much to disclose the operative "rationality" found in court societies that directs the actions and affective expressions of their members. This rationality has its genesis in the need of individuals to adapt their behavior, down to the minutest detail, to the exigencies of the hierarchical structure of the court in order to survive within it. Both the desire to gain and then to maintain status and the necessity to be aware constantly of the actions of others require foresight, careful calculation, and most important, self-restraint. According to Elias:

> Why this attitude becomes important to court people is easily seen: affective outbursts are difficult to control and calculate. They reveal the true feelings of the person to a degree that, because not calculated, can be damaging; they hand over trump cards to rivals for favour and prestige. Above all, they are a sign of weakness; and that is the position the court person fears most of all. *In this way the competition of court life enforces a curbing of the affects in favour of calculated and finely shaded behaviour in dealing with people.* The structure of social life within this figuration left relatively little room for spontaneous expressions of feeling.[72]

If this was the case in the court of early Japan, then one must assume that public poems such as MYS 1: 5–6 had a socio-political dimension, in addition to any individual psychological and emotional aspects. Indeed, I am prepared to go further and to argue that the intention[73] behind public poems of longing was to demonstrate to significant others one's own status and prestige, and that aim took precedence over the "pure" expression of personal emotion. Presentations of personal emotion in early Japan were made only in ways calculated ultimately to maintain or improve one's relative social standing. It is in this light that MYS 1: 5–6 and similar poems must be read and imaginatively recontextualized.

Prince Ikusa here may well have missed his wife, but in public poetry it was unimportant whether this was in fact the case or not. The public expressions of longing served larger purposes that are obscured if one focuses solely on the semantic content of the poetry and intrudes a personal lyrical voice. Here the public rehearsal of Ikusa's longing, in concert with stylized praise of the emperor ("My Lord/ that distant god"), for example, serves as a comment on and demonstration of the power of the sovereign as well as of Prince Ikusa's loyalty and obedience to him. Although Ikusa would like to be with his wife, a higher duty calls him on the imperial procession to serve his lord. The more the poet/singer emphasizes his love for his wife, the more his longing for her reflects on the power of the sovereign that could draw him away.

In the milieu of the court, Ikusa's protestations function in a variety of ways simultaneously to mark out distance and proximity, both spatially and socially. First, and most obviously, the generative occasion of the poem is Ikusa's physical separation from his wife. But the underlying point, which the prince himself calls to the audience's attention, is the reason for this separation—*he is with the emperor.* The public rehearsal of his longing includes the message of Ikusa's social proximity to the emperor, which translates into elevated status and prestige. At the same time, significant distance, again both physical and social, is created between Ikusa and others as he enjoys the privilege of traveling with the emperor while others presumably were left behind. It would be wrong, then, to take the "meaning" of this poem to be limited to a personal emotion or the love of a husband for his wife. It must be understood in the broader terms of the socio-political milieu of the imperial court. Locating the text in its performative context, one can see that there is an element of boastful pride in the prince's complaint.[74]

Thus, the public recitation of poems provided an important occasion for maneuvering in the ongoing social process to gain, then to maintain, prestige for oneself. For such poetry and for public recognition of prestige, an audience of significant others was absolutely essential, although ultimately everything depended on the disposition of the sovereign. (The sovereign, however, was himself constrained to a greater or lesser extent by the exigencies of his own situation in which he needed the support of sufficiently powerful clan leaders to survive.) Everyone in the court was necessarily and especially observant of the smallest shifts in the enmeshed social rank and status of its members, since any individual change affected the relative status of many contiguous others. A poem such as MYS 1: 5–6, for example, would have played a part in the internal gradation of status and prestige within the circle of the nobility and even within the smaller circle of imperial princes.[75] Although we do not know whether this was the case here or not, the *Nihonshoki* provides a number of examples of certain princes being selected to accompany the sovereign on a procession while others were left behind. We must remember that in the court it was important to be invited to attend the sovereign. The prestige value was such that to be granted the privilege of performing even menial service for him/her served to elevate one's own social stock.

The etymology of the English word "prestige" suggests how this poem might have functioned to create both social difference (distance) and similarity (proximity). According to *Webster's Seventh New Collegiate Dictionary*, "prestige" comes from Middle French (itself from the Late Latin *praestigium*) for "conjuror's trick" or "illusion." The "trick" is to get significant individuals to concur that one's own rank is deservedly higher than others in the same society, to create the illusion of difference and distinction that would then become a social reality. In this poem, and in others like it concerned with public prestige, there is a rhetorical sleight of hand at work. On the one hand, distance is created between the emperor and almost everyone else by declaring the sovereign's divinity, majesty, and so on; on the other, this distancing, like a magnet, draws others—notably those biologically related to the emperor and court functionaries—to the person of the emperor. While these individuals explicitly lower themselves relative to the sovereign, they raise themselves in terms of the whole society, creating distance in both directions. To appreciate why this is so it must be remembered that social prestige and status in a court society are based upon the two aspects of *mi* (vision) we saw earlier in association with the *kunimi* or land-viewing poems and ritual. First, it is important to be seen by others in the company of the sovereign (physical proximity); second, it is equally important to be seen by the sovereign in a good light (social intimacy). In such a prestige-conscious society, the public recitation of poetry during an imperial excursion would provide an excellent opportunity to realize both these goals. If one bears this in mind, it suddenly becomes clear that the public praise of one's lord, like the sovereign's praise of the land, also reflects on one's own social position.

All too often, poems from the early Japanese texts are read as individual expressions, that is, as poems by autonomous individuals free of any social constraints. In the "Introduction" to the Nippon Gakujutsu Shinkōkai translation of selections from the *Man'yōshū*, the editors assert that Man'yō poets frankly recorded their personal emotions, including the pain of separation from their wives, but "never a murmur of grudge or resentment" against the sovereign.[76] Yet if one understands the social structure of interdependence operative in the court, it is inappropriate to read these poems as expressions of private emotions. One should not compound this misreading by making unfounded assumptions as to why explicit complaints and criticism of the sovereign are not found in the extant poems. When they are understood as public poems, the reasons for the absence are obvious. It was not so much that early Japan was an idyllic society—even a cursory glance at the *Nihonshoki* would disabuse one of that conception—as that the court poets and courtiers were not fools. The emperor, empress, and others at the top of the socio-political structure had the power to make or break not only individuals but whole clans, as we shall see.

Only by keeping the social context of this poetry in mind can we understand why, as so many commentators have noted, poems of separation are based on journeys either with members of the imperial family or on their behalf.[77] Similarly, we can appreciate why poets sometimes express the fear of censure by others in the form of gossip for simply being with their wives. When Hitomaro, for example, in MYS 2: 207, a lament for his wife, says: "I desired to meet her intimately/ but if I went there too much/ the eyes of others would cluster around us/ and if I went there too often/ others would find us out,"[78] he is speaking as a member of the court society whose "private" life was subject to intense scrutiny and possible criticism by others. An individual who placed his personal desires above service to the imperial family was suspect and consequently in danger of a loss of social prestige through gossip and intrigue. In later chapters we will see how charges of sexual impropriety, incest, and disrespect toward some member of the imperial family or the power elite were also weapons in the political intrigues throughout the court.

To a great extent the actions and speech of every member of the court society were constrained by the awareness of the constant presence of "the eyes of others" (*hitome*).

Many of the poems in the *Man'yōshū*, if used properly, can serve historians and sociologists as documents demonstrating the figuration of early Japanese court society and the centripetal nature of the Court's power, a power that led individuals to channel even intensely felt private pain into rhetorically structured public expressions of status and prestige. Levy is quite right to emphasize the ways in which the public ritual poetry of Hitomaro functioned to create an "iconic image" of the imperial family,[79] but he fails to recognize that the poetry involves an undeniable element of self-aggrandizement as well. The public recitation of poetry of longing and separation provided an opportunity to display one's nobility, including a higher sensibility and sense of duty, through the social renunciation of private desires. One did this, of course, because of the promise of greater rewards of power, position, and prestige among one's peers.

Several poems by Hitomaro are best appreciated in this context. In looking at them, we may also be able to understand more fully the dynamic cultural function of public ritual poetry in the court milieu: MYS 2: 131–137 is a set of two *chōka* on Hitomaro's separation from his wife, each with two accompanying *hanka*, plus a variant of one of the envoys; MYS 2: 138–139 is a variant of 131–132. Scholars have long been at pains to explain why Hitomaro here adapts a public form, the *chōka*, to what they assume to be a lyrical expression of private emotion. In the Japanese literary tradition Hitomaro has been acclaimed for over a thousand years as a great, if not the greatest, poet. Such public/private poems as MYS 2: 131–139 have usually been interpreted as marking a signal creative development in Japanese literary history. Yet it is doubtful that the voice in Hitomaro's poetry is ever "entirely personal."[80]

The following example may demonstrate this point. The headnote preceding the set, MYS 2: 131–137, says: "Two poems by Kakinomoto Hitomaro when he parted from his wife in the land of Iwami and came up to the capital, with tanka." This suggests that Hitomaro had been summoned to the capital where he was employed, it seems, in the Island Palace (*Shima no miya*) of the Crown Prince Kusakabe.[81] Thus, these poems fit the pattern noted earlier of *Man'yōshū* poems of separation and longing in *chōka* form often involving performance of official duties in obedience to imperial commands. The second *chōka* of this set and the accompanying envoys, MYS 2: 135–137, read:

tsuno sahō   At Cape Kara
Iwami no umi no   on the sea of Iwami,

koto saeku	where the vines
Kara no saki naru	crawl on the rocks,
ikuri ni so	rockweed of the deep
fukamiru ouru	grows on the reefs
ariso ni so	and sleek seaweed
tamamo wa ouru	grows on the desolate shore.
tamamo nasu	As deeply do I
nabikineshi ko o	think of my wife
fukamiru no	who swayed toward me in sleep
fukamete moedo	like the lithe seaweed.
saneshi yo wa	Yet few were the nights
ikudamo arazu	we had slept together
hau tsuta no	before we were parted
wakareshi kureba	like crawling vines uncurled.
kimo mukau	And so I look back,
kokoro o itami	still thinking of her
omoitsutsu	with painful heart,
kaerimisuredo	this clench of inner flesh,
ōfune no	but in the storm
Watari no yama no	of fallen scarlet leaves
momijiba no	on Mount Watari,
chiri no magai ni	crossed as on
imo ga sode	a great ship,
saya ni mo miezu	I cannot make out the sleeves
tsuma gomoru	she waves in farewell.
Yakami no yama no[82]	For she, alas,
kumoma yori	is slowly hidden
watarau tsuki no	like the moon
oshike domo	in its crossing
kakuroi kureba	between the clouds
ama tsutau	over Ya[k]ami Mountain
irihi sashinure	just as the evening sun
masurao to	coursing through the heavens
omoeru ware mo	has begun to glow,
shikitae no	and even I
koromo no sode wa	who thought I was a brave man
toritenurenu	find the sleeves
	of my well-worn robe
	drenched with tears.
hanka nishu	Two envoys
aouma no	The quick gallop
agaki o hayami	of my dapple-blue steed
kumo i ni so	races me to the clouds,
imo ga atari o	passing far away
sugite kinikeru	from where my wife dwells.

akiyama ni	O scarlet leaves
ochitsuru momijiba	falling on the autumn mountainside:
shimashiku wa	stop, for a while, the storm
na chirimagai so	your strewing makes, that I might
imo ga atari mimu	glimpse
	the place where my wife dwells.[83]

If we read this poem in light of the points made above, then we can hear the expected stylized longing rehearsed here in a public voice. Service in the imperial court no doubt required some personal sacrifice, including at times separation from one's spouse, yet it would be premature to assume that such sacrifices were not finally willingly made. Poems such as these must be balanced by others such as MYS 3: 261–262:

Kakinomoto no Asomi no Hitomaro, Ni-itabe no miko ni tatematsuru uta isshu, narabe ni tanka	Poem presented by Kakinomoto Hitomaro to Prince Niitabe, with tanka
yasumishishi	Our Lord, sovereign
wago ōkimi	of the earth's eight corners,
takaterasu	child of the high-shining sun—
hi no miko	May I make my way to you
sakaemasu	like the snow
ōtono no ue ni	coursing through the far firmament
hisakata no	to fall upon the great halls
ama tsutaikuru	where your reign flourishes,
yuki ji mono	there to attend you
yuki kayoitsutsu	as the years pass to eternity.
iya tokoyo made	
hanka isshu	Envoy
Yatsuri yama	Through the streaming snow
kodachi mo miezu	that hides the grove of trees
furimagau	on Yatsuri Hill,
yuki ni ugutsuku	racing my steed to your halls:
ashita tanoshi mo	the mornings are my delight.[84]

The image of a racing steed, employed by Hitomaro in MYS 2: 136 to express the pain of separation from his wife, is here used to express the exhilaration of approaching the palace of the Imperial Prince Niitabe each morning. It is impossible to know which of these is Hitomaro's "real" feeling about his duties at court. There is probably a bit of truth in both, as well as some rhetorical posturing for public consumption. It is this latter point that requires emphasis, however, since it is usually overlooked. The poem refers to the daily ritual wherein the courtiers lined up in rank order before the palace to receive their orders for the day. It is at once a poem of praise of Prince Niitabe and a public proclamation of Hitomaro's fealty and joy in serving him. As such, it shares the dual function of creating social (and even ontological) distance between the prince and his subjects while also pointedly locating Hitomaro in proximity to the prince.[85] Although the immediate focus of the poem is on the courtier's loyal service, the overall effect of the poem is to reflect on the grandeur of Prince Niitabe, who inspires this loyalty and the "delight" the courtier supposedly feels.

The public recitation of poems of stylized longing and praise participated in the ongoing process of creating differences or gradations within the hierarchy of the court. In such public ritual occasions the members of the court, including the imperial family, the nobles, and the various court functionaries, continually reconstituted their society (in a Durkheimian sense) by representing the social order to themselves. This order was never constant but ever-changing in a continuous struggle for rank, status, and prestige. In MYS 3: 261–262, for instance, Hitomaro alludes to the daily morning ritual held in front of the palace. As the courtiers lined up in rank order, they displayed the hierarchy to themselves and to others. The rising or falling stock of an individual or family would have been immediately visible to everyone. Not only that; any single change would also affect the relative position (physically in the line and in relational terms of social status and prestige) of everyone else. In hierarchical groupings such as this, the proper form of address, the degree and form of social interaction, and so forth, were all dictated by the relative rank of any two persons who came into contact. Within the court, one's identity was in a very conspicuous manner a socially negotiated fact. The *Nihonshoki* is filled with entries detailing court promotions and demotions, for this was one of the sovereign's primary means of exercising and maintaining power. A single entry will indicate how the sovereign could use his power to promote individuals within the court, coupled with his knowledge of their intense desire for such promotions, to defuse a potentially dangerous situation. The entry comes from the reign of the Emperor Temmu in the late seventh century and, thus, is probably historically reliable. Characteristically vague and providing few details about the actual content and intention behind the actions recounted, it reads:

11th month, 3rd day [675 C.E.]. A certain man ascended the hill east of the Palace, and having uttered words of evil omen [*oyorozure koto shite*], cut his throat and died. Those who were on duty on that night received everyone a step in rank.[86]

Although this entry does not disclose the identity of the individual, it is clear that he was a member of the court. Moreover, his ritual curse and suicide were apparently a form of protest directed against the emperor. This political protest, expressed in ritual form, was taken seriously enough that the Emperor Temmu seems to have

felt compelled to promote the other courtiers immediately, an action probably designed to forestall their rallying to the rebel's cause. That is, Temmu was attempting
to pacify or, more crudely put, "buy off" the opposition; apparently the ploy
worked, for one hears no more of the affair.

Tama-*Related Rituals*

Hitomaro's poem of separation from his wife, introduced above, may serve as an
entry to the beliefs and practices surrounding the *tama*, the animating spirit that
gives life to the physical body. They constitute a central symbolic and ritual complex
in early Japan.[87] It will be recalled that MYS 2: 135 contained the lines "I cannot
make out the sleeves/ she waves in farewell" (*imo ga sode/ saya nimo miezu*). Although
it is not clear from the translation, this is an obvious reference to the performance
of a *tama-furi* (*tama*-shaking) ritual. The intention behind the action of Hitomaro's
wife is to guarantee his safe return. The belief in the efficacy of this action is related
in a general way to the familiar Western custom, now largely attenuated into metaphorical usage, of keeping a candle burning in the window while someone is away.
In both cases, the belief is that the action will help the absent person find his or her
way home again safely.

There are a large number of references to *tama-furi* rituals in the extant poetry
from early Japan, as well as in prose passages from the three texts. In MYS 2: 132,
one of the set of poems on parting from his wife, Hitomaro says:

Iwami no ya	O does my wife
Takatsuno-yama no	see the sleeves I wave
ki no ma yori	from between the trees
waga furu sode o	on Takatsuno Mountain
imo mitsuramu ka	in Iwami?[88]

Here again the ritual action of *tama-furi* is visible. The following are the last lines
of MYS 2: 207, a ritual funeral lament by Hitomaro on, according to the headnote,
the death of his wife. A messenger had just brought news of her passing.

iwamu sube	I did not know what to say,
namu sube shira ni	what to do,
oto nomi o	but simply could not listen
kikite ari eneba	and so, perhaps to solace
waga kouru	a single thousandth
chie no hito e mo	of my thousand-folded longing,
nagasamuru	I stood at the Karu market
kokoro mo ariya to	where often she had gone

wagimoko ga	and listened,
tomazu idemishi	but could not hear
Karu no ichi ni	the voices of the birds
waga tachikikeba	that cry on Unebi Mountain
tamatasuki	where the maidens
Unebi no yama ni	wear strands of jewels,
naku tori no	and of the ones who passed me
koi mo kiezu	on that road,
tamahoko no	straight as a jade spear,
michi yuku hito mo	not one resembled her.
hitori dani	I could do nothing
niteshi yukaneba	but call my wife's name
sube o nami	and wave my sleeves.[89]
imo ga na yobite	
sode so furitsuru	

Various elements of early Japanese belief and practice are found here. Note the frequent use of homonyms of *tama* here—*tamatasuki* and *tamahoko*—in addition to *tamazusa* earlier. The reference to the crying of birds alludes to the belief that the departing *tama* of the dead often assumed the form of a bird.[90] In waving his sleeves, Hitomaro was performing a *tama-furi* rite to call back his wife's spirit. Unless one understands this, Hitomaro's action of waving his sleeves is meaningless. The early Japanese did not consider death to be a permanent or irreversible state, at least for a short period after an individual had expired. Since death was believed to be a result of the *tama* having left the body, various *tama-furi*-related rituals were performed in an effort to attract the animating spirit back into the body. In this light, even in the twentieth century we can appreciate Hitomaro's action as a desperate attempt to deny the reality of the death of a loved one. Though the specific ritual expression is historically and culturally bound, the informing emotional response to death is recognizably more universal.

The mobility of the *tama* was a source of anxiety for the early Japanese, as we have seen. In addition to rituals to recall a departed spirit, they had rituals to bind it (*tama-musubu*) and others to restrict or impose boundaries on its movement. The latter practice is alluded to in two *banka*, MYS 2: 151 and 154, from the time of the temporary enshrinement of the corpse of the Emperor Tenji (r. 661–671):

(151)	
kakaramu no	If I had known
kokoro shiriseba	it would come to this,
ōmi-fune	I would have tied signs of interdiction
hateshi tomari ni	around the harbor
shimeyu wa mashi o	where the imperial craft did berth.

(154)

Sasanami no	For whom does the guardian
ōyamamori wa	of Sasanami's imperial mountains
taga tame ka	post his signs of interdiction,
yama ni shimeyuu	now that you, my Lord,
kimi mo aranaku ni	are no longer?[91]

Here following the death of Tenji, the imperial consorts retrospectively lament the fact that when he had fallen ill they had not had rituals performed that might have kept his life spirit from leaving his body and passing into the mountains, the realm of the dead.[92]

The word *musubi* or *musui* was originally written with a compound character generally taken to mean "spirit power." The first character clearly relates the term to birth or to producing or bearing something, and the latter character is *tama* or spirit. Another character is used to suggest the tying or binding of spirit to matter. Also pronounced *iwa(u)* and *yuwa(u)*, this word is conceptually related to the act of ritual celebration or commemoration. According to Kamstra, "In reality and origin this *iwau* . . . means: avoidance of the escape of the *musubi* from the material; the enclosure, coagulation of spirits in a certain (mag[ico]-religious) object."[93] The *musubi* belief complex also involves the element of sexuality and agricultural fertility and, thus, is deeply involved in the *niiname-sai*, the First Fruits or Harvest Festival and the imperial accession rituals, where the imperial *tama* is incorporated into the new sovereign. Linguistically, then, the term "*musubi*" was multivalent, carrying a rich symbolic content.

The textual references to binding the *tama* by tying knots are too numerous to list here, but a few examples will suffice. The poems MYS 2: 141, 143–144, and 146 all refer to *tama-musubi* rituals and may serve as an introduction to the ritual recitation of poetry in order to pacify the spirits of the dead. The entire set is also an excellent example of how the editors of the *Man'yōshū* employed earlier poems in their own historiographic project. Some historical background is necessary if we are to appreciate the significance of these poems. Saimei (r. [655]–661) was the former Empress Kōgyoku (r. [642]–645), and the Emperor Kōtoku (r. 645–654) was her younger brother by the same mother. Prince Arima was a son of Kōtoku, making Kōgyoku/Saimei his paternal aunt. Readers of the *Man'yōshū* in the late eighth century would have been familiar with the tale of Prince Arima from the *Nihonshoki* and other historical accounts, including perhaps oral histories.

The mid-seventh century was a time of intense intrigue in the court involving the very powerful Soga clan. The fortunes of the various clans and individual courtiers depended to a great extent on the eventual success or failure of their candidate in the constant jockeying for position and power. Those who for whatever reason were not in the faction in power tended to place their hopes in imperial princes by different mothers. Frequently courtiers skillful in the practice of palace intrigues sought to press their own claims and to improve their own fortunes by obliquely identifying their personal situation with the frustrations and complaints of a prince who had found his own desire for power and prestige effectively blocked in the court. The *Nihonshoki* provides occasional glimpses of this socio-political process. Unfortunately there are no memoirs from early Japan as extensive as those of Saint-Simon, a classic record of such intrigue within the French court of Louis XIV. In light of what we know from documentation of other court societies, however, the following passage rings true as to how a courtier was able to persuade Prince Arima to attempt to assassinate his aunt and seize the throne.

11th month, 3rd day [658]. Soga no Akae no Ōmi, the official who had charge during the Empress's absence, addressed the Imperial Prince Arima, saying:—"There are three faults in the Empress's administration of the affairs of Government. The first is that she builds the treasuries on a great scale, wherein she collects the riches of the people. The second is that she wastes the public grain revenue in digging long canals. The third is that she loads barges with stones and transports them to be piled up into a hill." The Imperial Prince Arima, recognizing Akae's friendly disposition towards himself, was gratified, and replied, saying:— "I have only now come to an age when I am fit to bear arms."[94]

The minister's criticisms of the empress must have struck a chord with Prince Arima. Though only nineteen at the time, Arima was encouraged by the suggestion that others shared his reservations about the empress's administration of the government, and a plot was hatched to usurp power. The plot was quickly revealed, however, and Prince Arima and his co-conspirators were captured and executed a few days later. It is out of this background that MYS 2: 141–142 must be understood.

Arima no miko, mizu kara itamite matsu ga
e o musubu uta nishu

Two poems by Prince Arima, in his sorrow
as he tied branches of a pine tree

Iwashiro no
hama matsu ga e o
hikimusubi
ma-sakiku araba
mata kaeri mimu

I draw and tie together
branches of the pine
on the beach at Iwashiro.
If all goes well
I shall return to see them again.

ie ni areba
ke ni moru ii o
kusamakura
tabi ni shi areba
shii no ha ni moru

The rice I would heap
into a lunch box
if I were home—
since I journey,
grass for pillow,
I heap into an oak leaf.

(143–144)
Naga no imiki Okimaro, musubimatsu o mite kanashibi musebu uta nishu

Two poems by Naga Okimaro, choked with sorrow upon seeing the pine with its branches tied

Iwashiro no
kishi no matsu ga e
musubikemu
hito wa kaerite
mata mikemu kamo

I wonder if he
who tied the branches of the pine
on the cliff
by Iwashiro's sea
returned to see them again.

Iwashiro no
no naka ni tateru
musubi matsu
kokoro mo tokezu
inishie omōyu

The pine
standing in the fields of Iwashiro
with its branches tied:
and my heart is undone
as my thoughts turn to the past.

(imada tsubahirakanarazu)

(The authorship is still uncertain.)[95]

(145)
Yamanoue no omi Okura, tsuite kotauru uta isshu

Poem by Yamanoue Okura at a later time responding to Okimaro's

tori kake na
ari gayoitsutsu
mirame domo
hito koso shirane
matsu wa shiruramu

Soaring like a bird
across the sky,
though he [is present and] sees,
men do not know it.
But the pine must know.

(migi no kudari no uta domo wa, hitsugi o hiku toki tsukuru tokoro ni arazu to ie domo, uta no kokoro o nazurau. soi ni banka no tagui ni nosu)

(Although the above poems are said not to be *banka* in the sense of "coffin-pulling poems," they share the same poetic intention, and therefore have been classified here with the *banka*.)

(146)
Taihō gannen kanoto ushi Ki no kuni ni idemashishi toki, musubi matsu o miru uta isshu. (Kakinomoto no Asomi no Hitomaro kashū no naka ni idezu)

Poem upon seeing the pine tree with its branches tied, at the time of the imperial procession to the land of Ki in the first year [junior metal-ox] of Taihō [701] (This poem is in the *Kakinomoto Hitomaro Collection*.)

nochi mimu to
kimi ga musuberu
Iwashiro no
komatsu ga ure o
mata mikemu kamo

Did you later see
the new growth on the branches
of the young pine at Iwashiro
you tied together in hopes
of seeing it again?[96]

In these poems one finds the ritual practice of tying together the branches of a tree associated with the tale of the aborted plan of an imperial prince to seize power. This blend of "timeless" ritual with current or recent political events is quite common in all the texts from early Japan. In one sense, every ritual of tying the branches was identical in action and in the informing belief system; but in another sense, Prince Arima's performance of this ritual action was a unique event, with specific intentions and meanings other performances did not have. The ritual performed here represents the hopes and fears not only of Prince Arima but of all his supporters. The social, political, and economic futures of an unknown number of families are involved in the intention behind this specific ritual performance.

Similarly, the poems that follow Prince Arima's "death poem" have a political aspect themselves, suggesting either that some individuals within the court had not yet reconciled themselves to Arima's death and possibly hoped to keep his factional aspirations alive, or alternatively, that those in power felt it necessary to pacify the spirit of the dead prince through the performance of public ritual laments. Whatever the case, because of the length of time that had elapsed since Arima's execution, it is impossible to believe that the cloth ties referred to in these poems were those used by Prince Arima. Rather, there are two possibilities: we have either (1) a case of later poets exercising poetic license or (2) a possible hint that others in the years following Arima's execution continued to tie the branches together as a political statement of their own. If the former was in fact the case, then there were not any actual *musubi-matsu* before the poets' eyes, and the extant verses represent a rhetorical fiction used to evoke a sense of pathos and tragedy in the readers. On the other hand, if the latter was the case, then we have an example of yet another way poetry could function in the public realm as a political tool, challenging the present status quo by recalling a perceived injustice from the past.

Moreover, the very fact that some of the poems were preserved in the *Man'yōshū* over a century after the events referred to is not without a political dimension of its own. The headnote to poem 141, Arima's death poem, locates his ritual performance at a specific time and place within the larger narrative frame of the tale of his conspiracy and execution. Purportedly Prince Arima ties the branches of the pine and recites the poem-prayer *after he has been arrested* and is being sent into exile and to his death. The sense of poignancy, even pathos, this poem evokes is a direct result of the reader's (or the listener's) knowledge of the outcome of the story—that Arima would be strangled and would not return to see the new growth of the pine in the spring. Neither the ritual act itself nor the poem in isolation would produce this effect. The "meaning" of the ritual act and of the poem is, then, generated by the larger context in which the action is reported to have been performed.

Our "facts" and data concerning this incident come from the extant texts, which are themselves temporally removed from the actual events. The paradox every historian faces is that the very texts that are one's only point of access to past events are also already interpretations of these events and not "pure" records. The authors or editors of each text tell their stories, giving narrative order and structure to the events, in order to convey their sense of history to the reader. In presenting and ordering poems 141–144, the editors of the *Man'yōshū* guide the reader's interpretation by contextualizing the embedded ritual acts in a larger narrative. In itself, poem 141 is almost generic, for with only a change in place name and possibly other minor alterations necessary to maintain the syllabic count, it could well be recited by anyone on any occasion of departing from a location to which one hoped to return safely. In that sense at least, the poem mirrors the ritual, which was also generic. Malinowski once said that every ritual performance is the same, and in a very limited sense he was right; but when history—human action in a specific time and place—is factored in, his statement is no longer true. Any event in time and space, including the performance of a ritual, does not in and of itself yield its own meaning. Meaning is supplied by the immediate context in which the event occurs, and by the interpretation of that event by others. For those who are removed spatially and/or temporally from the performance, the specific meaning of it is recoverable only through the retrospective narrative ordering of the ritual itself and the context and events surrounding it—and these may be altered over time.

The poem MYS 2: 141 may serve, then, to remind us that although it would be possible to extract references to ritual practices from these eighth-century texts and then to reconstruct in large measure the morphological structure of the rituals, unless they are then reinserted into the texts, specifically located in time and space, and studied individually in their respective performative and narrative contexts as well, much of the "meaning" will be lost. Thus, although it is important to know that *matsu* or "pine" is used ubiquitously in Japanese literature as a homonym of *matsu*, "to wait," and that the symbolic meaning or intention behind tying or binding is found in many religious traditions around the world,[97] it is also important to know the story of Prince Arima's conspiracy recounted in the *Nihonshoki* in order to appreciate what such a ritual action and poems would have meant to his followers and later generations. The meaning of MYS 2: 141 is not monolithic but multiple, with different readings by different individuals and groups over time. We cannot, then, ignore the fact that the processes of retrospective contextualization of poems and of anthologization possess ideological dimensions of their own.

One more point deserves mention. It will be recalled that the editorial note following MYS 3: 141–145 says: "Although the above poems are not *banka* in the sense of 'coffin-pulling poems,' they share the same poetic intention, and therefore have been classified with the *banka*." In seeking to understand these texts, we must try to appreciate the *emic* point of view, the "native" categories and classificatory systems by which the world was ordered, comprehended, and cognitively controlled. A classificatory term such as "*banka*" is expected to be a useful indicator as to the type of text one is looking at and how it should be read and interpreted. In the prose editorial note above, however, one finds that the *emic* classification—*banka*— is problematic. Rather than being stable, it appears unstable; rather than providing a ready key to the "map" of the world of meaning of early Japan, the editorial note suggests a changing topography. Yet this fact is important in itself, for it suggests that history has somehow entered into the picture; in the equivocation about the term "*banka*" we have evidence of an instance of historical change.

By the late eighth century when the *Man'yōshū* was anthologized, the editors seem to have realized that these poems were not really *banka* and yet, we are told, they shared something of the same "poetic intention" (*uta no kokoro*). To understand this editorial note the historian, whether of Japanese literature or religion, must first determine what an authentic *banka* was and then what element(s) constituted the shared poetic intention. Since this topic will be treated below in Chapter Four, let me simply say here that spatially, *banka* had their genesis and performance in the rituals performed around and in the *mogari no miya*, and in temporal terms during the period of the temporary enshrinement of the corpse. The two poems attributed to Prince Arima, 142 and 143, are presented as predating his death and burial, whereas the others postdate by several generations his execution in 658. (Poems 143 and 144 are attributed to Naga Okimaro, a contemporary of Hitomaro in the late seventh century, and 145 is said to be by Yamanoue Okura, 660?–733?.) Thus, none of the poems can be considered to have come out of the rituals of temporary en- shrinement. Moreover, by the time the *Man'yōshū* was compiled, the imperial court no longer practiced double burial in its previous form. At the time of the death of the Empress Jitō in 702, a *mogari no miya* was constructed; but a year later, instead of exhuming the corpse and reburying it elsewhere, as had been the prevailing prac- tice, the imperial family adopted the Buddhist practice of cremation. This instance marked the beginning of the rapid disappearance of the practice of double burial. Thus, within the court, the performative ritual locus of *banka* disappeared; as a re- sult, *banka* disappeared as an oral ritual form.

This editorial note with its equivocation concerning the genre of *banka* permits us to see how a shift in funerary practice led to a concomitant change in the param- eters of a literary classification. Whereas the designation *banka* apparently had once been restricted to funerary ritual laments, with the cessation of the practice of dou- ble burial other poems that simply referred to an individual's death came to be considered as like *banka*. Thus the classification was initially expanded. Very quickly, perhaps within a few years of the compilation of the *Man'yōshū*, however, the classification was abandoned completely, no doubt because without the ritual locus, it proved to be anachronistic and meaningless. Whatever the case may be, though, it is obvious that the history of such poetry cannot be separated from the history of the Japanese religious tradition.

Poems of Pacification of the Spirits of the Dead

The recitation of poems to pacify certain spirits, a major type of ritual poetry in early Japan, is found in different forms throughout the Japanese religious tradition.[98] Although most of the poems collected in the *Man'yōshū* concern the imperial family or courtiers, there are others that deal with anonymous figures. A good example of this type of poem is MYS 2: 220:

Sanuki no Samine no shima ni, ishi no naka ni mimakareru hito o mite, Kakinomoto Asomi no Hitomaro no tsukuru uta isshu narabe ni tanka

Poem by Kakinomoto Hitomaro upon seeing a dead man lying among the rocks on the island of Samine in Sanuki, with tanka

tamamo yoshi
Sanuki no kuni wa
kuni kara ka
miredomo akanu
kamu kara ka
kokoda tōtoki
ametsuchi
hi tsuki to tomo ni
tariyukamu
kami no mi-omo to
tsugite kuru
Naka no minato yu
funa ukete
waga kogi kureba
toki tsu kaze
kumo i ni fuku ni
oki mireba
toi nami tachi
he mireba
shiranami sawaku
isana tori
umi o kashikomi
yuku funa no
kajihiki orite
ochikochi no

The land of Sanuki,
fine in sleek seaweed:
is it for the beauty of the land
that we do not tire
to gaze upon it?
Is it for its divinity
that we deem it most noble?
Eternally flourishing,
with the heavens
and the earth,
with the sun
and the moon,
the very face of a god—
so it has come down
through the ages.

Casting off
from Naka harbor,
we came rowing.
Then tide winds
blew through the clouds;
on the offing
we saw the rustled waves,
on the strand
we saw the roaring crests.

shima wa ōke do

mei kuwashi

Samine no shima no

ariso mo ni

iorite mireba

nami no to no

shigeki hamabe o

shikitae no

makura ni nashite

ara doko ni

koro fusu kimi ga

ie shiraba

yukite mo tsugemu

tsuma shiraba

ki mo towamashi o

tamahoko no

michi dani shirazu

oboboshiku

machi ka kōramu

washiki tsumara wa

Fearing the whale-hunted seas,
our ship plunged through—
we bent those oars!
Many were the islands
near and far,
but we beached on Samine—
beautiful its name—
and built a shelter
on the rugged shore.

Looking around,
we saw you
lying there
on a jagged bed of stones,
the beach
for your finely woven pillow,
by the breakers' roar.
If I knew your home,
I would go and tell them.
If your wife knew,
she would come and seek you out.
But she does not even know the road
straight as a jade spear.
Does she not wait for you,
worrying and longing,
your beloved wife?

hanka nishu

[Two] envoys

tsuma mo araba

tsumite tagemashi

Sami no yamano no

e no uwagi

tōgi ni kerazu ya

If your wife were here,
she would gather and feed you
the starwort that grows
on the Sami hillsides,
but is its season not past?

okitsu nami

kiyoru ariso o

shikitae no

makura to makite

naseru kimi kamo

Making a finely woven pillow
of the rocky shore
where waves from the offing
draw near,
you, who sleep there![99]

The poet opens by praising the geographical place in terms reminiscent of the *kunimi* poems discussed earlier. This praise is not accidental, for the poem participates in the same symbolic and ritual complex. The headnote provides the purported occasion of the poem's genesis, yet the long first section does not introduce any human figures. Rather, it is devoted exclusively to praise of the land, which it declares beautiful and divine (*miredomo akanu/ kamu kara ka*, etc.). The identity of the drowning victim is unclear, as even Hitomaro does not know his name or home-town. Why, then, does Hitomaro use the *chōka* form for this *banka*? Most scholars agree that such poems must have been part of a ritual performed for the pacification of the spirit of the accident victim, whose fate had denied him the normal funeral rites. Itō Haku, for example, sees this *chōka* and the envoys as a product of Hito-maro's participation in the traditional belief and ritual complex surrounding travel and of his service in the imperial court.[100] Here Hitomaro seeks to pacify both the spirit of the land, through stylized praise, and the spirit of the dead, through recall-ing the love of the dead man's wife and suggesting that if only she knew where the corpse was, she would dutifully lament at his grave site.

The poem, however, is even more complex, for if the *chōka* is read carefully, one can see that Hitomaro also identifies himself with the drowning victim; he, too, is on a dangerous journey over the same seas that claimed this man's life. The effect of this rhetorical identification is once again to focus, although in a deflected or oblique manner, on the danger Hitomaro and his companions face in undertaking a journey ordered by a member of the imperial family. Ostensibly a poem on an anonymous drowning victim, Hitomaro takes the opportunity to turn it into another variety of a "boastful complaint" as he rehearses the horrors of the storm that forced his ship to beach on Samine. The poem, then, is quite complex in intention and in address, for it is directed in part to the *kami* of the place, praising the site's beauty and offering thanks for the party having found refuge there; in part to the spirit of the drowning victim; and in part to the assembled traveling companions of Hitomaro and ultimately to his patron in the imperial family. This fact suggests that Hitomaro was himself enmeshed in the rationality informing court society. In the middle sec-tion of the *chōka* he is not so much performing a ritual of pacification of the spirit of the dead man as he is rhetorically positioning himself within the ranks of court functionaries.

This internal "linkage" of the poet's own situation with that of the drowning victim was not lost on the compilers of the *Man'yōshū*, for the very next poem in the anthology, MYS 2: 223, is reputed to be Hitomaro's lament on his own impending death far from his wife and home.

Kakinomoto Asomi no Hitomaro, Iwami no kuni ni arite mimakaramu to suru toki, mizukara itamite tsukuru uta isshu	Poem by Kakinomoto Hitomaro in his own sorrow as he was about to die in the land of Iwami
Kamo yama no iwa neshi makeru ware o kamo shira ni to imo ga machi tsutsu aramu	Not knowing I am sleeping with the rocks on Mt. Kamo for a pillow, is my wife waiting, waiting for me?[101]

For the moment the historicity of this poem need not concern us, although we may note that the following four poems, MYS 2: 224–227, are all related through the prose headnotes to Hitomaro's death in exile, with verses 224 and 225 ascribed to his wife. It seems likely that this *banka* was part of a popular tale concerning Hitomaro, which some scholars have labeled the "Kakinomoto Hitomaro monogatari." In this regard it is important to remember that posthumously, Hitomaro became a legendary and cultic figure in Japan, akin to a patron saint of poetry.

A number of other *banka* in both *chōka* form and in the shorter *tanka* preserved in the *Man'yōshū* concern anonymous figures. For instance, MYS 3: 415 has the following headnote and editorial note: "Poem by Prince Uenomiya Shōtoku, in his grief when he found the body of a dead man on Tatsuta Mountain during his procession to Takaharanoi. (This was during the reign of the Sovereign, who ruled the realm under heaven from the palace at Owarita. The reign of the palace at Owarita was that of Empress Toyomike Kashiya-hime; her real name was Nukada, her posthumous name Suiko.)"[102] The poem itself, a *tanka*, is almost generic in form and expression.

ie ni araba	If he were home
imo ga te makamu	he would be pillowed
kusamakura	in his wife's arms,
tabi ni koyaseru	but here on a journey
kono tabito aware	he lies with grass for pillow—
	traveler, alas![103]

The poems MYS 3: 426–437 are all similar in theme, concerning both men and women whose corpses had been discovered, and all are categorized as *banka*. According to the headnotes, the corpses of the women in 428 and 429–430 were apparently cremated, indicating that this Buddhist practice was not unknown in Japan in Hitomaro's lifetime.

Poems of Pacification of Places

Ritual poems were recited not only to pacify the spirits of the dead but also to pacify the spirits of places associated with past events. One of the most famous sequences in the *Man'yōshū*, MYS 1: 29–31 is an example of such a poem. At first glance it has little political content, but only if it is understood in terms of both the socio-political situation of the court and the operative religious worldview can the poem be fully appreciated:

Ōmi no araretaru miya o suguru toki,	Poem by Kakinomoto Hitomaro on passing
Kakinomoto Asomi no Hitomaro no tsukuru uta	the ruined capital at Ōmi

tamatasuki
Unebi no yama no
Kashiwara no
hijiri no miyo yu
(aru wa iu, miya yu)
aremashishi
kami no kotogoto
tsuga no ki no
iya tsugitsugi ni
ame no shita
shirashimeshishi o
(aru wa iu, meshikeru)
sora ni mitsu
Yamato o okite
aoniyoshi
Nara yama o koe
(aru wa iu, sora mitsu
Yamato o oki aoniyoshi Nara
yama koete)
ikasama ni
omōshimeseka
(aru wa iu, omōshikemeka)
amazakaru
hina ni wa aredo
iwabashiru
Ōmi no kuni no
Sasanami no
Ōtsu no miya ni
ame no shita
shirashimeshikemu
Sumeroki no
kami no mikoto no
ōmiya wa
koko to kikedomo
ōtono wa
koko to iedomo
harugusa no
shigeku oitaru
kasumi tachi
haruhi no kireru
(aru wa iu, kasumi tachi
haruhi ka kireru natsugusa
ka shigeku narinuru)
momoshiki no
ōmiyadokoro
mireba kanashimo

Since the reign
(one source says, "the palace")
of the Master of the Sun
at Kashiwara
by Unebi Mountain
of the jeweled sleeve cords,[104]
all *kami* who have been born
have ruled the realm under heaven,
(one source says "[*shira*]-*meshikeru*")
each following each
like generations of the spruce,
in Yamato
that spreads to the sky.
What was in his mind
that he would leave it[105]
and cross beyond the hills of Nara
beautiful in blue earth?
(one source says "leave Yamato, seen
from the sky, and cross beyond
the hills of Nara, beautiful in
blue earth")
Though a barbarous place
at the far reach of the heavens,
here in the land of Ōmi
where the waters race on stone,
at the Ōtsu Palace
in Sasanami
by the rippling waves,
the Emperor,
the divine Prince,
ruled the realm under heaven.
Though we hear
this was the great palace,
though they tell us
here were the mighty halls,
now it is rank
with spring grasses.
Mist rises
and the spring sun is dimmed.
(one source says, "Mist rises and the
spring sun is dimmed. The summer
grasses have grown rank.")
Gazing on the ruins of the great
    palace,
its ramparts thick with wood and
    stone,

(aru wa iu, mireba
sabushimo)

I am filled with sorrow.
(one source says, "gazing on . . . I am
filled with lonely melancholy")

hanka

Envoys

Sasanami no
Shiga no Karasaki
sakiku aredo
ōmiyabito no
fune machikanetsu

Cape Kara in Shiga
at Sasanami
you are as before, but
you wait for the courtiers'
boats in vain.

Sasanami no
Shiga no (hitotsu ni iu,
Hira no) ōwada
yodomu tomo
mukashi no hito ni
mata mo awameyamo
(hitotsu ni iu, awamu to moe ya)

Waters in the deep bends
of Shiga's (one source says "Hira's")
lake at Sasanami[106]
you are calm, yet
you can never meet again
those people from the past.[107]
(one source says, "you think you will
never meet")

This verse has generated a large amount of critical study and commentary over the years. In English, only Levy has treated it at any length.[108] It is impossible to review all the readings offered, and only that which appears to be the modern consensus will be presented here.[109] This *chōka* and the accompanying envoys can, of course, be read and interpreted in isolation, but they take on a deeper and fuller texture and meaning if they are located in their generative and performative context. The *chōka* form suggests the poem was a formal public performative piece. Unless there is clear internal or other evidence to the contrary, this should be one's initial assumption.

Most Japanese literary critics concur that the occasion of these poems was not a casual happenstance that found Hitomaro passing the abandoned palace of the Emperor Tenji at Ōtsu. The first verse attributed to Hitomaro found in the *Man'yōshū*, this poem is located under the reign of Jitō and thus at a time when Hitomaro was in the imperial employ. He seems to have been associated with the Shima Palace (*Shima no miya*), built in the second decade of the seventh century by Soga no Umako and occupied in Hitomaro's time by the Crown Prince Kusakabe. The journey that took Hitomaro to Ōmi must have taken place after the death of Temmu in 686, but it is impossible to date it precisely. Scholars have come up with a number of theories as to the occasion of this poem. For instance, Yamamoto Kenkichi, building on the earlier work of scholars such as Origuchi Shinobu and Yanagita Kunio, has suggested that this set probably came out of a journey by Hitomaro to a semiannual gathering of various *uji*, extended clans, associated with the Wani and Ono clans for the performance of rituals offered to the clan *kami*.[110] Hitomaro's was one of the smaller clans that had become affiliated with the Ono clan. The various related clans were obligated to return to the homeland twice a year for ritual offerings and ceremonies at the shrine of the main clan *kami*. These rituals served as a means of drawing the various affiliated clans together and renewing their social, economic, and religio-political ties.

Yamamoto's thesis has much to suggest, but unfortunately neither the brief head-note nor any internal evidence makes it possible to pinpoint the generative occasion of these poems. Nevertheless, his thesis is useful insofar as it brings to our attention a point we might otherwise overlook: ritual poetry was found in many ritual loci other than those associated with the court. Few of these poems have survived in written form, though, since most of the extant texts focus their attention on the imperial family and the court. Ritual functionaries such as Hitomaro no doubt had many occasions to perform *uta* other than those specifically sponsored by the imperial family, although such verses were less likely to find a place in the texts of the eighth-century historiographic project.

Other scholars have suggested that MYS 1: 29–31 may have been performed on a journey sponsored by the Empress Jitō as part of an attempt to pacify the spirits of the dead. This hypothesis is based upon the recognition that Jitō had a vested inter-est in the performance of rituals of pacification at the site of the former palace of the Emperor Tenji, since the establishment of the Temmu-Jitō line had involved violent confrontation leading to the death of Kōbun and the subsequent abandon-ment of his capital.[111] Although it is impossible to determine the precise occasion of Hitomaro's journey to the abandoned capital, it is extremely unlikely that it was a private or a pleasure trip. Indeed, even if one decides to translate the verses into English in the first-person singular, it must be understood that Hitomaro would still have been expressing the thoughts and emotions of many members of Jitō's court.[112]

Let us look at a few elements of the rhetorical content and structure of MYS 1: 29–31. The *chōka* opens by recalling the history of the imperial family from the first human emperor, Jimmu, "the Master of the Sun/ at Kashiwara/ by Unebi Moun-tain." In the broad temporal sweep of the opening lines, the spatial focus is on Yamato, the heartland of early Japan. It moves quickly, however, to note a disloca-tion in the reign of the Emperor Tenji, who had moved the capital to the Sasanami area and there built the Ōtsu Palace. This is not to be understood as criticism of Tenji, even though one finds the area characterized as "a barbarous place/ at the far reach of the heavens" and Hitomaro avers that it is difficult to know "what was in [the emperor's] mind/ that he would leave [Yamato]." Before the establishment of Nara, the first permanent seat of the government, in 710, the capital was moved after the death of each sovereign and even occasionally in the midst of a reign. Such moves must have always caused considerable inconvenience and hardship for thousands of persons, and Tenji's own move to Ōmi was no different in this regard. In formal public poetry, however, this fact could not be expressed except in the most oblique fashion, although popular songs frequently contained satirical comments on this and other events in the court. The implication is clear that the mere presence of the sovereign is enough to transform a wild and barbarous site into the political, economic, and cultural center of the universe. The same rhetorical strategy is employed in MYS 1: 50 in regard to Jitō's construction of the Fujiwara Palace. Here in MYS 1: 29, however, as in many *banka*, the effect of having rhetorically emphasized the absolute importance of the sovereign's presence is to heighten the sense of radical disjunction and dislocation that the sovereign's death occasioned. The *chōka* draws a sharp contrast between the past glory of the site of the imperial palace and its present desolation, a contrast that affects the living, who are moved to sadness or a sense of lonely melancholy. The envoys, spoken directly to the spirits of the place, pick up this theme, noting that although the geography itself has not changed, the vicissitudes of human history have intervened and led to the abandonment of the capital. Hitomaro, speaking for the members of Jitō's court, suggests that the abandonment of the capital was not the result of an intentional act of the living but rather a response to Tenji's death, an inexplicable event.

According to the *Nihonshoki*, Tenji moved the capital to Ōmi in the sixth year of his reign. This move apparently was not well received, as the following passage suggests:

At this time the common people of the Empire did not desire the removal of the capital. Many made satirical remonstrance, and there were also many popular songs [*soe azamuku mono ōshi. wazauta mata ōshi*]. Every day and every night there were numerous conflagrations.[113]

Unfortunately we do not know precisely what the content was of the *wazauta* or popular songs that circulated at this time, but the implication is clear that they were satirical and critical in tone.[114] This tone contrasts sharply with what was found in the public performative poetry of the court poets. The fact that popular oral songs were used as vehicles of social and political comment is important, for it suggests that even when the written texts from the court are largely silent on certain topics (or when certain things are repressed or cannot be expressed), the silence does not necessarily mean that the texts represent the positions of everyone. We may assume, for example, that various divergent versions of historical events, both recent and more distant, circulated among the populace. In light of these competing versions, we may also assume that in their public performances those oral poets employed by the imperial family and other members of the court were engaged in a form of public relations. That is, their employ was based not only on the aesthetic interests of their patrons but also on the poets' usefulness in promoting their patrons' political interests.

To return to Hitomaro's poem, let us recall the situation in the court following Tenji's death in 671. As we have already seen, when Tenji fell seriously ill, his younger brother, Imperial Prince Ōama (the future Emperor Temmu), found it advisable to withdraw from the capital and go into retreat in the mountains of Yoshino, ostensibly removing himself from the succession. His main rival in the succession was the Imperial Prince Ōtomo (now recognized as the Emperor Kōbun). The *Nihonshoki* provides some insight into one of the ways Ōtomo attempted to consolidate his position while Tenji lay seriously ill. He had the five most powerful ministers of the court, including Soga no Akae and Nakatomi no Kane, swear oaths of loyalty before an image of the Buddha installed in the imperial palace and again a few days later in the presence of the dying Tenji.[115] After he succeeded Tenji, Ōtomo's capital remained in Ōmi while the Temmu faction's base of operations was the detached palace in Yoshino. Thus, from the perspective of the Temmu-Jitō faction after the Jinshin War, Ōmi was the locus of ambiguous and mixed emotions. On the one hand, it was impossible to forget that initially, at least, many powerful ministers and courtiers in that capital had supported Ōtomo's claim to be the rightful successor. On the other hand, although from their point of view Temmu's victory in the Jinshin War was a restoration of the proper lineage of succession from Tenji, the destruction of his palace and the human carnage that took place there required ritual expiation. There is a collective historical memory, then, that informs this verse and the place itself. It is not a dispassionate memory, or even a nostalgic one, but a memory that had been emotionally colored by the blood spilled in succession disputes over the years.

It has often been noted that these verses contain *banka*-like expressions, including the phrase "What was in his mind" (*ikasama ni omōshimeseka*). This phrase is found in other *Man'yōshū* poems, such as MYS 2: 162, 167, and 217; MYS 3: 443 and 460; and MYS 13: 3326, all of which are *banka*. The poem MYS 2: 162 is attributed to the widowed Empress Jitō and is said to be a verse that came to her in a dream following a Buddhist memorial ritual on the eighth anniversary of Temmu's death. The poem MYS 2: 167 is Hitomaro's famous lament at the time of the temporary enshrinement of the Crown Prince Kusakabe. Verse 217, also attributed to Hitomaro, is the lament on "the maiden of Tsu in Kibi." It is impossible to believe that the phrase "what was in his mind" is found incidentally in the *chōka* on the abandoned capital at Ōmi. It is a clear rhetorical marker that this verse is a public ritual lament expressing collective emotions and concerns, not "an unmistakably personal voice of lament," as Levy would have it.[116]

Similarly the phrase *tsure mo naki* ("remote"), found in 167, 460, and 3326, in two instances is used to modify the site of a *mogari no miya* and expresses the sense that the deceased person interred there has gone to some place "foreign" and, thus, broken established relationships. (The exception is MYS 2: 460, where it is used to suggest that at the time a Korean Buddhist nun had immigrated to Japan, it was a foreign land for her.) This usage is similar to the phrase "though a barbarous place/ at the far reach of the heavens" in MYS 1: 29, where the referent is Ōmi. Yamamoto Kenkichi has argued that this verse is to be understood as part of a *chinkon* ritual to pacify the spirits of Tenji and others associated with the site. The journey to Ōmi recorded here displays *michi-yuki*-like (i.e., "going on the road," a set piece noting sites passed on a journey) elements as well, with a string of five-syllable *makurakotoba* ("pillow words," epithets attached to place names) reminiscent of Princess Kage's lament found in the Buretsu Chapter of the *Nihonshoki*[117]—"of the jeweled sleeve cords" (*tamatasuki*), "that spreads to the sky" (*sora ni mitsu*), "beautiful in blue earth" (*aoniyoshi*), "at the far reach of the heavens" (*amazakaru*), "where the waters race on stone" (*iwabashira*), and "by the rippling waves" internally in the place name Sasa-nami.

All these elements suggest that Hitomaro's journey is to a site associated with death. It is not hard to understand why the victors in the succession dispute may have found it necessary to sponsor rituals of pacification of the dead at the site of the abandoned capital. In addition to the blood shed in the ensuing power struggle, we have seen that public oaths of loyalty to certain individuals had been made; these oaths frequently included curses that if the vows were broken, the offending individuals' lines should become extinct and their clans come to ruin. In a world where such magical vows were believed to be efficacious, the necessity of performing counter rites or of finding some other ritual antidotes is clear. Functionaries like Hitomaro were employed in exactly such ritual capacities, although their functions were clearly not limited to the performance of rituals of pacification. Some modern readers, though, may be skeptical about ritual laments being performed for cities or similar sites, yet there is a venerable tradition of precisely such laments in Greece, for instance, from antiquity down to the present.[118]

One final point concerning MYS 1: 29–31 bears mention here: the rituals of pacification of the spirits of the dead included the aim of making the deceased aware that they were indeed dead and could not (or should not) expect to return to the world of the living. This message is the essential burden of the two envoys. They are not expressions of nostalgia on Hitomaro's part but instances of a widely held belief that the dead, especially those who died violent or unnatural deaths, are not always easily reconciled to their new status. Thus, rituals of pacification often involved both attempts to convince the spirits of the deceased that they belonged in the land of the dead rather than among the living and efforts to send them on their way. The "courtiers" (*ōmiyabito*) of 30 and the "men of ancient times" (*mukashi no hito*) of 31 no doubt refer to the deceased members of the Ōmi court. Thus, like so much of the extant public poetry, this set of poems is not univocal; its message is at once directed to the *kami* of the place, to the spirits of the deceased that still lingered there, and to the living. The poem MYS 1: 29–31 is not the only example of a ritual pacification poem for a place. Among others, the reader may compare MYS 3: 257–259, a *chōka* and two envoys, attributed to Kamo Tarihito, on the abandoned palace of Prince Takechi (d. 696).

Two Types of Imperial Funeral Laments

The discernible differences in rhetorical content and effect in *banka* are a function of the respective positions of the deceased in the line of succession. For those who occupied critical positions in the court hierarchy *banka* tend to be much more political and mythological, in an effort to legitimate the succession and the newly reconstituted court hierarchy. On the other hand, for individuals who were neither serious contenders in the succession nor pivotal figures in its determination *banka* tend to rehearse the sense of loss felt by a surviving spouse. Such *banka* are much closer to the type of laments performed for individuals outside the imperial family.

The poem MYS 2: 199–202 is an example of the *banka* concerned with the imperial succession, whereas MYS 2: 196–198 is an example of the second type of imperial *banka*. The latter reads:

Asuka no himemiko Kinoe no araki no miya no toki, Kakinomoto Asomi no Hitomaro no tsukuru uta isshu narabe ni tanka	Poem by Kakinomoto Hitomaro during the period of the temporary enshrinement palace of Princess Asuka, with tanka
tobu tori no	Crossing a bridge of stone
Asuka no kawa no	(one source says "stepping stones")
kamitsu se ni	over the upper shallows
iwahashi watashi	of the Asuka River,
(hitotsu ni iu, iwanami)	where the birds fly,
shimotsu se ni	crossing a plank bridge
uchihashi watasu	over the lower shallows.
iwahashi ni	Even when the *tamamo* [water plants]
(hitotsu ni iu, iwa nami ni)	trailing from
oinabikeru	the bridge of stone
tamamo mo zo	(one source says "stepping stones")
tayureba ouru	breaks, it grows;
uchihashi ni	even when the river weeds
oi o oreru	spreading
kawamo mo zo	beneath the plank bridge
karureba hayuru	withers, it sprouts again.

nani shi kamo	Why, then,
wago ōkimi no	do you, our Princess,
tataseba	forget
tamamo no mokoro	the morning palace
koyaseba	of our splendid Lord
kawatamo no gotoku	who, when you rose,
nabikaishi	yielded to you
yoroshiki kimi ga	like the *tamamo*,
asamiya o	who, when you lay down,
wasuretamau ya	stretched out
yūmiya o	like the river weeds?
somukitamau ya	And turn away from
utsusomi to	the evening palace?
omoishi toki	I recall the time
harube wa	you were in this world,
hana orikazashi	how in spring
aki tateba	you broke off and decorated your-
momijiba kazashi	self with blossoms,
shikitae no	and when autumn came
sode tazusawari	decorated yourself with colored
kagami nasu	leaves,
miredomo akazu	how your hempen sleeves
mochitsuki no	crossed.
iya mezurashimi	Like a mirror
omōshishi	you never tired of gazing on the
kimi to tokidoki	Lord,
idemashite	who you thought
asobitamaishi	as precious as
mi-ke mukau	the full-moon.
Kinoe no miya o	Sometimes with the Lord
toko miya to	you would go out
sadametamaite	on formal excursions
ajisawau	to the palace at Kinoe,
megoto mo taenu	where the sacred food trays face
shikare kamo	each other.
(hitotsu ni iu, soko oshimo)	But now that you have established
aya ni kanashimi	that palace for all eternity,
nuetori no	gone are the eyes that met him,
katakoi tsuma	your words he heard.
(hitotsu ni iu, shitsutsu)	Is that why our Lord,
asatori no	(one source says "in deep regret")
(hitotsu ni iu, asakiri no)	choked with sorrow,
kayowasu kimi ga	moaning his unrequited love
natsukusa no	like the tiger thrush,
omoishinaete	goes back and forth,
yūtsutsu no	like the morning birds,

kayuki kakuyuki
ōbune no
tayutau mireba
nagasamuru
kokoro mo aranu
soko yue ni
semu sube shireya
oto nomi mo
na nomi mo taezu
ametsuchi no
iya tōnagaku
shinoiyukamu
mi-na ni kakaseru
Asuka-gawa
yorozuyo made ni
hashikiyashi
wago ōkimi no
katami ka koko o

(one source says "the morning mist")
to attend you?
When we see him
wilting like the summer grass,
staggering
like an evening star,
reeling
like a great ship,
with a heart that cannot be
    consoled,
we know not what to do.
Thus, at least let us remember
if only the sound,
if only the name,
forever far and long
as heaven and earth.
Let us remember
for ten thousand years
the Asuka River
that bears her precious name—
this the *katami*
of our beloved Princess!

tanka nishu

Asuka-gawa
shigaramiwatashi
seka maseba
nagaruru mizu mo
nodo ni ka aramashi
(hitotsu ni iu, mizu no
yodo ni ka aramashi)

Two tanka

If they had piled branches
across the Asuka River
to stop its course,
even the streaming waters
would have become quiet.
(one source says "would have
become a pool")

Asuka-gawa
ashita dani (hitotsu ni iu, sae) mimu
to omoeyamo
(hitotsu ni iu, omoe kamo)
wago ōkimi no
mi-na wasuresenu
(hitotsu ni iu, mi-na
Wasuraenu)

Asuka River!
even tomorrow alone
(one source says "if only")
I want to see you!
(one source says "hope to")
I cannot forget
the precious name of my Princess.
(one source says "I will not
forget the precious name")[119]

This lament was probably presented by Hitomaro as a surrogate for the husband of Princess Asuka. Princess Asuka, a daughter of the Emperor Tenji and Tachibana no Iratsume, died on 4/4/700. The lament comes out of the period of temporary interment of the corpse in the *mogari no miya*. The number of variants mentioned in the interlinear notes suggest that this lament may have been performed numerous times, either at this temporary enshrinement palace or, quite possibly, for others who had died at other times. If the early Japanese practice was similar to other cultures where oral laments are performed, a number of reciters or singers probably offered the same basic lament.

The *chōka* opens by recounting the journey to the site of the princess's *katami*, a site that is especially associated with the deceased and where it was believed to be especially easy to make contact with the spirit of the deceased. Misaki Hisashi has pointed out that the term *uchihashi*, here rendered as "a plank bridge," is found in five other *Man'yōshū* verses (4: 528, 7: 1193, 10: 2056 and 2062, and 17: 3909), four of which refer to the meeting of lovers. Thus, the basic theme of the *banka*, the love of the bereaved prince and the deceased Princess Asuka, is heightened by even the nouns used.[120] The poet then draws a pointed contrast between two types of water plants that seem to die yet return to life and the death of Princess Asuka. Then in accusatory form the deceased is reprimanded: "Why, then,/ do you, our Princess/ forget/ the morning palace/ of our splendid Lord?" The tone may strike the modern reader as irreverent, but oral laments often include this type of recrimination.[121]

A prose endnote appended to MYS 2: 202, an envoy to a *banka* for Prince Takechi, clearly indicates that the early Japanese themselves recognized this emotional aspect of the grieving process in the performance of oral laments. The widowed princess presents offerings at the shrine for her husband but also voices her bitterness at his death. The endnote says: "*The Forest of Classified Verse* says the above poem is 'by Princess Hinokuma in her resentment against the Nakisawa Shrine.' "[122] The speaker, here said to be Hitomaro, is a surrogate standing in for the bereaved. Thus, we must not be misled into assuming that the first-person "I" in such verses refers to the poet and indicates his personal emotional responses;[123] rather, such an "I" often indicates the surviving spouse and at times even the deceased.

The *chōka* then goes on to recall the past and the joyous times the princess and her husband had. Aoki Takako has argued that *banka* on a deceased spouse often recall an idyllic past. Although not mythical per se, it is described in such a way that the "ravages of time" do not appear.[124] The idyllic love of the prince and princess, which would seem to have lasted forever, is recalled in order to bring out in stark contrast the emotional desolation the princess's death has caused. The tone is still accusatory in that in dying, Princess Asuka is said to have turned her back on her faithful and loving husband. The responsibility for the suffering he is experiencing, as well as the sense of disorientation everyone in the court feels, is laid squarely at the princess's feet. But then the lament shifts to note the fact that the Asuka River shares the princess's name and flows by the palace at Kinoe where the couple used to travel together. Thus, this place has become her *katami*. In addition to expressing regret, the envoys (termed *tanka*, although they function here as *hanka*) seem to allude to ritual efforts to pacify the spirit of the deceased (*tama-shizume*) and to call it back. If only the prince had done something differently, perhaps time, like the flow of the river, could have been stopped and the princess's *tama*, like the once-surging water, could have become calm and settled. Note, though, that the poem as a whole focuses not only on the deceased but also on the living. Part of the professional poet's duty in such cases seems to have been to declare formally the undying love of the surviving spouse for the deceased.

Nowhere in the entire poem, though, is there ever any mention of other contemporary historical events. The focus is entirely on the imperial couple and their love. The imperial succession and the survivor's relative status in the court hierarchy find no mention. In this, MYS 2: 196–198 is similar to another *banka*, MYS 2: 194–195, performed by Hitomaro for Princess Hatsusebe and Prince Osakabe. This poem is in sharp contrast, however, to MYS 2: 199–202, a *banka* for Prince Takechi, a son of the Emperor Temmu. It is the longest sequence in the *Man'yōshū* and has been stirringly rendered by Levy.[125] It is not necessary to cite the entire sequence here. Instead, I will merely draw out a few of the elements that distinguish this type of "political" public *banka* from what we have just seen.

Prince Takechi was a son of Temmu and led his father's troops in the Jinshin War in 672 in which Temmu (then Prince Ōama) gained the throne. He was married to a daughter of the Emperor Tenji, Princess Minabe. Following the death of the Emperor Temmu in 686, the Crown Prince Kusakabe was to have succeeded to the throne, but he died on 4/13/689 and Temmu's widowed empress acceded as the Empress Jitō. There is some evidence to suggest that at this point Takechi became the heir apparent. An entry in the *Nihonshoki* for 7/5/690 says, "The Imperial Prince Takechi was made Prime Minister [*miko Takechi o motte, Ōmatsurigoto no Ōmae Tsukimi to su*]."[126] This entry indicates that Takechi would have been in control of much of the daily administration of the government. He died, however, on 7/10/696 at the age of forty-two or forty-three. The *Nihonshoki* entry recording his death is, like that for Kusakabe's death, very brief: "His Highness the Later Imperial Prince died."[127] The reference to Takechi as *nochi no miko no mikoto*, the Later Imperial Prince, suggests that he succeeded Kusakabe as the heir apparent. Whatever the case may have been, it is clear that he was a major figure in the court and that his death would have had a great impact on the future succession. As it turned out, his demise made much easier the abdication of Jitō in favor of her grandson, Prince Karu (the Emperor Mommu), almost a year later.[128]

With this brief background, it is easier to understand why the public performative *banka* at Takechi's temporary enshrinement palace would center on the imperial succession. The poem MYS 2: 199 evokes recent history in mythological terms. First, the death of the Emperor Temmu is recorded in mythic terms:

Asuka no	Our Lord,
Makami no hara ni	who, while we trembled,
hisakata no	fixed the far and heavenly
amatsu mi-kado o	halls of his shrine
kashikoku mo	on the fields of Makami in Asuka
sadametamaite	and, godlike, has secluded himself
kamusabu to	in the rocks there[129]
iwagakurimasu	

Dying is itself transformed into the intentional act of a divinity (*kamusabu to iwa-gakurimasu*)—an act that parallels Amaterasu's secluding herself in the "heavenly rock-grotto."[130] The *chōka* then says that the emperor "went down/ as from heaven/ to the provinces," again recalling the descent of the grandson of Amaterasu, Ninigi no mikoto, from the High Heavens to the earth. Then, like Amaterasu, the *banka* says he "gave the task to his son, he being an imperial prince [*miko nagara*]/ to pacify the raging rebels/ and subdue the land."[131] This section is followed by a long passage in which the swirl and terror of battle are conjured up. Once again, though, the historical events are remembered and recounted in mythic terms: the victory of Temmu's troops is described as a result of divine assistance.

yuku tori no	As they struggled
arasou hashi ni	like zooming birds,
Watarai no	the divine wind
itsuki no miya yu	from the Shrine of our offerings
kamukaze ni	at Ise in Watarai
ifuki matowashi	blew confusion upon them,
amakumo o	hiding the very light of day
hi no me mo misezu	as clouds blanketed the heavens
tokoyami ni	in eternal darkness[132]
ōitamaite	

This rhetorical device gives the reign of the Emperor Temmu and that of his descendants legitimacy through appeal to the intervention of the *kami* in human history. The *chōka* then alters its focus and moves to Prince Takechi. It bewails the fact that Takechi was positioned to succeed and establish his own rule when he passed away. It also describes an interesting ritual mourning practice in the court:

Haniyasu no	On the fields
mi-kado no hara ni	before the Haniyasu Palace Gate
akane sasu	[we] crawl and stumble like the deer

hi no kotogoto	as long as the sun
shishi ji mono	still streams its crimson,
ihaifushitsutsu	and when pitch-black night descends
nubatama no	[we] crawl around like quail,
yūbe ni nareba	turning to look up at the great
ōtono o	hall [ōtono].[133]
furisakemitsutsu	
uzura nasu	
ihaimotōri	

The focus of the *chōka* is now on the desolation and disorientation the prince's death has occasioned. This focus is similar to what we saw in the *banka* for Princess Asuka, and indeed it will be found in almost all such laments. Then the emphasis and focus shift to the site of the *mogari no miya*. Once again the frustrated expectations of the living are rehearsed, and the deceased is assured that he will never be forgotten by the living. In sharp contrast to the lament for Princess Asuka, there is no mention of the love his wives and consorts had for Takechi. Instead, his career is rhetorically situated in a larger mythistory.

To appreciate this lament, we must imagine the poem recited in the presence of a large assembly of members of the court who occupied critical positions in the hierarchy, as Takechi did. The public *banka* on the occasion of Takechi's temporary enshrinement were used to legitimate Temmu's violent assumption of power in the Jinshin War by rhetorically transforming the events surrounding it into a mythistory. In this way, in their public performative roles, poets like Hitomaro helped to give legitimacy to Temmu's successors as well.

In this chapter several different forms of ritual poetry from the imperial court have been introduced. Oral performative poetry was an important expression of the ceremonial nature of the court, a daily spectacle of sight and sound. It was also a resource that could be used in performance by different individuals for different purposes; it served still others when some *uta* were committed to writing and recontextualized. Most important, this poetry gained its coherence and meaning in a dynamic world of political ceremony and intrigue, designed to create and demonstrate power and prestige. Rather than merely reflecting a timeless or static collective ideal, it served as a means of articulating responses to incongruities experienced by the community and of pressing individual and factional claims. In the following chapter the intertwined mythological complex of death and the First Fruits Festival, the *niiname-sai*, will be the focus of attention, for it is a critical component of the early Japanese cultural discourse on the politics of death.

CHAPTER TWO

The Mythology of Death
and the *Niiname-sai*

Death is always a central element of a culture's understanding of the world and humankind's place in it, inevitably altering the social relations that obtain among the living. This effect takes on a heightened importance when death removes an influential political figure from the scene. In any hierarchical court society, the death of a high-ranking member affects the relative status of large numbers of contiguous others. Such alterations involve a redistribution of power, position, and prestige that is not easily or "naturally" achieved, since most of the members of the court are in one way or another competing with each other. It is this social process that I have called the politics of death, a process that is recounted in mythic narratives from early Japan and that was played out in human history.

The problem of legitimating the imperial succession and putting a good light on certain events in the court related to the politics of death was one of the socio-political forces behind the compilation of the *Kojiki*, the *Nihonshoki*, and the *Man'yōshū*. The mythic narratives of early Japan often mirror the historical reality of the court in the wake of the death of a sovereign or crown prince. The Izanagi–Izanami myth, for instance, will be found not only to present an ideal model of the imperial funeral practices, but also to portray the "reality" of the politics of death in the court. Similarly, the narrative detail of Susano-o's excessive mourning for the deceased Izanami and his expressed desire to visit her tomb will be found to provide the mythic charter for various forms of symbolically charged political acts in the court during the period of temporary interment. I will argue that Susano-o provided a model for imperial princes desiring to claim the throne in the wake of the death of a sovereign, while the Amaterasu–Susano-o myth links the celebration of the *niiname-sai* with the full exercise of the power and prerogatives of the sovereign.

Myths are by definition authorless, but that does not mean they are innocent of any personal or factional elements. Just as a specific oral telling of a myth can and often does have a particular "slant" put on it, when early Japanese myths were committed to writing at the imperial command to "correct" erroneous accounts, the result was a factional act of signification. Today it would be futile, as well as wrongheaded, to search for the "original" myths behind these written texts, for there never was an original myth, unadulterated by contemporary socio-political

concerns and factional aspirations. Every telling of a myth participates in the historical process in a dialectical manner. By carefully noting the "mythical," "historical,"
and "literary" traces of this dialectic in the texts, we can best understand the world
of the imperial court in early Japan.

Marshall Sahlins has observed that most studies of the way that structures are
realized in culture and over time have tended to give priority to institutional forms
over their associated ritual actions while ignoring the fact that patterned (and thus
significant) acts by historical agents can also precipitate or change social forms.[1]
Ironically, perhaps, although the mythology of death preserved in the three texts
was used, to borrow Sahlins's terms, in a "prescriptive" mode to legitimate the
socio-political order by denying history or change, these myths prove to be an important source of information about historical change. By the time the mythology of
death was committed to writing in the early eighth century, the ritual practice of
double burial inscribed within it had been abandoned in the court. Highlighting a
political "reading" placed on these myths by individuals who were necessarily political beings, if they were to survive in the court, helps us to understand a number of
"events" during the period of temporary interment of different sovereigns. This is
not, of course, to deny the religious or spiritual significance of these myths.

The Image of Death in the Man'yōshū

No one would deny that death is a central concern of human beings as they seek to
understand "ultimate reality." It would be wrong, however, to assume that a culture
first comes to some conception of death and then proceeds to commemorate this
conception ritually. That is, people do not first have an idea about death that they
then act on (or act out) in ritual. Rather, as Clifford Geertz has demonstrated,
culture patterns or symbolic complexes, including those surrounding death, are both
models of and models for reality. "Unlike genes, and other nonsymbolic information
sources, which are only models *for*, not models *of*, culture patterns have an intrinsic
double aspect: they give meaning, that is, objective conceptual form, to social and
psychological reality both by shaping themselves to it and by shaping it to themselves."[2]

There has been a renewed interest in the comparative study of the variety of
symbolic and ritual complexes surrounding death.[3] The present work may contribute
in a modest way to this larger cross-cultural project by providing some insight into
the early Japanese beliefs and ritual practices dealing with death. A proper understanding of these beliefs and practices is essential for any inquiry into the early
Japanese worldview and, perhaps less obviously, into the historiographic project of
the imperial court. Death is a common theme in all the extant works from early
Japan. Even a cursory glance at the contents of the *Man'yōshū* will reveal that to a

significant extent it is a collection of poetry on death. The topic is found not only in the *banka* or ritual funeral laments, where it is to be expected, but also in all the other poetic forms gathered there. Even pieces that were apparently love poems sometimes concerned the relationship of a living individual with a deceased loved one. Yet in the *Man'yōshū*, instead of the blunt verb *shinu*, "to die," a variety of alternative expressions are used, as the examples below demonstrate.

Most of the poems in the *Man'yōshū* concern members of the imperial court. Rather than having died, though, the nobility are often said to have gone some-where, be it to another land or distant place or somewhere beyond the clouds.

. . . such sadness now that you are gone
like the scattered leaves of autumn.

(MYS 3: 459)

The Prince who crossed the sleeves
of his evening robes with hers
has passed beyond the jewel-trailed
fields of Ochi. How could she hope
to meet him again?

(MYS 2: 195)[4]

At the Nakisawa Shrine
I offer sacred wine
and pray, but
you, my Lord,
now rule the high heavens.

(MYS 2: 202)

The second verse suggests a horizontal cosmology in that the deceased is located across the fields of Ochi. The last verse, however, says that the deceased imperial prince has gone up to the High Heavens, the realm of Amaterasu, suggesting an apparently vertical cosmology. In many poems a deceased emperor or the crown prince ascends to heaven after having performed some mighty feat:

He ruled as a god
at the Kiyomi Palace
in Asuka,
where the birds fly,
until he opened heaven's gate of stone
and rose, godlike, to those fields,
dwelling of Emperors. . . .

(MYS 2: 167)

Our Lord, who ruled
in peace,

our child
of the high-shining sun,
a very god,
dwells as a divinity
in the far heavenly palace. . . .

(MYS 2: 204)[5]

The land of the dead, though, is not always conceived of as located in the heavens. Sometimes the deceased are thought to reside elsewhere on this cosmological plane, either in the mountains or beyond the sea, though members of the imperial family are frequently spoken of as having returned to the High Heavens.

Did it suit my Prince's spirit well
that you should choose Kagami Mountain,
in the land of Toyo,
as your eternal shrine?

It seems you have raised a door of stone
before your tomb on Kagami Mountain
in the land of Toyo,
and concealed yourself inside.
Though I wait for you, you do not come.

(MYS 3: 417–418)[6]

Here the deceased is described as having concealed himself. This rhetorical expression and image of death is widely used in the *Man'yōshū*, as the following examples suggest:

Our Lord,
a very god,
conceals himself
behind five hundred
folds of cloud.

(MYS 2: 205)

Our Lord,
who, while we trembled,
fixed the far and heavenly
halls of his shrine
on the fields of Makami in Asuka
and, godlike, has secluded himself
in the rocks there. . . .

(MYS 2: 199)

Life's course cannot be stopped,
and so she is gone

out from the house
where she kept her well-woven pillow,
and is hidden in the clouds.

(MYS 3: 461)[7]

The dead are also often portrayed as sleeping:

Making a finely woven pillow
of the rocky shore
where the waves from the offing
draw near,
you, who sleep there!

(MYS 2: 222)

If you were home
you would be pillowed
in your wife's arms,
but here on a journey
you lie with grass for pillow—
traveler, alas!

(MYS 3: 415)[8]

In presenting excerpts of only a few of the many poems I might have cited on death in the *Man'yōshū*, I have done little more than use these poems in terms of a simple content analysis. Yet preliminary attention to these and other poems reveals several points of interest. First, the poems do not concern human death per se as a general philosophical or existential problem; rather, each of the poems concerns a specific deceased individual. This fact is not a result of an inadequate selection of poems or of some statistical anomaly. Most of the poems in the *Man'yōshū*, with the exception of some late and highly Sinified examples, are either addressed directly to the deceased or they praise him or her. Death is rarely dealt with at a general or universal level.

For the early Japanese, death was not an immediate, complete, and permanent break with the world of the living. Rather, communication between the living and the dead was assumed to be possible through various ritual practices—divination, oracles, possession—as well as through dreams.[9] The early Japanese performed various *tama-furi*-related rituals in order to call back the spirit of the deceased. The extant poems tend to deal with specific persons because the ritual loci out of which many of these came were part of the mortuary rites for individuals and not, for instance, a more general cult of the ancestors. Moreover, the dead mentioned in the *Man'yōshū* poems are usually members of the imperial family or nobility. We should use the internal evidence from these poems to speak about the religious worldview and ritual practices of the early Japanese elite rather than attributing our findings to all levels of society. Although brief glimpses of popular practice are sometimes possible in the texts, more often the written records concern only the elite.

Any attempt to use the *Man'yōshū* poems as historical documents cannot stop at a content analysis. We need to read and understand these poems as at once coming out of and re-creating a religious worldview in terms of Geertz's famous definition of religion.[10] We can say with a good measure of certainty that in early Japan the spirits of the dead were believed to return to the world of the living at specific times and seasons, notably in spring and autumn, to participate in religious rituals. Hori Ichiro has pointed out both the antiquity of this belief and its continuity over the centuries in Japan.[11] These texts suggest that when the spirit (*tama*) of the dead leaves the human body, it can either assume various forms or inhere in preexisting ones. One of the most common forms assumed is that of a bird, as found in the "Yamato-takeru uta monogatari." For example, in MYS 2: 153, a *banka* attributed to the widowed empress of the Emperor Tenji (r. 661–671), one finds:

. . . Oars on the offing,
do not splash so hard.
Oars by the strand,
do not splash so hard,
or the bird
beloved of my husband [*tsuma no/ omou tori tatsu*],
who was gentle
like the young grass,
will fly away.[12]

Modern scholars are largely in agreement that the bird here is to be understood as the repository of the just-deceased emperor's spirit, which might still be recalled.[13] The poems MYS 2: 170, 172, 180, 182, and 192, all *banka* by servingmen (*toneri*) of the newly deceased Crown Prince Kusakabe, refer to birds in similar fashion and must also be interpreted in light of the *tama*-belief and ritual complex. Similarly, when Hitomaro laments the death of his wife in MYS 2: 207, cited earlier, and says: "I stood at the Karu market/ where often she had gone,/ and listened,/ but could not even hear/ the voices of the birds/ that cry on Unebi Mountain," he is alluding to the belief that the cry of certain birds was the voice of the deceased.[14] The mourners in early Japanese funeral rituals were often equated with birds, though it is still unclear whether they actually dressed as birds and imitated them in some fashion or whether the reference is simply metaphorical.

The *Man'yōshū* is also an invaluable source of other information on the religious beliefs and ritual practices surrounding death in early Japan. The early Japanese believed that for a certain period of time death was only provisional and, thus, potentially reversible. One finds traces of the practice of individuals going into the mountains, for example, to call back and meet the spirit (*tama*) of the dead. The poem MYS 2: 85, traditionally attributed to Empress Iwanohime, is a clear expression of this belief. It is one of a set of poems with the prose headnote, "Four poems by Empress Iwanohime, thinking of the Emperor." The emperor in question here is Nintoku (r. 313–399).

kimi ga yuki	You journey, and the days
ke nagaku narinu	have turned long.
yamatazune	Shall I go into the mountains,
mukae ka yukamu	there to greet you,
machi ni ka matamu	or shall I wait and wait?[15]

The phrase *yamatazune* is literally to "visit" or "go into the mountains." As Hori has reminded us, however, the *kofun* or huge burial mounds found in early Japan were, in effect, artificial mountains and were regarded as and referred to as mountains. Well into the Heian period, long after the practice of raising *kofun* had disappeared, the mausoleums of the imperial family were still referred to as *yama* or mountains. Thus, *yamatazune* does not always refer to travel to actual mountains but also to imperial burial mounds. Even today in certain rural areas, related linguistic references to mountains in association with death and funeral rituals may be found, such as *yama-yuki*, literally "going to the mountain" for "visiting a grave site," or *yama-shigoto*, "mountain work" for "preparing a grave site."[16]

The poem MYS 2: 85 can be read as the Empress Iwanohime simply talking (sighing?) to herself in longing for her husband who is away on a trip, *or* it can be read as the empress imploring the spirit of her deceased husband, thought to be out wandering in the mountains, to return and revivify the corpse. Modern Japanese scholarship overwhelmingly endorses the latter reading.

The content of the poems in the *Man'yōshū*, combined with the prose headnotes and endnotes, can provide the reader with a considerable amount of information. The full meaning of the poems, however, is located not only in what they say but also in the silence of the texts (i.e., in the underlying and informing assumptions or common sense of the period that did not have to be verbalized). In order to appreciate properly the poems in the *Man'yōshū*, then, it is necessary to go outside the anthology to gather information concerning the early Japanese worldview. To that end we will now turn our attention to some of the central myths dealing with the origin of death and the subsequent politics of death. These myths will then be used in a dialectical fashion to disclose more of the meaning inherent in the historical chronicles and the extant poetry from early Japan.

The Myth of the Origin of Death

Historians of religions have long stressed the fact that the early Japanese (and thus, it is frequently implied, Shinto) have no myth of the Fall and, consequently, no concept of sin (*tsumi*) equivalent to that found in the Jewish and Christian traditions. Instead, we are told, the Japanese have developed a sense of pollution (*kegare*) and purity, and consequently they practice a variety of ritual means of purification. The mythic origin of purification rites is narratively connected to the first death, so that one cannot understand the Japanese concepts of purity and pollution without understanding their views of death.

In their comparative study of mortuary ritual Huntington and Metcalf have recently reminded us that "In centralized kingdoms everywhere—Africa, Europe, Asia—events surrounding the death of the king reveal most strikingly the nature of each polity and the structure of its political competition."[17] This is certainly the case in early Japan, although we can go even further and say that the narrative accounts of events surrounding the death of the sovereign often display the same structure or pattern as certain myths.

Turning to the well-known Izanami–Izanagi myth will enable us to see the political ramifications of death in both the divine and the human realms, or in terms of the early Japanese ideology, the interface of these realms in the imperial family— the living *kami*. It is not necessary to rehearse the entire myth of Izanagi and Izanami here. It is enough to recall that in the myth the heavenly *kami* command the male creator, Izanagi no mikoto, and the female creatrix, Izanami no mikoto, to descend from the heavens in order to complete and solidify the land. This they do, creating the earth by standing on the Heavenly Floating Bridge, lowering a jeweled spear into the cosmogonic brine, and stirring. The first island created comes from salt that drips off the end of the spear and coagulates. (Here and in most of this section for the sake of convenience I will follow the *Kojiki* version. In citing Philippi's translation I will silently modify the names to modern Japanese form.) They then erect a heavenly pillar (*ame no mi-hashira*), which they circumambulate, leading to copulation and the birth of a multitude of islands and then *kami*. The long list of the names of these *kami* need not concern us here.[18] The myth says, however, that in bearing the Fire Kami, Izanami's genitals were burned and she "died" shortly thereafter. This first death recorded in the *Kojiki* merits special attention.

Because [Izanami no mikoto] bore this child, her genitals were burned, and she lay down sick.

In her vomit there came into existence the deity Kana-yama-biko-no-kami; next, Kana-yama-bime-no-kami.

Next, in her faeces there came into existence the deity Hani-yasu-biko-no-kami; next, Hani-yasu-bime-no-kami.

Next, in her urine there came into existence the deity Mitsu-ha-no-me-no-kami; next, Waku-musubi-no-kami. The child of this deity is Toyo-uke-bime-no-kami.

Thus at last, Izanami-no-kami, because she had borne the fire-deity, divinely passed away. . . .

At this time Izanagi-no-mikoto said: "Alas, I have given my beloved spouse in exchange for a mere child!"

Then he crawled around her head and around her feet, weeping.

At this time in his tears there came into existence the deity who dwells at the foot of the trees in the foothills of Mount Kagu, named Naki-sawa-me-no-kami.

Then he buried the departed Izanami-no-kami on Mount Hiba, the border between the land of Izumo and the land of Hahaki.[19]

In this opening passage death is not presented as wholly negative but rather as a creative stage involving the transformation of matter, not its final destruction. Out of Izanami's vomit come two *kami* thought to be related somehow to metal (*kane*); from her faeces come a pair of *kami* believed related to clay or fertilizer; and from her urine come a female water or irrigation *kami* and a male *kami* of generation. In each case pairs of *kami*, composed of a male and a female, come into being. The death of Izanami also displays a widespread mythic pattern found in agricultural societies in which a primordial death or murder of a divinity results in the creation of staple foodstuffs and cultural techniques.[20]

In the description of Izanagi crawling around the corpse on all fours and weeping, we have the first mention in the text of a funeral ritual. Philippi says of the mention of Nakisawa-me, the *kami* who comes into being from Izanagi's tears, "This account undoubtedly reflects the practice of using female lamenters or professional mourners (*naki-me*, 'weeping woman') at funerals."[21] The important role of women in the funeral rituals, especially in the tradition of offering laments, will be a central focus of attention in Chapter Four. It may be mentioned that Nakisawa is a location at the foot of Kagu-yama, where many imperial family members were buried. Kagu-yama is a site associated with the imperial cult and succession.

One of the *Nihonshoki* variants of this myth suggests that when Izanami lay dying after having given birth to the Fire Kami, she also bore Hani-yama-hime (the Earth Goddess) and Mizu-ha-no-me (the Water Goddess). The Fire Kami is said to have then taken his sister, the Earth Goddess, as wife and they had a daughter, Waka-musubi. The five kinds of grain were produced from her navel, and the silkworm and the mulberry tree (i.e., sericulture) were produced from her crown.[22] Whatever the variant, however, life or the necessities of life come out of death. This point is given further expression in the myth when Izanagi, angry over Izanami's death, takes his sword and decapitates his son, the Fire Kami, whose birth had caused Izanami's death. In the same kind of metamorphosis whereby life comes out of death, still other *kami* are produced from the blood spilled.

The myth continues with Izanagi journeying to Yomi, the land of the dead, to visit his deceased spouse. He calls her to return with him to the land of the living: "O, my beloved spouse, the lands which you and I were making have not yet been completed; you must come back!"[23] Izanami responds that she desires to return but cannot, since she has already eaten of the hearth of Yomi. She must first obtain the permission of the *kami* of Yomi. She tells Izanagi to wait for her outside and not to enter the hall (*tono*) and view her there. Izanagi, though, is too impatient; he enters the hall and views the rotting corpse, which is covered with maggots. At this sight, he flees in fright and is pursued by ugly women of Yomi, the eight Thunder Kami, and the army of the underworld. Eventually Izanagi manages to escape outside and pulls a huge boulder in front of the entrance to Yomi, sealing the final separation of himself and his spouse. In anger, Izanami curses him and thus introduces death into the human world.

Once back in the land of the living, Izanagi says, "I have been to a most unpleasant land, a horrible, unclean land. Therefore I shall purify myself."[24] Out of every action then performed by Izanagi more *kami* come into existence, including the ancestors of the *muraji* of Azumi.[25] At this point in the mythic narrative, we come to an important juncture—the creation of new *kami* is now achieved through *ritual actions*, not "naturally" through metamorphosis at death. Performing ritual ablutions (*misogi semu*), Izanagi washes his left eye, and Amaterasu, the Sun Goddess, comes into existence; washing his right eye, Tsuku-yomi-no-mikoto, the Moon Deity, comes into existence; and finally, from his nose comes Susano-o-no-mikoto.

At each stage death and the death rituals *create* new *kami* and order out of disorder. The elements expelled from the body of the dying Izanami become *kami*; the blood and various body parts of the decapitated Fire Kami become *kami*; Izanagi's discarded clothes and each act of ritual purification yield *kami*. In short, in these myths death itself is not conceived of as merely the absence of life; rather, death in one physical or phenomenal form yields new life in another. But following the creation of a break—a radical disjunction between the realm of the dead and that of the living—the metamorphosis is now accomplished through ritual means. In the myth, Izanami's entry into Yomi and her "death" are not viewed as permanent until Izanagi breaks the taboo of entering the burial hall and views the corpse. The significance of this point has not, I think, been sufficiently appreciated. *The finality of death is a result of the actions of the living.*

If we take the burial chamber in the myth of the death of Izanami as the prototype of the temporary burial palace in the human realm, then we can readily appreciate that, just as in the myth, it is the viewing of the corpse that makes death final.

In cultures that practice double burial it is the viewing of the disinterred corpse immediately before final burial that marks the end of the period of intense public mourning and the point at which the living must reconcile themselves to the finality of the death. In the myth, Izanagi's action is described as the violation of a taboo, yet it is precisely this transgression that, from the larger perspective of the mythic narrative as a whole, yields purification rituals and consequently other *kami*, including especially Amaterasu, Tsuku-yomi, and Susano-o. In the myth, death is not a static state but a transformative, generative one. Moreover, while death rends the social fabric it simultaneously leads to the re-weaving of new social relations. This last comment bears special attention.

Let us return to the myth at the point right after Izanagi, having fled the land of Yomi, has performed his ablutions. To bring out significant details, I quote at some length from Philippi's translation of the *Kojiki* version.

At this time Izanagi-no-mikoto, rejoicing greatly, said: "I have borne child after child, and finally in the last bearing I have obtained three noble children."

Then he removed his necklace, shaking the beads on the string so that they jingled [*mi-kubitama no tama no omoyurani*], and, giving it to Amaterasu-o-mi-kami, he entrusted her with her mission, saying:

"You shall rule Takama no hara."

The name of the necklace is Mi-kura-tani-no-kami.

Next he said to Tsuku-yomi-no-mikoto, entrusting him with his mission:

"You shall rule the realms of the night."

Next he said to Take-haya-Susano-o-no-mikoto, entrusting him with his mission:

"You shall rule the ocean."

While (the other deities) ruled (their realms) in obedience to the commands entrusted to them, Haya-Susano-o-no-mikoto did not rule the land entrusted to him. (Instead), he wept and howled (even) until his beard eight hands long extended down over his chest.

His weeping was such that it caused the verdant mountains to wither and all the rivers and seas to dry up. At this, the cries of the malevolent deities were everywhere abundant like summer flies; and all sorts of calamities arose in all things.[26]

Then Izanagi-no-o-mi-kami said to Haya-Susano-o-no-mikoto:

"Why is it you do not rule the land entrusted to you, but (instead) weep and howl?"

Then (Haya-Susano-o-no-mikoto) replied:

"I wish to go to the land of my mother, Ne-no-katasu-kuni. That is why I weep."

Then Izanagi-no-o-mi-kami, greatly enraged, said:

"In that case, you may not live in this land!"

Thus [saying], he expelled him with a divine expulsion.[27]

The main concern of this section of the myth is the redistribution of power following the death of Izanami, one of the rulers of the world. The myth is a paradigmatic model for succession disputes thereafter in both the divine and the human realms. In the myth, Susano-o's mourning is considered to be excessive and widely disruptive precisely because, unlike Amaterasu and Tsuku-yomi, *he does not take up his newly assigned political role*. In other words, Susano-o arouses the anger of Izanagi because he does not accept the new political alignment and the redistribution of power that Izanagi seeks to impose in the wake of Izanami's (the sovereign's) death. Izanagi's rule also comes to an end shortly after the death of his spouse, since his own position and power are ambiguous. In the *Kojiki* version of the myth, he simply disappears from the text with the notice, immediately following the section cited above, that: "This Izanagi-no-o-kami is enshrined in Taga of Ōmi [or "Awaji" in the Ise manuscript]."[28] The *Nihonshoki* account says:

After this, Izanagi no Mikoto, his divine task having been accomplished, and his spirit career about to suffer a change, built himself an abode in the gloom in the island of Awaji, where he dwelt for ever in silence and concealment.

Another account says:—"Izanagi no Mikoto, his task having been accomplished, and his power great, ascended to Heaven and made report of his mission. There he dwelt in the smaller palace of the Sun." (By smaller palace is meant the palace of a prince.)[29]

The interlinear note here indicates that the compilers of the *Nihonshoki* recognized a parallel between the myths and the situation in the imperial court, although it is unclear precisely what is meant by referring to Izanagi here as a prince. For whatever reason, he seems unable or unwilling to rule on his own. Susano-o's refusal to accept the new status quo in some ways replicates the actions of Izanagi in the preceding episode. Indeed, Izanagi may feel threatened by Susano-o's recalcitrance and by the parallel he recognizes (consciously or unconsciously) between Susano-o's proposed actions and his own earlier ones. The reason why Susano-o's "excessive" mourning angers Izanagi is perfectly clear: Izanagi's final exercise of power is to inaugurate ritually the new ruling order, but Izanagi's ability to control the succession is contingent upon his ability to terminate the mourning rituals for the deceased. A decent period of mourning is acceptable, but interminable grief and mourning threatened the whole universe. In this light the permanent and complete break or "divorce" between Izanagi and Izanami, which is itself ritually accomplished, is a necessary first step in re-creating order and returning to a normalized state—both emotionally and politically. Continued mourning, not "letting go" of the dead, is clearly viewed in the myth as both psychologically and politically dangerous.

According to the logic of the myth, death became permanent for Izanami, and a rupture between Yomi and the world of the living occurred because of the actions and decisions of the living rather than of the dead. That is, even though Izanami had eaten of the hearth of Yomi, before Izanagi viewed the corpse the possibility was still held out by her that the separation of the couple occasioned by death might be only temporary. Izanagi's actions, however, cumulatively seal Izanami's—and hu-

manity's—fate, both literally and figuratively; after escaping from the land of the
dead, he rolls a huge boulder in front of the entrance to Yomi and the tomb. Her
death is then final, and humanity is thereafter characterized by mortality. Equally
important, the *kami* themselves, including the living human *kami* or the imperial
family, also become mortal.

Let us note the specific ritual action performed by Izanagi as he turned over the
authority to rule to Amaterasu:

Then he [Izanagi] removed his necklace, shaking the beads on the string so that they jingled,
and giving it to Amaterasu-o-mi-kami, he entrusted her with her mission.

Philippi cites Hirata Atsutane in saying that by this action, Izanagi ceded his
power to Amaterasu.[30] This assertion seems to me to be uncontestable. The ritual
action of *tama-furi* was practiced in Japan well into the Heian period. It is known
most popularly as *chinkon* or spirit pacification. The *chinkon-sai* or spirit pacification
ritual or festival was, when practiced for a member of the imperial family, also
known as the *mitamafuri no matsuri*. In the court, it was normally held the day before
the *niiname-sai* or the First Fruits Festival. In the myth, the *tama* (beads) of the
necklace are homonyms with *tama*, spirit or soul. The fact that Izanagi disappears
from the scene after Izanami's death suggests that the *tama* and power he attempts
to transfer are not only his but Izanami's as well. It will be recalled that Izanagi and
Izanami came into being as a paired couple rather than as individual *kami*. When
Izanagi seeks to distribute power among his noble children, however, this decision
apparently has to be consensual.

When one looks at the distribution of power among the three noble children that
Izanagi proposes, it does not seem to be equitable, for Amaterasu emerges (potentially, at least) as first among equals. It is not surprising, then, that Susano-o challenges this arrangement. He does this through the only means immediately available
to him: (1) by continuing the mourning for Izanami, *and* (2) by threatening (the term
may not be too strong) to go to her—that is, to enter the burial hall as Izanagi had
earlier done. The latter action seems to have been interpreted by Izanagi as politically
threatening, probably because of a fear that Susano-o would thereby have been able
to appropriate Izanami's *tama* and power (in Weberian terms, her charisma) onto
himself exclusively. All these actions lead one to conclude that after the sovereign's
death, one of the first crucial steps in the transfer of power and the establishment
of a new hierarchical order is to effect the conclusion of mourning. Izanagi cannot
accomplish this, however, without first banishing the recalcitrant Susano-o. But even
then, a smooth succession is not guaranteed.

Other political maneuvers also reportedly surround the death of Izanami. According to the *Kojiki*, after he had been ordered into exile, Susano-o asks permission

to visit Amaterasu. This goddess is suspicious of her brother's motives, saying: "It is certainly not with any good intentions that my brother is coming up. He must wish to usurp my lands."[31] Amaterasu then ties her hair up in a masculine style, puts on *maga-tama* or crescent-shaped beads, arms herself, and strikes a martial pose. When Susano-o arrives, she demands to know why he has come. Susano-o replies that he has no sinister ulterior motives but has come only to say "goodbye." To prove his innocence, he challenges Amaterasu to take an oath with him after which they are both to bear children, the nature of which will determine the winner and prove or disprove his veracity. Susano-o ultimately emerges victorious or at least claims to be the victor. Once again the actions of these two figures yield *kami* who are reckoned the ancestors of specific human families and clans. Yet as Alan Miller has rightly noted:

The contest narrowly conceived is a draw; both produce "children." But Susano-o understands it as a victory for him and "rages" in exultation, with the result that he commits violent and destructive acts that threaten the ongoing life of the created world by destroying the order on which it depends. Thus the contest taken in its entirety proves the superiority of Amaterasu and affirms her claim to sovereignty.[32]

Miller has put his finger on an important point: the *Kojiki* myth and all of the *Nihonshoki* variants view Amaterasu as the rightful ruler. She and not Susano-o is considered to be the ancestor of the imperial family. This "contest," then, bears further close study in terms of its relation to the problem of the succession and the legitimacy of the imperial family. In this regard both Amaterasu and Susano-o apparently need to borrow some of the power of the other in order to produce children. In the *Kojiki* version, Amaterasu takes the sword Susano-o wears, breaks it into three pieces, rinses these in *Ame no mana-i*, the Heavenly Well, and then chews and spits them out.[33] Her children come into being in the misty spray (*ibuki no sagiri*). In similar fashion, Susano-o bears children from various *maga-tama*, crescent-shaped beads worn in Amaterasu's hair. Here one glimpses both another expression of the *tama*-belief complex and a suggestion of incestuous relations, not unlike those between Izanagi and Izanami.[34] The next section of the myth is important.

Then Haya-Susano-o-no-mikoto said to Amaterasu-o-mi-kami: "It was because my intentions were pure and bright that in the children I begot I obtained graceful maidens. By this it is obvious that I have won."

Thus saying, he raged with victory, breaking down the ridges between the rice paddies of Amaterasu-o-mi-kami and covering up the ditches.

Also he defecated and strewed the faeces about in the hall where the first fruits were tasted [*ōnihe*].

Even though he did this, Amaterasu-o-mi-kami did not reprove him, but said:

"That which appears to be faeces must be what my brother has vomited and strewn about while drunk. Also his breaking down the ridges of the paddies and covering up their ditches—my brother must have done this because he thought it was wasteful to use the land thus."

Even though she thus spoke with good intention [*nori-naoshi*], his misdeeds did not cease, but became even more flagrant.

When Amaterasu-o-mi-kami was inside the sacred weaving hall seeing to the weaving of the divine garments, he opened a hole in the roof of the sacred weaving hall and dropped down into it the heavenly dappled pony which he had skinned with a backwards skinning.

The heavenly weaving maiden, seeing this, was afraid, and opening the heavenly rock-cave door, went in and shut herself inside.

Then Takama-no-hara was completely dark, and the Central Land of the Reed Plains was entirely dark.

Because of this, constant night reigned, and the cries of the myriad deities were everywhere abundant, like summer flies; and all manner of calamities arose.[35]

This episode of the myth has long occasioned much scholarly debate and commentary. Here, however, we are interested in the specific narrative framing (which is itself a "reading") of the myth preserved in the *Kojiki* and the *Nihonshoki* (i.e., not only in an ahistorical structural analysis but also in the possible ways in which the socio-political situation in the court may have affected the details in the narrative form given to this myth as it was committed to writing in the early eighth century). Thus, it is of paramount importance to note that although, as Miller pointed out, both *kami* bore children, Susano-o proceeds to perform acts that disqualify him in the eyes of the myriad *kami* as a legitimate ruler. It is finally not the actions of either Amaterasu or Susano-o that settle the succession issue but the actions of the other lesser *kami*, those who may be thought of as equivalent to the nobles and courtiers in the imperial court. These figures finally restore order by successfully plotting to trick Amaterasu into emerging from the rock-grotto where she has secluded herself and by capturing, trying, and ultimately banishing Susano-o. To understand why this should be the case according to the internal logic of the myth, let us note first the three "sins" performed by Susano-o (the list differs depending on the version, but I will use the main version cited earlier):

(1) he breaks down the ridges between rice paddies created by Amaterasu and covers up irrigation ditches;

(2) he defecates in the Hall of the First Fruits; and

(3) he drops a pony, which had been skinned backwards, down a hole into the sacred weaving hall.

The first offense involves interference with the cultivation of the sacred rice fields where the rice for the *niiname* is grown; the second involves interference with the harvest festival; and the third involves the *Kammiso-sai* or Festival of the August

Garments of the *kami*, celebrated in both the spring and the fall and on the latter occasion on the day preceding the *niiname-sai*. It is extremely significant that the myth locates this attempt by Susano-o to upset the new order in the world at the time of the *niiname-sai* or First Fruits Festival, yet surprisingly few scholars have recognized this fact. Nelly Naumann, for example, in an otherwise excellent analysis of the myth that discloses much of the significance of the ritual action of reverse slaying (*sakahagi*), seems to have missed the crucial symbolic import of this temporal locus. She writes:

it should be pointed out that the reverse flaying and its utmost disastrous consequences are in full accord with the character of Susanowo as depicted at the outset of the myth, namely, that is as the weeping god who caused the death of every living thing on earth—this, at least, is what we may infer from the accounts. In complete consistency with his character as the great destroyer of life on earth, he ascends to the heavens before entering the realm of the dead, his true domain, in order that he might complete his work of destruction in the heavens, too. Given the range of this tremendous context, bearing as it does on the essential questions of life and death, the remaining misdeeds of Susanowo—his interference with the cultivation of the rice-fields and defecation in the hall for tasting the first-fruits—seem only trivial and out of place.[36]

Although Naumann may feel these other elements are "trivial and out of place," in fact, all of them participate in a central informing ritual complex wherein the death/rebirth symbolism found in the agricultural cycle is conflated with that of the succession following the death of a divine sovereign. Rather than being out of place, these other elements are "natural" parts of the politics of death in early Japan. The sovereign was considered the final guarantor of peace, prosperity, and fertility in the land. It was the sovereign in his special religio-political capacity who performed the *niiname-sai*. Since all Susano-o's actions are designed specifically to disrupt the performance of the *niiname-sai*, closely associated with the imperial accession ceremony, we can say that through these actions Susano-o sought to keep Amaterasu from formally assuming the full ritual prerogatives of her newly appointed office. As Miller has shown, in the myth the weaving maiden was weaving the *ōfusuma*, the sacred shawl spread over a would-be sovereign or his couch in the imperial accession ritual. Thus, all Susano-o's "sins" would seem to be part of a conscious program of disrupting the rituals designed to effect a transfer of power and to legitimate a new political hierarchy. Susano-o's misdeeds, and most especially his reverse flaying of the piebald horse and flinging it down into the sacred weaving hall, lead to the death of the heavenly weaving maiden and Amaterasu's retreat into the cave.

Then Takama-no-hara was completely dark, and the Central Land of Reed Plains was entirely dark.

Because of this, constant night reigned, and the cries of the myriad deities were everywhere abundant, like summer flies; and all manner of calamities arose.

This description follows very closely that found after the demise of Izanami when Susano-o mourns excessively and refuses to take up his newly assigned position. In that earlier episode we read that:

His weeping was such that it caused the verdant mountains to wither and all the rivers and seas to dry up. At this, the cries of the malevolent deities were everywhere abundant like summer flies and all sorts of calamities arose in all things.

The immediate parallel is more than just a narrative convention for describing a disordered and chaotic world; it is *an intentional redundancy* that indicates the unchanging character of Susano-o. These parallel descriptive passages lead us to conclude, as Amaterasu had suspected from the beginning, that Susano-o's ultimate goal remains unchanged. Though initially frustrated, he still seeks the position of supreme ruler. He first attempts to realize his ambitions by refusing to cease mourning and seeking to go to the temporary burial site of Izanami. When he is blocked in this effort by Izanagi, however, and the scene shifts to the heavens and Amaterasu's palace, the action is in one sense reversed. In the former instance one may assume that Susano-o's professed desire to enter the *mogari no miya* of Izanami was publicly presented as a desire to continue the ritual attempt to resurrect the deceased and thus to maintain the old political order; in the latter instance, his desire to enter the palace of Amaterasu is ostensibly to recognize formally the new status quo and, thus, implicitly to accept Izanami's permanent death. Yet his intrusion into the residence of this living female *kami* and his subsequent misdeeds drive his sister into a rock-cave/tomb or, if we are to believe Matsumae Takeshi and others, to her death.[37]

Once again the myth presents a paradigm for symbolically meaningful acts in the imperial court: following the death of a ruler, the physical entry of a male contender for the throne into the residence of a female intimately associated with the throne, be it the temporary burial palace of a deceased sovereign or the palace of a living *kami*, is an act that is meant to enable the male to usurp power. Several narratives found in the *Nihonshoki* and elsewhere that share this narrative detail can be understood only in light of this myth.

At this point in the myth Susano-o has been able to achieve, temporarily at least, what he was unable to do during the period of mourning for Izanami—he has apparently disposed of his major opposition. The myth, of course, does not end at this point but goes on to recount how Amaterasu was drawn out of the cave, order was restored, and Susano-o was punished and exiled. What is crucial is that this myth provides a paradigmatic model for overcoming two critical problems in both the divine and the human realms: (1) the radical socio-political disjunction and crisis occasioned by the death of a sovereign, and (2) the presence of an "illegitimate" person in power. (In Hitomaro's famous *banka* performed at the time of the temporary interment of Prince Takeru, MYS 2: 199–201, discussed in the previous chapter, Hitomaro explicitly identifies Prince Ōama's [Temmu's] flight into the Yoshino mountains following the death of the Emperor Tenji with Amaterasu's seclusion within the heavenly rock-grotto. This use of a myth to inform the narrative structure and interpretive frame put on historical occurrences is one of the most common and significant historiographic techniques used in these texts.)

The myth of Amaterasu and the rock-grotto includes, then, a "charter myth" for the *chinkon-sai* (Chinese reading) or *tama-furi* (Japanese) rituals to call back the spirit of the deceased and then to bind it and/or transfer it in the imperial accession ceremony. It is a paradigmatic "solution" to the cognitive dissonance between the claims of the imperial family's direct descent from Amaterasu and an unbroken line and the biological "fact" of death. The divine *tama* is one across the generations and ages as the imperial *tama* is transferred to the new sovereign as part of the *daijō-sai*, the accession ritual. At the same time, Amaterasu's "retreat" and later return to the throne, as well as Susano-o's banishment, may be seen as a model for and a model of a number of incidents in the imperial court and their retrospective narration.

It should be noted that Susano-o is not upset by the results of his actions in either the excessive weeping episode or in the instances of ritual defilement aimed against Amaterasu. In fact, just the opposite seems to be the case. Susano-o seems to be perfectly aware of the fact that his actions will create disorder and throw the world into a state of dangerous chaos, which it would not be able to endure for very long. It is clear that he performs all his acts precisely with the intention of creating such havoc. In spite of Susano-o's protestations to the contrary, his goal is to usurp the power and throne of Amaterasu. Thus, the myth narrates an attempted coup d'état, albeit on a cosmic scale.

It would be a mistake, however, to equate prematurely Susano-o with the natural powers of darkness, death, and destruction, and Amaterasu with light and fertility, as some scholars have done in reading this myth as an allegory of either a basic cosmic duality or a natural celestial phenomenon.[38] Without denying the possible value of such interpretations, we must realize that the early Japanese also read the socio-political situation in the court into these cosmic myths and vice versa. Myths may indeed have universal and timeless messages, but they are also given specific interpretations and are used in specific and intentional ways by conscious human agents in history. At the same time, myths are subject to being changed by human agents in time. If it is naive to assume that the myths in the *Kojiki* and the *Nihonshoki* are timeless, it is equally erroneous to suggest that they are simply an attempt by certain factions in the court to pull the "silk" over someone's eyes. An important aspect of the effective exercise of power is the ability to reach a consensus on the legitimate distribution of prestige and position. This could be achieved only by utilizing culturally available and valorized interpretive frames and paradigms (mythic and other) to contextualize and give narrative form to developments in the court.

In the myth of Amaterasu and Susano-o, after Amaterasu has retreated into the rock-grotto, plunging the world into darkness, the myriad *kami* gather together in consternation to decide what to do. After having recourse to a form of divination (*uranai*) involving the firing of the shoulder bones of deer and reading the resultant crack lines, they devise a plan to draw Amaterasu out of the cave/tomb. Some *kami* make a mirror while others make *maga-tama*, two of the three imperial regalia. (The third item of the regalia, the famous Kusanagi sword, is at this point still held by Susano-o. In a later episode of the myth, he presents the sword to Amaterasu after slaying an eight-tailed dragon.) The *kami* then set up sacred *sasaki* branches before the cave and hang the mirror, *maga-tama*, and strips of white and blue cloth from these. They next have cocks (*naga-naki tori*) crow in an effort to cause the sun (Amaterasu) to appear. Futo-tama no mikoto ("Strong-*tama kami*," ancestor of the Imbe, a powerful ritual guild aligned with the Soga) holds these sacred objects while Ame-no-koyane no mikoto (mythical ancestor of the Nakatomi) intones ritual prayers (*norito*). Meanwhile, a male *kami* hides by the door to the rock-grotto and Ame-no-uzume no mikoto, often described as the paradigmatic female shaman or *miko*, dances on top of an overturned barrel (*ukefune*, an instrument used, according to Matsumae, only in the *chinkon-sai*[39]), becomes possessed (*kamu-gakari*), and exposes her breasts and genitals. At this the myriad *kami* laugh and the sound of their laughter perplexes Amaterasu. She narrowly opens the door to the rock-cave and says:

"Because I have shut myself in, I thought that Takama-no-hara would be dark, and that the Central Land of the Reed Plains would be completely dark. But why is it that Ame-no-uzume sings and dances [*asobi*], and all the eight-hundred myriad deities laugh?"

Then Ame-no-uzume said:

"We rejoice and dance because there is here a deity superior to you."

While she was saying this, Ame-no-koyane-no-mikoto and Futo-tama-no-mikoto brought out the mirror and showed it to Amaterasu-o-mi-kami.

Then Amaterasu-o-mi-kami, thinking this more and more strange, gradually came out of the door and approached (the mirror).

Then the hidden Ame-no-ta-jikara-o-no-kami took her hand and pulled her out. Immediately Futo-tama-no-mikoto extended a shiri-kume rope behind her, and said:

"You may go back no further than this!"

When Amaterasu-o-mi-kami came forth, Takama-no-hara and the Central Land of the Reed Plains of themselves became light.

At this time the eight-hundred myriad deities deliberated together, imposed upon Haya-Susano-o-no-mikoto a fine of a thousand tables of restitutive gifts, and also, cutting off his beard and the nails of his hands and feet, had him exorcised and expelled with a divine expulsion.[40]

Scholars have long recognized Ame-no-uzume as a kind of shaman and related her dance to the *chinkon-sai* or spirit pacification ritual. One also finds in this "scene" a complex ritual being prepared and performed by *kami* held to be the ancestors of ritual specialists of the sacred in early Japan, specifically the five clans of the Yamato court, who also figure in the narrative of the descent of Ninigi no mikoto, Amaterasu's grandson, as they carry the imperial regalia to earth, marking the transition from the Age of the Gods to that of the divine-human sovereigns. Finally, one sees that Susano-o's beard and nails are cut before he is banished. Philippi, following Japanese scholarship, has suggested that this was done "to punish him or, rather, in order to exorcise him and thus remove the sins and pollution adhering to him."[41] We may, however, also see these actions as forcibly removing the signs of continued mourning, since many cultures prohibit persons in mourning to cut their hair and nails, to bathe, to change clothes, and so on.

In the Amaterasu–Susano-o myth, Amaterasu, like Susano-o, apparently knows precisely what she is doing when she conceals herself in the cave. She fully expects the world to be thrown into darkness and disarray and, not without a dash of self-importance, expects that the world will not survive without her. This latter expectation is frustrated when the myriad *kami* are heard laughing outside the cave—a situation that confuses Amaterasu. Her confusion is compounded when Ame-no-uzume informs her that the *kami* have found a deity superior even to Amaterasu. These elements combine to draw Amaterasu out of the cave, wondering, perhaps, if she had misjudged Susano-o's power. What is of import is the fact that Amaterasu is tricked into reemerging; that is, she is not brought out by woeful laments of the *kami* on the desperate condition of the world without her, or by pleas that only she can save the world, which one might expect—and which Amaterasu specifically seems to have expected.

If Amaterasu's concealment in the cave is taken as a kind of death, then her reemergence represents a return to life. If we follow the *Kojiki* version, although Susano-o's actions are disturbing to be sure, in the final consideration Amaterasu enters the cave or "dies" of her own volition. Yet she is drawn out through an elaborate ruse and not on her own terms. If this is so, then the rituals to recall the spirit of Amaterasu created by Ume-no-uzume and the other *kami* have a core element of trickery about them, an element that would then be found in the *chinkon* or *tama-furi* rituals when these are transferred to the human realm. There is a hint here that religious ritual involves an element of tricking the *kami* into acting as the ritualists want them to.

The Shared Patterns in the Izanagi–Izanami and the
Amaterasu–Susano-o Myths

In many ways the Amaterasu–Susano-o mythic narrative appears to replicate the essential structure of the Izanami–Izanagi sequence. This initial impression, however, requires closer study. The myths are obviously related but in precisely what manner is not immediately apparent. In the Izanami–Izanagi sequence one finds Izanagi (the living) performing specific ritual actions to keep Izanami (the dead) in the land of Yomi. These rituals constitute examples of what Van Gennep called rites of separation, since they are intended to demarcate and differentiate the realms of the living and the dead. Final or permanent death is not chosen by Izanami but is effected by the actions of Izanagi, first in breaking a taboo concerning the "dead" and then in the series of defensive actions he takes fleeing Yomi. The reverse situation is found in the Amaterasu–Susano-o portion of the myth: (1) death or entering the land of the dead is freely chosen by Amaterasu; (2) the taboos violated by the male and living *kami* (Susano-o) are clearly associated with rituals of fertility and life; and (3) other living *kami* (Ame-no-uzume et al.) initiate actions first to bring the deceased back to the world of the living and then to bar Amaterasu from entering, not leaving, the cave again.

It will be useful to look at a simple chart comparing the significant narrative patterns of the Izanami–Izanagi myth with those of the Amaterasu–Susano-o sequence.

Izanami–Izanagi Myth	*Amaterasu–Susano-o Myth*
Brother and sister assigned to rule shared realm	Brother and sister assigned to rule separate realms
Cooperative "incest" yields male and female pairs of *kami* children	Competitive "incest" yields *kami* children of one sex
Progeny recognized as children of both parents	Progeny recognized as children of only one parent
Female "dies" involuntarily in giving birth to Fire Kami	Female "dies" voluntarily after birthing contest
Female enters land of Yomi	Female enters rock-cave
Male is upset by female's death	Male not upset with female's death
Male attempts to get deceased to return	Male makes no attempt to get deceased to return
Izanami requires permission to return to land of the living	Amaterasu requires no permission to return to land of the living
Izanagi kills son, the Fire Kami, for having caused "death" of mother (father's sister)—cuts off head	Other *kami* punish Susano-o for having caused "death" of sister—cut off beard and nails

Izanagi (male) violates ritual taboo concerning temporary death, causing permanent death

Izanagi views the corpse of Izanami and is repulsed

Izanagi flees realm of dead

Izanagi tricks the ugly hags of Yomi by throwing down objects that turn into food

Izanagi performs rituals to keep the dead sovereign, Izanami, from returning to the land of the living

Izanami pronounces a curse, introducing death into the world

End result is permanent separation and death and new political status quo

Izanagi bears Noble Children independently and assigns them realms to rule

Sister/spouse and her children disqualified as legitimate heirs

Izanagi disappears from narrative

Susano-o (male) violates ritual taboos concerning life and fertility, causing temporary death

Amaterasu views herself, a "living corpse," in mirror and is attracted

Amaterasu is tricked into inching out of grotto/realm of the dead

The myriad kami trick Amaterasu by laughing and showing her her own countenance in the mirror

The kami perform ritual actions to keep the "resurrected" Amaterasu from returning to the land of the dead

The kami pronounce a spell that keeps life in the world

End result is return to original political status quo as ordered by Izanagi

Amaterasu names one of her sons to rule on earth

Brother/"spouse" and his children disqualified as legitimate heirs

Susano-o exiled, but narrative presence continues

Although the Amaterasu–Susano-o myth in some ways replicates the Izanami–Izanagi myth, in other ways certain elements represent an inversion. The first four items above, for instance, all mark out the Amaterasu–Susano-o myth as the inverse of the former. The myths converge, however, at the fifth item as the female protagonist in each undergoes a "temporary" or "provisional" death. Both Izanami and Amaterasu enter a place we may take to be a *mogari no miya* or temporary enshrinement palace. Although the *Kojiki* version of these myths is not explicit on this point, the internal evidence is overwhelming for adopting this reading. Moreover, one version of the death of Izanami preserved in the *Nihonshoki* explicitly says: "Izanagi no Mikoto, wishing to see his younger sister, went to the temporary burial-place [*mogari no tokoro*]."[42]

If this is the case, then the actions performed at that location, by Izanagi in the former case and by the myriad *kami* in the latter, are ritual actions during the time of temporary enshrinement. The Amaterasu–Susano-o narrative, then, serves as the charter myth for the *chinkon-sai* or *tama-furi* rituals, whereas the Izanami–Izanagi narrative is the charter myth for the rituals of final burial that confirm the death as permanent. The critical act on Izanagi's part that seals Izanami's fate is his viewing the rotting corpse, a thing of horror now and obviously unsuitable for life in the realm of the living. This narrative element finds its ritual expression in cultures that practice double burial when the temporarily interred corpse or the skeletal remains are disinterred and then given final burial, at which time mourning ceases.[43] Izanagi is able to create his own "noble children" and designated heirs only after the boulder is used to seal the tomb and entrance to Yomi and the final rites of separation are performed. Amaterasu is ritually installed as ruler of the heavens only at this point in the narrative. The sequential unfolding of this mythic narrative provided the rationale for the preferred timing of the conclusion of the period of temporary interment and for the performance of final burial rites in the court.

Death and the Niiname-sai

In the myth the "three sins" of Susano-o, which caused Amaterasu to withdraw into the heavenly rock-grotto, all centered temporally and spatially around the harvest festival or *niiname-sai*. The Amaterasu–Susano-o sequence, then, does not serve as a charter myth for the *niiname-sai*, since the ritual is said to have already existed in the High Heavens. We must look for its first performance on earth. The mythological archetype of the *niiname-sai* on earth is found in the "Age of the Gods" or *kami no yo* section of the *Nihonshoki* in one version of the myth of the descent from the High Heavens of Amatsuhiko-ho no Ninigi no mikoto (hereafter referred to as Ninigi), a grandson of Amaterasu.[44] In this myth Ninigi, rather than his father, is sent by Takami-musubi no kami and/or Amaterasu to rule the earth. He descends with the imperial regalia to a mountain peak and begins wandering around until he discovers a beautiful young woman, Kami-ataka-ashi-tsu-hime (more popularly known as Ko-no-hana-sakuya-hime), and desires to possess her. She demurs, asking him to request permission from her father. When Ninigi does so, the father sends both the beautiful young woman and her elder sister, Iwa-naga-hime, to be Ninigi's wives, as well as food and drink to entertain him.

The names of the two sisters play an important role in the myth. Ko-no-hana-sakuya-hime is "Princess Who Blossoms Like the Flowers on the Trees," and Iwa-naga-hime is "Rock-long Princess." According to the *Nihonshoki*:

Now the August Grandchild [Ninigi] thought the elder sister ugly, and would not take her. So she went away. But the younger sister was a noted beauty. So he took her with him and favoured her, and in one night she became pregnant.[45]

The elder sister and/or her family are humiliated by Ninigi's rejection of her. In several versions she curses Ninigi, in others the father does, but in each case the result is the mortality of humans and of the imperial family as well. One version, for example, has Iwa-naga-hime say:

If the August Grandchild had taken me and not rejected me, the children born to him would have been long-lived and would have endured for ever like the mossy rocks. But seeing that he has not done so, but has married my younger sister only, the children born to him will surely be decadent like the flowers of the trees.[46]

Another version is even more explicit in asserting that Ninigi's rejection of the elder sister was the cause of human mortality:

Iwa-naga-hime, in her shame and resentment, spat and wept. She said:—"The race of visible mankind shall change swiftly like the flowers of the trees, and shall decay and pass away." This is the reason why the life of man is so short.[47]

Here too death—or human mortality—is a direct result of the actions of a male figure. Yet, while death is introduced into the world life is also introduced in the pregnancy of Ko-no-hana-sakuya-hime. In other words, although individual immortality is no longer possible, a different sort of generational immortality is introduced through the lives of one's heirs and descendants. This was, of course, to become an important element of the imperial religio-political ideology in early Japan. This change, however, is not readily accepted by Ninigi. The myth continues with the famous passage in which Ninigi tries to deny his paternity.

Kami-ataka-ashi-tsu-hime saw the August Grandchild, and said:—"Thy handmaiden has conceived a child by the August Grandchild. It is not meet that it should be born privately." The August Grandchild said:—"Child of the Heavenly Deity though I am, how could I in one night cause anyone to be with child? Now it cannot be my child." Ko-no-hana-sakuya-hime was exceedingly ashamed and angry. She straightaway made a doorless muro [a windowless wooden structure], and thereupon made a vow [ukei], saying:—"If the child which I have conceived is the child of another Deity, may it surely be unfortunate. But if it is truly the offspring of the Heavenly Grandchild, may it surely be alive and unhurt." So she entered the muro, and burnt it with fire.[48]

She then gives birth to three (one version has four) male children, all of whom are of course unharmed. In written form, all their names include the character for "fire" to signify the nature of their birth. This section once again introduces the problem of legitimacy in the succession process. The myth continues:

Then with a bamboo knife [Ko-no-hana-sakuya-hime] cut their navel-strings. From the bamboo knife which she threw away, there eventually sprang up a bamboo grove. Therefore that place was called Taka-ya [i.e., Bamboo House]. Now Kami-ataka-ashi-tsu-hime by divination fixed upon a rice-field to which she gave the name Sanada, and from the rice grown there brewed Heavenly sweet sake, with which she entertained him [i.e., Ninigi]. Moreover, with the rice from the Nunada rice-field she made boiled rice and entertained him therewith.[49]

Some elements found here are also in the narrative of Ninigi's own birth. Ninigi's father, Ame-no-oshi-ho-mimi no mikoto, had originally been selected to rule the earth. In preparation for this undertaking Amaterasu presented him with the sacred mirror and the other imperial regalia.

She further gave command, saying:—"I will give over to my child the rice-ears of the sacred garden [*yu-niwa*, the plot where the sacred rice for the *niiname-sai* is grown] of which I partake in the Plain of High Heaven. And she straightaway took the daughter of Takami-musubi no mikoto, by name Yorozu-hata-hime, and uniting her to Ame-no-oshi-ho-mimi no mikoto as his consort, sent her down. Therefore while she was still in the Void of Heaven [i.e., in the sky between the High Heavens and earth], she gave birth to a child, who was called Amatsu-hiko-ho-ho-Ninigi no mikoto. She accordingly desired to send down this child instead of his parents.[50]

Here the sacred rice fields are granted to the heir apparent as part of the necessary trappings of his soon-to-be-assumed office. When the mantle shifts to his son—and the phrase is apposite here in light of the central role of the *ōfusuma* or sacred shawl—these fields are transferred as well. Clearly the *niiname-sai* is closely related to the complex of divine kingship, though the precise relationship is not immediately obvious.[51] In the Ninigi/Ko-no-hana-sakuya-hime myth, *she* establishes the sacred fields and institutes the prototypical harvest festival. Interestingly enough, this is not done after Ninigi has proved his legitimacy, since as the chosen representative of Amaterasu and as a result of the subjugation of the unruly earthly *kami*, there is no dispute over his right to rule. Rather, the *niiname-sai* is performed after the legitimacy of potential heirs—the products of the union of a heavenly being and an earthly one—has been called into question. The first performance of the *niiname-sai*, then, certifies the legitimacy of the heir(s) to the throne.

In all the myths we have looked at so far, the female character enters some dark windowless enclosure and undergoes either a kind of death or an ordeal that could lead to death—Izanagi enters Yomi, Amaterasu the rock-grotto, and Ko-no-hana-sakuya-hime the *muro*. Furthermore, each case involves the bearing of children or the creation of heirs: Izanami dies in giving birth to the Fire Kami, whereas Izanagi creates his own "noble children" independently; Amaterasu enters the rock-grotto after the birthing contest with Susano-o; and Ko-no-hana-sakuya-hime bears her children in the burning *muro*. In addition, discord between the female and male protagonists always develops.

The Ninigi–Ko-no-hana-sakuya-hime myth is clearly related to both the Izanagi–Izanami and Amaterasu–Susano-o myths. Although the incest theme is absent from the Ninigi myth, this myth shares with the Amaterasu–Susano-o myth the narrative detail that the first children produced of the union are not recognized, initially at least, as the offspring of both parents. The Ninigi–Ko-no-hana-sakuya-hime myth is, however, finally the inverse of the Izanagi–Izanami myth insofar as in the former the progeny are eventually recognized as the children of both parents, whereas in the latter Izanagi goes on to produce heirs by himself, although Susano-o continues to refer to Izanami as his mother. The Ninigi myth, however, replicates the Izanagi–Izanami narrative insofar as the female protagonist in each—Iwa-naga-hime and Izanami respectively—pronounces a curse that introduces death into the human realm.

Finally, let us note how the denouement of each of these myths affects the political status or legitimacy of the children. In the Izanagi–Izanami myth the female and her children are effectively disqualified, whereas the "noble children" of Izanagi are presented as legitimate heirs, with Susano-o falling from grace by identifying with his "mother." In the Ninigi–Ko-no-hana-sakuya-hime myth, after the ordeal of the burning *muro* the children are recognized as rightful heirs and as the offspring of both parents, though there is intense competition and tension between the two main contenders for the position of heir apparent.

It is only in the Amaterasu–Susano-o myth, though, that we find the female protagonist's "death" presented as that of a sovereign rather than as the death of a spouse/empress-consort. If Amaterasu's retreat into the cave is a temporary death, then one finds an apparent connection in the myth between the ritual harvest festival and the death of the sovereign that needs to be more fully explored. Comparative and cross-cultural studies since at least the time of Frazer have disclosed a symbolic complex surrounding divine kingship in which agricultural symbols of degeneration and putrescence are often related to other symbols of rebirth and fertility.[52]

The apparent connection between sudden death and the Harvest Festival in early Japan has long been noted,[53] but in a recent short essay, "Niiname ni shutsugen suru ōja, korosareru ōja" ("Sovereigns Who Appear and Sovereigns Who Are Killed in the *Niiname*")[54] Obayashi Taryo has refocused attention on this complex. Obayashi argues that in early Japan the time surrounding the *niiname-sai* was a "season" of murder and assassination, as well as of renewal of the socio-political order. Insofar as this is correct—and Obayashi presents a convincing case—we have an instance of the classic Frazerian symbolic complex of sacred kingship. The *Nihonshoki* is filled with accounts of executions, assassinations, suicides, and other violent deaths in the imperial court. Such events were the "stuff" of history for the early Japanese, as they retrospectively ordered and narrated those significant events that defined their present. Although not all the accounts of the events surrounding violent deaths in the court temporally locate them around the time of the *niiname-sai*, a significant number do so.

Robert Ellwood, one of the major Western scholars of the history of early Japanese religion, has noted the centrality of the *niiname-sai* in the early Japanese world of meaning, asserting that "The major festival in Shinto since the introduction of agriculture—both court and popular, archaic and historic—is the harvest festival,

the *Niiname*. All the other fundamental institutions of Shinto, including its connection with the sovereign and the state, revolve around the *Niiname* just as the Christian calendar revolves around Easter."[55] Ellwood's comparison of the *niiname-sai* to
Easter is appropriate, especially insofar as it serves immediately to underscore the
presence of a victim of a violent death together with rebirth and fertility symbolism.
These elements are found in the Izanami–Izanagi and Amaterasu–Susano-o myths
because Susano-o defiles the sacred rice paddies and the palace in which Amaterasu
is celebrating the *niiname-sai* by secretly defecating either there or, in other versions,
under Amaterasu's seat. In addition, the sacred weaving hall where the ritual garments for the festival are being prepared is defiled when Susano-o throws the back-
ward-skinned pony down into it. The final result in all versions, however, is the
interruption of the ritual, an act that plunges the world into a state of turmoil,
chaos, and darkness. At the same time, either Amaterasu or the Heavenly Weaving
Maiden dies, in some versions after the shuttle of a loom strikes her genitals.

A second mythic narrative that relates the *niiname-sai* to the politics of death
centers on the question of the legitimate ruler of the Central Land of Reed Plains,
another name for Japan. In the *Kojiki* this myth follows the rather lengthy Okuninushi sequence, which we will pass over for the moment. It is found in slightly
different versions in both the *Kojiki* and the *Nihonshoki*, as well as in a different,
clearly factional version in the *Engi-shiki*.[56] Amaterasu and/or Taka-mi-musubi-no-
kami desire(s) to send a son, Ame-no-oshi-ho-mimi-no-mikoto, one of the children
born in the contest with Susano-o, down from the High Heavens to rule this world.
This is a central episode linking the imperial family directly to the Sun Goddess.
Amaterasu's son descends to the Heavenly Floating Bridge (*Ame no uke-hashi*) but
then returns to the High Heavens to report that he was unable to take up his rule.
The description of the chaotic state of the world found in the *Nihonshoki* is a familiar
one:

But in that Land there were numerous Deities which shone with a lustre like that of fireflies,
and evil Deities which buzzed like flies. There were also trees and herbs all of which could
speak.[57]

This description recalls those found earlier when Susano-o, weeping and howling,
mourned excessively following the death of Izanami, and again when Amaterasu
retreated into the heavenly rock-grotto. After reviewing this passage, Alan Miller has
suggested that "The central image is that of unbridled motion and alienness." Moreover, he rightly notes that "The condition of the universe that results from Susano-
o's actions is characterized in these texts as not a universe at all, not a cosmos, but
chaos, that is, disorder, a random motion that results in desolation and death either
by means of withering or by means of unbridled growth."[58]

If one puts a political interpretation on this situation, the world is chaotic precisely because there is as yet no legitimate ruler to establish and then maintain order. After consulting with the myriad deities, it is decided that Ame-no-ho-hi-no-kami, another son of Amaterasu from the contest with Susano-o, should be sent to subdue the unruly earthly *kami* (*kunitsu-kami*). Instead of performing his assigned task, however, this *kami* curries favor with Okuninushi and fails to report on his mission. After three years, another son of Ame-no-ho-hi-no-kami, named Ame-no-waka-hiko, is sent. According to the *Kojiki*:

> Then they [Amaterasu, Taka-mi-musubi and the myriad *kami*] bestowed upon Ame-no-waka-hiko the heavenly deer(-slaying) bow and the heavenly feathered arrows and dispatched him. Then Ame-no-waka-hiko descended to the land and soon took as wife the daughter of Okuninushi-no-kami, Shita-teru-hime. He also plotted to gain the land (for himself) [*kuni o emu to tomoi hakarite*] and for eight years did not return and report (on his mission).[59]

The *Nihonshoki* account is similar.[60] The narrative continues with Taka-mi-musubi sending a pheasant, named Naki-me (literally, "Weeping Woman") in the *Kojiki* and Na-nashi ("Nameless") in the *Nihonshoki*,[61] down to earth to find out what has kept Ame-no-waka-hiko. The pheasant flies to earth, perches on a branch of the sacred *katsura* tree just outside the door of Ame-no-waka-hiko, and recites the words precisely as instructed by the heavenly *kami*. Then a mysterious female figure, Ama-no-sagume,[62] reports these to Ame-no-waka-hiko, adding that they are evil words and that the pheasant should be killed. Ame-no-waka-hiko proceeds to do this, using the sacred bow and arrow bestowed on him by the heavenly *kami* prior to his descent. The fatal arrow passes through the body of the pheasant and shoots up backward (*sakashima ni iageraete*) to the High Heavens, where it lands at the feet of Amaterasu and Taka-mi-musubi (called Taka-ki-no-kami in the *Kojiki*). The *Kojiki* version continues:

> When Taka-ki-no-kami picked up the arrow and looked at it, there was blood on its feathers. Then Taka-ki-no-kami said: "This is the arrow which was bestowed upon Ame-no-waka-hiko." Then, showing it to all the deities, he said: "If Ame-no-waka-hiko has not failed his trust, and if (this) arrow be one which was shot at the evil deities, then let it not strike Ame-no-waka-hiko! But if he has a treacherous heart [*moshi kitanaki kokoro araba*], then let him be cursed in this arrow!" Thus saying, he took the arrow and thrust it back down through the arrow-hole; then it hit Ame-no-waka-hiko in the chest as he lay in his bed in the morning [*asatoko ni ineshi*], and he died.

> [Ed. gloss:] This is the origin of (the saying:) "the returning arrow." Also, the pheasant never returned. Therefore even today there is a saying: "The one-way errand of the pheasant [*kigishi no hitazukai*]."[63]

The *Nihonshoki* version of the last part of this episode is especially important. It reads:

Thereupon Taka-mi-musubi no Mikoto took up the arrow and flung it back down (to earth). This arrow, when it fell, hit Ame-waka-hiko on top of his breast. At this time Ame-waka-hiko was lying down after the feast of first fruits [*toki ni, Ame-waka-hiko niinahe shite nefuseru toki nari*], and when hit by the arrow died immediately.[64]

Several elements here are of special significance. The precise time of Ame-no-waka-hiko's death is not given in the *Kojiki* version, which merely says he was lying down in the morning. The *Nihonshoki*, however, explicitly locates his death *after* he had performed the *niiname-sai*, an important narrative linkage of the Harvest Festival with the death of a (would-be) ruler. Indeed, the linkage may be intended to suggest that Ame-no-waka-hiko's performance of this ritual was an attempt to show him exercising one of the prerogatives of the ruler. Insofar as the narrator/recorder of the myth does not consider Ame-no-waka-hiko to be the rightful ruler, there is an element of poetic justice in the manner, timing, and place of this character's death.

In addition, as Philippi notes, the words Taka-mi-musubi pronounces before he casts the arrow back to earth are a form of magical oath known as *ukei*, the same magical form used by Amaterasu and Susano-o in their contest of childbearing.[65] Such an oath was supposed to have the unequivocal power of determining a person's innocence or guilt, or as the *Kojiki* passage above puts it, whether his heart is impure (*kitanaishi*). The muted suggestion in these narratives of a ritual ordeal associated with the *niiname-sai* and divine kingship has not gone unnoticed. Ellwood, for example, after reviewing the evidence suggests that Ame-no-waka-hiko failed some test that involved reclining on a couch during the *niiname-sai*. A legitimate ruler or heir would have been wrapped in the *matoko ōfusuma*, which Aston renders "coverlet spread on the true couch."[66] Alan Miller has pointed out that this was the garment that the Heavenly Weaving Maiden/Amaterasu was weaving when Susano-o cast the dappled pony skinned backward down through a hole in the sacred weaving hall. This point is important when one recalls that in the *daijō-sai*, the imperial accession ceremony, the new sovereign spends the night before his accession in the Kairyūden, a building symbolically equated with the rock-cave of Amaterasu, and there wraps himself in the *madoko* (or *matoko*) *ōfusuma*.[67]

The myth of Ame-no-waka-hiko continues with his family building a temporary mortuary house (*mo-ya*), establishing several birds as ritual functionaries, and then mourning his death by singing and dancing (*asobu*) for eight days and nights. The death of Ame-no-waka-hiko, who is presented as an illegitimate ruler, is narratively related to the *niiname-sai*. Moreover, his burial is seemingly necessary before the establishment of the proper imperial lineage through Ninigi, who begins the line leading to the Emperor Jimmu and the subsequent human rulers. Ninigi is said to be the second son of Ame-no-oshi-ho-mimi and a daughter of Taka-mi-musubi.

A third narrative, this one not from the Age of the Gods but from that of human sovereigns, clearly displays the symbolic complex of the imperial succession, death, and the *niiname-sai*. Tagishimimi-no-mikoto, a son of the Emperor Jimmu by a concubine, plots to do away with the three full imperial princes and to claim the throne for himself. The *Kojiki* version is of little immediate interest here since it is again vague as to the time Tagishimimi was killed after his intentions became known.[68] It does, however, contain two *uta* by which Jimmu's widow is to have warned her sons of their half-brother's intentions against them, and it notes that Tagishimimi took his father's widow and his own stepmother as wife.

The *Nihonshoki* version, however, locates the events following the death of the Emperor Jimmu around the time of the *niiname-sai*, and this narration takes up two-thirds of the Suizei Chapter.

When [the Emperor Suizei] reached the age of forty-eight, the Emperor [Jimmu] died. Now [Suizei's] disposition was profoundly filial, and his grief and longing knew no bounds. He made the funeral ceremonies his especial care.

His elder half-brother, Tagishi-mimi no mikoto, was not advanced in years, and had a long experience of matters of state. Therefore he was again charged with the conduct of affairs, and the Emperor [Suizei] treated him as an intimate friend. This prince, however, was of a perverse disposition, and his natural bent was opposed to justice. During the period of sincere seclusion [*mi-mono omoi no kiwa ni*] his authority at last became independent, and concealing his malicious purposes, he plotted the destruction of his two younger brothers.

Now in the year Tsuchinoto U of the cycle, Winter, the 11th month, Kamu-nunagawa-mimi no mikoto [Suizei] and his elder brother Kamu-yai-mimi no mikoto learnt privately his intentions and effectively prevented him. *When the business of the misagi had ended*, they caused Yuge-no-waka-hikoto to *make a bow*, and Yamato-no-kanuchi-amatsu-mara to *make a true-deer arrow point*, and Ya-wagi-be to prepare arrows. When the bow and arrows were ready, Kamu-nunagawa-mimi no mikoto wished therewith to shoot to death Tagishi-mimi no mikoto, *who happened just then to be in a great muro at Kataoka, lying alone on a great couch* [*tamatama . . . Kataoka no ōmuro no naka ni mashite, hitori ōmitoko ni mashimasu*]. Then Kamu-nunagawa-mimi no mikoto spake to Kamu-yai-mimi no mikoto, saying:—"*The right time has now arrived* [*ima tamatama sono toki nari*]. In words, secrecy is to be prized: in deeds, caution is advisable. Therefore, we have never had any partner in our conspiracy, and the enterprise of today is to be carried out by thee and me alone. I will first open the door of the muro. Do thou then shoot him." They accordingly went forward and entered in together.

Kamu-nunagawa-mimi no mikoto pushed open the door, while Kamu-yai-mimi no mikoto's arms and legs trembled so that he was unable to let fly the arrow. Then Kamu-nunagawa-mimi no mikoto snatched the bow and arrows which his elder brother held and shot Tagishi-mimi no mikoto. *The first shot struck him on the breast*, the second on the back, and so at length he killed him.[69]

As a result of the fiasco in the *muro*, the elder brother realizes that he is unsuited to rule and he cedes the kingship to his younger brother, who is formally installed within two months. Several elements of the narrative that are especially relevant to our immediate concerns have been italicized above and may be summarized here:

(1) The events occur "when the business of the *misagi* had ended," that is, after the burial and funeral ceremonies for the deceased emperor;

(2) the princes have a special ritual bow and arrows made;

(3) when the would-be ruler is killed, he is lying on a great couch;

(4) Prince Kamu-nunagawa-mimi (Suizei) announces, "*tamatama sono toki nari*," literally "now is the (or 'that') time," but the sense has been captured by Aston in his translation as "the right time";

(5) the arrow strikes the victim, the illegitimate claimant, in the chest.

The weapons here are the same as those in the myth of Ame-no-waka-hiko. In addition, like Ame-no-waka-hiko, Tagishimimi is described as lying alone on a couch in a great building, though it is not specifically identified as the First Fruits Hall. Note, however, that the *Nihonshoki* explicitly locates the events in the eleventh lunar month or precisely when one would expect the *niiname-sai* to be performed. The validity of this "reading" is strengthened by the evidence (cited below) that the final burial of a deceased emperor ideally should have been concluded prior to the performance of the *niiname-sai* by his successor. This ideal ritual scenario of the proper order of things would be consistent with the timing reported here in the *Nihonshoki*—the events occur after the funeral ceremonies and in the eleventh lunar month. Note, too, that Tagishimimi's purported plot to seize the throne is also located during the period of temporary burial and mourning for Jimmu.

A fourth relevant narrative, found in both the *Kojiki* and the *Nihonshoki*, involves the Emperor Suinin (r. [29 B.C.E.]–70 C.E.).[70] In both versions Prince Sao-biko, an elder brother of Suinin's empress, Sao-biko-hime, is said to have plotted to have his sister assassinate the emperor as he slept. The *Nihonshoki* reports that Prince Sao-biko approached his sister with his plan on the twenty-third day of the ninth month of the fourth year of Suinin's reign (i.e., 26 B.C.E.), whereas the deed was attempted over a year later on the first day of the tenth month of the fifth year of the reign. The empress was ready to stab her husband as he slept in her lap in Taka-miya, apparently some kind of shrine, but before she could bring herself to commit the murder tears welled up in her eyes and then fell onto the sleeping emperor's face. He awoke and recounted a dream he had just had and this led the empress to confess to the conspiracy. The brother, Sao-biko no mikoto, then built an *inaki* or granary that he entered and there sought to stave off the attack of Suinin's troops.

At this point in the narrative the *Kojiki* and the *Nihonshoki* diverge significantly.

The *Kojiki* version has Sao-biko-bime giving birth to a son after entering the granary with her brother and after the emperor had set it on fire; the *Nihonshoki* has her carry an infant into the granary with her. Whatever the version, however, it is the inclusion of the element of the granary or "rice palace," as well as the autumn temporal locus, that leads one to associate this narrative with the others we have seen. The child is named Homutsu-wake (*Nihonshoki*) or Homuchi-wake (*Kojiki*), with the character *ho* ("fire") referring to the fire in which he was born. Although Suinin recognizes this child as his son in both versions, Homutsu-wake does not succeed him. Moreover, Homotsu-wake is presented as having been dumb well into adulthood. He gains the ability to speak only when, while standing with the emperor before the Great Hall (*ōtono*), a swan flies overhead and cries. This event is said to have occurred on the eighth day of the tenth month, which again would place it around the time of the Harvest Festival. Some commentators have suggested that this bird was from Tokoyo, the underworld, and that it carried the *tama* of a deceased individual that could revivify and give power to the person it entered. If this is correct, then this passage is another expression of the *tama*-belief complex. Finally, in the texts, Homutsu-wake is not treated as just another prince. This has led some scholars to suggest that he was, in fact, the ancestor of an imperial line. Quite possibly, then, we have here hints that elements suggestive of the *niiname-sai* were incorporated into the narrative as a device to give legitimacy to claims made for this prince as the heir apparent.

A fifth narrative, found in the *Kojiki*, concerns a failed attempt to murder the Emperor Richū (r. [400]–405). According to this account:

> When [the Emperor Richū] was first dwelling in the palace of Naniwa, he celebrated the [festival of the] first-fruits [*ōnihe*] and held a state banquet.
>
> At the time, he rejoiced greatly in the great wine and went to sleep.
>
> Then his younger brother Suminoe-no-nakutsu-miko, seeking to kill the emperor, set fire to the great hall.
>
> At this time, the ancestor of the Atae of the Aya of Yamato, the Atae Achi, spirited him out, put him on horseback, and took him to Yamato.[71]

Once again we find several of the central elements of the symbolic complex: the attempt on the emperor's life takes place precisely when he is (1) performing the *niiname-sai* and (2) lying down (although the sacred couch is not explicitly mentioned). The *Nihonshoki* does not temporally locate these events at the time of the *niiname-sai* but rather after the period of mourning for the recently deceased Emperor Nintoku and prior to Richū's formal ritual accession to the throne. It records, however, a competition among the two brothers for one Kurohime, the daughter of Hata no Yashiro no Sukune, a nobleman.[72] Competition for a woman is another element often associated with the symbolic complex of death, the *niiname-sai*, and the succession. Just as in the myths recounted earlier, the messenger (here Prince Nakutsu) does not perform his duties as ordered but instead possesses for himself the woman destined for the emperor, an act that the narrative explicitly associates with a political power play. The conspirator, Prince Nakutsu, is himself later killed when he is in the privy, a detail that immediately recalls the Yamato-takeru tale wherein Yamato-takeru kills his elder brother, who also had possessed two women intended for the emperor, in the same location. The association with faeces, of course, also links this narrative with the myth of Susano-o.

A sixth narrative involves the eldest son of the Emperor Richū, Ichinobe-no-Oshiwa, and the Emperor Yūryaku. Yūryaku (r. 456–479) managed to gain the throne through a series of ruthless assassinations of his brothers and other possible contenders. According to the *Nihonshoki* account, Yūryaku never forgot that the Emperor Ankō had intended that Prince Ichinobe should succeed him. Thus, Yūryaku plotted to kill this prince by luring him out into the countryside on a hunt. This scheme was reportedly realized on the first day of the tenth lunar month of 456 when Ichinobe was killed in a "hunting accident." Only after this was Yūryaku able to accede formally to the imperial reign on the thirteenth of the following month. Although Ichinobe never became emperor himself, he was the father of the Emperors Kenzō (r. [485]–487) and Ninken (r. [488]–498).

The Ichinobe narrative is of interest not only because of the timing of the assassination but also because it introduces the imperial hunt as yet another element in the symbolic complex of sacred kingship, death, and the *niiname-sai*. Imperial hunts were large-scale ceremonial events, with many princes, ministers of state, courtiers, and so on accompanying the imperial prince or the sovereign. It was "natural" to carry arms on such a hunt, so their presence would not necessarily arouse suspicion. Moreover, a hunt provided greater opportunity for individuals to speak privately and in confidence than was possible in the capital, where one had to be ever on guard against even the slightest word of criticism reaching the sovereign's ears or those of other powerful persons in the court. Thus, it is not surprising to find a number of narratives concerning plots and political schemes that were conceived on such hunts.

A final example requires only brief mention. The *Nihonshoki* reports that on the third day of the eleventh month of 592, the Emperor Sushun was assassinated at the instigation of Soga no Umako, the powerful patriarch of the Soga clan. An editorial gloss in the *Kojiki* preserves the date as the thirteenth rather than the third, but gives no details at all surrounding Sushun's death.[73] Nevertheless, the temporal location of this assassination around the time of the *niiname-sai* suggests this narrative is related to the others we have seen.

Death and the Niiname-sai: *The Narrative Frame*

Obayashi notes that in each of these cases the assassination, whether realized or only attempted, is narratively located either specifically at the time of the *niiname-sai* or between the tenth and eleventh lunar months. To be sure, not all the assassinations reported in the three texts occurred at this time, but a definite narrative pattern seems to exist. There is no need for us to assume, though, that all these events actually occurred at this time of the year. Although it is ultimately impossible to determine with any precision "what really happened," we are more interested in the ways the early Japanese retrospectively structured and ordered events to make sense of their past and their present. Our object of study is the texts as they are given, or the ways in which they are structured to convey a readily recognizable meaning. Hence, it is precisely the presence of narrative patterns and significant deviations from them that are of the utmost concern.

Nevertheless, we must ask what relation these narratives may have to attempted and realized assassinations that may be presumed to have occurred in early Japan. Obayashi notes three distinct possibilities:

(1) The events narrated may actually have occurred on the dates given in the texts, but the timing of the events was coincidental without any specific intention on the part of the assassins. This possibility requires one to assume that the texts are straightforward and accurate records of events. When two or more texts differ, one must be mistaken, whether because of scribal error, inadequate documentation on the editors' part, or some other factor;

(2) The events may have happened, though not necessarily at the season of the *niiname-sai*. This temporal locus was retrospectively assigned by something like narrative convention or tradition;

(3) If the time surrounding the celebration of the *niiname-sai* was related to a culturally operative death/rebirth symbolic complex, then the early Japanese may have considered this the "proper season" to kill a ruler or contender/pretender, and political conspirators may have waited for this time to put their political intrigues into action. If this was the case, then the temporal locus found in our examples would be anything but coincidental.[74]

Of these three possibilities the first can be readily dismissed. The shared symbolic complex is too obviously a "package" and too common to have been a result of sheer happenstance. Moreover, the extant texts are in many ways factional documents, not objective factual reports. No historian is willing to accept everything in these texts at face value, and certainly not the contents of either the mythological or the early reign sections. The truth probably lies in the conflation of the second and third possibilities. The third possibility by itself is perhaps too Frazerian. It assumes that the historical actors consciously imitated mythological patterns. Yet if this were the case, one might expect each of the emperors to be portrayed like Frazer's priest of Nemi, red-eyed and nervously pacing outside his shrine (here the First Fruits Hall), ever fearful of attack and especially at the time of the niiname-sai.[75] As we have seen, though, the textual descriptions of even those emperors reportedly killed while performing the niiname-sai give no hint that the emperors were aware that it was an especially dangerous season; nor do they seem to have taken special precautions, such as stationing armed troops around the sacred hall, at this time.

This leads one to surmise that the second possibility is the most likely. While the Kojiki and the Nihonshoki are at once our major sources of information on this period of early Japanese history, at the same time they stand as the major stumbling blocks to our having access to "what really happened." These texts are already interpretations. They are ordered and determined by narrative conventions and the ideology of the period, expressed in symbolic terms. Thus, they do not provide immediate access to the "hard facts." Nevertheless they are invaluable, if properly handled, in understanding how the early Japanese made sense of their world. What the historian of religions can obtain by subjecting these texts to a careful analysis of the narrative patterns and strategies adopted and adapted is an outline of some of the constituent elements of the symbolic universe of early Japan and how such ritual and narrative structures are themselves historical and, thus, subject to change.

It is too simplistic, then, to argue that there is a "symbolic logic" at work in agricultural societies like early Japan that necessarily finds expression in some form of a death/rebirth complex. Nor can one simply assume that when urbanization and political and economic centralization occur, the symbolic complex of sacred kingship will be conjoined with this agricultural symbolism. Discernible patterns or structures should finally not be separated from historical praxis, for such structures inform both intentional action in history and the retrospective narrative ordering of events.

In the fourth example cited above concerning the attempt on the life of the Emperor Suinin, his son, Homutsu-wake, was born in a fire (Kojiki); or he was carried into the granary as an infant but was brought out before it was burned to the ground, killing his mother, her brother, and their supporters (Nihonshoki). It has often been noted that this tale shares certain features with that of Susano-o. First, both Homutsu-wake and Susano-o were born out of a strained marital relationship—in fact, a relationship that in each case was to end with the death of the mother brought about by the father's actions. From another point of view, each was in effect abandoned by his mother shortly after birth. In addition, both children were retarded in some way: Susano-o was childlike, weeping long past the proper mourning period until his beard was "eight hands long" and extended down over his chest;

Homutsu-wake was unable to speak, even though (note the same phrase) his beard was "eight hands long." Significantly, neither Susano-o nor Homutsu-wake succeeded their fathers. Susano-o refused to take up his assigned realm, sought to gain Amaterasu's realm, and was exiled, whereas Homutsu-wake simply disappears from the narrative after miraculously regaining his speech through worshiping at Izumo.

Susano-o's actions were especially destructive immediately before and during the time of the *niiname-sai*, and in the Homutsu-wake narrative the Empress Sao-bime was about to assassinate the emperor around this same time. What one can glimpse here is perhaps not only the mythic expression of the ambiguous nature of sacred kingship but more specifically the ambivalent socio-political status of certain princes in early Japan. One need not resort to Freudian Oedipal interpretations to see that sons—especially those of wives or concubines out of favor, or alternatively, with powerful and politically ambitious relatives—could be perceived as a threat to other princes and their supporters who also had political aspirations. In this sense both the "myths" and "histories" mirror the political reality in early Japan. It is difficult to say whether the mythic narratives of the *Kojiki* and the *Nihonshoki* replicate historical situations in some sort of euhemerism, or whether, conversely, actions in history were played out, consciously or unconsciously, according to a mythic pattern or "script." Whatever position one ultimately takes, the shared patterns are undeniable and merit serious study.

Returning to the comparison of Susano-o and Homutsu-wake, one finds that their births are narratively related to specific actions of the respective fathers that tend to sever any relationship with the mother: Susano-o is born out of Izanagi's ritual bath to purify himself of the pollution associated with Izanami's corpse; Homutsu-wake is born in the fire set by his father (or reborn in the *Nihonshoki* version, insofar as he is brought back out of the granary before it is set afire). In the Susano-o myth it is ostensibly the action of the father that leads to a permanent break with the mother, whereas in the Homutsu-wake story it is the action of the mother/wife/sister, following her brother's suggestion, that leads to the break. Again, the hint of an incestuous relationship between a brother and sister is found in both stories, though in the case of Izanagi and Izanami it is creative, whereas in that of Sao-hiko and Sao-bime it is destructive.

A closer analysis, however, shows that in each case the narrative element that moves the plot along and "triggers" the breakdown of the couple is a transference of primary allegiance by the female figure. In the Izanagi–Izanami myth, Izanami ultimately pays primary allegiance to the *kami* of Yomi. Though Izanagi asks her to return with him to complete their work of creation, Izanami does not comply with the request but responds that she must first seek the permission of Yomi no kami. It is this development that leads Izanagi to enter the inner chamber where he sees the corpse, resulting in the unintentional introduction of death into the human world. In a parallel manner Susano-o's primary allegiance is problematic and the cause of his break with Izanagi, for he refuses to obey his father's command, seeking instead to go to the land of his "mother," Izanami. By way of comparison, in the Homutsu-wake narrative one sees that Sao-bime's primary allegiance is to her brother. The *Kojiki* version opens as follows:

When this emperor [Suinin] made Sao-bime his empress, Sao-biko-no-miko, the elder brother of Sao-bime-no-mikoto, asked his younger sister:
"Which do you love more, your husband or your elder brother?"
She answered:
"I love my elder brother more."
Then Sao-biko-no-miko plotted, saying:
"If you truly love me, then you and I will rule the kingdom."[76]

In both cases the shift in allegiance of one or more of the characters stirs the wrath of the sovereign, leading to a radical rupture: Susano-o is expelled and thus, homeless, is forced to wander the earth; Sao-bime and her brother perish in the flames of the granary.

The element of fire figures not only in several of the narratives above but in others as well. In the Seinei Chapter of the *Nihonshoki*, for instance, we are told that after the death of the Emperor Yūryaku in the eighth lunar month of 479, one of his three senior concubines, Kibi-no-waka-hime, maneuvered to have a young son, Prince Hoshikawa, succeed to the throne rather than the crown prince appointed by Yūryaku. The following excerpt summarizes both the action that takes place after Yūryaku died on the seventh day of the eighth month and the first dated entry of the Seinei Chapter, the fourth day of the tenth lunar month when Seinei ascended to the emperorship:

The Emperor Ōhatsuse [i.e., Yūryaku] died in the 8th month of the 23rd year of his reign. Then Kibi-no-waka-hime secretly addressed the Imperial Prince, the younger son Hoshikawa, saying:—"If thou dost desire to ascend to the Imperial rank, do thou first of all take the office of the Treasury." . . . [Prince Hoshikawa] rashly followed the advice of the Lady his mother. Finally he took possession of the Treasury, and locked the outer door, therewith making provision against disaster. He exercised arbitrary authority, and squandered the official property.[77]

At this point, several high-ranking court officials and their troops surrounded and besieged the Treasury, setting fire to it, and thus killing Prince Hoshikawa, his mother, an elder half-brother, and other supporters. Once again these events are said to have taken place shortly after the death of the Emperor Yūryaku and before his final burial. According to the *Nihonshoki* chronology, Yūryaku was buried in a mausoleum on the ninth day of the tenth lunar month of the following year (480). According to this narrative, the succession was disputed, with one claimant seeking to grab power by occupying and securing the Treasury, a building architecturally related to the granary in early Japan. This detail makes us realize that the Homutsu-wake tale, among others, is even more closely connected to those cited above than the shared element of fire alone suggests.

Based on the narrative pattern of claimants to the throne being born out of fire or surviving an ordeal by fire, we might posit the existence of some sort of ritual ordeal through which a would-be emperor had to pass to demonstrate his fitness for the position. Unfortunately, conclusive evidence for the historical existence of such a rite does not exist. Nevertheless, we may say with much more certainty that Prince Hoshikawa's death by fire here is probably offered as "proof" by narrative convention that his claim to the throne was invalid. That is, the actual circumstances of Prince Hoshikawa's death may not be preserved here; rather, what we have is an instance of a narrative convention, based on a mythological paradigm, used by the editors of the eighth-century histories to order retrospectively the story of this prince's death for the purpose of justifying it. Had his legitimacy been accepted by those compiling the *Nihonshoki*, one would expect Prince Hoshikawa to have survived the fire miraculously. This sequence would follow the pattern established by the vow of Ko-no-hana-sakuya-hime when, to prove the paternity of the child(ren) she was carrying, she pronounced a vow (*ukei*), entered a doorless structure, and set it on fire.

Other tales of individuals surviving a fire that had been deliberately set come to mind immediately: Okuninushi survives a fire set by Susano-o, and Yamato-takeru survives a fire started on a grassy plain by the ruler of the land of Sagamu. The fact that this same narrative element is found both in myths and in the chronicles of "historical" emperors is another example of the open boundary between myth and history in early Japan. When the early Japanese set out to tell of past events, specific mythic and narrative conventions and related symbolic complexes often suggested themselves as interpretive frames. Temporally locating the assassination of an emperor around the time of the *niiname-sai*, for example, served several purposes. Not only was this time the symbolically appropriate "season" for the assassination of the ruler, it was also that for the appearance of new rulers or claimants to the throne. The death of any ruler upsets the political status quo and the sense of social stability. In early Japan the large number of imperial children resulting from the practice of polygamy inevitably led to a mad scramble for position within the court hierarchy following the death of a significant member of the power elite. Assassination, fratricide, and so on, were endemic to this situation.

If we take the Ninigi–Ko-no-hana-sakuya-hime narrative as the mythic paradigm and origin of the *niiname-sai*, then we must also note that within the logic of the symbolic complex informing that narrative, the birth of the three sons in a fire associated with a granary and their survival legitimates both their royal status and their claim to the succession. The element of fire, *ho* or *hi*, is incorporated into the names of each of these princes—Ho-no-akari (or Ho-deri), Ho-no-susumi (or Ho-no-suseri), and Ho-no-orihiko-hoho-demi (or Amatsu-hiko-hiko-hoho-demi). The name Hiko-hoho-demi, moreover, is also given in the *Nihonshoki* as the personal name of the Emperor Jimmu, the first "human" ruler, indicating an attempt to create a sense of identity or direct descent from that lineage.

Ellwood has noted the ancient association of fire with the *niiname-sai*, writing: "One feels the *Niiname* may have been a New Year's rite of the renewal of tribal succession and spirit pacification with a new fire, as at Izumo, before it was a harvest festival."[78] This suggestion is intriguing, but whether or not it is correct in historical terms, it is now clear that a "link" was consciously made by the early Japanese for historiographic purposes. One of the narratives that provides the strongest evidence for this assertion comes from the Seinei Chapter of the *Nihonshoki* following the tale of the ill-fated Prince Hoshikawa recounted above. After the death of Hoshikawa and his brother in the fire, the third son of the Emperor Yūryaku succeeded to the throne as the Emperor Seinei (r. [480]–484). Seinei, however, had no children, a situation that portended yet another uneasy succession. And, indeed, after the emperor's death on 1/16/484, an elder sister held the reigns of power for about ten months, although she was never formally installed and thus is not recognized in the official list of sovereigns. Strikingly enough, this princess is reported to have died in the eleventh lunar month (i.e., once again around the time of the *niiname-sai*, though the text provides no details of how she died). Based on what we have learned so far, however, one might well be suspicious of the circumstances.

In order to appreciate the socio-political circumstances related in this narrative, we must go back in time to a point prior to Seinei's reign. According to the *Nihonshoki* the Emperor Ankō was assassinated on 8/9/456 by a child, Prince Mayuwa. This action triggered a rash of killings by one of the other imperial princes, who was to emerge as the Emperor Yūryaku. Again, all these events occurred during the period of temporary enshrinement and before the formal accession of a successor to Ankō. On the first day of the tenth lunar month, less than two months after Ankō had been killed, Yūryaku (still a prince known by another name at this time) enticed the heir apparent, Prince Ichinobe no Oshiwa, to join him on a hunt where he staged a "hunting accident" in which the prince was killed. When reports of the "accident" reached two of the assassinated prince's sons, Prince Ōke and Oke, they fled to the countryside, where they concealed their identities and worked as commoners.[79] The Yūryaku Chapter is silent about these two princes, but their story is taken up again in the Seinei and Kenzō Chapters. (Parenthetically, it is worth reminding ourselves that Yūryaku is one of only two sovereigns who are censored by the *Nihonshoki* for their cruelty.) The Seinei Chapter includes the following relevant entries:

2nd year [481], Spring, 2nd month. The Emperor [Seinei], vexed that he had no children, sent the Ōmuraji, Ōtomo no Muroya, to the provinces, and established the Shirakabe *toneri*, the Shirakabe *kashiwade*, and the Shirakabe *yukei*, in the hope of leaving a trace which might be seen of posterity.

Winter, 11th month. For the purpose of the offerings of the feast of first-fruits [*ōnihe tame-matsuru shiro ni yorite*] Odate, of the Be of Kume of Iyō, ancestor of the Yamabe no Muraji and Governor of Harima, was sent thither. In the new muro of Hosome, Miyatsuko of the Oshinomi Be and Ōbito of the granary of Shijimi in the district of Akashi, he saw Ōke and Oke, sons of the Imperial Prince Oshiwa of Ichinobe. He took them together reverently to his bosom, recognized them as his lords, and attended to their nurture with extreme care. From his own private income he arranged for the construction of a palace of brushwood [*shiba no miya*] in which he lodged them temporarily, and mounting a swift steed, hastened to inform the Emperor. The Emperor was astonished, and after exclaiming for a good while, he said with emotion:—"Admirable! Delightful! Heaven in its bountiful love has bestowed on us two children." In this month he sent Odate with a token of authority [*shirushi o mochite*], and *toneri* of the left and right in attendance on him, to Akashi to meet them [and escort them back]. . . .

[482] 3rd year, 1st month, 1st day. Odate and his companions arrived in the province of Tsu, escorting Ōke and Oke. Then Omi and Muraji were sent, with emblems of authority and a royal green-canopied carriage, to meet them and bring them into the Palace.

Summer, 4th month, 7th day. Prince Ōke was appointed Prince Imperial [i.e., heir apparent], and Prince Oke was made an Imperial Prince.[80]

The princes-in-hiding are discovered by Odate when he is sent as the emperor's representative to perform the *niiname-sai*. Moreover, the temporary palace of brushwood is reminiscent of the temporary rough wooden structures built for use in the royal accession ceremonies. Ellwood has noted that such structures were found in the early harvest rituals:

At harvest time, what may have been the first shrine, a *yashiro*, or temporary house, was erected in the fields. Here the deity was housed, and it was like a parturition hut in which the harvest-child was brought forth, just as if he were a successor to sovereignty. This house, modeled after the early granary, was the harvest lodge of the deity who otherwise dwelt at his high *shiki* (or else the *shiki* of his mate); he moved to and from it with the grain and with ceremony, the flavor of which is preserved in part of the *Daijō-sai*.[81]

This house clearly is the same structure found in the narrative of Prince Ōke and Prince Oke. Furthermore, the "tokens of authority" referred to suggest that a simple ceremony of some sort was held to proclaim the identities and royal status of the two princes. Then, too, the two princes are officially introduced into the imperial palace on New Year's Day, when the *Nihonshoki* reports many formal accession ceremonies to have been held. Finally, Prince Ōke, the elder brother, is named the heir apparent, though it would ultimately be the younger brother who would succeed first to the throne as the Emperor Kenzō.

The Kenzō Chapter, which immediately follows that devoted to Seinei's reign, is much fuller and preserves more of a *monogatari*-like flavor. In the following passage, for example, one can easily imagine a performance of this tale with the dialogue spoken by different actors. What we have here, however, is not a verbatim report of actual conversations but a retrospective imaginative re-creation, whether from the minds of the editors of the *Nihonshoki* or from an earlier source (written or oral). The narrative opens by retelling briefly how the two young princes were forced to flee to the countryside in 456. It then skips to 481 and their discovery by Odate.

In Winter, the 11th month of the 2nd year of the reign of Emperor Shiraka [Seinei], the Governor of the province of Harima, Odate Iyo no Kumebe, ancestor of the Yamabe no Muraji, went to the district of Akashi to make arrangements for the offerings of the festival of first fruits. (One writing says:—"Went on a circuit to the districts of Kohori and Agata to collect the land tax.") It so happened that he arrived just when the Ōbito of the granaries of Shijimi was holding a house-warming for a new muro [*niimuro ni asobi shite*] and was extending the day by adding to it the night [*yo o mote hiru ni tsugeru ni ainu*]. Hereupon the Emperor [i.e., Prince Oke at this time] spake to his elder brother, Prince Ōke, saying:—"Many years have passed since we fled hither to escape ruin. It belongs to this very evening [*masa ni ko yoi ni atareri*] to reveal our names and to disclose our high rank." Prince Ōke exclaimed with pity:—"To make such an announcement ourselves would be fatal. Which of us could keep safe his person and avoid danger?" The Emperor said:—"We, the grandsons of the Emperor Izahowake, are a man's drudges, and feed his horses and kine. What better can we do than make known our names and be slain?" At length he and Prince Ōke fell into each other's arms and wept, being unable to contain their emotion. Prince Ōke said:—"In that case who else but thou, my younger brother, is capable of making a heroic effort, and is therefore fit to make this disclosure?" The Emperor refused firmly, saying:— "Thy servant has no ability. How can he make so bold as to display virtuous action?" Prince Ōke said:—"There are here none to excel my younger brother in ability and wisdom." And in this way they mutually held back each in favour of the other for two or three times. It was ultimately arranged, with the Emperor's consent, that he should make the announcement. Together they went to the outside of the muro and sat down in the lowest place.[82]

The *niimuro* here may well be the same type of ritual structure we saw above. This possibility is strengthened by the use of the verb *asobi shite* ("celebrated"), which often indicates ritual song and dance. At the same time, the phrase "extending the day by adding it to the night" probably indicates an all-night ritual. In terms of the passage as a whole, we can say that it is a rather stylized history of the virtuous princes. This passage, like many others in the *Nihonshoki*, owes much to the tradition of Chinese dynastic histories. The brothers display almost no ambition to gain power for personal ends, ceding the position of heir apparent to each other. As the passage continues, the intention of this style of historiography is made explicit as the meaning of the actions (or perhaps nonactions) of the princes is given in the "recorded" dialogue of a character:

The Ōbito of the granary ordered [the two princes] to sit beside the cooking-place and hold lights to the right and left. When the night had become profound, and the revel was at its height, and every one had danced in turn, the Ōbito of the granary addressed Odate, saying:—"Thy servant observes that these light-holders honour others, and abase themselves; they put others before, and themselves behind. By their respectfulness they show their observance of just principles; by their retiring behaviour they illustrate courtesy. They are worthy of the name of gentlemen."[83]

The behavior of the princes and their public demeanor display their true nature and the correctness of their reassuming their rightful places in the line of the imperial succession. Such a stylized history does not represent a full and accurate report of what actually happened, yet we should not summarily dismiss the tale as completely fictional, since it is also possible that the recounted events were staged according to the ideals informing the operative symbolic system of the period. Although it is ultimately impossible to ascertain which if any of these possibilities was the case without corroborative independent testimony, it is enough—for our purposes—to note that the elements of the succession, the *niiname-sai*, the death of a sovereign, fire, and so forth, are all incorporated into the narrative.

It is the "timing" of the events in this narrative, though, that seems most significant. We are told that Odate went to Harima to prepare for the *niiname-sai*. Moreover, the crucial revelation of the identity of the princes also seems to have occurred in the evening, more specifically at midnight "when the night had become profound, and the revel was at its height." Let us pick up the *Nihonshoki* narrative again.

Upon this Odate played on the lute and gave orders to the light-holders, saying:—"Get up and dance." Then the elder and younger brothers declined in each other's favour for a good while and did not get up. Odate urged them, saying:—"Wherefore all this delay? Get up quickly and dance." Prince Ōke got up and danced. When he had done, the Emperor stood up in his turn, and having adjusted his dress and girdle, proposed a health for the Muro, saying:—[the following is in song form]

"The Dolichos roots [the reference is to ropes] of the new muro which he has upbuilt—
These are the calm of the august heart of the master of the house:
The ridge-poles which he has raised aloft—
These are the grove of the august heart of the master of the house:
The laths which he has placed—

These are the fairness of the august heart of the master of the house:
The Dolichos cords which he has tied—
These are the endurance of the august life of the master of the house:
The reed-leaves it is thatched with—
These are the superabundance of the august wealth of the master of the house:
[Izumo is newly cultivated;][84]
With the ten-span rice-ears,
Of these fresh fields,
In a shallow pan
We have brewed sake.
With gusto let us drink it,
O my boys!
Whenever we dance
Uplifting the horns of a buck
Of these secluded hills
(Weary to the foot) [*ashibiki no*]
Sweet sake from Eka market-town
Not buying with a price,
To the clear ring of hand-palms
Ye will revel,
Oh! my immortal ones! [*Tokoyo-tachi*]"

When he had ended proposing this health, he sang to the accompaniment of music, saying:—

"The willow
Growing by the river—
As the water flows,
It bends, then rises up,
But does not lose its roots."[85]

Odate addressed him, saying:—"Capital! Pray let us hear something more." The Emperor at length made a special dance (This is what was anciently called a Tatsutsu dance. The manner of it was that it was danced while standing up and sitting down.), and striking an attitude, said:—

"Of Yamato
soso chihara
asa chihara
The younger Prince am I."[86]

Hereupon Odate thought this profoundly strange and asked him to say more. The Emperor, striking an attitude, said:—

"The sacred cedar
Of Furu in Isonokami—
Its stem is severed,
Its branches are stripped off.
Of him who in the Palace of Ichinobe
Governed all under Heaven,[87]

The myriad Heavens,
The myriad lands—
Of Oshiwa no Mikoto
The august children are we."[88]

The *Nihonshoki* account then goes on to say that Odate was astonished at these developments but that he quickly paid obeisance to the two princes, had a temporary palace built for them, and informed the emperor of their existence. This narrative is found in similar form, though with significant differences and some expansions, in both the *Kojiki* and the *Harima fudoki*.[89] These texts do not explicitly say that the time of this event was the *niiname-sai*. Nevertheless, the presence of the granary and the "new" *muro* in both suggests as much. It is important to note that the *Nihonshoki* makes this explicit, though it is unclear whether this detail was added or simply brought to the fore.

Ellwood and a number of Japanese scholars have noted the conflation of solar symbolism with the agricultural symbolism of death and rebirth in the sacred kingship system of early Japan. In this chapter we have focused on several major myths concerning the origin of death and the politics of death while bearing in mind that the legitimation of the Temmu–Jitō line of the imperial family was one of the primary intentions behind the commissioning of the *Kojiki*, the *Nihonshoki*, and the *Man'yōshū*. In the process of the realization of the historiographic project of the imperial family, the editors of these texts had available for their use not only written documents and various clan histories but also oral histories, myths, legends, and a large corpus of poetry. We can assume that if their history was to be believable, they could not use a crude "cut-and-paste" method with complete abandon. Rather, certain narrative structures and paradigms were culturally available when these texts were committed to writing and given their final textual form. One such structure or paradigm was the ordeal at the time of the *niiname-sai* that proved the legitimacy or illegitimacy of an individual's claim to the throne. The narratives studied above will permit us to appreciate more fully other narratives related to the politics of death in early Japan as we turn next to the funeral practices of the imperial court.

CHAPTER THREE

The Liminal Period of Temporary Enshrinement

Few Japanese and even fewer Western scholars have recognized the full significance of the practice of double burial for the political history of early Japan and for the history of Japanese literature.[1] Yet the period of the temporary enshrinement of a deceased sovereign was one of the most important loci for religious ritual performances, the recitation of ritual poetry, and political maneuvering on the part of various figures in the court to determine the succession. We have seen above that various public rituals, including the recitation of poetry, participated in the sociopolitical drama of the succession. Unfortunately, the available information on the rituals performed in and around the *mogari no miya* is both scant and scattered within the three texts. Nevertheless, by collating the data among the texts it is possible to reconstruct, in skeletal form at least, some of the *mogari no miya* rituals. Rather than take the reader through a step-by-step reconstruction of this ritual complex, however, I shall summarize the cumulative results of modern Japanese scholarship and my own research.

The nature of the extant data makes it impossible to demonstrate that any individual historical performance of the *mogari no miya* ritual, which may have been spread out over several months or several years, included each and every element to be mentioned, in precisely the same order. This description, then, should be understood as portraying an ideal or generic ritual complex reconstructed from the fragmentary records of a number of temporary enshrinements. In spite of their generally conservative nature, ritual performances often change over time. Specific political and other historical contingencies, such as the date of the sovereign's death, frequently resulted in changes in the performances and in their timing. Beyond this, the available data hold certain implications for the picture that emerges. As might be expected, the *Nihonshoki* records from the reigns of some of the rulers are fuller than those for others. The reigns of the Emperors Bidatsu (r. [572]–585), Tenji (r. [662]–671), and Temmu (r. [673]–686), for example, provide a large portion of our information concerning the *mogari no miya* complex. This fact is a mixed blessing. On the positive side, since these are relatively late sovereigns, the data are probably more reliable. On the negative side, however, the fact that all these sovereigns are male means that the ritual complex we are able to reconstruct tends to reflect that performed for male rather than female sovereigns. Unfortunately, we do not have sufficient data to say with any certainty in what ways, if any, the rituals for a female sovereign differed. The best we can do is to make a few tentative inferences based on comparative material from other cultures.

The first record of funeral ceremonies in the texts is found in both the *Kojiki* and the *Nihonshoki* and concerns Ame-no-waka-hiko. This *kami* had descended to the earth to subdue the land in preparation for the descent of Ninigi, but instead he married the daughter of a local ruler and sought to obtain the land for himself. He was slain while performing the *niiname-sai* when the sacred arrow that he had used to kill the pheasant messenger was cast back down to earth by Taka-mi-musubi-no-kami and struck him in the chest. Let us pick up the *Kojiki* narrative at this point:

At that time, the sound of the weeping of Shitateru-hime, Ame-no-waka-hiko's wife, was carried by the wind and sounded again and again in the heavens. Then the father in the heavens of Ame-no-waka-hiko, Ama-tsu-kuni-tama-no-kami, as well as his wife and children, heard (this) and, descending, wept and lamented.

Immediately in that place they built a funeral house [*moya*]. They made a wild goose of the river the bearer of the funeral offerings [*kisari-mochi*]; a heron the broom-bearer [*hahaki-mochi*]; a kingfisher the bearer of the food offerings [*mike-bito*]; a sparrow the grinding woman [*usu-me*]; and a pheasant the weeping-woman [*naki-me*].

Having thus determined the role (of each), they sang and danced [*asobiki*] for eight days and nights.

At this time, Aji-shiki-taka-hiko-ne-no-kami arrived to participate in the mourning [*mo o toburaitamau*] for Ame-no-waka-hiko.

Then Ame-no-waka-hiko's father, and his wife who had descended from the heavens, wept and said:

"My child is not dead after all!" [*waga ko wa shinzute ari keri*]

"My lord has not died after all!" [*waga kimi wa shinzute mashi keri*]

Thus saying, they clung to his hands and feet and wept and lamented.

The reason for their mistake was that the appearance of these two deities was extremely similar; for this reason they mistook him.

Then Aji-shiki-hiko-ne-no-kami was greatly enraged and said:

"I have come to mourn him because I am his beloved friend; why do you liken me to an unclean corpse [*kitanaki shinibito*]?" Thus saying, he unsheathed the sword ten hands long which he was wearing at his side, and cut down that funeral house and with his foot kicked it away.

This is the mountain Mo-yama in the upper reaches of the Aimi River in the land of Mino.

The sword which he used to cut it down was named Ōhakari ["The Great Leaf Cutter"]; it was also named Kamu-dono-tsurugi.

When Aji-shiki-hiko-ne-no-kami, enraged, flew away, his younger sister, Taka-hime-no-mikoto, wishing to reveal his name, sang:

ame naru ya	Ah, the large jewel
oto tanabata no	Strung on the cord
unagaseru	Worn around the neck

tama no misumaru	Of the heavenly
misumau ni	Young weaving maiden!
ana-dama ha ya	Like this is he
mi-tani	Who crosses
futa-watarasu	Two valleys at once,
Aji-shiki-	The god Aji-shiki-
taka-hiko-ne-no-kami zo	taka-hiko-ne!

This song is *hina-buri*.[2]

The *moya* or "mourning house" mentioned here has been conclusively identified with the *mogari no miya*.[3] The *Nihonshoki* version, in fact, says explicitly: "Forthwith a mortuary house was made, in which [the corpse] was temporarily deposited [*sunawachi moya o tsukurite mogarisu*]."[4] The funeral ceremonies, extending over eight days, required several persons performing different ritual roles, suggesting some social complexity and specialization. The last sentence reports that the single *uta* preserved in this text was performed in *hina-buri* style. Although the precise meaning of *hina-buri* is unclear, it is significant that this *uta*, which we may presume was one of a set, was traditionally performed in the court by the time the *Kojiki* was committed to writing.

The reactions of the parents of Ame-no-waka-hiko express the belief that death was not initially permanent. When Aji-shiki-taka-hiko-ne appears at the *mogari no miya*, the grieving parents embrace him as their own son. The lines immediately following this act that explain their "mistake" are a later editorial addition.[5] The mourning rituals, complete with professional mourners, involved singing and dancing. The ritual role of the grinding woman, *usu-me*, is of interest, because "*usu*" is also found in the original name of the prince more popularly known as Yamato-takeru. His tale may help to elucidate this narrative as well as others.

"The Yamato-takeru no mikoto uta monogatari" is the longest tale in the *Kojiki*. As such, it has occasioned much study and commentary. The hero of the tale, Prince Yamato-takeru, has been called the paradigmatic tragic hero of Japan.[6] Yamato-takeru, at this time known as Prince Ousu, appears as the second son of the Emperor Keikō (r. [71]–130). In a now familiar pattern, the emperor sends his elder son, Prince Ōusu, to summon two beautiful sisters to the capital to serve as his consorts. This son, however, possesses the women himself, an act that is a direct challenge to the throne. The emperor then tells Prince Ousu (Yamato-takeru) to return his brother to court, but Ousu slays him instead, initiating his heroic career. For the moment, however, we are more interested in the *Kojiki* account of events following Yamato-takeru's death.

At this time [Yamato-takeru's] empresses and children who were in Yamato came down [to the plain of Nobo] and constructed his tomb.

Then, crawling around the neighboring rice paddies [*nazukida*], they sang while weeping:

nazuki no	The vines of the *tokoro*
ta no inagara ni	Crawl around
inagara ni	Among the rice stems,
hai-motohorou	The rice stems in the rice paddies
tokoro-zura	Bordering on [the tomb].

At this time he was transformed into a giant white bird [*yahiro-shiro chidori*] and, soaring through the skies, flew away towards the beach.

Then the wives and children, though their feet were cut by the stumps of the bamboo reeds, forgot the pain and ran after (the bird), weeping.

At this time they sang this song:

asaji no hara	Moving with difficulty, up to our waists
koshi nazumu	In the field of low bamboo stalks,
sora wa yukazu	We cannot go through the skies—
ashi yo yuku na	But, alas, must go by foot!

Again, when they waded into the sea and moved (through the waves) with difficulty, they sang:

umi ga yukeba	Going by sea, waist-deep in the water,
koshi nazumu	We move forward with difficulty;
ōkawara no	(Like) plants growing
ue-gusa	By a large river,
umi gawa	(We) drift aimlessly
isayou	In the ocean currents.

Again, when (the bird) had flown to the rocky shores, they sang:

hamatsu chidori	The plover of the beach
hama yo wa yukazu	Does not go by the beaches,
iso zutau	But follows along the rocky shores.

These four songs were sung at his funeral [*mi-hafuri*]. For this reason, even today these songs are sung at the funeral of an emperor.

From that land (the bird) flew away and stopped at Shiki in the land of K[ō]chi.

For this reason they built his tomb at that place and enshrined him there [*mi-hafuri o tsukurite shizumari-isashimeki*]. This tomb is called the White Bird Tomb.

However, from that place (the bird) again soared through the heavens and flew away.[7]

Once again we note the presence of *uta* in the funeral rituals. The belief that the animating spirit or *tama* of the deceased turned into a white bird seems to have been widely held in early Japan, for it is also found in other places in the *Kojiki* and the *Nihonshoki*, including an intriguing entry from the Chūai Chapter of the latter.[8] Here the mourners attempt to follow the white bird and to get it to settle down. Indeed, the phrase "to settle down" captures one aspect of the meaning of the verb *shizumu*, literally, "to pacify, to quiet." Philippi has glossed this as "enshrined." To pacify the spirit of the deceased is to get it to stop wandering and to rest in a stable location.

Several ritual activities associated with mourning are also visible in this passage— the mourners crawl around the temporary enshrinement tomb, singing and weeping. The reference to the mourners' feet being cut may be an allusion to ritual mortification, a practice that once existed in the court. Finally, the *uta* themselves contain some interesting information. To mention only one point, through their songs and actions the mourners portray themselves to the deceased as disoriented. This imagery is quite common in *banka* and seems to constitute a distinctive form of praise of the dead by stressing the extent to which the deceased's absence has affected the living. Here it is combined with the image of seaweed moved by the water currents, a common *Man'yōshū* metaphor in both poetry of longing and *banka*.[9]

The *mogari no miya* was constructed immediately following the death of a member of the imperial family. In the case of a sovereign, it was built in the courtyard of the main imperial palace, usually in the South Courtyard, though it is reported in the North Courtyard as well.[10] The corpse was deposited inside. The Chinese character used here suggests the corpse was buried, but there is also Chinese precedent for laying out the corpse. When an adult male member of the imperial family died, all the women who had been sexually intimate with the deceased—his primary wife and his concubines—were apparently secluded within the *mogari no miya* for an extended period of time, often for several months. In addition to these noble women, their servants and handmaidens were probably secluded as well. It is clear, though, that the interior of the *mogari no miya* was a distinctively and exclusively female preserve. It was a locus of both special ritual activity, including *tama-furi* rituals designed to recall the spirit of the deceased, and political intrigue. Below we will see that the unique position of the women secluded with the corpse of the deceased emperor seems to have translated into significant power leverage in the determination of the succession.

Outside the *mogari no miya* in the surrounding space, one found a mixed-gender ritual area, though the activity of males is especially evident in the texts. Whereas the interior of the *mogari no miya* was characterized by a sense of privacy and even intimacy, expressed for instance in the familiar forms of address used with the deceased, the area surrounding the *mogari no miya* was a locus of public ritual activity. It was there that most of the important public mourning rituals were held, eulogies were pronounced, assertions of clan loyalty to the throne were made, the genealogy of the succession from Amaterasu to the present was recited, and so on. It, too, was an arena for intense political maneuvering in the succession process.

The *mogari no miya* seems to have been surrounded by a high wall or fence and, indeed, had something of the appearance and even function of a fortress. Guards were located in the space outside the temporary enshrinement palace itself but within the surrounding walls. The *mogari no miya* was heavily guarded, though, not so much to protect the corpse from desecration or to guard any treasures deposited there as to protect the secluded women from sexual attack. Below we will discover that within the operative symbolic and mythistorical world of meaning of early Japan, the fear of such an attack was justified. Even after the period of ritual seclusion for the women ended, guards continued to be posted at the *mogari no miya*, probably until the time of final burial. These guards seem to have been considered by the rest of society as no longer belonging to the world of the living, since their names were removed from the official census. The following entry from the chronicle of the reign of the Emperor Kenzō (r. [485]–487) is often cited in this regard:

[485] 5th month. Karafukuro no Sukune, Kimi of Mount Sasaki, who was implicated in the assassination of the Imperial Prince Oshiwa, when about to be executed, bowed down his head to the ground, and his words expressed extreme sorrow. The Emperor could not bear to put him to death, so he added him to the *misazagi* [mausoleum] guardians [*misazagi no e ni ate*], making him at the same time mountain-warden, and erasing his name from the census registers [*e no fumita o kezuri sutete*]. He was then handed over to the jurisdiction of the Yamabe no Muraji.[11]

In addition, other guards or *toneri* seem to have continued to serve the deceased prince or emperor in a more ritual fashion, traveling before dawn each morning from the palace where the deceased had lived to the *mogari no miya* and then returning at dusk. These courtiers continued to line up, in rank order no doubt, to receive their morning orders and again to be dismissed ritually at night, just as they had done while the prince or emperor was alive. This daily routine provided the occasion for special formalized recitation of poems of praise and of mourning, including the famous set of twenty-three poems by *toneri* lamenting the death of the Crown Prince Kusakabe (d. 4/13/689), MYS 2: 171–193. These and other poems from the period of temporary enshrinement will be treated in the next chapter.

The rituals that have been mentioned so far, while based on the *tama*-related belief system, are not exclusively Shinto ceremonies insofar as the prayers and other invocations were addressed to both *kami* and various buddhas and bodhisattvas. At the same time, the majority of the rituals were directed as much, if not more, to the living as to the deceased. For example, when representatives of the major clans recited their respective genealogies before the *mogari no miya*, this was not so much for the benefit of the soul of the deceased as it was to proclaim or assert publicly the high status of the reciters' families. Such public recitations were intended to buttress or even improve the relative positions of the speakers' clans in the inevitable reshuffling of the socio-political hierarchy in the aftermath of the death of the prince or emperor. Similarly, eulogies praising the deceased were phrased in ways that associated the speaker and his family or patron with the imperial family and emphasized past loyal service that would merit promotion or some other special consideration in the future.

Baldly stating this aspect of the ritual situation is not to deny that genuine emotions of grief were felt and expressed at these ritual occasions, nor is it to suggest that the words of praise for the deceased offered in the eulogies were so much empty hyperbole pronounced only for purposes of self-aggrandizement. Clearly many individuals were profoundly affected by the death of a loved one or their leader. Nevertheless, we must recognize that a distinctive court rationality was also operative during the time of the *mogari no miya*. The courtiers who found themselves enmeshed in the socio-political network in the court operated under severe constraints in public. The expression of emotion was restricted to accepted and expected modes and consequently was both highly stylized and formalized. Below we will have occasion to see that such public expressions of grief, praise, and so on, were subject to criticism, censure, and even mockery by others. Moreover, such public performances following the death of a high-ranking figure were not to be taken lightly, for the volatile and unstable condition in the court, fueled by suspicion and rumors, made such occasions potentially dangerous.

There is clear evidence that Buddhist rituals were an integral part both of efforts to cure the individual before his/her death and of the *mogari no miya* rituals. One finds records of various sutra recitations, purification ceremonies, the commissioning of Buddhist statues for purposes of merit accrual and transfer, land grants to temples, and hundreds of men and women taking the tonsure at one time, all related to the serious illness or death of the sovereign. Buddhist monks and nuns held mourning rituals and memorial services at the *mogari no miya*. This is significant because we are talking about a period of time prior to the adoption of the Buddhist practice of cremation in the court. Thus, in its incipient stages Buddhism adapted itself to and participated in the ritual complex of double burial found in Japan. The records clearly indicate that within the court both the *kami* cults and Buddhist practices existed side by side and, indeed, often within the same immediate ritual locus.

There does not seem to have been a set length of time for the *mogari no miya* to serve as a locus for the performance of rituals before the final burial of the corpse. According to the *Nihonshoki*, the periods of temporary enshrinement varied from as short as two months to over six years. There is a demonstrable connection between the timing of the final burial of a deceased sovereign and the formal accession of the successor. Table 1, based on information provided by the *Nihonshoki*, presents the chronology of double burial in early Japan. Whenever such information is available, it contains the dates of the enthronement, death, and final burial of each sovereign.

TABLE 1

The Chronology of Double Burial

Emperor/ empress	Date of enthronement	Date of death	Date of burial	Length of temporary interment	
Jimmu	?	3/11/585 B.C.E.	9/12/584		6 mos.
Suizei	1/8/581	5/10/549	10/11/548	1 yr.	5 mos.
Annei	7/3/549	11/6/511	8/1/510		9 mos.
Itoku	2/4/510	9/8/477	10/13/476	1 yr.	1 mo.
Kōshō	1/9/475	8/5/393	8/14/355	38 yrs.	
Kōan	1/7/392	1/9/291	9/13/291		8 mos.
Kōrei	1/12/290	2/8/215	9/6/209	6 yrs.	7 mos.
Kōgen	1/14/214	9/2/158	2/6/153	5 yrs.	5 mos.
Kaika	11/12/158	4/9/98	10/3/98		6 mos.
Sujin	1/13/97	12/5/30	8/11/29 or 10/11/29		8 or 10 mos.
Suinin	1/2/29 B.C.E.	7/14/70 C.E.	12/10/70		5 mos.
Keikō	7/11/71	11/7/130	11/10/132	2 yrs.	
Seimu	1/5/131	6/11/190	9/6/191	1 yr.	3 mos.
Chūai	1/11/192	2/5/200	11/8/202	2 yrs.	9 mos.
Jingū	(regent)	4/17/269	10/15/269		6 mos.
Ōjin	1/1/270	2/15/310	?		?
Nintoku	1/3/313	1/16/399	10/7/399		9 mos.
Richū	2/1/400	3/15/405	10/4/405		6 mos.
Hanzei	1/2/406	1/29/410	11/11/416	6 yrs.	10 mos.
Ingyō	12/?/412	1/14/453	10/10/453		9 mos.
Ankō	12/14/453	8/9/456	?/?/459	3 yrs.	
Yūryaku	11/13/456	8/7/479	10/9/480	1 yr.	2 mos.
Seinei	1/15/480	1/16/484	11/9/484		10 mos.
Kenzō	1/1/485	4/25/487	10/3/488	1 yr.	6 mos.
Ninken	1/5/488	8/8/498	10/5/498		2 mos.
Buretsu	12/?/498	12/8/506	10/3/508	1 yr.	10 mos.
Keitai	1/4/507	2/7/531	12/5/531		10 mos.
Ankan	2/7/531?	12/17/535	12/?/535		<1 mo.
Senka	12/?/535	2/10/539	11/17/539		9 mos.
Kimmei	12/5/539	4/15/571	9/?/571		5 mos.
Bidatsu	4/3/572	8/15/585	4/12/591	5 yrs.	8 mos.
Yōmei	9/5/585	4/9/587	7/21/587		3 mos.
Sushun	8/2/587	11/3/592	11/3/592	buried same day	
Suiko	12/8/592	3/7/628	9/24/628		6 mos.
Jomei	1/4/629	10/9/641	12/21/642	1 yr.	2 mos.
Kōgyoku	1/15/642	abdicated 4/14/645			?
Kōtoku	6/14/645	10/10/654	12/8/654		2 mos.
Saimei	1/3/655	7/24/661	2/27/667	5 yrs.	7 mos.
Tenji	1/3/668	12/3/671	?		?
Temmu	2/27/673	9/9/686	11/11/688	2 yrs.	2 mos.
Jitō	1/1/690	12/22/702	cremated 12/17/703	1 yr.	

By calculating the time lapse between the last two dates, the length of the period of temporary enshrinement can also be calculated.

Examining the data in the table, one finds 35 cases in which the relation between the timing of the final burial of a sovereign and the ritual accession of the successor can be determined. In 21 (or 60%) of these instances, final burial of the deceased sovereign preceded the accession of the successor. This figure may not seem overly significant in itself, but if one looks only at the data from the later reigns, which are generally recognized as more historically reliable, the percentage rises dramatically.[12]

Many historians have seriously questioned the historicity of a large number of the traditionally recognized sovereigns appearing in the *Nihonshoki* (and included in the chart). Robert Ellwood, for example, has characterized the emperors following Jimmu (r. [660]–585 B.C.E.) up to the time of Sujin (r. [97]–30 B.C.E.) as "a series of clearly contrived nonentities,"[13] dismissing some five-and-a-half centuries of *Nihonshoki* "history" as spurious. No one would deny that the *Nihonshoki* is not always reliable as "hard history," especially in the earlier sections, and that certain narratives "ring true" while others do not. But by focusing upon narrative patterns found *precisely* in the "history" of contrived emperors, we may be able to discover what the Japanese of the eighth century held to be the *ideal* order of religio-political ritual events following the death of a sovereign, an order that various contingencies in the *real* world of early Japan often made it impossible to realize in human history. In addition, in the series of abbreviated chapters on these fictional rulers we may discover what the compilers of the *Nihonshoki* felt were the minimum "facts" necessary to write a convincing functional history. Regarding this last point, in studying the records of the reigns between those of the Emperors Jimmu and Sujin (i.e., those that are the strongest candidates for being characterized as fictional creations), one discovers the following narrative pattern of entries for each sovereign:

(1) Following the death of his predecessor, the crown prince assumes the throne;

(2) the deceased emperor is given final burial;

(3) the widowed empress is honored with a new title;

(4) the capital is moved;

(5) a new empress is appointed and the birth of a male child or the births of several children are noted;

(6) a new crown prince is appointed;

(7) the emperor dies; and the pattern begins all over again in the next reign.

Several points of interest emerge from this pattern. First, fully half of the eight "contrived" emperors—Suizei, Itoku, Kōan, and Kaika—are not the eldest but rather the second sons. Yet, except for the case of the Emperor Suizei, there is no hint in the text of a difficult succession, and even there the full-blood elder brother readily recognizes Suizei's innate superiority and demurs to him, whereas the troublemaker is an evil half-brother. If anything, it is this pattern of consistently smooth successions that makes the chronicle of these five-and-a-half centuries suspicious as hard history, since the more reliable sections of the *Nihonshoki* are filled with murders, fraternal jealousies, attempted coups d'état, ruthless political schemes, and so on. Having recognized this, one is then able to see that what we have here is someone's ideal pattern of what the imperial succession should be like: it should proceed smoothly and amicably, with the "natural" successor universally recognized for his superior qualities. By taking careful note of such fictional patterns (presented as factual) we can begin to appreciate more fully the ways in which the eighth-century Japanese retrospectively structured actual events. Historians, including the editors of the *Nihonshoki* and the *kataribe* or oral reciters, never simply record what happens; they turn occurrences into "events" by placing interpretive frames, embedded in the narrative structures and strategies employed to tell their story, around the "facts." If the fictional sections cannot provide historians with hard facts, they can yield a wealth of information about the historiographic process in early Japan.

In Table 1 in those cases following the reign of the Emperor Suinin, one finds that in 18 of 25 instances, or 72% of the time, final burial of the deceased sovereign preceded the formal accession of the successor. Furthermore, in the seven instances in which this pattern does not obtain, in every case except one (which I will discuss in a moment) the period of temporary enshrinement was over 18 months long. The six emperors in question and the respective lengths of the period of their temporary enshrinement are as follows: Keikō—2 yrs.; Hanzei—6 yrs. 10 mos.; Ankō—3 yrs.; Kenzō—1 yr. 6 mos.; Buretsu—1 yr. 10 mos.; and Bidatsu—5 yrs. 8 mos. The one exception to the pattern and temporal order noted above is that involving the Emperor Keitai and his successor, Ankan. There the period of temporary enshrinement for Keitai is reported as having been less than 18 months (10 months, to be exact), but the accession of Ankan is reported to have preceded Bidatsu's final burial. Upon closer inspection, however, this exception is found to be more apparent than real. It is reported that Keitai died on 2/7/531 and was buried 10 months later on 12/5/531. The date for the accession of Ankan, 2/7/531, is taken from the following entry in the Ankan Chapter of the *Nihonshoki*:

In the 25th year of his reign [i.e., 531], Spring, the 2nd month, the 7th day, the Emperor Ōdo [i.e., Keitai] established Ōye [i.e., Ankan] as Emperor, and on the same day he died.[14]

The *Nihonshoki*, however, is internally inconsistent, for the first year of the reign of Ankan is reported as 534, or three years after the death of his predecessor. Thus, we may assume that the entry cited above should be understood as a retrospective attempt to justify Ankan's succession to the throne by claiming that on his deathbed

Keitai shifted the mantle of the sacral kingship to him. For reasons that will soon become clear, we may surmise with some certainty that Ankan's formal ritual accession probably took place late in 533, shortly before the date for the celebration of the *niiname-sai*. If these assumptions are correct, then this case is in fact not an exception to the pattern noted above but rather a confirmation of it, as once again the final burial of the deceased emperor would have preceded the successor's formal accession. (Parenthetically, we may note that the addition of this case would raise the percentage of cases following the temporal ritual order from 72% to 76%.) In light of this evidence, we can conclude that in early Japan the formal accession *after* the final burial was the preferred ritual order. Moreover, the data collected in the table suggest that in general the period of the temporary enshrinement of the corpse of a deceased sovereign was less than 18 months. When the period was longer than this, the succession appears to have been uneasy and not readily accomplished.

Several other points of interest and possible significance emerge from a close study of the table. For example, the first month seems to have been preferred for the accession of the sovereign, since 21 of the 39 rulers (54%) for whom dates are recorded were formally installed then. This month is followed in terms of frequency by six accession ceremonies in the twelfth lunar month, four in the second month, and one each in the fourth, sixth, eighth, and ninth months. There are none recorded for the third, fifth, seventh, tenth, and eleventh months. As far as the figures for the timing of final burial are concerned, they too show some clustering: ten sovereigns were buried in the tenth month, seven in the eleventh, six in the ninth, five in the twelfth, two in the second, two in the eighth, one in the fourth, and one in the seventh month. There are no final burials reported in the first, third, fifth, or sixth lunar months. Even with these facts in hand, though, one must still ask whether there is any significance to these distributions.

To begin to answer this question, we may note that most of the final burials—in fact, an overwhelming 5:1 ratio—occur between the ninth and twelfth lunar months. This is clearly more than a slight wrinkle in a graph of statistical probability. Kikuchi Takeo has recently argued convincingly that the timing of final burial, which brought the period of temporary enshrinement and mourning to an end, was connected with the performance of the *niiname-sai*, the primary autumn ritual in early Japan. It was celebrated on the *shimo-u no hi* or "lower day of the hare," the fourth zodiac sign, of the eleventh month. Kikuchi points out that the final burials of the six emperors that were performed in the eleventh month all occurred *prior to* the *niiname-sai*.[15] Those emperors, the respective months and days of final burial, and the dates on which the *niiname-sai* would have fallen in the respective years are as follows:

Emperor	Date of burial	Date of niiname-sai
Keikō	11/10	11/19
Chūai	11/8	11/17
Hanzei	11/11	11/18
Seinei	11/9	11/22
Senka	11/17	11/18
Temmu	11/11	11/25

Although these dates are indeed suggestive of an immediate relation between the timing of the final burial and the *niiname-sai*, the fact that five burials took place in the twelfth month (i.e., *after* the *niiname-sai*) needs to be considered. Unless this fact can be explained, Kikuchi's thesis that an important connection existed between final burial and the successor's celebration of the *niiname-sai* is severely weakened. On the other hand, those final burials that fall in the first ten months pose no such problems. The emperors buried in the twelfth month and their dates of final burial are Suinin, 12/10; Keitai, 12/5; Ankan, 12/?; Jomei, 12/21; and Kōtoku, 12/8.

Glancing back at Table 1 above, we see that both Suinin and Kōtoku were temporarily enshrined for relatively brief periods of five and two months respectively. Perhaps in these cases the requisite preparations and rituals surrounding the *mogari no miya* were not completed before the calendrical date for celebrating the *niiname-sai*. In other words, the proximity of these emperors' deaths to the dates on which the *niiname-sai* fell that year may have put impossible pressure on the ritual calendar. If Kikuchi is correct, final burial ideally should have taken place prior to the *niiname-sai*; but if and when this order was impossible, the date of the celebration of the *niiname-sai* seems to have taken precedence.

Emperor Ankan, who died on 12/17, was given final burial almost immediately. No precise date is given in the text, but it must have been within two weeks. The reason for this extraordinary step is unclear, but again the pressure of the ritual calendar may have been a factor. The case of Emperor Keitai is even more problematic, though, because he died in the second lunar month, so final burial in the eleventh month should not have occasioned severe calendrical pressure. On the basis of negative evidence, however, it may be surmised that the state of the land was unsettled for an extended period of time after Keitai's death. Although the *Nihonshoki* is silent about conditions in the court after the emperor's death on 2/7/531, the fact that the first year of Ankan, Keitai's official successor, is recorded as being 534, or three years later, strongly suggests a lengthy period of political instability and turmoil before Ankan could be formally installed. The three-year gap in the record between this entry and the first year of Ankan may bespeak the fact that not everyone had accepted Ankan's claim and that a formal accession ceremony was only possible much later. Ankan's own reign was very short, indicating that the unsettled political situation had continued almost unabated. Because of the paucity of information in the *Nihonshoki*, however, this must remain nothing more than a hypothesis. It is worthy of note, though, that this period (i.e., the early sixth century) would seem to be too early for the Chinese practice of a three-year period of mourning to have been adopted by the Japanese imperial family. Moreover, if the three-year period were a narrative convention, it would be found in more than this isolated instance.

Among the sovereigns in question only the Emperor Jomei remains to be considered. Jomei died on 10/6/641 and was given final burial on 12/21/642, some fourteen months later. Of importance for our immediate purposes is the following entry in the *Nihonshoki* for 10/18/641:

Emperor Jomei was temporarily interred north of the Palace. This was called "the great temporary tomb" [*ōmogari*] of Kudara. At this time the Heir Apparent, the Imperial Prince Hirakasu-wake, was sixteen years old, and pronounced the funeral eulogium.[16]

Normally the prince who led the mourning rituals would have succeeded his father. Perhaps because of the heir apparent's youth, however, Jomei's widow succeeded as the Empress Kyōgoku. It is unfortunate that the text is silent about the role the empress-consort played in these developments—whether such political maneuvering was accomplished from within the *mogari no miya* and a state of ritual seclusion, or whether the widow frequently left the temporary enshrinement palace. What is apparent from other entries in the *Nihonshoki* text, though, is that the heavy hand of the Soga was involved. The Kyōgoku Chapter says, for example:

[642] 1st year, Spring, 1st month, 15th day. The Empress-consort assumed the Imperial Dignity. Emishi, Soga no Ōmi, was made Ōmi as before. The Ōmi's son, Iruka (also called Karatsukuri), took into his own hands the reins of government, and his power was greater than his father's. Therefore thieves and robbers were in dread of him, and things dropped on the highways were not picked up.[17]

On the basis of all the available evidence, Kikuchi concluded that in early Japan when final burial was not smoothly completed before the celebration of the *niiname-sai* by the new sovereign, the lapse indicates an uneasy succession.[18] This finding underscores the point that the final burial of an imperial predecessor was an important transitional rite in the process of consolidating and ritually confirming the power and position of the new ruler. This sequence conforms to the pattern found in the *Kojiki* and *Nihonshoki* myths, as we saw in Chapter Two. The successor could fully perform the *niiname-sai* only as the emperor, a status ritually realized by passing through the formal accession ritual. As Ellwood has pointed out, in early Japan these two rituals were not yet completely differentiated. Thus, the performance of the *niiname-sai* had more immediate political significance in terms of the succession than it was to have later after these rituals were clearly distinguished. Moreover, we have already seen more than one myth in which an individual who would be king, or who would at least appropriate some of the imperial prerogatives unto himself, attempted to realize these goals by performing the *niiname-sai*.

Nihonshoki *Records of Political Maneuvering During the Period of the* Mogari no Miya

The first record found in the *Nihonshoki* of the temporary enshrinement of the corpse of a ruler is that for the Emperor Chūai (r. 192–200).[19] This case is peculiar, however, in that the temporary interment of the corpse was performed for purposes of political expediency rather than out of some religious worldview. Chūai was the husband of the redoubtable Empress Jingū, who, according to the text, became possessed by a *kami* who told her the imperial army should attack the Korean kingdom of Silla. Chūai balked at following the instructions of the *kami* but died shortly thereafter. It is possible that, like a number of other rulers, he was killed by certain factions within the court. Nevertheless, all mourning for the deceased emperor was suppressed so that the planned military campaign against Silla could be carried out.[20] This record, then, is of no help for our purposes.

The next reference to temporary enshrinement is found in the Ingyō Chapter and concerns the Emperor Hanzei (r. 406–410). Little information is found therein, however, other than a report that a temporary interment shrine had been erected and that in 416 the superintendent of the *mogari no miya*, one Tamata no Sukune, had been lax in the performance of his duties, was discovered absent from his post, and was consequently executed.[21] Nevertheless, this brief entry does tell us that there was an official charged with overseeing and guarding the *mogari no miya*. If the chronology is to be believed, this official and his guards were still assigned to the *mogari no miya* six years after the emperor's death.

The record for the Emperor Kimmei (r. 539–571) is equally brief and of no help for our immediate interests.[22] The record concerning the Emperor Bidatsu (r. 572–585), however, provides some intriguing and unexpected insight into the socio-political situation surrounding the period of temporary interment and the performance of public rituals at the *mogari no miya*. Indeed, it is so critical to our understanding of this liminal period that it merits citation at length:

[585] Autumn, 8th month, 15th day. The Emperor's disease having become more and more inveterate, he died in the Great Hall. At this time a Palace of temporary interment was erected at Hirose. Umako no Sukune delivered a funeral oration with his sword girded on. Mononobe no Yugei no Moriya no Ōmuraji burst out laughing, and said:—"He is like a

sparrow pierced by a hunting shaft." Next Yugei no Moriya no Ōmuraji, with trembling hands and legs, delivered his funeral oration. The Ōmi, Umako no Sukune, laughed and said:—"He ought to have bells hung upon him." From this small beginning the two Ministers conceived a hatred of each other. Sakō, Miwa no Kimi sent Hayato [i.e., armed guards] for the protection of the Courtyard of the temporary tomb. The Imperial Prince Anahobe, who wished to possess himself of the empire, flew into a rage, and declared, saying:—"Why do ye serve the Court of a dead King, and do no service where the living King is?"[23]

It is clear that public ritual orations were an important part of the rituals performed at the *mogari no miya*—so important, in fact, that in presenting them, Great Ministers (Ōmi) were reduced to quivering bundles of nerves. Such public funeral orations were not only significant elements of a religious ritual; they also had decisive political dimensions. By and large, however, scholars have failed to consider the full implications of this fact. In light of what we saw in Chapter One concerning the socio-political dimensions of public performative poetry of praise, of stylized longing, of land viewing, and so on, it is hardly surprising to find that similar dimensions are found in the spatio-temporal locus of the *mogari no miya*. In this passage, for example, the reader sees how, at least according to the editors of the *Nihonshoki*, the enmity between two powerful ministers of the Soga and Mononobe clans surfaced publicly in disparaging remarks about each other's performance and appearance in the ritual eulogization of the deceased emperor. Of course, we need not believe this was the actual origin of the bad blood between the two men. Indeed, the *Nihonshoki* itself reports that earlier the Mononobe chieftain had blamed a widespread pestilence on the Soga clan's patronage of Buddhism. He consequently gained the permission of the Emperor Bidatsu to burn down the Soga temples, destroy the enshrined Buddhist images, and defrock and flog Soga women who had become nuns.[24]

The public performance of each minister provided the occasion for belittling the other before members of the court and provincial clans whose respect and support were needed. The rituals of temporary enshrinement were, then, also vehicles for political maneuvering in the immediate aftermath of the sovereign's death and a venue for actors engaged in political theater. At the same time, those in control of the ritual proceedings felt it necessary to guard the *mogari no miya*. One might assume that the intention was to guard against grave robbers or to ward off evil spirits, but the real reason was that the *mogari no miya* was held to be the locus of the deceased sovereign's *tama*. Guards were posted not so much to keep the spirit in as to keep out those among the living who would try to appropriate it onto themselves.

Finally, the reader learns that Imperial Prince Anahobe, a younger paternal half-brother of the deceased Emperor Bidatsu, had designs on the throne himself. Moreover, Anahobe was reportedly angered by those who served at the *mogari no miya*, where the corpse of Bidatsu was enshrined, instead of taking up what he saw as their proper roles of serving "the living king," a term by which Anahobe, of course, referred to himself. One cannot help but notice the parallel here with the myth of the death of Izanami where, as we have seen, Susano-o runs afoul of Izanagi precisely because he continues to weep and mourn the deceased Izanami and refuses to take up his proper station in the new ruling alignment as dictated by Izanagi. In both cases Anahobe and Izanagi take declarations of loyalty or attachment to the deceased by others as a personal affront and a threat to the smooth transition to a new status quo and power alignment they desire.

Arnold van Gennep pointed out many years ago that funerary rituals are essentially rites of passage or transitional rites, accomplishing the transformation from one state to another. Such rites of passage are characterized by three distinct phases or stages—separation, transition, and reincorporation—with concomitant rites that both create these stages and propel their development into the next one. In the ritual complex surrounding the practice of double burial, the period of temporary enshrinement or interment clearly is the transitional or liminal period,[25] an inherently dangerous and chaotic time between the old order and the new one that is to emerge. A new order, however, does not come into being naturally; it has to be ritually created. If the liminal period is extended for very long or not brought to a close, the subsequent rites of reincorporation and the establishment of a renewed order cannot be realized. In the myth of the death of Izanami, Susano-o's mourning becomes threatening to the entire cosmos precisely when it continues for an inordinately long period of time. Whether it is in the world of myth or in human society, the liminal rite of mourning, which is essential as a transitional stage, becomes disruptive when its continuation blocks the realization of the next stage of reestablishing order.

However brief, the whole episode surrounding the temporary enshrinement of Emperor Bidatsu is filled with tantalizing hints of what was going on beneath the surface of the text. Fortunately, by using the scattered evidence in the three texts it is possible to reconstruct the details with a good measure of certainty. In the following pages this record will serve as an entrée into the liminal period of temporary interment, a period of special concern in the *Kojiki*, the *Nihonshoki*, and even the *Man'yōshū*. Incidents such as the one cited above involving Prince Anahobe need to be viewed not only in general terms of the *mogari no miya* ritual but also in terms of the specific socio-political situation during this period of Japanese history. Since a critical point in the ongoing struggle for political hegemony among the powerful Soga, Mononobe, and Nakatomi clans was reached precisely in the reign of the Emperor Bidatsu, it may be useful to give a brief sketch of the socio-political circumstances within the court at this time.

Most histories of Japan locate the formal introduction of Buddhism into the country in 552 C.E., when the king of the Korean kingdom of Paekche sent a bronze statue of the Buddha, sutras, various ritual items, and gifts to the Japanese emperor. Buddhism had, of course, been carried into Japan much earlier by Korean immigrants and refugees from the continent. Nevertheless, the introduction of Buddhism into the court seems to have led to a polarization of members of the ruling elite around the Soga and Nakatomi clan factions. The Nakatomi were a clan of hereditary specialists of the sacred whose duties centered around the imperial cult and the worship of the *kami*. The Soga, on the other hand, were the first influential clan to adopt Buddhism, which they went on to promote along with other Chinese cultural arts and forms of political administrative structure. Sansom has succinctly characterized the situation that obtained between the Soga and the Nakatomi factions in the sixth century:

The underlying conflict, it need hardly be said, was a clash of political interests; though it would be a mistake to assume that no genuine religious feelings were involved. The Nakatomi clan naturally stood for the indigenous faith. The Monobe, a military clan, joined, and indeed led, the resistance to Buddhism, not so much on religious grounds as on what today we should describe as nationalistic grounds. They did not approve of foreign ideas, and they believed in the use of armed force as the proper instrument of policy. Opposed to this conservative school was the Soga clan, whose leader, the Great Minister Iname, was convinced of the need for a new system of government which would break the autonomy of the clans and assert the authority of the Crown and its appointed ministers. This was a line which the Soga family could afford to take, since . . . they had already established their own position by means of marriage relationships with the imperial family.[26]

Predictably, the death of the Emperor Bidatsu, who had vacillated in various ways during his reign between support of the cult of the *kami* and Buddhism, brought matters to a head, since each of the competing factions had a vested interest in seeing an individual sympathetic to its cause crowned as Bidatsu's successor. Significantly, the individual who emerged and was crowned as the Emperor Yōmei seems to have been either a compromise candidate or someone politically astute in placating both factions. The opening of the Yōmei Chapter of the *Nihonshoki*, for instance, clearly states: "The Emperor believed in the Law of the Buddha and reverenced the Way of the Gods." (*Sumeramikoto hotoke no minori o uketamai kami no michi o totobitamu.*)[27] This is the well-known line in which the term *kami no michi* or "Shinto" appears for the first time in the written records of early Japan. The tussle between the contending factions, though, does not seem to have diminished with Yōmei's succession.

The shadowy, somewhat sinister figure of Prince Anahobe reappears in the Yōmei Chapter of the *Nihonshoki*, which in standard fashion returns to the time of the death of the previous emperor to pick up the thread of the narrative. It sheds further light on both the ritual practices during the period of temporary interment and their socio-political context. Although the Yōmei Chapter deals specifically only with the transition between the reigns of Bidatsu and Yōmei, we may assume that the general situation described was characteristic of most such liminal periods. Work on the construction of the *mogari no miya* began immediately after Bidatsu died on 8/15/585. The first dated entries of the Yōmei Chapter read:

[585] 9th month, 5th day. The Emperor [Yōmei] assumed the Imperial dignity, and made his capital at Iware, calling it the Palace of Namitsuki in Ikenoe. Soga no Umako no Sukune was made Ōmi, and Mononobe no Yuge no Moriya no Ōmuraji was made Ōmuraji, both as before.

19th day. The Emperor made command, saying:—etc., etc.—appointing the Imperial Princess Sukate-hime to the charge of the Shrine of Ise and to attend to the worship of the Sun-goddess.

(This Imperial Princess, from the time of this Emperor until the reign of the Empress Kashikiya-hime [i.e., Suiko], attended to the divine service of the Sun-goddess. She then retired of her own accord to Kazuraki, and there died. See the reign of the Empress Kashikiya-hime. [In fact, no reference to this incident is found there.] One book says:—"Having attended to the worship of the Sun-goddess for the space of thirty-seven years, she then retired of her own accord and died.")[28]

Although the text says that Yōmei "assumed the imperial dignity" within a month of Bidatsu's death, the ritual performed was probably the *sokui-rei*, a simple civil ceremony, and not a full-fledged enthronement ceremony because of the elaborate preparations that would have been required. Yōmei seems to have attempted to maintain the balance between the Soga and Mononobe by reappointing the clan heads to the positions they had held under Bidatsu. The next entry is devoted exclusively to the appointment of a new imperial princess to serve as the head priestess of the cult of Amaterasu at the Ise Shrine. The editors of the *Nihonshoki* felt it necessary, though, to state explicitly, not once but twice, that the princess later left this ritual position "of her own accord" (*mizukara*). One senses that the text protests too much here, suggesting that the real reason for the princess's leaving the ritual position may have been something else.

Imperial Princess Sukate-hime, appointed to this critical ritual position at Ise, was the daughter of Yōmei and one of his consorts, Ishikina, a daughter of Soga no Umako. The *Nihonshoki* does not indicate the identity of the Imperial Virgin she replaced. Interestingly enough, however, an entry in the seventh year of Bidatsu's reign (3/5/578) says that Imperial Princess Uji had been appointed to serve ritually at Ise but was recalled after having an "intrigue" (sexual relations are implied) with Prince Ikenoe (*Ikenoe no miko ni okasarenu*). Such an "intrigue" involving the Ise

Priestess seems to allude to the Ise Virgin as a potential locus of symbolic power in the succession. If this hypothesis is correct, the appointment and the dismissal of the Ise Virgin would have had political implications. Prince Ikenoe is not mentioned anywhere else in the *Nihonshoki*, but Ikenoe is the name of the place where Yōmei located his palace and capital. Since many individuals in early Japan took the name of their homeland as their own name, this prince may have come from that area.

The next passage where Prince Anahobe surfaces again is dated some eight months after the presumed *sokui-rei* of Yōmei and reads as follows:

[586] Summer, 5th month. The Imperial Prince Anahobe tried to force his way into the Palace of temporary interment in order to ravish [*okasamu toshite*] the Empress Consort Kashikiya-hime. But the favourite Minister, Sakō (or "Sakafu") Miwa no Kimi, called out the guards, who firmly fastened the Palace Gate, and resisting his entrance, would not let him in. The Imperial Prince Anahobe demanded of them, saying:—"Who is it that is here?" The guards answered and said:—"Sakō, Miwa no Kimi, is here." Seven times he shouted at them to open the gate, but they steadily refused to admit him. Hereupon the Imperial Prince Anahobe addressed the Ōmi [Soga no Umako] and the Ōmuraji [Mononobe no Moriya], saying:—"Sakō is incessantly insulting me. In the funeral eulogy delivered by him at the Court of temporary interment [*mogari no miya*] he said:—'Thy Court shall not be left desolate, but shall be kept pure as the surface of a mirror, and thy servant will preserve peace in dutiful service to thee.' This is an insult. At this moment there are many young men of the Emperor's family, and there are two Chief Ministers present. Who has any right wantonly to monopolize talk of dutiful service? Moreover when I wished to see the interior of the palace of temporary interment, I was prevented, and not allowed to enter. Seven times I myself called out, 'Open the gate,' but there was no answer. I request that I may be allowed to put him to death." The two Chief Ministers said:—"Be it as thou hast commanded." Upon this, the Imperial Prince Anahobe, while secretly planning to make himself ruler of the Empire, falsely gave out that his object was to kill Sakō no Kimi. At length, along with Mononobe no Moriya no Omuraji, he led troops with which they surrounded Ikenoe in Iware.[29]

Once again Anahobe takes umbrage at another's public declaration of loyalty to the deceased sovereign. As in the myth concerning events following the death of Izanami, this declaration is taken as an attempt somehow to control the succession and to block another's political ambitions. Moreover, the verbal "insult" Prince Anahobe claims to have suffered is exacerbated by the fact that he is denied entry to the *mogari no miya*. This element of the narrative once again immediately parallels Susano-o's expressed desire to visit the deceased Izanami, which was also blocked. Prince Anahobe cleverly appeals to *both* Soga no Umako and Mononobe no Moriya when they are together, making it impossible for Soga no Umako to declare publicly his true feelings on the matter. Anahobe seems to have skillfully maneuvered Umako into approving his plan to do away with Sakō no Kimi by suggesting that both Sakō's public statements in his eulogy and his actions in denying Anahobe entrance to the *mogari no miya* were not slights directed only at Anahobe but were also attempts to detract from the relative prestige of the two ministers. In effect, Anahobe represented Sakō's eulogy and subsequent actions as a concerted attempt at one-upmanship on his part by implying that he was somehow more loyal than all the others, including the imperial princes and great ministers (*Ōmi*). Sakō's claim that he had been personally commissioned by the emperor did not sit well with others in the court. It would be a mistake, then, to assume that Soga no Umako and Mononobe no Moriya united at least temporarily in order to eliminate another player from the political stage. A more careful reading of the text suggests that Soga no Umako was temporarily outmaneuvered at this point and forced to accede to an act of which he did not really approve.

The slant[30] placed on Sakō's public eulogy by Prince Anahobe resulted in Sakō's execution. It is little wonder, then, that both Soga no Umako and Mononobe no Moriya were reportedly nervous, as we have seen above, when it was their turn to present a funeral oration. They were fully conscious of the fact that Sakō's funeral eulogy—and those of every other courtier—though ostensibly addressed to the deceased emperor were equally addressed to the living, giving these rituals a decidedly political dimension.

By focusing on the manner in which Prince Anahobe seized upon the opportunity presented by Sakō's public performance to manipulate, through the clever use of insinuation, two of the most powerful ministers in the court to give him permission to execute Sakō, one can see the extent to which the court rationality referred to in Chapter One was operative. Within this social milieu, in such liminal periods, an affront to one's status and prestige, whether real or imagined, was sufficient reason to justify the execution of a powerful nobleman or even an imperial prince. The seriousness of the affront may have been a manufactured fiction among friends—and even enemies—but the complex network of interdependencies obtaining among the courtiers quickly transformed it into a dangerous and deadly reality.

Sakō initially managed to escape the grasp of the troops of Prince Anahobe and Mononobe no Moriya and sought refuge in the summer palace of Kashikiya-hime, Bidatsu's widow. Precisely what happened thereafter is unclear, for the *Nihonshoki* records two different versions: either Mononobe no Moriya killed Sakō and his family, or Prince Anahobe did so himself. Whatever the case may have been, however, this incident once again set the Soga openly at odds with the Mononobe. Let us return to the text at this point:

[Mononobe no Moriya] arrived with his troops and reported the result of his commission, saying:—"I have executed Sakō and the others." (One book says:—"The Imperial Prince went in person and shot them dead.") Hereupon Umako no Sukune broke into bitter lamentations, saying:—"Civil disorder in the Empire is not far off." The Ōmuraji [Mononobe] hearing this, answered and said:—"Thy position is that of a small minister; thou dost not know."[31]

This verbal jab must have stung Umako, for by calling him a "small minister" Mononobe no Moriya implied that Umako was unfit to occupy the rank of a Great Minister. Although it is impossible to accept much of the dialogue recorded in the *Nihonshoki* as verbatim accounts, in general this passage rings true in terms of what we know of court society. The open display of emotion by Umako played into the hands of his rival, who used it to belittle him publicly before an important imperial prince and, we may assume, other members of the court. The Soga were, of course, to have their revenge shortly, defeating the Mononobe on the battlefield and utterly destroying their power base. But not all the struggles for power, position, and prestige were played out on the battlefield. Much more frequently, perhaps even on a daily basis, there were public verbal joustings among the courtiers, ministers, and princes in the constant process of the creation and destruction of their social status within the court.

In presenting this history, however, the editors of the *Nihonshoki*—written in a Soga-dominated court—were not about to take a chance with their readers' loyalty, for they follow the narrative quoted above with an interlinear note:

This Sakō, Miwa no Kimi, was a favourite of the Emperor Ōsada [i.e., Bidatsu], and he was charged with all matters both internal and external. In consequence of this the Empress-consort Kashikiya-hime and Umako no Sukune both conceived enmity against the Imperial Prince Anahobe.[32]

This note makes it clear that Sakō had indeed been following the wishes of the deceased Emperor Bidatsu, the widowed Empress (a Soga daughter), and very probably Soga no Umako himself in denying entrance to the *mogari no miya* to Prince Anahobe. Here, then, we have the answer to the question as to whom the posted *hayato* or guards were guarding the *mogari no miya* against. We can now say with some certainty that the decision to deny Anahobe entrance to the interior of the temporary enshrinement palace was a strategic move in the succession struggle on the part of the Soga faction designed to block Anahobe's efforts. This conclusion lends further credence to the assertion that the *mogari no miya*, both in the interior female space and in the exterior public ritual space, was a critical locus of activity in the politics of death in early Japan.

The Interplay of Myth and History in the Anahobe Tale

The narrative patterns and strategy informing the "historical chronicle" and those found in the myths recounted above reflect back on each other, each illuminating elements of the other that are not visible on the surface of the texts. If Susano-o's desire to go to the land of his deceased "mother" is the equivalent of entering the *mogari no miya*, then the reactions of Izanagi to this stated intention parallel those of Soga no Umako and others opposed to Anahobe. Although we know *who* the temporary enshrinement palace was being guarded against, it is still not clear *why* Anahobe's (or for that matter any other prince's) entering the *mogari no miya* would potentially have resulted in control of the succession. In an effort to understand why this was the case, let us review a few key elements of the political situation following the death of the Emperor Bidatsu by refreshing our memory of the chronology of events.

8/15/585   Emperor Bidatsu dies

shortly thereafter the corpse is temporarily enshrined and Soga no Umako and Mononobe no Moriya exchange insults concerning each other's public oration

Prince Anahobe is angered that guards are posted around the *mogari no miya*

9/5/585   Yōmei assumes power (in a *sokui-rei?*)

9/19/585   Yōmei appoints Sukate-hime as the imperial priestess of the Ise Shrine

5/586   Prince Anahobe attempts to force his way into the *mogari no miya* to possess the Emperor Bidatsu's widow; Sakō no Kimi stops him

Anahobe convinces Umako and Moriya to permit the execution of Sakō.

If we assume that at this time a full formal accession ceremony had not yet taken place, then Prince Anahobe may have continued to believe that he had time and room to maneuver to gain the throne without attacking Yōmei directly. If Yōmei had not been formally installed, then he was not yet "really" the emperor. Or, one might say that he was the emperor *de facto* but not yet fully *de jure*.

Heretofore we have concentrated on Anahobe's actions, but it is also important to look carefully at those of Yōmei, for these two individuals and their supporters were engaged in an ongoing struggle for political power, making moves and countermoves, sometimes executing preemptive strikes and at other times strategic retreats. If we look at Yōmei's actions reported up until this point, we find only three listed:

9/5/585   he reappointed Soga no Umakao and Mononobe no Moriya to their positions previously held under Bidatsu

9/19/585   he appointed a new Ise Priestess

1/1/586   he appointed his empress-consort.

Of these actions, only the second stands out as somewhat unusual. Relatively few sovereigns appointed a new priestess immediately after assuming power. Here this should be understood as a preemptive defensive action, taken once again to thwart the political ambitions of Prince Anahobe. Yōmei's action hints, perhaps, that not only was the female realm of the interior of the *mogari no miya* somehow a repository of the charisma (*tama*) of the sacred kingship, but so too was the Ise Shrine and the person of its imperial priestess. There are hints that in addition to *tama-furi* rituals performed by the sexual partners of the deceased emperor inside the *mogari no miya*, the Ise Priestess also had some kind of power to recall the imperial spirit and transfer it to another individual. Specific details in the Yamato-takeru tale point to this conclusion, as does the story of Imperial Prince Ōtsu in the days immediately following the death of his father, the Emperor Temmu, in 686, found in the *Nihonshoki* and the *Man'yōshū*.

While the *mogari no miya* rituals continued to be performed, the would-be successor or successors could hardly afford to be seen as forcibly or prematurely ending the mourning rituals. But at the same time, as long as the *mogari no miya* rituals continued, the contending players in the court could pursue a variety of strategies, both military and symbolic, in positioning themselves for the succession. The data collected in the chart above support this contention, as do mythic parallels such as the account of the events following the death of Izanami.

Let us return, though, to the *Nihonshoki* record of the denouement of Prince Anahobe's persistent and varied attempts to become the emperor. Following the interlinear note from 5/586 cited above, there are no entries in the *Nihonshoki* for almost a year. Then suddenly the pace of the report picks up dramatically with the following entry:

[587] 2nd year, Spring, 4th month, 2nd day. The Emperor [Yōmei] performed the ceremony of tasting the new rice [*niinae kikoshimesu*] on the river-bank of Iware. On this day the Emperor took ill and returned to the Palace. All the Ministers were in attendance. The Emperor addressed them, saying:—"It is Our desire to give our adherence to the three precious things [i.e., Buddhism]. Do ye Our Ministers advise upon this." All the Ministers entered the Court and consulted together. Mononobe no Moriya no Ōmuraji and Nakatomi no Katsumi no Muraji opposed the Imperial proposal, and advised, saying:—"Why should we reverence strange deities, and turn our backs upon the gods of our country? Of course we know naught of any such thing." The Ōmi Soga no Umako no Sukune said:—"Let us render assistance in compliance with the Imperial command. Who shall offer advice to the contrary?" Hereupon the Imperial Prince the Emperor's younger brother [Anahobe] introduced into the interior [of the imperial palace] a priest of the Land of Toyo (the personal name is wanting). Mononobe no Moriya no Ōmuraji glared at them in great wrath.[33]

Since Anahobe was the candidate of the conservative Mononobe and most probably of the Nakatomi as well, it is perhaps surprising to see him so quickly acquiesce to the Soga and bring a Buddhist priest into the imperial palace. Anahobe may have been merely an opportunist who sensed the political tide shifting, or perhaps he was cleverly introducing (or better, "planting") a Buddhist priest he felt he could control. From the information provided by the text it is impossible to determine the actual case, though later events suggest that Anahobe remained the Mononobe candidate. Mononobe no Moriya's reported glaring at Anahobe and the Buddhist priest may have been another act of political theater staged for public consumption. At the same time, though, one must also note the manner in which Soga no Umako effectively blocked the Mononobe and Nakatomi faction's total opposition to introducing Buddhism into the imperial palace: he cleverly stated his own position in such a way that to disagree with it would have made the others appear to be disloyal to the emperor himself—something no one, of course, could afford to suggest publicly in any way. This strategy was in many ways similar to that which Anahobe had successfully used earlier in getting Umako to acquiesce to the execution of Sakō no Kimi. Following this encounter another minister, who no doubt had been present, conveyed his own interpretation of the ever-shifting and treacherous political situation to Mononobe no Moriya, suggesting that the other ministers were plotting against Moriya and planned to arrest him.

In what was becoming a predictable pattern in times of uneasy succession, Mononobe no Moriya withdrew from the capital into the country, where he gathered troops. There he was soon joined by Nakatomi no Katsumi and his troops. An intriguing entry reports that Katsumi fashioned figurines of the heir apparent, Prince Hikohito, and another prince, Takeda, and practiced some kind of black magic on them. When this ploy was ineffective in bringing them down, however, he proceeded to the palace of Prince Hikohito apparently to assassinate him. Word of the plot preceded Katsumi, though, and it was he who was slain.[34] After Katsumi's death, Mononobe no Moriya sent a message to Soga no Umako and other leaders, saying, "Hearing that the Ministers have designs against me, I am keeping out of the way."[35] Umako, though, was not fooled for a moment by this statement or lulled into complacency. He was not politically naive any more than Amaterasu had been when Susano-o ascended to her in heaven ostensibly, it will be remembered, to bid her farewell and to get out of the way. Umako immediately saw through this doubletalk and had a special twenty-four-hour guard placed around his palace.

The final showdown between these two factions was fast approaching as Emperor Yōmei lay on his deathbed and was to die only a week later. Needless to say, the circumstances of his death are suspicious. It is quite possible, for example, that he was poisoned at the *niiname-sai*. If so, the Mononobe and especially the Nakatomi would be prime suspects, since they were intimately involved with the preparations of the food and implements for this ritual, and certainly both had motive. In fact, if one were to plan a murder of the sovereign, the *niiname-sai* provided a perfect opportunity, for whereas the emperor could employ food tasters at all other meals, in this ritual the emperor and the emperor alone as a living god was permitted to serve the *kami* ritually and to feast with them. In at least one prominent version of the Amaterasu–Susano-o myth recorded in the *Nihonshoki*, Amaterasu falls sick and "dies" during the *niiname-sai* because of the excrement Susano-o had secretly strewn under her seat. This may well be a mythic parallel to the death of the Emperor Yōmei.

In the record of the death of Yōmei, however, there is a peculiar detail that merits mention. The *niiname-sai*, a harvest festival, is normally performed in the eleventh lunar month, yet the *Nihonshoki* states that Yōmei fell ill while celebrating it in the fourth month. Celebrating the ritual at a date this far out of place on the liturgical calendar is very irregular. Because of the centrality and importance of the *niiname-sai* in early Japan, it is impossible to explain away this curious detail by appeal to scribal error. It is much more likely that the inclusion of the *niiname-sai* here may have been a narrative convention used to explain away, as it were, the somewhat awkward, even suspicious, death of a sovereign, since in the myths a sovereign or would-be sovereign who died during its performance was thus shown to have been ultimately unsuited to serve as the sacred king. The editors of the *Nihonshoki*, however, do not in any way portray Yōmei in a negative light or even hint that he received his just deserts in suddenly dying early in his reign.

The detail about the emperor falling ill during the *niiname-sai* may have been a survival from an earlier narrative version of Yōmei's death, or a detail from another factional history, one with an interest in showing that the *kami* punished those who forsook them for alien cults. Although it is impossible to say anything definite one way or the other, in the *Nihonshoki* Yōmei's celebration of the *niiname-sai* is narratively related to his announcement to the assembled ministers that he intended to embrace Buddhism. If this policy had been adopted, it would have constituted a significant move away from his earlier even-handed treatment of the *kami* cults and Buddhism. It is conceivable that the knowledge on the part of some members of the court of Yōmei's intentions in this regard may have led them to take drastic measures to block their realization. On the other hand, even if one assumes no correlation between Yōmei's announcement that he intended to embrace Buddhism and his death, there is yet another possibility. A performance of the *niiname-sai* by Yōmei would have in and of itself been a conscious attempt to demonstrate ritually that he was indeed the emperor. Certainly this action would have been so interpreted by those who opposed him and may have been sufficient impetus to assassinate him.

Whatever the case, after the brief reign of Yōmei the court was once again thrown into a dangerous, chaotic, and liminal state.

The story of Anahobe continues in the following chapter of the *Nihonshoki*, covering the reign of Emperor Sushun (r. 587–592), where we find the following intriguing passage:

The Emperor Tachibana no Toyohi [Yōmei] died in the second year of his reign, Summer, the 4th month. In the 5th month the army of the Mononobe no Ōmuraji made a disturbance thrice. The Ōmuraji from the first wished to set aside the other Imperial Princes and to establish the Imperial Prince Anahobe as Emperor. He now hoped to make use of a hunting party [*kari suru ni yorite*] to devise a plan for raising him to the throne instead. So he secretly [*shinobi ni*] sent a messenger to the Imperial Prince Anahobe, to say:—"I should like to hunt with the Imperial Prince in Awaji." The plot leaked out.[36]

Soga no Umako and the Empress-Consort Kashikiya-hime had Prince Anahobe executed on the seventh day of the sixth month, and Imperial Prince Yakabe was put to death the following day for having supported him. Anahobe's fate presaged that of the Mononobe clan. Within a month the Soga clan and their allies routed the Mononobe forces at Shigisen. With the Mononobe candidate, Anahobe, out of the way, Soga no Umako moved quickly to have a son of Emperor Kimmei by a Soga daughter succeed to the throne as the Emperor Sushun on the second day of the eighth month. The *Nihonshoki* records that Yōmei had been buried on the twenty-first day of the seventh month. We may perhaps assume, then, that the decisive defeat of the Mononobe in this month occurred before this date. Within weeks of Yomei's burial, Sushun was on the throne, though once again not for long. Only five years later, Soga no Umako was to have Sushun assassinated on 11/3/592. Barely a month later on the eighth day of the twelfth month, Kashikiya-hime, the widow of Bidatsu and herself a Soga daughter, succeeded to the throne as the Empress Suiko, with Prince Shōtoku as regent. Kashikiya-hime, it will be recalled, was the widowed empress whom, according to the *Nihonshoki*, Anahobe had sought to possess while she was secluded in Bidatsu's *mogari no miya*. The reign of the Empress Suiko (and of Prince Shōtoku as regent) was to see many significant changes occur in Japan, including the court's full embrace and promotion of Buddhism as an imperial and national religion.

In the tale of Anahobe and related narratives in the *Nihonshoki*, one finds the stuff of a grand historical epic, with the main plot, the ongoing struggle over the generations for political hegemony among the Soga faction and the Mononobe and Nakatomi, tying together a large number of subplots. The historical chronicle is replete with a steamy storyline and characters motivated by lust and ambition, love triangles, assassinations, and "incest." The Anahobe narrative represents one such subplot that

weaves itself through the reigns of three emperors. To be sure, what we have preserved in the *Nihonshoki* narrative is little more than a plot outline, yet the character
sketches are sufficiently intriguing to capture the reader's imagination. The story is
believable and the characters' motives plausible insofar as the reports of many of the
courtiers' actions and reactions conform to a predictable pattern as a result of the
operative court rationality. While nevertheless "history," what we have here is a
very literary human history. Yet it is essential to realize that these tales were intended to serve as fundamental elements of the official (i.e., correct) national history.
The Anahobe tale has no doubt been preserved in the *Nihonshoki* largely because the
Soga faction wanted to justify the succession at this point. At the same time it was
a central event leading to the final triumph of the Soga over the Mononobe clan and
their candidate.

The tale of Anahobe is crucial in achieving a better understanding of not only the
central socio-political importance the period of temporary enshrinement held in the
imperial succession but also the intention informing the genesis and the structure of
each of these three basic texts. Various details from the Anahobe narrative will
enable us to answer certain questions surrounding the politics of death in early
Japan.

It will be recalled that Anahobe first appears on the scene—that is, on the surface of the text—at the *mogari no miya* of Emperor Bidatsu in the entry dated 8/15/
585, where he is angered because guards are posted around the *mogari no miya*. At
that point, however, his anger is aroused because the guards and their commander,
Sakō Miwa no Kimi, seem to be loyal to the deceased emperor and not to himself.
There is no report that Anahobe attempted to enter the *mogari no miya* forcibly in
order to possess the widowed empress, an event only related nine months later as
follows:

[586] Summer, 5th month. The Imperial Prince Anahobe tried to force his way into the
Palace of temporary interment in order to ravish [*okasamu toshite*] the Empress Consort Kashikiya-hime.

Concerning this entry, Aston rightly notes that "The motive was probably not
lust, but ambition,"[37] yet he does not expand on why this is a political act. At first
glance, Anahobe's reported behavior appears to be irrational, an act of sheer mad-
ness. He may have been mad, of course, but in that case one would hardly expect
to find a number of powerful political figures, including the heads of the Mononobe
and Nakatomi clans, supporting him. One must also entertain the possibility that
the report was a crass attempt to discredit Anahobe and besmirch his character.
Ultimately, one cannot help but feel that the *Nihonshoki* text obfuscates as much as
it reveals on this subject. If one assumes the events described to have actually taken

place, however, then one may presume that Anahobe's contemporaries could read between the lines, as it were, to discern the meaning and intention behind this act. Alternatively, even if one assumes the story to be fictional, the early Japanese readers of the *Nihonshoki* would have recognized the deep meaning of this narrative element. In either case, the symbolism of the act, whether it occurred or not, would have been obvious to the early Japanese and, thus, did not have to be explained explicitly. Within a larger symbolic context, the act was meaningful, not irrational.

To recover the early Japanese world of meaning within which the Anahobe narrative is to be located and interpreted, we must study the specific cultural symbols that inform this and related narratives and learn to read the narrative—insofar as it is possible—in the same way the early Japanese may be presumed to have read it. To do this, though, requires reconstructing a heretofore largely ignored aspect of the symbolic and ritual center of early Japan.

Female Power in the Liminal Period of the Mogari no Miya

We have already isolated dual female loci of the imperial charisma during this period in the interior of the *mogari no miya* and in the position of the Ise Priestess. The conflation of sexual imagery with political power is, of course, not unique to Japan. The practice of royal incest, for example, was widespread in Melanesian and South Pacific cultures. The sexual relations involved or alluded to in a number of narratives from the early Japanese texts have led me to put the term "incest" in quotation marks, since these cases are not incest proper. It is unclear, for example, how we are to understand the "brother and sister" relationship of Izanagi and Izanami or what to make of the term *imo*, "wife" but also "younger sister."[38] The same can be said of the childbearing contest between Susano-o and Amaterasu, though once again the suggestion of "incest" is present, if one should choose to take it in that sense. Individually none of the narratives might warrant this reading, but cumulatively the weight of the evidence is such that the existence of some form (albeit attenuated) of ritual incest must be entertained as at least one of the levels of meaning in these records.

Let us turn to a few relevant myths. In one *Nihonshoki* version of the myth of O-kuni-nushi, this *kami* is presented as Susano-o's son.[39] In the *Kojiki* version it is unclear whether he is Susano-o's son or a sixth-generation descendent.[40] Certain elements in this myth parallel those found in the Izanami–Izanagi and Amaterasu–Susano-o myths. O-kuni-nushi's brothers, the eighty deities, plot to kill him and even do so twice. His mother, however, is able to intervene both times and have him brought back to life. He then escapes a third attempt on his life by slipping through the fork of a tree and is sent by his mother (or another sympathetic *kami*) to *ne no katasu kuni*, the underworld, with the promise that Susano-o would help him there. Thus, in this myth O-kuni-nushi, too, descends to the underworld where Susano-o had been banished after his abortive attempt to seize Amaterasu's realm. Japanese scholars have long noted that the description of Susano-o's palace and the great hall recalls the great burial tumuli or *kofun*.

In the underworld O-kuni-nushi meets Suseri-bime, Susano-o's daughter—thus, his own sister or at least half-sister—and they become husband and wife. When Susano-o attempts to kill O-kuni-nushi, Suseri-bime possesses the power to save him. When O-kuni-nushi is made to sleep in a snake-filled chamber (*hemi no mu-roya*),[41] she presents him with a magical snake-repelling scarf (*hemi no hire*), saying "When the snakes are about to bite, drive them away by waving this scarf three times" (*sono hemi kuwamu to seba, kono hire o san-tabi furite uchi-harai tamae*).[42] Again the next night she gives O-kuni-nushi another magical scarf to pacify bees and centipedes placed in his sleeping chamber. Note that once again the incestuous relationship between this brother and (half-)sister seems to be the key to power. It is the sister who gives the male magical objects and the instructions for their use in *tama-furi*-like rituals. Philippi has translated an important passage from the *Kujiki*, another historical chronicle covering the period from the Age of the Gods to the reign of the Empress Suiko. The extant manuscript is from the Heian period. It lists precisely these scarves as two of the ten imperial regalia presented by Amaterasu to Ninigi prior to his descent from the High Heaven. It reads:

The Ancestress of the Heavenly Deities (thus) commanded, bestowing Ten Precious Treasures as the Heavenly Regalia. These were: the Mirror of the Deep, the Mirror of the Shore, the Sword Eight Hands Long, the Jewel of Life, the Jewel of Resuscitation, the Jewel of Plenty, the Jewel of Turning Back on the Road, the Snake(-repelling) Scarf [*hemi no hire*], the Bee(-repelling) Scarf [*hachi no hire*], and the Scarf (to ward off) Various Things.

The Ancestress of the Heavenly Deities commanded, saying: "If there should be any pain anywhere, take these ten treasures, and while saying: 'One, two, three, four, five, six, seven, eight, nine, ten,' wave them, wave them in a leisurely manner. If this is done, the dead will return to life." This is the origin of the word *furu*, "to wave."[43]

Philippi rightly notes that "This is no doubt a description of an actual ceremony connected with the *Chinkon-sai* (Spirit-pacification Festival), in which articles of the emperor's clothing are known to have been waved or shaken."[44] Thus, Suseri-bime is transferring to her brother articles of the imperial regalia that have the power to bring the deceased back to life but also to *transfer the imperial charisma* or *tama*. The significance of this point cannot be emphasized too much, though it must be viewed with other attending details. For example, the third time Susano-o tries to kill O-kuni-nushi, he sends him into a grassy plain to return a special arrow but then sets the plain on fire. As we have seen, an ordeal by fire is frequently a test of the legitimacy of would-be imperial heirs. Here O-kuni-nushi survives the fire by seek-ing refuge in an underground hole. If we assume that the narrative pattern of the rightful heir surviving such an ordeal by fire was well known in early Japan, then the audience would have understood the encoded meaning in this myth.[45]

In the *Kojiki* version of the myth, O-kuni-nushi is thought to be dead after Su-sano-o sets the plain on fire, so Suseri-bime carries funeral goods (*hafuritsu mono*) out onto the plain. Once again the third time is a charm for O-kuni-nushi, because after he is invited back to Susano-o's palace, he and Suseri-bime escape the underworld for good by tricking Susano-o. As they leave, O-kuni-nushi takes Susano-o's sword of life (*iku tachi*) and bow-and-arrow of life (*iku yumi-ya*). The first two of these powerful magical objects recall the Jewel of Life and the Jewel of Resuscitation mentioned in the *Kujiki* passage above. Like Izanagi before him, O-kuni-nushi rolls a large boulder in front of the entrance to the underworld to keep the dangerous other (here Susano-o) from emerging. At the Yomotsuhira-saka, the pass separating the land of Yomi from the land of the living, Susano-o finally, if perhaps reluctantly, gives O-kuni-nushi the promised counsel, telling him:

Using the sword of life and the bow-and-arrow of life which you are holding, pursue and subdue your half-brothers on the side of the hill; and pursue and sweep them down at the rapids of the river. Then becoming O-kuni-nushi-no-kami, and becoming Utsushi-kuni-tama-no-kami [i.e., ruler of the land], make my daughter Suseri-bime your chief wife. Dwell at the foot of Mount Uka, root the posts of your palace firmly in the bedrock below, and raise high the crossbeams unto Takama no Hara itself, you scoundrel![46]

O-kuni-nushi emerges from these dangerous situations with his (half-)sister as his spouse and with the power and mandate to defeat all the other contenders in estab-lishing his rule on earth. Only with his sister's assistance is he finally able to take up the creation of the land left incomplete at the time of the death of Izanami.

On the basis of the myths we have looked at, we may tentatively conclude that through "incestuous" relations certain women had the ability to transfer power to a male relative. A few details passed over earlier in the Ame-no-waka-hiko myth add further support to this conclusion. First, it is important to note the relationships of the main figures in this myth. In the *Kojiki* we find the following line: "Then Ame-no-waka-hiko descended to the land and soon took as wife the daughter of O-kuni-nushi-no-kami, Shitateru-hime [and] . . . plotted to gain the land (for him-self)."[47] Shitateru-hime is the younger sister of Aji-shiki-taka-hikone, the *kami* mis-taken for the deceased at the temporary burial palace. In the *Kojiki* version it is the parents of Ame-no-waka-hiko who mistake him for their son, whereas in another *Nihonshoki* version it is Ame-no-waka-hiko's wife (i.e., Shitateru-hime) and children who cling to him saying, "Our Lord is still alive."[48]

Is it possible that the brother enters the temporary enshrinement palace here *in order to appropriate* the position of his deceased brother-in-law and perhaps his wife/ sister as well? To be sure, the extant versions seem to suggest the opposite, and yet the myth seems somehow truncated as Aji-shiki-taka-hikone and his sister disappear from the narrative too quickly. In destroying the interment palace, perhaps the brother was seeking to end the funeral rituals so that he might take up the reins of power. This must remain no more than a hypothesis, but it is a suggestive one.

By following the tale of Prince Anahobe carefully and at length, we have been able to learn much of importance about the liminal period of the temporary enshrinement of a sovereign. Other relevant records from the *Nihonshoki* are pertinent to our effort to reconstruct the *mogari no miya* ritual complex and to understand better the socio-political situation in such times. The following, for example, is the last entry in the Sushun Chapter and involves the individual who, on the orders of Soga no Umako, had slain the Emperor Sushun on 11/3/592.

This month, Koma, Yamato no Aya no Atahi, had a clandestine amour [*nusumite*] with the Soga Imperial concubine Kawakami no Iratsume, and made her his wife. (Kawakami no Iratsume was the daughter of Soga no Umako no Sukune.) Soga no Sukune did not find out immediately that Kawakami no Iratsume had been clandestinely possessed by Koma, and supposed that she was dead. When Koma's unclean relation [*kegaseru koto*] with the Imperial concubine became known he was killed by the Ōmi.[49]

Koma's relationship with the concubine of the recently assassinated emperor was probably a symbolic political maneuver through which Koma hoped to gain more power. Soga no Umako may have been under the impression that his daughter had committed suicide following Sushun's death. The surviving sexual partners of the emperor would have been secluded in the *mogari no miya*, but Sushun was buried immediately, probably to forestall any possible attempts by his supporters to regain control during the liminal period of the *mogari no miya*.

The Suiko Chapter, which follows that covering the reign of Sushun, includes one of the few entries concerning final burial that contains any detail. It reads:

[612] 2nd month, 20th day. The body of the former Empress-consort Kitashi-hime was removed and re-interred in the Great Misagi of Hinokuma. On this day funeral orations were pronounced on the Karu highway. First of all, Tori, Ahe no Uchi no Omi, pronounced an eulogistic decree of the Empress, and made offerings to the spirit of the deceased [*sumera-mikoto no ōmikoto o shinobi-koto tatematsuru. sunawachi mitama ni mono muku*] of such things as sacred utensils [*mikemono*] and sacred garments [*mikeshi*], fifteen thousand kinds in all.

Secondly, the Imperial Princes, each in the order of their rank, pronounced funeral orations. Thirdly, Omaro, Nakatomi no Miyadokoro no Muraji, pronounced the eulogistic address of the Ōmi. Fourthly, the Ōmi, at the head of the Omi of the eight [i.e., "many" or "all"] families, caused Marise, Sakaibe no Omi, to read the written eulogiums of the nobility [*uji kabane no moto o shinobikoto mosashimu*]. The people of that time said that Marise and Omaro delivered their eulogiums well, but that Tori no Omi delivered his badly.[50]

As the final line makes clear, the public recitals of eulogies and so forth were subject to critical evaluation by the audience composed of other nobles and courtiers. Negative criticism could damage an individual's prestige in the court. This specific occasion, however, seems to have been much less politically charged than the rituals surrounding the *mogari no miya* of a sovereign or crown prince, since the succession was not immediately involved. Once again we can also see that the rank of the participants determined the order of their oral presentations in the ritual, with those of highest rank going first. This entry suggests that at this time at least some of the eulogies were apparently written. This observation is significant because it clearly indicates that by the early seventh century the court was already in a secondary or residually oral stage. Many people no doubt still maintained the ability to create and perform such pieces orally, but others were already relying on written texts from which they read. This development may have been spurred by the greatly increased practice of sutra recitation in the imperial palace and throughout the capital.

The records of the temporary enshrinement and final burial of the Empress Suiko (d. 3/7/628) are quite brief and provide no new information for our purposes. The heir apparent, Prince Shōtoku, however, had died earlier on 2/5/621, and in the interim no one had been named to this position. Consequently, the situation following Suiko's death was quite unsettled.[51] There was great controversy over what the last words of Suiko had been, with conflicting claims put forward as some individuals asserted that she had appointed Prince Tamura as her successor, whereas others maintained it had been Prince Yamashiro no Ōe. The Soga clan was itself divided over the issue, with Emishi supporting the candidacy of Prince Tamura and Sakaibe no Marise no Omi supporting Prince Yamashiro no Ōe.

When all the members of the extended Soga clan were gathered at the site of the tomb being constructed for Soga no Umako, Marise is reported to have knocked down the sheds surrounding the tomb. He then retired to the Soga homestead and refused to perform any official duties.[52] This behavior is strangely reminiscent of the act of Aji-shiki-hiko-ne-no-kami in the myth of the death of Ame-no-waka-hiko where he kicked down the *mogari no miya*. The precise import of Marise's actions is unclear, but they appear to have been directed against his elder brother, Emishi. In his refusal to perform official duties, Marise's protest also recalls Susano-o's refusal to take up his duties following Izanami's death. Thus, once again one finds a "historical" record sharing a series of details with those found in myths. This seems to have been an important historiographic method used in the court.

The opening sections of the Jomei Chapter devote extensive space to the political intrigues that followed the Empress Suiko's death but virtually none either to the *mogari no miya* rituals or to final burial other than to note the dates on which these events occurred. A bit more information is available concerning the rituals for Jomei. The Kōgyoku Chapter contains a brief reference to the final burial of the Emperor Jomei on 12/21/642.[53] Ministers and nobles pronounced eulogies at the tomb for the various imperial princes and for all the Omi. This type of surrogate oral presentation was quite common, with nobles and other ritual functionaries, such as the *asobibe*, who also recited eulogies and poems of praise, serving as representatives for other parties. These professional poets, singers, and reciters also created pieces for the princes and princesses to present themselves. The prose headnote to MYS 2: 194, a *banka*, may refer to this practice: "Poem presented by Kakinomoto Hitomaro to Princess Hatsusebe and Prince Osakabe" (*Kakinomoto Asomi no Hitomaro, Hatsusebe no himemiko Osakabe no miko ni tatematsuru uta isshu*).[54]

The next chapter in the *Nihonshoki*, covering the reign of the Emperor Kōtoku (r. 645–654), is of note because for the first time we find the court promulgating extensive legislation to regulate and control burial practices, including the size of tombs permitted individuals of various ranks, the number of forced laborers and length of time that could be employed in constructing the tombs, and so on.[55] Paradoxically, the prohibition of certain practices reported in this chapter is our best evidence of the existence and/or persistence of these practices in early Japan. We learn, for example, that in an earlier time pearls or jewels were placed in the mouths of the dead and jewel-shirts and jade armour were buried with the corpse. Then, too, there is the following notice:

When a man dies, there have been cases of people sacrificing themselves by strangulation, or of strangling others by way of sacrifice, or of compelling the dead man's horse to be sacrificed, or of burying valuables in the grave in honour of the dead, or of cutting off the hair, and stabbing the thighs and pronouncing an eulogy on the dead (while in this condition). Let all such old customs be entirely discontinued.[56]

The most important notice to be found in the regulations promulgated in Kōtoku's reign, however, is the following: "The construction of palaces of temporary interment is not allowed in any case, from Princes down to common people" (*ōyoso ōkimi yori shimotsukata, ōmitakara ni itaru made ni, mogariya tsukuru koto ezaru*).[57] Had this regulation been effectively and uniformly enforced immediately after its proclamation, the *mogari no miya* and the ritual complex surrounding it would have virtually disappeared after 646. Because of the tenacity of the people's attachment to the traditional practices and/or the lack of sufficient power on the part of the court to enforce this regulation, however, *mogari no miya* continued to be built for princes and princesses, as well as for emperors and empresses, until the early eighth century.

The desire on the part of the Emperor Kōtoku to control burial practices down to the minutest detail marks a heightened recognition in the court of the political dimensions of such funeral practices. Part of the intention behind the regulations Kōtoku sought to institute was to delineate clearly hierarchical distinctions in the life of the court.[58] The edicts were also an attempt by Kōtoku to assert his own power and position by circumscribing the privileges of even the Soga, the most powerful clan in the court. One entry seems to criticize Soga no Emishi precisely for the size of the tomb he had built for himself and his arrogance in commandeering a large force of corvée labor to build it.[59]

The politics of regulating funerary rituals has not received the full attention the topic deserves, although a few scholars have begun to explore it in other cultures and historical periods.[60] The control of death rituals is an important expression of centralized political power, so it is not surprising to see the early Japanese court moving in this direction. Death, though, was only one area over which the court tried to exercise control. The reign of Kōtoku shows an unprecedented concern to regulate every aspect of life in the court—titles, dress, housing, etiquette—through constant tinkering with the system of rank and prestige. The emperor, however, was enmeshed in a complex web of socio-political relations that constrained his power and the ability to dictate change. When Ahe no Ōmi died, for instance, the emperor himself, along with the empress, the crown prince, and all the princes and ministers, mourned the deceased at the South Gate.[61]

The next reference to the death of a sovereign is that for the Empress Saimei on 7/24/661. It is a somewhat unusual case in that the empress died in the Asakura Palace and the corpse was later carried back to Asuka. Though she died in the seventh lunar month, temporary interment did not take place until 11/7, some three-and-a-half months later. The first year of the reign of the Emperor Tenji is given as 1/1/662, even though he formally acceded to the throne only much later on 1/1/668 (another unnamed document alluded to in the *Nihonshoki* gave the date as 3/667). Since Saimei was given final burial on 2/27/667, either of these dates would follow the general pattern of final burial of the deceased sovereign preceding the successor's formal ritual accession. The *Nihonshoki* suggests quite clearly, however, that the crown prince (i.e., Tenji) was in control during the period of the *mogari no miya*. A sentence in the opening passage of the Tenji Chapter reads: "The Prince Imperial, clad in white garments, discharged the functions of government" (*hitsugi no mikoto, asamono misotate matsurite matsurigoto kikishimesu*).[62] The "white garments" here are mourning clothes. Aston asked in a note whether *matsurigoto kiko-shimesu* may not mean "announced the mourning for the Empress" rather than "attended to the government." In fact, these two readings or interpretations are not mutually exclusive, for to lead the mourning rituals was to lead the government. In these rituals the crown prince publicly presented himself as occupying the highest rank in the court hierarchy and as in control of his emotions and the ritual proceedings and thus, implicitly, the political situation. (Contemporary Soviet specialists and Sinologists similarly attach the greatest significance to the respective roles potential successors and other powerful figures occupy in the public funeral and memorial services for members of the ruling elite.) Interestingly enough, the Saimei record also contains a poem of longing for the deceased empress attributed to the Prince Imperial (Tenji). The relevant passage reads:

[661] Winter, 10th month, 7th day. The Empress' funeral train returning, put to sea. Hereupon the Prince Imperial, having come to an anchor [somewhere], was filled with grief and longing for the Empress. So he sang to himself, saying:—

kimi ga me no	Because of my yearning
kōshiki kara ni	To see your form,
hatete ite	Must I remain anchored here
kakuya koimu mo	And yearn thus—
kimi ga me o hori	Wishing to see your form?[63]

If this poem comes out of a *tama-furi* or *chinkon*-like ritual context—something that must remain only a hypothesis—and if the poem was part of an attempt to both pacify and recall the spirit of the empress, then the passage takes on additional significance.

Tenji only acceded after a period of five-and-a-half or six-and-a-half years from the temporary enshrinement of the Empress Saimei. We have already seen that a period of more than eighteen months usually signaled an uneasy succession. The lapse of time between Saimei's death and Tenji's accession ceremony might also be explained by pressing developments on the Korean peninsula that immediately affected Japan and occupied the attention of the court.[64] But even then, one must assume that Japan and her allies would have found it to their advantage to have had a formally installed emperor.

The Tenji Chapter has relatively little to say about Tenji's own death and the *mogari no miya* rituals. It does report, though, that after he fell gravely ill, an eye-opening or consecration ceremony for one hundred Buddhist statues was held in the imperial palace and special offerings were made to Hōkō-ji. Tenji supposedly offered the reins of government to the prince imperial, later the Emperor Temmu, but he refused them, saying he intended to take the tonsure and retire to the Yoshino mountains to pray for Tenji's recovery. In the next chapter, we will find that the *Man'yōshū* preserves important information not found elsewhere concerning the period of Tenji's *mogari no miya*. Before turning to that text, however, let us look at the final sovereign whose death is recorded in the *Nihonshoki*, namely, Temmu.

The Death of the Emperor Temmu and His Mogari no Miya

After the death of Tenji, his brother briefly succeeded him. The *Nihonshoki*, however, does not recognize the latter's reign as legitimate, so there is no Kōbun Chapter. Instead one finds a Temmu Chapter One (*jō*), covering the Kōbun period, and a Temmu Chapter Two (*kami*) on Temmu's reign proper. The second Temmu chapter and that covering the following reign of the Empress Jitō contain the largest number of entries recording ritual events surrounding the *mogari no miya*. Unfortunately, the *Kojiki* does not continue its coverage up to this period, nor does the *Man'yōshū* preserve many ritual poems from Temmu's *mogari no miya*. Nevertheless, because this prose record is especially full and in many ways more reliable as a historical document than others we have seen, it provides another glimpse into the politics of death in early Japan. If we are to believe the *Nihonshoki*—and I see no reason to doubt it on this score—Temmu's health began to fail in 685. The following entries in the Temmu Chapter either explicitly or probably concern the emperor's health: [685]—9/24, 10/24, 11/6; [686]—5/24, 6/10, 6/16, 6/19, 6/22, 7/28, 8/1, 8/2, 8/9, 8/13, 9/4, 9/9. This large number of entries indicates the critical importance attached to the emperor's health and the threat his deteriorating condition posed. Although we cannot look at every one of these notices, several deserve our attention. The initial report (9/24/685) of Temmu's illness says:

On account of the Emperor being unwell, Buddhist scriptures were read for three days in the Great Temple of the Great Palace, and in the Temples of Kawara and Asuka. Rice was accordingly given to these temples, in amounts varying in each case.[65]

Here we can see the emperor having recourse to Buddhist rituals to effect a cure. Subsequent notices report that a Korean Buddhist priest and a layman (*upasaka*) were dispatched to the Mino district to prepare an infusion of *okera* (*atractylis ovata*), a medicinal herb, for the emperor, and that they returned with it the following month. This detail recalls the story of the Emperor Suinin's illness and how he sent Tajima Mori to Tokoyo, the supernatural realm, to bring back the *tachibana* or the fruit of a tree bearing out of season to restore his health. Suinin reportedly died just before Tajima Mori returned.[66]

The next entry, dated 10/24/685, after reporting that the infusion of *okera* had been delivered, says: "On this day the ceremony of 'calling on the spirit' [*mitama-furi shiki*] was performed for the Emperor's sake."[67] The mythological origin of this ritual is found in the narrative of Ninigi's descent from Takama no Hara, the High

Heavens, to the lower earthly world recorded in the *Kujiki* (c. 620). According to the *Kujiki*, before sending Ninigi off on his divine mission, Amaterasu presented him with ten sacred articles, including the well-known three imperial regalia, and said: "In case of ailment, say to these ten treasures, '*Hi, fu, mi, yo, itsu, mu, nana, ya, kokono, tari*,' and shake them *yura-yura*. If thou doest so, the dead will come to life again."[68] According to Ban Nobutomo, the character for "ten," normally read "*to*" or "*ju*," is here read "*tari*" as a homonym for the verb *taru* or *tari*, "to be sufficient, full."[69] By repeating this counting from one to ten ten times (10 × 10 = 100), it was believed that one could "fill" the emperor's life and thus extend it. This *mitama-furi* ritual is related to the more general *tama-furi* and *tama-musubi* ritual complex, where the symbolism of "tying" or "knotting" (*musubi*) the life-cord is central.[70]

Although the *Nihonshoki* does not refer to the *mitama-furi* ritual in connection with the descent of Ninigi, there is some hint of it in the section covering the reign of the first human emperor, Jimmu. Significantly, the ritual was first performed on the same day Jimmu assumed the imperial dignity, thus indicating a close connection with the ritual accession complex. The relevant entry reads:

On the day on which he first began the Heavenly institution, Michi no Omi no Mikoto, the ancestor of the Ōtomo House, accompanied by the Ōkume Be, was enabled, by means of a secret device received from the Emperor, to use incantations and magic formulae so as to dissipate evil influences [*yoku soe-uta sakashima-goto o mote, wazawai o harai torakaseri*]. The use of magic formulae had its origin from this.[71]

This passage seems to refer to esoteric verbal formulas that would have a public or exoteric meaning but also a hidden meaning and intention. These magical formulas are specifically referred to as *uta*, further indicating the intimate relation between song/poetry and magico-religious practices in early Japan.

Similarly, as Japanese scholars have long pointed out, the name of the Mononobe clan seems to be related to early Japanese religious beliefs and ritual practices. The term "*mono*" is usually written with a character that originally referred to suprahuman or strange things, taboo objects, malevolent spirits, and so on. The Mono-no-be, literally the "guild of *mono*," then was probably a guild of specialists of the sacred whose ritual duties involved pacifying and controlling *mono*. There is quite a bit of evidence to suggest that by 685, the date of the entries cited above concerning Temmu's illness, the *mitama-furi* ritual had become regularized as part of the *chinkon-sai* or pacification ceremony, which immediately preceded the celebration of the *niiname-sai*.

As the agricultural ritual and symbolic complex based on the rice culture introduced in the Yayoi period became conflated with the emerging imperial cult with its solar symbolism, the sovereign took over many of the ritual functions, privileges, and powers related to fertility. As these ritual functions came to be centered on the person of the sovereign, his or her health was identified with the sun, especially in terms of the waning length of the day and the strength of the rays of the sun in autumn. Thus, it is not surprising to learn that the *mitama-furi* ritual was not only a ritual of affliction, to borrow Victor Turner's phrase, but also an annual ritual celebrated on or around the winter solstice. In the latter case, the intention behind its annual performance was to recall and capture the imperial *tama*, as found in the mythic paradigm of Amaterasu and her retreat into the rock-grotto. This ritual would ensure not only the health of the sovereign but the well-being and fertility of the entire country. To be sure, the *mitama-furi* rituals could be pressed into service in times of crisis and exceptional need when the sovereign fell ill, but in the annual ritual calendar the performance of this ritual functioned as a demonstration of the cosmic power of the sacred sovereign.

To return, however, to Temmu's illness, by 686 Temmu's deteriorating physical health was more than a ritual condition; it was a painful physical reality that must have thrown the court into disarray. The *Nihonshoki* entry for 5/24 says, "The Emperor's body was ill at ease. Accordingly the 'Sutra of Yakushi' was expounded in the Temple of Kawara, and a 'retreat' was held within the Palace [*miya no uchi ni ango seshimu*]."[72] Yakushi is the Healing Buddha and was one of the most popular buddhas in early Japan.[73] The task of diagnosing the cause of the emperor's illness fell to a diviner:

[6th month] 10th day. It was ascertained by divination that the Emperor's disease was owing to a curse from the Kusa-nagi sword. The same day it was sent to the shrine of Atsuta, in Owari, and deposited there.[74]

The Kusanagi sword plays an important role in the mythology of Susano-o, Ninigi, and Yamato-takeru as one of the imperial regalia. Here Temmu has the Kusanagi sword returned to the Atsuta Jingu in Owari (in present-day Nagoya). This is the homeland of Miyazu-hime, a consort of Yamato-takeru. In the myth Yamato-takeru is given the seemingly impossible task of single-handedly subduing and pacifying all the unruly *kami* and peoples of the East. After receiving the Kusanagi sword from his aunt, the chief priestess of the Ise Shrine, Yamato-takeru visits Miyazu-hime and promises to marry her on his return. When he does return, however, he finds her polluted by menstrual blood. Nevertheless, they are conjugally united. As he departs to subdue the *kami* of Mount Ibuki, he leaves the Kusanagi sword with Miyazu-hime. Yamato-takeru is then fatally injured by the *kami* of Mount Ibuki disguised as a white boar. We can only guess at what the phrase "a curse from the Kusanagi sword" in the divination reported above implied, but it may well be that Temmu, too, was judged guilty of having broken a sexual taboo. At any rate, he felt it advisable to return the Kusanagi sword to that area. This detail demonstrates how seriously myth was taken as history in early Japan.

The chronicle of Temmu's illness also suggests that he repeatedly turned to Buddhist rituals to effect a cure. The following entry is characteristic:

[6th month] 16th day. Prince Ise and a number of officials were sent to the Temple of Asuka, to communicate to the priests the Emperor's commands, as follows:—"Of late Our body is ill at ease, and We request that the dread power of the Three Precious Things may be invoked, in order to obtain repose for Our person. Let the Sōjō, the Sōzu, and the general body of priests therefore put up prayers." Offerings of rare and valuable things were accordingly made to the Three Precious Things. On this day the three higher ecclesiastics, with the Risshi and the abbots of the four temples, the directors, and the priests of professorial rank then in residence, received each alms of one suit of Imperial garments and one Imperial coverlet.[75]

It is clear that when he so desired, the emperor could command a powerful group of religious functionaries to act on his behalf. Among the articles presented as offerings to the various temples were imperial robes and coverlets (ōmi-fusuma), items that would have been used in mitama-furi rituals to restore the emperor's health. The remaining entries in the Temmu Chapter largely consist of reports of various Buddhist rituals and practices performed for him. These entries appear in rapid succession in the text, perhaps indicating the rising sense of urgency spawned by the emperor's health. The era name of Temmu's reign was retrospectively changed to Shuchō or Akamitori in the middle of 686, an action usually taken in times of crisis when there was a strongly felt need to make a new beginning. Following the entry for 6/16/686 one finds the following entries, all concerning Temmu's health:

6/19   offerings were made at the Kawara Temple and public officials lit expiatory lanterns there, and a great vegetarian feast was sponsored by the court and rites of repentance were held

7/2   Buddhist functionaries were called into the palace to perform penitential rites

7/3   the emperor ordered the Ōharai or Great Purification Ceremony to be performed in all the provinces

7/4   half of all taxes in the empire were remitted and forced labor was canceled

7/5   offerings were made to kuni-gakari no kami, the four shrines of Asuka, and to the deity of Sumiyoshi

7/8   100 Buddhist priests were called into the palace to read the Konkōmyokyō (Suvarna-prabhasa Sutra)

7/22   the era name was changed to Shuchō

7/28   70 persons were selected to take the tonsure and a vegetarian feast was held
      in front of Temmu's residence; various imperial princes and ministers had
      images of Kannon made for Temmu's sake; sutras were read in the palace

8/1   80 individuals took the tonsure for the sake of the emperor

8/2   100 men and women took the tonsure; 100 statues of Kannon were installed
      in the palace and the Kannon Sutra was read

8/9   prayers were offered to the *kami* of Heaven and Earth

8/13   offerings were made to the *ōkami* of Tosa; 400 houses were added to the fiefs
      of the Crown Prince Kusakabe and the Imperial Princes Ōtsu and Take-
      chi, and 100 houses were granted to two other princes

8/15   two imperial princes were granted 200 houses each, and the Temples of
      Hinokuma, Karu, and Ōkubo 100 houses for a period of 30 years

8/23   200 houses were granted to the Temple of Kose.

In an effort to regain his health, Temmu also distributed economic largess to various princes and temples. This action was a critical means by which Temmu could indicate the relative status and prestige each of the princes held in his eyes, something that would be crucial when the succession came to be determined. The grants to various temples held a similar importance, for each temple was identified with its main patron from among the nobility. The final entries from the Temmu Chapter illuminate certain additional aspects of the *mogari no miya* rituals. The first entry of import is from about ten days later:

9th month, 4th day. All, from the Princes of the Blood down to the Ministers, assembled in the Temple of Kawara, and put up vows for the Emperor's illness, etc., etc.

9th day. The Emperor's disease having shown no sign of abatement, he died in the principal Palace.

11th day. Lament was begun for him [*hajimete minetate matsuru*], and a temporary burial Palace erected in the South Court.

24th day. The Emperor was temporarily interred in the South Court and mourning began. At this time the Imperial Prince Ōtsu conspired against the Prince Imperial [Kusakabe].

27th day. At dawn, all the priests and nuns having made lament in the Court of Temporary Interment, retired. On this day, for the first time, offerings were made at the tomb and eulogies pronounced [*mike tatematsurete tsunawachi shinobikoto tatematsuru*]. First of all, Arakama, Ōshiama no Sukune, pronounced a eulogy regarding the Imperial Princes; next, Prince Ise, of Jō-dai-shi rank, pronounced a eulogy regarding the other Princes; next, Ōtomo, Agata no Inukai no Sukune, of Jiki-dai-samu rank, pronounced a eulogy regarding the officials of the Household generally; next, Prince Kawachi, of Jō-kwo-shi rank, pronounced a eulogy regarding the Ōtoneri of the right and the left; next, Kunimi, Tagima no Mahito, of Jiki-dai-samu rank, pronounced a eulogy regarding the Guards of the right and left; next, Tsukura, Uneme no Asomi, of Jiki-dai-shi rank, pronounced a eulogy regarding the lady officials of the Palace; and next, Mahito, Ki no Asomi, of Jiki-kwo-shi rank, pronounced a eulogy regarding the Stewards of the Palace.

28th day. All the priests and nuns again made lament in the Court of Temporary Interment [*mogari no miya*]. On this day, Minushi, Fuse no Asomi, of Jiki-dai-samu rank, pronounced a eulogy regarding the Council of State; next, Maro, Isonokami no Asomi, of Jiki-kwo-samu rank, pronounced a eulogy regarding the judicial officers; next, Takechimaro, Ōmiwa no Asomi, of Jiki-dai-shi rank, pronounced a eulogy regarding the administrative officials; next, Yasumaro, Ōtomo no Sukune, of Jiki-kwo-samu rank, pronounced a eulogy regarding the Treasury; and next, Ōshima, Fujiwara no Asomi, of Jiki-dai-shi rank, pronounced a eulogy regarding the war officials.

29th day. The priests and nuns again raised lament. On this day, Maro, Ahe no Kuno no Asomi, of Jiki-kwo-shi rank, pronounced a eulogy regarding the Board of Punishments; next, Yumihari, Ki no Asomi, of Jiki-kwo-shi rank, pronounced a eulogy regarding the Department of the Interior; next, Mushimaro, Hozumi no Asomi, of Jiki-kwo-shi rank, pronounced a eulogy regarding the Governors of Provinces; next, the Ōsumi, Ata no Hayahito, and the Umakai-be no Miyatsuko of Yamato and Kawachi each pronounced eulogies.

30th day. The priests and nuns made lament. On this day, the Paeche prince Ryōgu pronounced a eulogium on behalf of his father, Prince Zenkwo. Next, the Miyatsuko of the various provinces, as they came, each pronounced his eulogy. There were also performances of all manner of singing and dancing [*kusagusa no uta-mai o tsukae matsuru*].[76]

Once again the entire ritual sequence unfolded with the public pronouncements made in rank order. The amount of detail provided here allows one to appreciate how the hierarchical socio-political order was displayed throughout the *mogari no miya* rituals. In one sense the occasion allowed the court society to represent itself to itself. As events in the recent past and the interdependencies of the various courtiers with the deceased sovereign were publicly recalled in the eulogies, the court both retrospectively ordered the past and created possibilities for the future. In this process factional differences frequently surfaced. Eulogizing the deceased, then, was not only a backward-looking act but yet another form of expressing—and ideally realizing—one's personal and clan aspirations for the future.

The extent to which Temmu had recourse to Buddhist rituals and texts demonstrates that Buddhism played a central part in the daily life of the court in the late seventh century, though the cults of the *kami* were certainly not ignored. We must begin to take seriously the fact that Buddhism and the cults of the *kami* were already interrelated by the seventh century and probably from earlier than that. Large numbers of Buddhist priests and nuns were involved in rituals to restore the emperor's health and then, following his death, in the rituals of the *mogari no miya*. The *Nihonshoki* reports that Buddhist priests and nuns offered laments at the *mogari no miya* daily from the twenty-seventh through the thirtieth (i.e., every day for which there is an entry), where we may assume *mitama-furi* rituals were also being performed.

Many of the poems preserved in the *Shoki-Man'yōshū* come out of the period of the temporary enshrinement of members of the imperial family. In light of the conspicuous presence of Buddhist priests and nuns in the ritual locus of the *mogari no miya*, one must question the traditional assumption that the poetry of the *Man'yōshū* is "pre-Buddhist" or the expression of a "pure" indigenous worldview. Watase Masatada is one of the few Japanese scholars to have raised this question seriously. He argues persuasively, I think, that no individual in the capital in the late seventh century could have remained completely immune to Buddhist influence or ignorant of Buddhist beliefs and practices. More specifically, Watase argues that Hitomaro's poetry was affected by the heavy presence of Buddhism in the court and by its ritual expressions. Indeed, he goes so far as to suggest that some of Hitomaro's poetry may have been performed in a Buddhist ritual context.[77] If Watase is correct, the *mogari no miya* rituals—while they lasted—were a unique blend of elements from the cults of the *kami* and Buddhism.

Additional records of rituals related to the death of the Emperor Temmu are found in the Jitō Chapter. The following entries all directly concern public rituals at the *mogari no miya* or other related events: [686]—12/19, 12/26; [687]—1/1, 1/5, 1/19, 1/20, 5/22, 8/5, 8/6, 8/28, 9/9, 9/10, 10/22; and [688]—1/1, 1/2, 1/8, 1/23, 1/16, 3/22, 8/10, 8/11, 11/4, 11/5, 11/11.

Only those entries that explicitly refer to events related to the death and funeral rituals of Temmu have been listed here. Many others no doubt are also related, including the reports of imperial amnesties, tax abatements, imperial gifts to various individuals and religious institutions, imperial acts of charity, and so on, most of which were probably intended to accrue merit for the deceased sovereign as well as support for Jitō. The sheer number of such entries—and it should be remembered that the *Nihonshoki* is not a daily chronicle—indicates that the *mogari no miya* rituals occupied a major part of the attention, time, and effort of the court for almost two years following Temmu's death. By studying these entries we discern still other significant points.

The monthly anniversary of Temmu's death was observed as a national day of mourning. An imperial decree reported for 2/16/688 suggests that a fast was also to be observed on this day.[78] The entry for 1/1/687 indicates that the New Year following Temmu's death began with the Prince Imperial Kusakabe leading a procession to the *mogari no miya* where ritual mourning was held and eulogies were offered, again in rank order. We find there for the first time mention of commoners actively participating in the rituals. These rituals were repeated on the fifth day and possibly daily in the intervening days.[79] It is significant that the Crown Prince Kusakabe is explicitly said to have led the mourning, since this indicates that he was in line to succeed his father.

The entry for 3/20/687 is of special interest. It reads: "An ornamental chaplet [*hanakazura*] was offered at the Palace of temporary interment. This was called Mikage."[80] "*Mikage*" is accurately glossed by Aston as "august shade." Scholars have long pointed to MYS 2: 149, attributed to the empress following the death of the Emperor Tenji, as a poem coming out of an identical ritual locus. It reads:

sumeramikoto kamuagari-mashishi nochi, Yamato no ōkisaki no tsukuri-mashishi mi-uta isshu	Poem by the Yamato Express after the death of the Sovereign
hito wa yoshi	People say, "Enough,
omoi yamu to mo	stop thinking of him,"
tamakazura	yet I cannot forget
kage ni mietsutsu	while I see [your] image
wasuraenu kamo	in the wreath of jewels.[81]

The *tamakazura* or "jeweled wreath" here serves as a *katami*, an object that is used both to recall the deceased to mind for the living and, more important, as a repository for the deceased's *tama*. It is intriguing to note that the mourning empress is urged by others to stop grieving for her deceased husband, to "let go" and get on with her life. The identity of these persons is unclear, but two possibilities come to mind: they may have been female companions of the empress, or individuals who wished to see the *mogari no miya* rituals brought to a conclusion so that a successor could be formally installed. At the same time, these possibilities are not mutually exclusive; that is, some of the empress's female companions in the *mogari no miya*, ladies-in-waiting and others, may well have pressed her to act in ways that would benefit their own family interests. More than most, though, this poem skillfully captures in miniature something of the tension, both emotional and political, inherent in the period of temporary interment. Various psychological and socio-political forces pulled a widowed empress in different directions at this time. We have seen how myths as well as records of imperial reigns suggest that extended grieving that does not come to a timely conclusion can be dangerous for everyone concerned.

The Jitō Chapter of the *Nihonshoki* is especially important in this inquiry into the liminal period of temporary enshrinement because of the extent and detail of the records therein. It also provides further hints that the widowed empress and the emperor's consorts were largely secluded during this period. In this regard, it is significant that the *Nihonshoki* does not record a single journey by the empress during the more than two years of the *mogari no miya*. In fact, the empress is not explicitly mentioned during this period except in the oblique form of entries to the effect that an imperial decree was issued, various gifts and ritual offerings—including robes of the deceased emperor—were made to certain temples, and so on. At no time does the text ever report that "the empress did so-and-so." This curious detail might be insignificant in itself were it not for the fact that immediately after the final burial of Temmu on 11/11/688, one finds a large number of entries in rapid succession stating that "The Empress gave audience to the ten-thousand lands in the Front Hall" (1/1/689); "The Empress gave orders to the Governor of the province of Izumo" (1/9); "The Empress visited the Palace of Yoshino" (1/18); and so forth.[82] In other words, the empress appears in public only *after* the final burial of Temmu. Thereafter, the empress's location is regularly noted, yet in the more than two years of the *mogari no miya*, the *Nihonshoki* never informs the reader of her whereabouts.

How is this seclusion to be understood and how much significance should be attached to it? Ultimately the answers depend in large measure on whether one adopts a "strong" or a "weak" reading of the evidence. The strong reading would suggest that Jitō was actually secluded in the *mogari no miya* for the entire period of the temporary enshrinement, hence making it unnecessary to state the empress's location because it would have been assumed. The weak reading would acknowledge that the empress did not occupy the public stage during this period, but it would question the implication that she was, then, ritually confined within the *mogari no miya*. In the absence of clear positive evidence that the empress was secluded in the *mogari no miya*, the weak reading is easier to maintain in the face of possible challenges. Nevertheless, during the two-plus years of Temmu's *mogari no miya* (and in striking contrast to the silence concerning the public appearances and activities of the empress), the Crown Prince Kusakabe is repeatedly reported to have led various rituals of mourning. The entries for 1/1, 1/5, and 5/22/687 clearly state that, accompanied by all the ministers and other public functionaries, Prince Kusakabe proceeded to the *mogari no miya* and led the offering of ritual laments. The entry for 10/22/687, for instance, reports that

The Prince Imperial, accompanied by the Ministers and public functionaries, as well as by the Governors of provinces, and the Kuni no Miyatsuko, together with common people, both men and women, began the construction of the Ōuchi Misasagi.[83]

This entry says quite explicitly, as if it were worthy of note, that both men and women followed in the train of the prince. Yet although female mourners were found among the commoners, there is no mention of any of the princesses or other female members of the court.

In the following year (688), the entries for 1/1 and 11/4 also explicitly report Kusakabe's publicly leading the *mogari no miya* rituals, but during this period the empress and other princes merit specific mention only twice. The first comes in an enigmatic entry (8/26/687) that reports that the empress sent robes made from the emperor's garments to Buddhist priests at the Asuka Temple. Unfortunately there is no indication whether this command was issued from within the *mogari no miya* or from the imperial palace. The second exception is found in the entry for 8/11/688, which reads: "Prince Ise, of Jo-dai-shi rank, was commanded to announce the state to be observed at the funeral."[84] Even here, though, it is clear that Prince Ise was commanded to perform this public act; he was not in command. We learn, however, that the details of the final burial were finalized and announced exactly one month prior to the ceremony.

Considering the above information, it is still impossible to make any definite statement about whether the widowed empress was actually in ritual seclusion for this entire period or not. On the other hand, it is very clear that Jitō was firmly in charge of the political situation, whether from the interior of the *mogari no miya* or simply out of public view. The repeated references to Prince Kusakabe also indicate that it was Jitō's firm intention that he should succeed Temmu. Within days of Temmu's death, she swiftly and ruthlessly arrested and executed Kusakabe's major challenger, his half-brother Prince Ōtsu. In spite of her plans, however, Crown Prince Kusakabe died suddenly on 4/8/689, shortly before he was to go through the formal imperial accession ceremony.

Lengthy ritual seclusions following death are found in many other cultures, but there is no incontrovertible evidence that the widowed empress was so secluded in early Japan. It seems likely, though, that at a minimum the widowed empress occupied the *mogari no miya* daily. The ritual necessity for her presence there would have precluded any trips outside the capital during the period of temporary enshrinement. This practice helps to explain why a number of poems in the *Man'yōshū* attributed to Jitō come out of the *mogari no miya* ritual complex. We will turn to this topic in the next chapter.

Earlier we saw that the Emperor Temmu had recourse to a large number of Buddhist rituals in order to restore his health. The *Nihonshoki* entry for the first anniversary of Temmu's death and that for the following day indicate that Buddhist rituals continued to be performed after his death.

[687] 9th month, 9th day. A national feast of vegetable food was given in the Temples of the capital [*hate no miogami o miyako no teradera ni moku*].

10th day. A maigre [a special Buddhist vegetarian meal] entertainment was given at the Palace of temporary interment [*mogari no miya no ogamisu*].[85]

The brevity of these two entries pointedly illustrates one of the problems encountered in trying to reconstruct precisely what went on in the rituals of the *mogari no miya*. At best, the *Nihonshoki*, the single most important source of information we have for this period, is parsimonious in providing details. Although we learn that

Buddhist rituals were performed, we do not know who was in attendance, who performed them, who sponsored them, and so on.

There are no entries for the second anniversary of Temmu's death. Whereas the *Nihonshoki* is silent, the *Man'yōshū* provides a tantalizing hint of ritual activity in the court on this anniversary years later. The headnote to MYS 2: 162 says: "On the ninth day of the ninth month in the eighth year after the Emperor's death [i.e., 693], a Buddhist feast was held in his memory. That night the following poem came to the Empress in a dream. (This poem is in *An Anthology of Ancient Poems*)."[86] The *Nihonshoki* has no entry for this date, but the entry for the following day, the tenth, says: "On behalf of the Kiyomihara Emperor [i.e., Temmu] a public great-congregation [*mushae*] was held within the inner precincts [of the imperial palace]. All prisoners were released."[87] If the *Man'yōshū* headnote is to be believed, then MYS 2: 162 comes out of a time filled with Buddhist memorial services, sutra readings, other rituals, and a general amnesty offered for the deceased emperor's sake. In her dream the empress may have recalled this poem from one of these ritual occasions. On the other hand, the reference to the dream may be spurious and the poem one that was commissioned from a professional poet for Jitō. What is significant is that Buddhist rituals continued to be associated with the deceased *after* final burial, and moreover, these rituals were sometimes the generative and/or performative loci of *uta*.

The *Nihonshoki* entry for 8/28/687, a day that fell in the middle of extensive daily rituals leading up to the first anniversary of Temmu's death, merits our attention:

28th day. The Empress sent Ōshima, Fujiwara no Asomi, of Jiki-dai-shi rank, and Ōtomo Kyūmi no Muraji, of Jiki-dai-shi rank, to invite together 300 high priests [*ogoshiki hoshi-tara*] to the Temple of Asuka, and to present to each a priestly robe [*kesa*], saying:—"This was made of the august garments [*ōmiso*] of the Emperor Ama no Nunahara oki no Mahito." The language of the Imperial message was so pathetic that it may not be set forth in full [*mikoto-nori no kotoba karaku itashi. tsubusa ni nobu bekarazu*].[88]

The clothing of the deceased sovereign seems to have had special value or power attached to it. It may well be that, like the entry cited earlier from the period of Temmu's illness, it was believed that these garments were especially efficacious in helping to recall the *tama* of the emperor. It is intriguing that the editors of the *Nihonshoki* found it inappropriate to record the full text of the imperial edict because the language employed was too "pathetic" (*kotoba karaku itashi*, literally "painful and bitter"). Not only does this editorial restraint serve to report the extent to which the widowed empress still grieved for her husband; it is perhaps more effective through indirection than a literal rehearsal of the empress's words. Moreover, in this one case where the empress is reported to have expressly commanded a ritual offering to be made, it is directed outward (the source is again unclear), not to the *mogari no miya* but to a Buddhist temple.

One part of the public rituals held outside the *mogari no miya* was the recitation by ministers and representatives of the various clans of their clan histories, genealogies, and past loyal service to the throne. One week before the final burial of Temmu we find the following entry:

Winter, 11th month, 4th day. The Prince Imperial, accompanied by the Ministers and public functionaries, as well as by the guests from the frontier lands, went to the Palace of temporary interment and made lamentation. On this occasion offerings of food were made, and the *tate-fushi* dance performed. The Ministers each advanced in turn and pronounced a eulogy, setting forth the circumstances of the services rendered by their ancestors.[89]

These eulogies and the public recollection of the loyal service rendered by their respective clans were directed to the audience of the living in attendance as well as to the deceased emperor's spirit. In some ways it was no doubt more important for the nobles to win the recognition of the Crown Prince Kusakabe of their loyalty and past service than it was to pacify the spirit of the deceased through praise. The former, however, could be accomplished in part precisely through the public ritual praise of Temmu.

The *mogari no miya* rituals also provided an occasion for the court to pursue international relations, since emissaries and official delegations were sent to attend these rituals from the various Korean kingdoms, China, and elsewhere. These delegates offered official condolences, sponsored memorial rituals, and conveyed greetings from their own rulers. They were entertained by the court while in Japan and usually carried messages back with them. Occasionally the Court took umbrage at what it considered to be slights in rank and/or number of the members of official delegations sent to the funerary rites. For example, the Empress Jitō is reported to have sent a rather bluntly worded message to the King of Silla after a relatively small and lower ranking delegation arrived in the wake of the death of the Crown Prince Kusakabe.[90] Not incidentally, the public announcement of this imperial rebuke no doubt also served to remind others that Kusakabe was to be considered and treated in death as an emperor, even though he had never formally been installed as such. The public display of anger in the immediate and strongly worded response was most certainly intended as a message to both the Asian continent and the domestic audience that Jitō remained in firm control of the court and, indeed, remained a formidable force to reckon with in spite of her advanced age.

In this chapter we have seen that the death of the sovereign created a liminal socio-political situation that was characterized by danger and uncertainty, but which was simultaneously a time of opportunity, a time for maneuvering for position at all levels of the hierarchical court society. In many ways the ambiguous ontological status of the deceased sovereign between life and death during this period reproduced (or mirrored?) the precarious positions among the living in the court. The actions of these individuals and the intentions behind them during this liminal period were sometimes interpreted through paradigmatic narrative frames. Moreover, ritual poetry, both public and private, played a significant—if heretofore seldom recognized—role in legitimating the new socio-political order. In the next chapter, "The Poetry of the *Mogari no Miya*," some of this poetry will be explored in greater depth in order to understand better the ways in which it participated in the politics of death.

CHAPTER FOUR

The Poetry of the
Mogari No Miya

The *Shoki-Man'yōshū* is an especially important source of the poetry of the *mogari no miya* in preserving examples from a number of different imperial reigns and ritual contexts. Some scholars, including Konishi and Levy, have argued that the extant poems are evidence of a change in the consciousness of the Japanese as they evolved from a primitive stage of culture, characterized by a collective mythic voice, to a lyrical age characterized by individual consciousness and voice freed from the constraints of collective ritual. But as we will see, this position is untenable because it is based on false assumptions and a serious misunderstanding of religious ritual.

The loci of the larger *mogari no miya* ritual complex may be distinguished in a variety of ways—by space, by gender, and as either predominantly public or private in nature. As we will see, poems by women secluded within the *mogari no miya* or the palace are frequently characterized by intimacy of voice and form of address. Those by *toneri* (servingmen) and court women from outside the temporary enshrinement palace, or from the former palace of the deceased, are more public in nature and draw on formal epitaphs for the deceased. We will look first at the poetry from within the *mogari no miya*.

Female Banka *from the* Mogari no Miya

Earlier it was suggested that the interior of the *mogari no miya* was essentially a female preserve, where women who had been sexually intimate with the deceased sovereign were secluded with the corpse for an unspecified period of time. These women participated in *tama-shizume* and *tama-furi*-like rituals with the aim of attracting the absent spirit of the deceased back into the corpse, pacifying it, and getting it to remain in a specific site or object. Once again full and precise details concerning the content and order of performance of these activities are either lacking or obscure, yet it is clear that the rituals were all related to the *tama*-belief complex. In essence, the women performed ritual functions that many commentators have pointed out display elements of shamanic practice.[1] Scholars cite a number of different texts as preserving evidence of shamanism—the myth of Amaterasu's seclusion in the rock-grotto, and more specifically the character of Ame no Uzume and her erotic dance, the description found in the *Nihonshoki* of the Empress Jingū going into trance, and so forth. A strong case can and has been made for this interpretation. But whether the women actually entered a shamanic trance or exhibited other traits of shamanic ecstasy is difficult to judge from the extant texts. One need not assume, however, that first-person and direct dialogue with the dead is possible only in shamanic trance. Evidence from cultures with living oral lament traditions clearly demonstrates that the lament provides a vehicle for a seeming dialogue with the deceased without the person entering a trance state.

Book 2 of the *Man'yōshū* preserves an extraordinary set of poems by women (147–155) that sharpens our focus on the ritual functions of female laments during the period of at least partial seclusion (*imi*) following the death of an emperor. The poems are collected under the genre category of *banka* and under the reign of the Emperor Tenji (r. [662]–671). These poems, like so many others in the *Man'yōshū*, have been the subject of intensive study by Japanese scholars, which I have drawn upon in offering the reading below.[2]

Comparative data from the oral lament tradition of contemporary rural Greece are especially helpful in informing the reconstruction of the performative context of the Man'yō *banka* because of several important parallels in the two religio-aesthetic traditions. First, in rural Greece not only is double burial still practiced, but the conjoined tradition of oral female laments has survived from at least the sixth century B.C.E. This living tradition has been the subject of a number of recent anthropological fieldwork studies that shed invaluable light on the role of women in the practice of double burial, the genesis of oral laments and their circulation, the use of forms of direct address to and from the dead in these laments, as well as the multiple functions (religious, psychological, social), both collective and individual, that laments serve. Because the Man'yō *banka* survive only as written texts and largely out of their generative and performative contexts, the Greek evidence is useful in imaginatively restoring these contexts.

Let us begin, then, with MYS 2: 147 and the prose editorial note attached to it:

sumeramikoto miyamai shitamau no toki,   Poem presented by the Empress when the
ōkisaki no matsuru mi-uta isshu   Sovereign was ill

ama no hara   Turning to gaze
furisake mireba   upon the fields of heaven,
ōkimi no   I see my Lord's long life
mi-inochi wa nagaku stretch to fill the firmament.[3]
ama tarashitari

The headnote suggests that this *uta* was recited or sung by the empress when the Emperor Tenji was ill. Since it is categorized as a *banka*, however, we may assume that at the time the *Man'yōshū* was compiled in the late eighth century, this poem was understood by the editors to have come from the period of the fatal illness of Tenji. As we saw in Chapter Three, the *Nihonshoki* reports that Tenji fell ill in the ninth (or eighth) lunar month of 671 and died on 12/3 of the same year. If these dates and the *Man'yōshū* headnote are reliable, the poem comes from the period between these two dates and, thus, can be fairly precisely located temporally. Although strictly speaking the poem does not come from the period of the *mogari no miya*, apparently it was nevertheless included in the set of *banka* by the editors of the *Man'yōshū* because of its temporal proximity to Tenji's death and its thematic connection.

Poem 147 itself is of historical interest because it indicates that in a time of crisis, such as the grave illness of the emperor, the empress performed a ritual that included the recitation of a poem or poems in order to restore his health and to ensure his longevity. Insofar as this verse seeks to realize a given state by both envisioning it *and* verbally proclaiming it—"I see my Lord's life/ stretch to fill the firmament"— the verse participates in the same religious worldview and ritual pattern we saw earlier in the *kunimi* ritual poetry. Because the empress can still "see" the life (*inochi*) of the emperor, she hopes this life might be restored to him. If one might borrow an English phrase here, the empress has not yet allowed her husband to "give up the ghost."

Scholars differ over the referent of the prose note following verse 147. Some, including the editors of the *Nihon koten bungaku taikei*, take it to be an endnote to 147,[4] whereas others, like Levy, assume it to be a headnote to verse 148.[5] The note reads: *isho ni iwaku, Ōmi no sumeramikoto, seitai shitamau mi-yamai niwaka naru toki, Ōkisaki no tatematsuru mi-uta isshu*—"According to one source, a poem by the Empress when the illness of the Ōmi Sovereign [i.e., Tenji] suddenly took a turn for the worse." The NKBT editors suggest that this note is inappropriate for verse 148, although they do not indicate why they feel this to be the case. They argue that it should be read as referring to the previous poem. Adopting this course, however, means that of all the poems in this set, verse 148 alone would have no headnote. If one assumes the editors would have striven for uniformity, then one must assume in turn that either the headnote was missing at the time the *Man'yōshū* was compiled or that for some unknown reason it was omitted by the editors of the anthology. Yet there is no need to create this irregularity. In light of the prevailing *tama*-related beliefs found in early Japan, the prose note in question "fits" with verse 148 quite nicely. That poem reads:

aohata no   My eyes can see
Kohata no ue o   your presence hovering

kayō to wa	over Kohata,
me ni wa miredomo	of the blue flags,
tada ni awanu kamo	but I cannot meet you in the flesh.[6]

If one recalls that in early Japan serious illness or death was thought to be due to the spirit leaving the physical body and wandering outside, then attaching the prose note to this poem makes perfect sense. Moreover, the poem as ordered in the *Man'yōshū* allows the reader to follow sequentially the progress of the Emperor Tenji's illness.[7] (Whether each of the poems in sequence mirrors the actual progress of Tenji's illness, death, and funeral rituals, or whether this effect is a later editorial creation remains open to question.) Although in verse 148 it seems the empress can still see the emperor's spirit, as was the case in verse 147, there is nevertheless a sense of growing desperation. Perhaps the emperor had lost consciousness; but whatever the case, it seems clear that the disputed prose note may indeed be considered a headnote to this verse. Even if the emperor had expired by this time, the note could still be considered a headnote since, as we have seen, in early Japan death was not considered immediately permanent or irreversible. In this regard it is significant that both these poems are addressed to the emperor.

Poem 149 continues the sequence, skillfully capturing not only the unfolding developments concerning Tenji's fatal illness and death but also the mental state of the empress and the pressure she was under from those around her in the court. It reads:

| sumeramikoto kamuagarimashishi ato, Ya-
mato no ōkisaki no tsukurimashishi mi-uta
isshu | Poem by the Yamato Express after the
death of the Sovereign |

hito wa yoshi	People say, "Enough,
omoi yamu to mo	stop thinking of him,"
tamakazura	yet I cannot forget
kage ni mietsutsu	while I [still] see your image
wasuraenu kamo	in the *tamakazura*[8]

The *tamakazura*, rendered as "wreath of jewels" by Levy, seems to have served as a *katami*, a ritual object used to recall the spirit of a deceased individual. *Katami* is a compound noun composed of the characters *kata*, "form" or "shape," and *mi*, "to see," indicating the intention behind the usage of such objects. As we have already had occasion to see, the *Nihonshoki* entry for 3/20/687 records that a similar wreath of flowers (*hanakazura*) was offered at the *mogari no miya* of the Emperor Temmu.[9] Other related references to similar ritual leaves (*oshiki no tamakazura*, *tachikazura*, and *iwaki no kazura*) are found in the Ankō Chapter,[10] and the same object, *tamakazura*, reappears in the Yūryaku Chapter.[11] *Tama* or "jewel" is, of course, homonymous with *tama* or "spirit." The Ankō-Yūryaku references suggest that it is also related to sexual relations and the succession. In giving verse 149, I have adopted Levy's translation by substituting "your" for "his" in the fourth line to capture the fact that the empress continues to address the spirit of her deceased husband directly. Presumably the wreath was ritually offered at the *mogari no miya*, so that within the poetic sequence the spatial locus has now shifted there from the imperial palace. Bearing this in mind, let us turn to the next poem, 150, which reads:

sumeramikoto kamuagari mashishi toki,	Poem upon the death of the Sovereign by
taoyame ga tsukuru uta isshu seishi imada	one of his concubines (Her name is yet un-
tsubairaka narazu	clear.)

utsusemishi	As the living are unfit
kami ni aeneba	for commune with the gods,
sakari ite	so I am separated from you
asa nageku kimi	Lord whom I grieve for in the morning,
sakari ite	so I am kept from you,
waga kouru kimi	Lord whom I long for.
tama naraba	If you were a jewel,
te ni maki mochite	I would wrap you round my wrist.
kinu naraba	If you were a robe,
nuku toki mo naku	I would never take you off.
waga kouru	Lord whom I long for,
kimi so kizo no yo	last night I saw you
ime ni mietsuru	in a dream.[12]

Several points of interest are found in this poem. First, the prose headnote clearly suggests that other sexual partners of the deceased emperor besides the empress offered such laments. Then, too, we can see that contact or communication with the spirit of the dead was sought not only through ritually induced states of waking consciousness, trance, or reverie, but also through dreams. Finally, there is a strong suggestion that jewels (*tama*) were sometimes worn to serve as repositories of the spirit (*tama*) of the deceased, while certain articles of clothing could also serve as *katami*. Levy has commented at some length on this poem, but since my own interpretation differs significantly from his, some explanation may be in order. Levy notes that the term "*utsusemi*"

is the word Tenji himself had used in his "Poem on the three hills" [MYS 1: 13] to distinguish, and thus to draw an analogy between, the realm of mortals living in the present and that of the gods who had lived in the mythic past. In this poem by his concubine, "utsusemi" is followed by the emphatic "shi," and thus is stated a separation between the deified Emperor and the bereaved mortal he has left behind, a separation as absolute as that between Yamato Takeru and his bereaved wives. But now the bereaved mortal is thrown back on her own imagination, and the result is an imaginative transposition of the departed soul into material objects. This transposition is not a magical one, as was the transformation of Yamato Takeru into a white plover, but a conscious act of metaphorical creation achieved through the parallel conditional propositions "tama naraba" and "kinu naraba" ("if you were a jewel" and "if you were a robe"). It is an attempt, literary *par excellence*, to recapture the soul by hypothetically binding it in a metaphor. This is an imaginative construction, the product of the poet's own creative intent.[13]

The conditional propositions Levy cites may well be read as metaphors here, but at the same time one must not overlook the fact that in the religious worldview and ritual practices of the early Japanese, physical objects, geographical sites, children, and so forth, were all considered to be possible repositories for the spirit of the deceased. The *tamakazura* or ritual wreath in the preceding poem, for example, in which the spirit or shade of the deceased emperor is visible to the widowed empress, is not merely an imaginative metaphor; ritually and psychologically the presence of the deceased emperor in this object is experienced as real by the empress. Thus, the separation of the living and the dead is not "absolute," as Levy would have it, but rather one that could be overcome or mediated through ritual means. Much of the evidence seems to suggest that this is not a case of an original literary creation but rather a common ritual expression.

Earlier in our survey of several myths from the *Kojiki* and the *Nihonshoki* we saw that scarves, necklaces, combs, and other personal articles were frequently used to transfer magical powers, political legitimacy, and the charisma of office. Such objects (as well as places and individuals) could come to be invested with both spiritual and evocative emotional power. This was not something found only in an earlier and primitive stage of Japanese culture that had disappeared by the time of Tenji. The *Nihonshoki* entry for 8/28/687, as we saw in the previous chapter, notes that in the course of preparations for the first anniversary of the death of the Emperor Temmu, the widowed Empress Jitō had three-hundred robes made from the garments of her deceased husband to be distributed to high-ranking Buddhist priests.

Although MYS 2: 150 may be rhetorically more sophisticated than the prose narrative of the Yamato-takeru myth, this does not imply that a change in the consciousness of the early Japanese had occurred between the genesis of these two, as Levy would have it. Instead, it may well be that the difference is the result of the rhetorical natures of the genres of myth and poetry. Whereas the conditional voice is possible in poetry, myth is declarative. Moreover, Levy's argument is based upon the false assumption that myth—and specifically the Yamato-takeru myth—is ancient if not timeless. Scholars have argued persuasively, however, that the Yamato-takeru myth probably gained currency and its present (or close to present) form around the same time as the genesis/performance of this set of *banka*.[14] On the basis of all these considerations, this poem should be read, along with the rest of the set, as a poem recited or sung at the *mogari no miya* as part of the complex of ritual performances held during the period of temporary enshrinement.

To return to the set of *Man'yōshū banka*, the next two poems, MYS 2: 151–152, read:

sumeramikoto no ōaraki no toki no uta nishu

Two poems from the time of the Sovereign's temporary mausoleum

kakaramu no
kokoro shiriseba
ōmi-fune
hateshi tomari ni
shimeyuwamashi o
(Nukata-ō)

If I had known
it would come to this,
I would have tied signs of
        interdiction
around the harbor
where the imperial craft did berth.
(Princess Nukata)

yasumishishi
wago ōkimi no
ōmi-fune
machi ka kōramu
Shiga no Kara saki
(Sekibito Kine [?])

Does Cape Kara in Shiga
wait in longing
for the imperial craft
of our Lord, sovereign
of the earth's eight corners?
(Sekibito Kine)[15]

Like the woman in verse 150, these two women seem to have served as consorts of the deceased emperor. Though virtually nothing is known about the second woman or even if the prose reading of her name ("Sekibito Kine") is correct, the first, Princess Nukata, is a well-known poetess. Verse 151 laments the fact that Nukata-o had not taken ritual precautions that might have kept the emperor's spirit from wandering off. Verse 152 adopts a more formal voice in suggesting that even the *kami* or local divinity of Cape Kara must long for the return of the emperor. This is another rhetorical device used to emphasize the sovereignty of the deceased emperor as even the land (i.e., the local *kami*) feels a deep sense of loss whenever he is absent. It also functions in the ritual context to draw the spirit of the deceased back to this place so closely connected with his life. The poem has a more formal tone with its use of a standard epithet for the emperor—"our Lord/ sovereign of the earth's eight corners"—and an honorific—"the imperial craft" (*ōmi-fune*).

Verse 153 is again imputed to be by the widowed empress and contains another important example of a *katami*, here a bird or birds. It reads:

ōkisaki no mi-uta isshu

Poem by the Empress

isana tori
Ōmi no umi o
oki sakete
kogi kuru fune

Ships that come rowing
far on the offing,
ships that come rowing
close by the strand

e tsukite	on Ōmi's whale-hunted seas:
kogi kuru fune	Oars on the offing,
okitsu kai	do not splash so hard.
itakuna hane so	Oars by the strand,
etsu kai	do not splash so hard,
itakuna hane so	or the bird
wakagusa no	beloved of my husband,
tsuma no	who was gentle
omou tori tatsu	like the young grass,
	will fly away.[16]

This poem displays elements of near parallelism as well as rhetorical inflation. An example of the latter is found in the fixed adjectival phrase (*joshi*), *isana tori*, preceding the place name Ōmi, rendered by Levy as "Ōmi's whale-hunted seas." This most probably refers not to the sea but to the waters of Lake Biwa. More important, however, for our concerns is the question of whether the bird here was believed to be a repository of the emperor's *tama* or was merely employed, as Levy suggests, as a rhetorical device devoid of any religious significance or conviction. Levy again argues that this poem may be used as historical evidence of a positive mental development from an earlier magico-religious and mythic worldview to a lyrical and self-conscious age.[17] For Levy, ritual implies the mindless or slavish repetition of earlier patterned actions and forms of verbal expression. Yet as Sally Moore and Barbara Myerhoff have said, "Ritual may do much more than mirror existing social arrangements and existing modes of thought. It can act to reorganize them or even help to create them."[18] In speaking of cultural images of death expressed in myth and ritual, Lévi-Strauss has noted that "the imagery with which a society pictures to itself the relations between the dead and the living can always be broken down in terms of an attempt to hide, embellish or justify, on the religious level, the relations prevailing in that society among the living."[19] In early Japan each and every ritual performance in the court, which often included oral poetry, had reference to the "age of the *kami*" as well as to the immediate and particular historical situation. Similarly, ritual poetry from the *mogari no miya* was directed *both* to the deceased and to the living. This is an important fact that Levy ignores.

Returning to the *banka* from the *mogari no miya* of the Emperor Tenji, one may note that verse 154 is again attributed to a woman identified as "the concubine of the Ishikawa family" (*Ishikawa no bunin*). Ishikawa is another name for the Soga, one of the most powerful clans of this period. The practice of marrying daughters from powerful clans into the imperial family was a practice that was to continue throughout the Man'yō and into the Heian period as well. It will be treated in the following chapter. It is quite possible that this Ishikawa/Soga daughter and Princess Nukata are one and the same individual. The poem, with its headnote, reads:

Ishikawa no bunin no uta isshu

Poem by the concubine of the Ishikawa family

Sasanami no
ōyama mori wa
taga tame ka
yama ni shimeyū
kimi mo aranaku ni

For whom does the guardian
of Sasanami's imperial mountains
post there his signs of interdiction,
now that you, my Lord, are no longer?[20]

This poem picks up the theme of verse 151, suggesting again that ritual actions such as those mentioned are meaningless now that the emperor has departed this life. This expression of anger at the futility of the rituals and at the fact that, for others, life goes on largely as before rings true to what we know about both the grieving process and other lament traditions. For the princess in her grief, the existence of others has little meaning. Her thoughts and emotions remain invested almost exclusively in the deceased emperor.

The final verse of this set of *banka*, 155, is a short *chōka* attributed to Princess Nukata. It is an important source of information about the *mogari no miya* ritual complex for several reasons. First, the fact that it is in *chōka* form suggests it was part of a public performance by one of the women secluded in the mausoleum. In this respect it is similar to verse 150, although it is much more formal in tone and expression. It reads:

Yamashina no mi-haka yori soki arakuru toki, Nukata no ōkimi no tsukuru uta isshu

Poem by Princess Nukata when the mourners withdrew from the Yamashina tomb and dispersed

yasumishishi
wago ōkimi no
kashikoki ya
mi-haka tsukauru
Yamashina no
Kagami no yama ni
yoru wa mo
yoru no kotogoto
hiru wa mo
hi no kotogoto
ne nomi o
nakitsutsu tsukarite ya
momoshiki no
ōmiyabito wa
yuki-wakarenamu

In awe [we] serve the tomb
of our Lord, sovereign
of the earth's eight corners,
on Kagami Mountain
in Yamashina.
There through the night,
each night,
through the day,
each day,
[we] have stayed,
weeping and crying aloud.
Now have the courtiers
of [your] great palace,
its ramparts thick with stone,
left and gone apart?[21]

The Yamashina tomb referred to here was the site of the final burial of the Emperor Tenji. The *Nihonshoki* does not contain any information about the dates on which the rituals of temporary enshrinement occurred or when final burial took place. Since the reign of Tenji is so late compared with those covered by the chronicle, this omission is somewhat surprising. One would expect a fairly full account of the rituals performed. Following Tenji's death, however, the court was thrown into an extended period of turmoil. The set of *banka* constituting MYS 2: 147–155 would have come out of this time of political upheaval and, moreover, may well have played a role in the succession dispute as well. Verse 155 must be viewed in this light. If the continuation of the *mogari no miya* rituals could at times play an important role in the politics of death, then one might hear a certain bitterness in the last lines noting that the courtiers and other members of the court were abandoning the mourning rituals. At the same time, this recrimination against others reflects on Nukata's own continued mourning as an expression of loyalty and devotion to the deceased sovereign.

Following the death of the Emperor Tenji, his brother, Prince Ōtomo, held power for a brief period as the Emperor Kōbun, but this period in the imperial court has been completely effaced from the *Nihonshoki*, which covers the succession dispute from the perspective of the Temmu faction. Almost all the action in the text takes place in the Yoshino mountains where Prince Ōama (Temmu) had withdrawn to bide his time and gather his forces. Following the accepted cultural pattern of the capital being where the sovereign resides, the locus of the first Temmu Chapter, covering Kōbun's reign and the Jinshin War, is in the Yoshino mountains. Since Prince Ōama had departed the capital before his father's demise, we may presume that to a large extent the *mogari no miya* rituals for Tenji must have been controlled by the Kōbun faction. With the eventual victory of Temmu's forces in the Jinshin War, the records of Kōbun's reign were suppressed, accounting for the fact that, except for these poems from the *Man'yōshū*, virtually no textual evidence has survived from this period or from the locus of Tenji's *mogari no miya*.

The Performative Loci of Banka

The consensus of Japanese scholars is that these poems, as well as many other *banka*, were recited or sung at the *mogari no miya*. A few scholars, however, dissent on this issue, most notably Yoshinaga Noboru.[22] He argues, among other points, the following: (1) the prose headnotes to the set above and others say simply "*mogari no miya no toki*" ("at the time of the *mogari no miya*"), locating the poems temporally but not necessarily spatially; (2) the fact that the meritorious acts of the deceased are praised in some *banka* is not sufficient evidence to say that a poem was recited/sung at the *mogari no miya*; (3) some *banka*, like MYS 2: 194, are reported to have been presented to the surviving spouse, not to the deceased, by a poet and thus should not be thought of as having been performed at the *mogari no miya*; (4) the belief in the possibility of resuscitating the dead had run its course in Japan by the time of the Emperor Tenji; and (5) the personal emotion expressed in poems like MYS 2: 149 militates against our considering them as part of a public ritual.

Yoshinaga's arguments are not convincing individually or cumulatively. Even granting his first two points to the effect that neither the prose headnotes nor the contents of most of the *banka* absolutely preclude other locations for their recitation, the *mogari no miya* nevertheless remains the most likely locus. The evidence for this assumption is quite strong, yet Yoshinaga can respond only that it is not airtight. If one asked for positive evidence that ruled out all other possibilities on almost any point concerning the history of early Japan (or any history for that matter), then as historians we would be paralyzed and unable to say anything. In other words, to point out that one cannot be absolutely certain that the *banka* were recited or sung at the *mogari no miya* does not diminish the high probability that they were. It is essential that we form educated hypotheses based on the limited evidence available, though certainly this must be done with due caution.

Before looking further at the socio-political situation following the death of Tenji, I would like to focus closer attention on the other points Yoshinaga raises. All of them relate in one way or another to his conception of ritual, a conception that is inaccurate in critical ways. First, he seems to assume that personal emotion would be out of place in public or religious rituals. *Banka*, however, represent a different case because there the expression of grief and longing is not only natural, it is prescribed. Even if a minister, clan head, or courtier were not at all dismayed by the death of the sovereign, in the public presentation of laments, such an individual would still have been constrained rhetorically to express grief and a sense of loss and disorientation.

Yoshinaga also suggests that only *banka* performed before the spirit of the deceased and addressed to it are appropriate for the ritual locus of the *mogari no miya*. Yet we have already found that public ritual poetry, including *banka*, were directed not only to the spirit of the deceased but equally to the audience of the living in attendance. Finally, we must recognize that there are important differences between "private" and "public" laments but that these are not always neatly separated. Heretofore I have emphasized the political dimensions of ritual laments, yet we must not forget that the death of an emperor or a crown prince was also the death of a husband, son, or patron. The death of an important political figure in the imperial court emotionally affected certain individuals personally and deeply, even while it had wider socio-political ramifications. Thus, it should not be surprising that such a death may have occasioned both individual and collective responses. One may assume that frequently the "private" grief of immediate relatives of the deceased also found expression in public forums. In this complex situation we cannot presume to know what forms of expression would have been appropriate or inappropriate without considering all the available evidence about the practice of temporary enshrinement in early Japan.

Yoshinaga specifically points to MYS 2: 149, one of the *banka* from the set we looked at above, as the type of poem expressing personal emotion that he suggests cannot be considered to have been part of a public ritual. In that poem unidentified persons urged the widowed empress to cease her mourning.

In order to appreciate this *banka*, we must do two things: (1) attempt to understand the psychological process of grieving and mourning following the death of a close family member, and (2) bear in mind the socio-political dimensions of the *mogari no miya* ritual complex. On the latter point, we have seen that in the liminal period of the *mogari no miya* for an emperor, the widowed empress and the imperial consorts exercised significant political power due to their pivotal position in the mourning rituals, especially insofar as they were central figures in the *tama-furi* rituals performed in an attempt to resuscitate the deceased. These women could exercise considerable political leverage by continuing such rituals. This is not to say, however, that the women would not have been under pressure from some persons in the court to terminate the rituals at a point that would be advantageous to those persons, or that a widowed empress may not have used her position and prerogatives for her own ends. In this light, it is possible to read the poem as capturing some of the pressure the widowed empress felt from such quarters—"People say, 'Enough, stop thinking of him!' "—or, to paraphrase, "Let go of him. End the *mogari no miya* rituals and let us get on with life." Here the perturbed cry of Prince Anahobe, directed to the guards at the *mogari no miya* after the death of the Emperor Bidatsu— "Why do you serve a dead king, and do no service for the living king?"—finds a strong resonance. Yet we can also glimpse one way in which the widowed empress resisted this pressure.

The reading suggested here has much to recommend it, yet it is not the only one possible. Although the empress would no doubt have been under pressure from some quarters to end the temporary burial rituals, one might also argue that this poem captures a common situation in which a grieving individual is unable psychologically to "let go" of a deceased loved one. Friends or relatives then have to intervene gently to pry the individual away from the dominant emotional attachment to the dead and to refocus the person's attention on the task of getting on with his/her own life. If the grieving process is presumed to be universal (an assumption that itself begs for corroborative evidence), then such a scene could well be imagined at any socio-economic level, time, and place. Thus, the poem may mirror a specific point in the psychological process of grieving through which the empress or anyone must pass rather than an explicitly and exclusively political situation. Without further corroborative evidence, it is difficult if not impossible to determine which of these readings is "correct." Both may be valid, in that the empress was after all still the empress, so that whether intentional or not, her actions and reactions following the death of the sovereign would have had political implications. Friends, relatives, or others may well have had the empress's interests at heart and urged her to stop thinking of her deceased husband; but it is impossible to believe that any intervention in this situation could have been free of political ramifications.

Multiple Performances of Banka

If the *Man'yōshū banka* are to be used as historical documents for the study of early Japan, then the "voice" of these poems must be recovered by carefully, yet imaginatively, recreating their performative contexts using the scant and scattered evidence available in the texts from early Japan. The intentional goal of recalling the spirit of the deceased in the *tama-furi* rituals seems clear enough, and we have seen that the performance of these and the related *tama-shizume* rituals had other political dimensions as well. The psychological functions the performance of such funeral laments may have served, however, are less immediately evident or accessible to the modern scholar. For one thing, the editors of both the *Nihonshoki* and the *Man'yōshū* did not have as their primary goal the simple recording of the emotional reactions of members of the court to various stimuli and events, although a little over a century later, in his famous Japanese preface to the *Kokinshū* (c. 905), Ki no Tsurayuki was to assert that spontaneous emotional reaction to external stimuli was the basis of all poetry. Emotions are recorded, to be sure, but usually for specific narrative and historiographic purposes—to arouse sympathy in the readers for the plight of a character, or to characterize negatively or positively a given actor.

There is, however, at least one critical passage from the *Nihonshoki* that may suggest an important psychological function of oral laments, though once again it is never far removed from political motives and machinations. The *Nihonshoki* entry for the fifth month of the fourth year of the reign of the Empress Saimei (i.e., 658) reads:

5th month. A grandson of the Empress named Prince Takeru died. He was eight years of age. His remains were deposited in a temporary tomb [*mogari*] which was raised for him over the Imaki valley. The Empress had always esteemed her grandson highly for his obedient conduct. She was therefore beside herself with grief, and her emotion was exceeding[ly] great. Sending for the Ministers, she said:—

"After ten thousand years and a thousand autumns he must be interred along with us in our own misasagi."

So she made songs, saying:—

Imaki naru	On the hill of Omure
Omure ga ue ni	in Imaki—
kumo dani mo	if a cloud
shirukushi tataba	arose, plain to be seen,
nani ka nagekamu	how would I grieve!
(sore hitotsu)	(This was the first song.)
iyu shishi o	I did not think of you
tsunagu kawa e no	as being a mere child, young
wakakusa no	like the young grass
wakaku ariki to	by the river bank, where they track
a ga mowanaku ni	the wounded deer.
(sore futatsu)	(This was the second song.)
Asuka-gawa	Like the swollen
minagirai tsutsu	waters of the Asuka River
yuku mizu no	flowing on and on
aida mo naku mo	without break
omōyuru kamo	I long for you.
(sore mitsu)	(This was the third song.)

The Empress sang these songs from time to time, and lamented bitterly.[23]

Among other things, this passage clearly indicates that the empress sang these laments to express and assuage her grief. Moreover, we are told that she *often* sang them, indicating that *banka* were intended for multiple performances. This possibility is strengthened by what we know from other cultures with oral lament traditions. Five months later another entry in the *Nihonshoki* returns to the subject of the empress's continued lamenting for her deceased grandson. This entry reads:

Winter, 10th month, 15th day. The Empress visited the hot baths of Ki. The Empress, remembering her Imperial grandson, Prince Takeru, grieved and lamented. She exclaimed, saying:—

yama koete	Though I pass over the mountains
umi wataru tomo	and cross the seas,
omoshiroki	yet can I never forget
Imaki no uchi wa	the pleasant
wasurayumashiji	region of Imaki.
(sore hitotsu)	(The first)
minato no	With the harbor's
ushio no kudari	ebbing tide,
unakudari	as the sea goes down,
ushiro mo kure ni	with the darkness behind me

okite ka yukamu	must I leave and go?
(sore futatsu)	(The second)
utsukushiki	Beautiful one,
a ga wakaki ko o	my young child
okite ka yukamu	must I leave you and go?
(sore mitsu)	(The third)

She commanded Maro, Hada no Ōkura no Miyatsuko, saying:—"Let these songs be handed down and let them not be forgotten by the world."[24]

An earlier passage suggests that Imperial Prince Arima, a son of Emperor Kōtoku, conspired to get the empress to travel to the hot springs in Ki by feigning insanity himself and then saying that the miraculous powers of the springs had cured him.[25] The hot springs were later to be the site of her young grandson's *mogari*. The paradox that this locus of supposed curative powers was later to be a prime locus of the grief the empress still suffered is skillfully brought out with a minimum of narrative. Indeed, the repeated use of "etc., etc." (*shikashika iu*) in the prose passage suggesting Prince Arima's conspiratorial nature indicates that the full narrative was well known when the *Nihonshoki* was committed to writing in its present form in 720. It is likely that this tale, including the songs presented above, had been orally preserved and performed over the intervening years by ritual reciters. Thus, it is possible that some *banka* may have been preserved not only in their oral performance in ritual contexts but thereafter also in what Japanese scholars have come to call "*rekishi uta monogatari*" or historical poetic prose tales.

It is significant that the *Nihonshoki* maintains that a Soga minister used the empress's absence from the capital during a stay in Ki to plot with Prince Arima to seize the throne. This assertion is a further indication of just how pervasive the politics of death were in early Japan, for in many ways Saimei was herself a Soga political creation. It is unclear whether as the plot progressed Soga no Akae got cold feet, as it were, and thus betrayed Prince Arima, or whether he had set up Arima from the start in order to discover the identity of others in the court who were prepared to challenge Saimei's rule. At any rate, Akae reportedly played a major role in placing Arima under house arrest and turning him over to the crown prince, later the Emperor Tenji, who had Prince Arima and a large number of others involved in the plot executed.

The imperial grandson had died in the fifth month of 658; the second set of songs presented above is dated some five months later. This dating suggests that the mourning rituals continued at least that long, a time span falling well within the parameters we saw earlier. Akima Toshio has recently done much to elucidate the context and meaning of these laments, especially the second set attributed to the Empress Saimei.[26] He convincingly argues that these *banka* include dialogue placed in the mouth of the deceased. Regarding the second lament of the first set, he points out that the first three lines (in translation) are virtually identical to lines in MYS 16: 3874. The verse in the *Nihonshoki* reads:

iyu shishi o	I did not think of you
tsunagu kawabe no	as being a mere child, young
wakakusa no	like the young grass
wakaku ariki to	by the river bank, where they track
a ga mowanaku ni	the wounded deer.

and MYS 16: 3874 reads:

iyu shishi o	How I yearn for the woman
tsunagu kawabe no	I slept with, when we were young
nikogusa no	as the soft grass
mi no wakakae ni	by the river bank, where they track
saneshi kora wa mo	the wounded deer.[27]

The phrase *iyu shishi*, "the wounded deer," here is thought to refer to the law that the rights to such wounded game belonged to the hunter whose arrow first drew blood, even if the wounded animal had to be tracked for a great distance and into anothers' hunting territory before it fell. This seems to be an especially appropriate metaphor to describe the feelings of someone grieving for a dead loved one or an absent lover, insofar as the deceased has gone to another land while the survivor desperately hopes to call that person back again. The use of love songs as laments for the dead is a well-documented phenomenon in a number of cultures.[28] In this *Nihonshoki* passage we have a strong hint that these *uta* were part of an oral repertoire that could be adapted in performance to specific circumstances.[29] This suggestion of multiple and adapted performances in turn implies that the application of the concept of authorship may be inappropriate in connection with such *banka* insofar as an individual might borrow an earlier *uta* and change it to meet her/his immediate needs. Though the laments are said to be "by the Empress," this may mean only that she performed them or had them performed, not that she was the creator. This is a point that will merit further consideration below.

Akima has suggested that the poems above attributed to the Empress Saimei were sung by *asobibe*, whom he describes as "a group of shamans in charge of the appeasement of the spirits of dead emperors."[30] The first two songs in the second set are to be regarded as "sung by the dead man's [*sic.* actually in this case the child's] spirit as it descends into the nether world leaving its beloved family behind in this world."[31] This reading is an important corrective to the prevailing interpretation on which Philippi based his English translation.[32]

Everything we have seen so far supports Akima's thesis. Indeed, one could go further and suggest that the second set of *uta* may have come from the ritual of final burial. Once again the Greek lament tradition suggests support for this conjecture. The following is part of a lament sung by a grieving mother at the grave site when the skull of her daughter who had been killed in an accident was exhumed: "Now I have set out. Now I am about to depart from the black and cobwebbed earth."[33] This ritual of exhuming the skeletal remains immediately preceded final burial. The speaker here is the deceased daughter, although in performance it was the mother who sang these lines. This situation would parallel the Empress Saimei's giving a voice to her deceased grandson in her lament. In this way funeral laments not only allow the living to give vent to their grief; they also provide a vehicle for sustaining a vital conversation with the dead.[34]

Many Japanese scholars, following the lead of Origuchi Shinobu, have argued for the existence in early Japan of female mediums or shamans who acted as mouthpieces for the deceased while in trance. Yet, one need not appeal to instances of shamanic trance to explain the existence of such first-person songs of the dead. Although the *Nihonshoki* suggests that the Empress Jingu participated in shamanic rituals, these were not related to funerary rites. It is more difficult to argue that the seventh-century female sovereigns were shamans. There is no evidence, for example, that Saimei had shamanic powers, such as having mastered techniques of ecstasy, magical flight, and so on. The *Nihonshoki* account we have just seen indicates that *banka* attributed to Saimei were then handed down by professional performers on her orders. Maro Hada no Ōkura, the official the empress ordered to preserve the poems, was probably a member of a traditional clan of reciters (*kataribe*) or *utaibito*, the oral performers of *uta*. As such he would have been a court functionary similar to the type Kakinomoto Hitomaro was.

The *Nihonshoki* contains an even clearer indication that surrogate singers could create laments in the first person for another individual. In the Kōtoku Chapter an entry for 3/25/649 says that the wife of the crown prince died shortly after learning that her husband had led her father to commit suicide by falsely accusing him of plotting against the imperial family. The passage of immediate relevance reads:

When the Prince Imperial heard that she had passed away, he was grieved and deeply shocked, and bewailed her loss exceedingly. Upon this Mitsu, Nunaka Kawara no Fubito, came forward and presented verses of poetry as follows [*susumite uta o tatematsu. utaite iwaku*]:

yamakawa ni	On the mountain stream
oshi futatsu ite	is a pair of mandarin ducks,
tagui yoku	well matched
tagueru imo o	like you, my love, and I—
tare ka inikemu	who has taken you away?

(sore hitotsu)   (This was the first verse.)

motogoto ni   Although on each tree
hana wa sakedomo   the blossoms are in bloom,
nani to kamo   how can it be
utsukushi imo ga   that you, my beautiful one,
mata sakide konu   will never come out in bloom again?

(sore futatsu)   (This was the second verse.)

The Prince Imperial, with a sigh of deep despair, praised the verses, saying:—"How beautiful! How pathetic!" ["*yoki kana, kanashiki kana*"] So he gave him his lute [*mi-koto*] and made
him sing them. He also presented him with four hiki of silk, twenty tan of cloth, and two
bags of floss silk.[35]

Here a third person generates verses for the grieving crown prince (later the
Emperor Tenji), who finds they precisely capture or express his sorrow and pain.
The fact that the prince praises the laments as affectively moving is a clear indication
of their status as a verbal art of performance. Note that he does not write the verses
down; rather he has them performed again to music. Moreover, they are judged not
solely on the semantic content but also in terms of the aesthetics of performance
and emotive power they have over the audience. If we bear this in mind it is easier
to appreciate why certain verses that, on the basis of their semantic content, do not
seem to refer to death or funerary rites are nevertheless designated as *banka*. One
thinks immediately, for example, of the *Kojiki* verses associated with the death of
Yamato-takeru. Note, too, that the term of endearment, "my love" (*imo*), found in
these laments is used only for one's own sister, wife, or lover. Yet here it is used by
Fubito to refer to Prince Naka no Ōe's wife, indicating that such first-person *banka*
were often generated by surrogates for the bereaved. Were this not the case, the use
of such terms in the prince's presence would have been extremely dangerous. The
implications of the practice of surrogate generation of such verses for the study and
critical reading of early Japanese poetry are far-reaching.

The vagueness of the Japanese language when taken out of its full communicative
context leads to a situation in which poems such as these, in their textual and
anthologized form, are open to divergent interpretations. The choice of different
subjects can, as we have already seen, give the poems a very different sense and
voice.

The results of our inquiry so far suggest the possibilities that (1) the *banka* were
performed quite often; (2) they were circulated by professional reciters/singers and
others; (3) they could be adapted for use for different individuals and occasions, just
as was the case with the laments from the tale of Yamato-takeru; (4) such orally
circulating verses were used not only in ritual situations but also in oral (and later

written) histories; and (5) the dead were sometimes given a voice in the laments, allowing direct "dialogue" between the living and the dead to be sustained.

Above we turned to the songs recorded in the Saimei Chapter of the *Nihonshoki* in an effort to read MYS 2: 149 as direct dialogue with the spirit of the dead, as well as to restore the performative voice of the set of *banka* from Tenji's *mogari no miya* by suggesting these *uta* came out of real life (and death) situations. Such *banka* served both as public ritual, with important socio-political as well as religious dimensions, *and* as individual expressions of and vehicles for the psychological process of grieving. Only by conjoining these two aspects can we fully appreciate this type of ritual poetry.

Unfortunately, the number of *banka* extant in the texts is relatively small. Moreover, all the texts postdate the court's adoption of the practice of cremation. By the time the *Man'yōshū* was compiled, the practice of double burial was already in many ways a thing of the past. As a result, although there are records to the effect that *mogari no miya* rituals were performed, little concerning the sequential unfolding of these rituals is available. Nor do we have much detail concerning the interaction of the participants in the rituals or of these persons and the audience. It seems that adoption of the practice of cremation, coupled with the rapid change into a literate culture in the court, led to the sudden decline of *banka*, first as a performative ritual genre and then as a meaningful literary category.

Greek Funeral Laments and Banka

Among the large number of cultures where oral laments are still performed, the Greek oral funeral lament tradition offers several advantages for this study. First and foremost, the practice of double burial has been conjoined with oral laments in an unbroken tradition in rural Greece since at least the sixth century B.C.E., although with the expected regional variations and changes over time. As was the case in early Japan, in Greece the corpse is initially buried in a grave, which becomes the site of family and communal grieving, including the singing of laments. Laments are sung at the grave site, sometimes daily, for a period of three to five years until the skeletal remains are exhumed, cleaned, and then either reburied elsewhere or committed to the village ossuary.[36] This period may be considered the equivalent of the *Man'yōshū*'s "the time of the *mogari no miya*."

Recent fieldwork studies of the death rituals of rural Greece provide clues to a number of the critical missing components in the early Japanese materials—a sense of the live performative contexts of funeral laments; the psychological functions of performing and listening to such laments; the social interactions of female participants; the processes by which laments are orally generated, adopted, adapted, and transmitted; the relation of various major themes and metaphors found in laments and other genres; and the special role of women in the rituals of temporary burial. We cannot, of course, assume that the Greek ritual practice is identical to that of the early Japanese in all respects. Rather, one must use the Greek tradition to demonstrate certain suggestive parallels that may permit us to fill in crucial gaps in the data concerning the *mogari no miya* ritual complex. Rather than superimposing the Greek picture onto the Japanese, we use the modern studies to enhance the picture we have developed of early Japan, based on all the available evidence, much as scientists today use computer enhancement, based on other bodies of data, to fill in details of a satellite, laser, or sonar picture.

Here we are interested first of all in recovering the meaning of the *banka* for their performers and listening audience in their ritual contexts. To say this is to suggest that the meaning of a song/poem is to be found not only in its semantic content or textual form but, equally important, in its performance. The meaning of any given oral poem was created out of the performative/communicative event in toto. Meaning in this sense was transactionally negotiated between the performer and audience, not unilaterally "composed" by any individual. This interpretation is so different from the textual assumptions that have long prevailed in *Man'yōshū* scholarship that it merits repeating.

Banka and other ritual poems can be (and often have been) studied as purely literary texts; but something extremely important is lost, in that ritual poems not only *say* different things, they *do* things. Anna Caraveli-Chaves, in her excellent study of Greek laments, has rightly pointed out that laments do not merely describe the behavior of the mourners or of the deceased; they have the capacity to affect and even prescribe such behavior.[37] Furthermore, laments do more than mirror or recount the suffering of the deceased in the grave or the underworld, for that, too, would still be a form of descriptive poetry. Through the identification of the deceased's life with the lives of the living, the oral lament is transformed into a social and communicative event. In focusing on the ways such laments affect the women who regularly visit the grave site, Caraveli-Chaves found that the ritual performance served a number of different purposes. According to her, "the death of a specific woman is utilized to affect the female participants in a variety of ways: to affirm kinship ties, to cement bonding among the women, to heighten the meaning of female roles, and to reinforce survival strategies."[38]

Loring Danforth has also clearly demonstrated the ways in which oral laments in rural Greece affect the living. He draws on Clifford Geertz's distinction between a "religious perspective" based on "a sense of the 'really real' . . . which the symbolic activities of religion as a cultural system are devoted to producing, intensifying, and so far as possible, rendering inviolable by the discordant revelations of secular experience"[39] and the commonsense perspective of the world. He then argues that oral performative laments serve as a means of subjectively establishing and maintaining communication between the living and the dead within the religious perspective. In terms of an individual psychology of grieving, he contends that funeral laments and the associated ritual complex reflect both the denial of death, and the anguished recognition of its reality (or perhaps finality), and ultimately the acceptance of it—contradictory emotions *held simultaneously*, even though at any given moment one takes primacy.

Although Danforth was writing about contemporary rural Greece, the following passage might well be used in refererence to early Japan:

During the early portions of the long liminal period that lasts from the time of death until the exhumation, the attitudes of those in mourning tend to be dominated by the religious perspective . . . in spite of the occasional expression of an awareness of the contradictions between this religious perspective and the [biological] reality of death. As long as the religious perspective is subjectively maintained, a woman in mourning can continue to inhabit the socially constructed reality that existed prior to the death of the relevant significant other. She can continue to interact with the deceased; she can carry on a reality-sustaining conversation with him through the performance of death rituals in his memory.

With the passage of time, however, the religious perspective becomes increasingly more difficult to maintain. In the face of everyday reality and the objective [biological] facts of death, it gives way to a common-sense perspective in which the reality of death is accepted. This shift from a religious to a common-sense perspective brings about, by the time of the rite of exhumation, which concludes the liminal period, an end to the social relationships between the living and the dead. The conversation is concluded as a new social reality is constructed, one that does not include the significant other, who is now long dead.[40]

Death rituals also reflect social contradictions and realities, as noted by Lévi-Strauss and many others. In the case of early Japan, the *mogari no miya* ritual complex was an attempt to maintain the ideology or social fictions of the imperial family as *kami* and of an unbroken line of succession by, among other things, denying that the members of the imperial family "really" died. The associated *tama*-belief system and symbols expressed in the temporary burial rituals and the accession rites reflect this incongruity. The performance of the *mogari no miya* rituals helped to generate the collectively shared religious belief that the deceased continued to exist in this world in another form *and* continued to have significant relations with the living. A "new social reality" emerged only after final burial and the formal accession of a successor. For others not in immediate line for the succession, the parallel to the Greek case would have been even closer.

Danforth's discovery that individuals in mourning do not consistently maintain either a religious perspective or a commonsense one is of special significance for scholars of Japanese literature. According to Danforth, the mourners shift back and forth between these two perspectives, sometimes within the same sentence of a lament or in conversation at the temporary grave site:

Paradoxically, the religious perspective and the common sense perspective, two "radically contrasting ways of looking at the world" (Geertz), at times seem to be held jointly by the women of rural Greece, so rapidly do they move back and forth between them. . . . The juxtaposition of these two conflicting perspectives is occasionally revealed in the comments of women in mourning as they discuss death and the death rituals that occupy so much of their time. For example, a woman trying to comfort a widow who was industriously sweeping the ground around the grave of her dead husband said, "Tonight your husband will sleep all tucked in and nicely cared for," but then she added sadly: "It's all useless. It's all for nothing." [and] "We're wasting our time. We're not accomplishing anything at all." Such comments suggest that some women are aware of the futility of their actions at the very moment they are performing them.[41]

This ambivalence, this sudden swing of moods, is reflected in *Man'yōshū banka* as well. The fact that some Man'yō *banka* explicitly express a sense of futility as to the efficacy of the rituals, while others suggest, even as some *tama-furi* ritual is being performed, a seeming resignation to the fact that the poet can never meet the deceased again, has long puzzled commentators and critics and led to more than a few farfetched explanations. These have included "historical" explanations to the effect that these poems reflect a clear shift from an earlier primitive and mythical consciousness to a kind of enlightened lyricism, or that they are evidence that the belief in the possibility of recalling the spirit of the dead had disappeared by that time (Yoshinaga). If, however, the evidence from Greece is any indication of the lived emotional reality of the mourners, we might take precisely such expressions of existential doubt and despair as evidence of the authenticity of those *banka*. A few examples from the *Man'yōshū* where this emotional ambivalence is evident must suffice here.

The following *banka* are purported to be by Hitomaro following the death of his wife. One expects to find personal grief expressed by the poet to a much greater extent in these poems than in the commissioned pieces. The verses in MYS 2: 207–209 read:

ama tobu ya	Soaring through the sky!
Karu no michi wa	On the Karu Road
wagimoko ga	is your village, my love;
sato ni shi areba	although I desired to meet you intimately,
nemokoro ni	if I went there too much
mimaku hoshikedo	the eyes of others would cluster
yamazu yukaba	around us,
hitome o ōmi	and if I went there too often
maneku yukaba	others would find us out.

hito shirinubemi	And so I hoped
sanekazura	that later we would meet
nochi mo awamu to	like tangling vines,
ōbune no	trusted we would
omoitanomite	as I would trust a great ship,
tama kagiru	and hid my love:
iwakaki fuchi no	faint as jewel's light,
komori nomi	a pool walled in by cliffs.
koitsutsu aru ni	Then came the messenger,
wataru hi no	his letter tied
kureyuku ga goto	to a jewelled catalpa staff,
teru tsuki no	to tell me,
kumogakuru goto	in a voice
okitsu mo no	like the sound
nabikishi imo wa	of a catalpa bow,
momichiba no	(a variant has "I heard only the
sugite iniki to	voice of the catalpa bow.")
tamazusa no	that you, my love
tsukai no ieba	who had swayed to me in sleep
azusayumi	like seaweed of the offing,
oto ni kikite	were gone
(hitotsu ni iu, oto	like the coursing sun
nomi kikite)	gliding into dusk,
iwamu sube	like the radiant moon
namusubeshira ni	secluding itself behind the clouds,
oto nomi o	gone like the yellow leaves of
kikite arieneba	autumn.
waga kōru	I did not know what to say,
chie no hitoe mo	what to do,
nagusamuru	but simply could not listen
kokoro mo ari ya to	and so, perhaps to solace
wagimoko ga	a single thousandth
tomazu idemishi	of my thousand-fold longing,
Karu no ichi ni	I stood at the Karu market
waga tachikikeba	where often you, my love, had gone,
tamatasuki	and listened,
Unebi no yama ni	but could not even hear
naku tori no	the voices of the birds
koi mo kiezu	that cry on Unebi Mountain,
tamahoko no	of the jewelled sleeve-cords,
michiyuku hito mo	and of the ones who passed me
hitori dani	on that road,
niteshi yukaneba	straight as a jewelled spear,
sube o nami	not one resembled you.
imo ga na yobite	I could do nothing
sode so furitsuru	but call your name

(aru hon, na nomi
kikite arieneba to
ieru uta ari)

(Another source has the following
verse: "All I could do was call
your name.")
and wave my sleeves.

hanka nishu

Two envoys

aki yama no
momichi o shigemi
motoinuru
imo o motomemu
yamaji shirazu mo

Too dense the yellow leaves
on the autumn mountain:
wandering,
not knowing the mountain path
to find you by, my love.

momichiba no
ochiriyuku nabe ni
tamazusa no
tsukai o mireba
aishi hi omōyu

With the falling away
of the yellow leaves,
I see the messenger
with his jewelled catalpa staff,
and recall the days we met.[42]

This is a powerful, moving set of poems. It is followed by others equally so (see MYS 2: 210–216). Rather than reading these as textual variants, with the implicit suggesion that one version must be the final and "correct" one (or that one must be the original—and thus correct—version, while the others are later and lesser variants or the results of scribal errors), these poems should be understood as orally generated variants from different occasions within a series where Hitomaro lamented at his wife's grave site. Note the central expressions of the devastating realization of the finality of his wife's death, the rude intrusion of the commonsense perspective that disrupts the social relationship, and continued dialogue with the deceased maintained through the ritual mourning process. Now let us look at the set above in more detail. The *chōka* MYS 2: 210 ends with:

nagekedomo
semu sube shira ni
kouru domo
au yoshi o nami
ōtori no
Hagai no yama ni
waga kouru
imo wa imasu to
hito no ieba
iwa nesakumite
nazumi koshi
yoke kumoso naki
utsusemi to
omoishi imo ga
tama kagiru

Lament as I may
I know nothing I can do.
Long for you as I may,
I have no way to meet you.
And so when someone said
you, my beloved wife,
dwelt on Hagai Mountain,
of the great bird,
I struggled up here,
kicking the rocks apart,
but it did no good:
my love, whom I thought
was of this world,
is less visible
than the faint light of a jewel.

honoka ni da ni mo
mienu omoeba

[or perhaps, "when I realize
that your *tama*, my love,
which I thought was of this world,
cannot be seen
but faintly."][13]

Here Hitomaro may be heard expressing the frustrated expectation of the promise proffered by the prevailing religious and ritual belief that he could indeed meet his wife again. This does not mean, however, that this verse or the associated verses mark a new stage of consciousness or the "true beginning"[44] of Japanese poetry freed of its collective ritual trappings. Hitomaro's voice here is, one may assume, true to the tradition of oral *banka*. Although the specific occasion of these laments—the death of Hitomaro's wife—is unique, the form of the expression of human grief seems to be shared across time and space, finding resonance even today in the laments of rural Greece.

There is a cruel irony in Hitomaro's realization that he can do nothing in the face of his wife's death, for as a member of the *asobibe*, the guild of ritual functionaries whose duties included performances in the death ritual complex, he was to have been a religious specialist who could effect communication with the dead. Hitomaro, however, did not step outside his ritual role when he recited, or more likely sang, these laments, any more than the women of rural Greece do when they move from performing laments at the grave site of another villager to that of an immediate relative. These *banka* by Hitomaro were indeed personal in that they involved his own wife, and in that sense they differ from the public or "professional" *banka* offered on commission for others; nevertheless, they are still ritual banka. Moreover, since Hitomaro was a relatively low ranking functionary within the court, he was not under the ideological obligation, as were members of the imperial family, to deny— in public at least—the finality of death. Hitomaro employs many of the same formal expressions found in imperial *banka*—"gone like the yellow leaves of autumn," "rise . . . like a bird/ and conceal yourself/ like the setting sun"—but here they function as a tragic and ironic comment on his immediate state.

The poem MYS 2: 213, a variant *chōka*, ends with the crushed realization by Hitomaro that "my love/ whom I thought was of this world/ has become ashes" (*utsusemi to/ omoishi imo ga/ hai nite naseba*).[45] If we assume this line refers to the time of final exhumation or to cremation, it may be usefully compared with the following description recorded by Danforth in rural Greece when a corpse was exhumed for final burial:

The rite of exhumation promises to return that which it cannot. It is "disjunctive," in the sense that it ritually declares passage where in fact there is simply the illusion of passage. The rite of exhumation does not return the dead person to the world of the living; it only returns the decomposed body of what had once been a person. This realization is dramatically expressed in [a] comment made by Elini's [a young woman killed five years earlier] mother: "Look what I put in and look what I take out! I put in a partridge, and I took out bones."[46]

It is erroneous to assume that the Japanese once lived wholly in a mythic consciousness in which they believed the dead truly came back to life, and that Hitomaro had outgrown the belief. The evidence from the texts indicates that this hope continued to be expressed ritually throughout the centuries in early Japan in spite of the recognition at another level of the "reality" or finality of death. (This hope continues to find expression in Japan even today, albeit in different form, in the Buddhist O-bon festival and related beliefs.) The inevitable frustration of this promised result at the time of exhumation must have been experienced in prehistorical Japan as well as in Hitomaro's age. To assume otherwise is to imply the existence of a "primitive mind." A more plausible understanding would be based upon the recognition that during the period of temporary interment, it was the religious perspective that continued to hold sway and to find expression in funeral laments and related ritual actions, although this perspective was never continuously maintained even in the period of the *mogari no miya*.

A few features of MYS 2: 207–209 make this set of poems especially powerful. The *chōka* opens by recalling the past when Hitomaro's wife was still alive; it is also spatially focused on her hometown, Karu, with its *makurakotoba* or standard ephitet, *ama tobu ya* ("Soaring through the sky!"). This calls to mind the image of the spirit of the deceased Yamato-takeru assuming the form of a bird and flying off through the sky where his mourning wife and children could not follow. The *chōka* then goes on to allude, with regret on Hitomaro's part, to the social constraints that had kept him from fully expressing his love for his wife. The phrase *tamakagiru* and the verb *komoru* ("to hide") are employed to express his love and perhaps retrospectively to justify to his wife his earlier reticence to spend too much time with her—"and [I] hid my love/ faint as jewel's light/ a pool walled in by cliffs" (*tamakagiru/ iwagakifuchi no/ komori nomi/ koitsutsu ari ni*). Both *tamakagiru* and *komoru* are used to telling effect again at the end of the second *chōka*, MYS 2: 210, where they now refer to the deceased wife. Hitomaro brings out the bitter irony that whereas he had once thought he would temporarily hide his love from the eyes of the world, now his wife is about to hide herself from his view forever for she is no longer of this world.

The associated *tama*-images in the early section of the *chōka*, MYS 2: 207, find another ironical echo later in the lines, "I stood and listened/ but could not even hear/ the voices of the birds/ that cry on Unebi Mountain/ of the jewelled sleeve-cords" (*waga tachikikeba/ tamatsuki/ Unebi no yama ni/ naku tori no/ koi mo kiezu*). The irony here is heightened by the coming of a messenger, carrying a jeweled catalpa staff, to announce with "the voice of a catalpa bow" the death of his wife. The catalpa bow was a common instrument used by shamans and mediums in Japan in rituals in which they served as mouthpieces for the dead. The repetition of the word *tama* throughout this set—*tama kagiru, tamazusa, tamahoko*—cumulatively builds up the intense expectation placed on (and the immanent frustration that would result from) the *tama-furi* ritual, "a desperate act that the poet knows is hopeless."[47] One need not disagree with Levy's suggestion here that even as Hitomaro performed this ritual action he must have realized its ultimate futility, for even if he were able to sustain some sort of dialogue with his wife, she would not return in the flesh. At the same time, however, one need not conclude, as Levy does, that "Hitomaro's opus leaves us with a sense of extraordinary originality."[48] The oral performative voice that comes through here is not original in the sense of being the first expression of individual pain; rather it is the authentic voice of the pain of all who have lost a loved one, the pain the Greeks call *ponos*.[49] Although these *banka*, then, cannot properly be used as historical evidence of a change in human consciousness in early Japan, they can and should be studied as culturally determined and styled expressions of the human grief caused by the death of a loved one.

Banka *by Servingmen*

The set of female *banka* from the *mogari no miya* of the deceased Emperor Tenji above probably came from the interior of the *mogari no miya*, although the *chōka* by Nukata-ō (MYS 2: 155) may have been from a public forum. In order to explicate the multidimensional functions and meaning of these laments, other *banka*, including those attributed to the Empress Saimei following the death of her grandson and laments by Hitomaro on the death of his wife were introduced. Saimei's laments seem to have come from the temporary grave site of her grandson, and Hitomaro's came from his wife's home village, though again this was also probably the grave site. Let us turn next to a formal public *chōka* and two envoys by Hitomaro at the time of the temporary enshrinement of the Crown Prince Kusakabe and a well-known set of *banka*, MYS 2: 167–193, from the period of Kusakabe's *mogari no miya* by *toneri*, servingmen or male guards, attached to this prince's palace. These poems seem to have been performed in the open public area around the *mogari no miya*.[50]

The earliest extant poems attributed to Hitomaro are MYS 2: 167–169. Their highly developed rhetorical style, however, suggests that at this time Hitomaro was already a masterly poet. When the Emperor Temmu died on 9/9/686, his widow, later the Empress Jitō, moved quickly to do away with the Imperial Prince Ōtsu in order that her only son, Kusakabe, might assume power. Temmu was given final burial on 11/11/688 and plans were laid for Kusakabe to succeed, but then he died unexpectedly on 4/13/689. This meant that the court, which had only recently completed more than two years of mourning for Temmu, once again found itself involved in elaborate public funeral rites for the deceased crown prince. Jitō had compelling reasons to make certain that the *mogari no miya* rituals were impressive and completely under her control. Kusakabe was her only son, so with his death her dynastic hopes devolved next upon her grandson, then about six years old. It is in this somewhat unusual situation that Jitō once again used the funeral rituals, among other venues available to her, to advance her faction's cause in the succession struggle. Bearing this background sketch in mind, let us turn to Hitomaro's public *banka* on Kusakabe's temporary burial, followed by the long sequence of short laments by *toneri*.

Hinamishi no miko no mikoto no araki no miya no toki, Kakinomoto no Asomi no Hitomaro no tsukuru uta isshu narabe ni tanka

Poem by Kakinomoto Hitomaro at the time of the temporary enshrinement of the Crown Prince Hinamishi (Peer of the Sun), with tanka

ametsuchi no
hajime no toki
hisakata no
ama no kawara ni
yaoyorozu
chiyorozu kami no
kamu tsudoi
tsudoi imashite
kamu hakari
hakarishi toki ni
Amaterasu
Hirume no mikoto
(hitotsu ni iu, sashi
noboru Hirume no sashi)
ama o ba
shirashimesu to
ashihara no
mizuho no kuni o
ametsuchi no
yoriai no kiwami
shirashimesu
kami no mikoto to
amakumo no
yaekaki wakite
(hitotsu ni iu, amakumo
no yaekumo wakite)
kamukudashi

In the beginning
of heaven and earth,
on the riverbanks
of the far firmament,
the eight million deities,
the ten million deities
gathered in godly assembly
and held divine council,
and judged that the Sun Goddess,
(a variant says: "the high-shining
Sun Goddess")
Amaterasu,
would rule the heavens
and, that he should rule
this land below,
where ears of rice flourish
on the reed plains,
until heaven and earth
draw together again.
He pushed apart the eight-fold
[banks of] clouds of heaven
(a variant says, "pushed apart the
eight-fold clouds of heaven")
and descended, a god.
The High-shining
Prince of the Sun
ruled as a god

imase matsurishi
takaterasu
Hi no miko wa
tobu tori no
Kiyomi no miya ni
kamunagara
futoshikimashite
sumeroki no
shikimasu kuni to
ama no hara
iwato o hiraki
kamuagari
agari imashinu
(hitotsu ni iu, kamu
nobori imashi ni shikaba)
wago ōkimi
miko no mikoto no
ame no shita
shirashimeshiseba
harubana no
tōtokaramu to
mochitsuki no
tatawashikemu to
ame no shita
(hitotsu ni iu,
osukuni)
yomo no hito no
ōfune no
omoi tanomite
amatsu mizu
aogite matsu ni
ikasama ni
omōshimeseka
tsure mo naki
Mayumi no oka ni
miyabashira
futoshikiimashi
mi-araka o
takashirimashite
asagoto ni
mikoto towasanu
hi tsuki no
maneku narinuru
soko yue ni
miko no miyahito
yukue shirazu mo

at the Kiyomi Palace
in Asuka,
where the birds fly,
until he opened
heaven's gate of stone
and rose, godlike,
rose to dwell
in those fields of heaven,
the land ruled
by Emperors past.
(A variant says, "until he
went up godlike.")
If you Lord, the Crown Prince,
had lived
to rule under the realm of heaven,
how, like the spring blossoms,
you would have been noble,
how, like the full moon,
you would have waxed great.
So the people
of the earth's four directions
(a variant says, "the imperially
ruled lands")
placed their hopes on you,
as on a great ship,
and looked up to you in expectation
as, in a drought,
to the [rain-]swollen sky.
But—what could have been
in your mind?—
you have driven thick palace pillars
by remote Mayumi Hill
and raised high your mausoleum hall.
Now many days and months
have passed
without your commands
given each morning,
and so
the imperial courtiers
do not know which way to turn.
(A variant has, "the courtiers of
the luxuriant bamboo Prince do not
know which way to turn.")[51]

(hitotsu ni iu, sasutake
no miko no miyahito
yukue shiranisu)

hanka nishu   Two envoys

hisakata no   That the palace
ame miru gotoku   of the Prince we held in awe
aogimishi   as we would look up
miko no mikado no   to the far firmament
aremaku oshi mo   should fall to ruins—alas!

akanesasu   The crimson-gleaming sun
hi wa teraseredo   still shines,
nubatama no   but that the moon is hidden
yo wataru tsuki no   in the pitch-black night it crosses—
kakuraku oshi mo   alas!

(aru hon, kudari no uta   (In one book, these poems are envoys
o mochite nochi no miko   to a poem from the time of the
no mikoto no araki no   temporary enshrinement of a later
miya no toki no uta no   Crown Prince.)[52]
han[ka] to naseri)

This set of *banka* is useful in providing insight into the function of public laments. One of the first things that strikes the modern reader of these poems is their highly developed rhetorical style and structure. This rhetoric, however, did not function in isolation; its power came in large part from the worldview out of which it came. The first part of the *chōka*, distinguished in the translation by a break, although none exists in the original manuscripts, rehearses the myth of the descent of Ninigi, the grandson of Amaterasu and the divine ancestor of the imperial family, from Takamagahara to the earth. This myth is recorded in both the *Kojiki* and in a number of versions in the *Nihonshoki*. It must be recalled, though, that both these texts were written down *after* this set of laments, including this *chōka* by Hitomaro, would have been performed. A precise dating of these poems is impossible, although internal evidence ("Now many days and months/ have passed/ without your commands/ given each morning") suggests that they could not have come out of the initial rite of temporary enshrinement but must come from later in this period. Some scholars have suggested that Hitomaro's *chōka* may come from the time of final burial, although there is no clear evidence for this. Watase Masatada has even suggested that *banka* may have continued to be performed after final burial but in a Buddhist ritual venue.[53] This suggestion is intriguing and not impossible to imagine as a transitional phase in the growing claim on the part of Buddhists to dominion over funeral rituals. We know from the *Shoku-Nihonshoki*, the historical chronicle that picks up from the reign of the Emperor Mommu, for example, that after the death of the Empress

Dowager Jitō, she was temporarily enshrined for about a year before the corpse was cremated. During this period many Buddhist rituals were performed at the *mogari no miya* and in various temples. Even if Watase's suggestion were to be found to have merit, however, this does not detract from the fact that the *mogari no miya* clearly continued to be the central locus for the offering of not only *banka* but also eulogies, words of praise, ritual songs, and dancing.

If we assume MYS 2: 167–169 to have been performed at the *mogari no miya* (or even some other public ritual site), can we reconstruct the intention(s) informing this performance, as well as its possible reception by the assembled audience? I think we can, at least to some extent. First, we must bear in mind the *tama*-related religious complex informing both the funerary practices and the accession rituals of the imperial court. Yamamoto Kenkichi has succinctly summarized this complex as well as its relation to this set of poems.[54] In brief, the religio-political ideology of early Japan was based on the premise of a single imperial *tama* that was ritually transferred from one sovereign to the next. Thus, while the individual physical bodies were different, the imperial *tama* that resided in the sitting sovereign's body was identical. The transferral of the *tama*, though, was not effected laterally, as it were, but rather finally through a vertical circuit. It is in this light that the frequently appearing terms such as *kamuagari* ("rising god-like") and *kamukudari* ("descending god-like") must be understood. The imperial *tama* first descended to the earth with Ninigi. At death it reascends to Takamagahara, the High Heavens, only to descend once again when the successor formally accedes to the throne. Kagu-yama, among others, seems to have been especially identified as a site where the imperial *tama* ascended to heaven. With the development and growth in importance of the Ise Shrine cult, the *tama* was called back down there during the imperial accession ceremony, though we will see that this was not the exclusive locus of *tama-furi*-associated accession rites.

The poem MYS 2: 167 is structured in terms of this understanding of the movement of the imperial *tama*. It opens by rehearsing the original divine assembly of the myriad *kami* and their collective decision that Amaterasu should rule the heavens and Ninigi no mikoto should descend to rule the world. Significantly, Ninigi is not explicitly identified here by name but is suggested only later by the phrase *kami no mikoto* ("the divine prince").[55] His identity, however, is clear. It is no accident that Ninigi's relative position in the myth as the grandson of Amaterasu precisely mirrors the immediate situation that obtained following the death of Kusakabe when the mantle fell on his son and Jitō's grandson, Prince Karu. In the myth up until the last moment, it was Ninigi's father who was to descend to rule the world, just as it was assumed Kusakabe would rule. When the *chōka*, in a rapid temporal sweep, moves on to focus on the Emperor Temmu, it is through the following lines:

takaterasu	The High-shining
hi no miko wa	Prince of the Sun
tobu tori no	ruled as a god
Kiyomi no miya ni	at the Kiyomi Palace
kamunagara	in Asuka,
futoshikimashite	where the birds fly,
sumeroki no	until he opened
shikimasu kuni to	heaven's gate of stone
ama no hara	and rose, godlike,
iwato o hiraki	rose to dwell
kamuagari	in those fields of heaven,
agari imashinu	the land ruled
	by Emperors past.

Yamamoto Kenkichi suggests that the *hi* ("Sun") in the phrase *takaterasu hi no mikoto* ("the High-shining Prince of the Sun") is the imperial *tama* that is passed on to the imperial successor in an unbroken line from Amaterasu.[56] If we accept this suggestion, we can better recognize part of the intention informing Hitomaro's rhetorical strategy. The opening section recalls the original descent of the imperial charisma or *tama* with Ninigi no mikoto and proceeds to link this genealogy with Temmu, the deceased emperor who had recently been given final burial. Everything we have been able to learn about the *mogari no miya* complex suggests that during the period of temporary enshrinement, the imperial *tama* was believed to be outside the imperial body but still in this world. Thus, *tama-furi* rituals were performed to attract the *tama* back into the body or into some other object (*katami*). Once the spirit was believed to rest in the corpse or in another ritual object, *tama-shizume* rituals were performed to pacify and to keep it in a stable location. At the time of exhumation and final burial, however, the *tama* was believed to reascend once again to Takamagahara, the High Heavens.

Since Temmu had been given final burial or, to say the same thing but to different effect, since the imperial *tama* had been returned to the High Heavens, the way had been prepared for a successor to be installed in a ritual accession ceremony in which the *tama* would be called down once again to reside in a new body. This ritual scenario—an important rite of passage—is the basis for Hitomaro's reference to the expectations that the people had held for the Crown Prince Kusakabe. His unexpected death, however, frustrated these hopes. It also prompted the thinly veiled protest, found in several *banka*, addressed to the deceased—"What could have been in your mind?" (*ikasama ni/omōshimeseka*).[57] This phrase can, of course, equally be taken as a statement that the divine will (here of Kusakabe) is beyond the comprehension of mere mortals. Without denying this possibility—indeed, while assuming that this was probably the interpretation of the phrase by some of Hitomaro's audience—it is nevertheless useful to note that after the sudden and unexpected death of a loved one, individuals often have feelings of anger and betrayal that are directed at the deceased.[58] In other words, the existence of a set phrase of regret does not preclude the possibility that at any given time it could be used to express a genuine emotional response to death.

Finally, it is significant that death, as it is rhetorically presented in public *banka* for members of the imperial family, does not happen to individuals; it is willed. In death, too, the imperial family exercises complete control. If a sovereign yields earthly power to another, it is only that she/he might rise to the High Heavens to rule with other past emperors and empresses (*sumeroki no/ shikimasu kuni to/ ama no hara*). This transformation from a living sovereign (*sumeramikoto*) in the Land of Reed Plains to a heavenly ruler (*sumeroki* or *sumerogi*) was ritually effected through the *mogari no miya* complex.

According to Hitomaro, the death of the Crown Prince Kusakabe leaves the courtiers disoriented (*miko no miyahito/ yukue shirazu mo*). This response is not only symbolically appropriate in the larger complex of the power of the ritual center; it also accurately represents the socio-political situation as experienced by the courtiers. The death of a central political figure, such as the crown prince, deeply affected the positions of those whose personal careers were associated with that individual and immediately introduced anxieties about future prospects for advancement and for even maintaining their respective rank privileges. It is in this light that we must read the set of laments offered by male servingmen and guards following Kusakabe's death.

This set of poems is usually given as MYS 2: 171–193. For reasons to be discussed shortly, I lean toward the suggestion of some modern scholars that 170, attributed to Hitomaro, should also be included in this set. These *banka* will be presented interspersed with interpretive comments as we go along. It is impossible to use the *Nihonshoki* for corroborative and supplementary information in association with what is the longest set of laments in the *Man'yōshū*, for the *Nihonshoki* contains no records at all on the *mogari no miya* rituals for Kusakabe. Indeed, his death is reported in a single line—"[689/4] 13th day. His Highness the Prince Imperial Kusakabe died."[59] The chronicle is curiously silent about the immediate impact of Kusakabe's death. There are also no female *banka* preserved in the *Man'yōshū*. This situation is the reverse of that concerning the death of Temmu where the *Nihonshoki* contains, as we have seen, extensive references to the mourning rituals. Although a number of *banka* on Temmu's death attributed to Jitō are preserved in the *Man'yōshū*, there are no male *banka* by either servingmen or ritual reciters from this period. The reasons for this situation are unknown. Nevertheless, the repeated references in the Temmu Chapter to the public offerings of eulogies and laments at the *mogari no miya* strongly suggest that *banka* such as those above by Hitomaro and others by servingmen must have been performed in a public ritual context even though they have not been preserved. One possible explanation is that the inclusion or exclusion of poems in the *Man'yōshū* was determined by the political needs of the Jitō faction. That is, Jitō figures prominently in the *Man'yōshū* record of Temmu's funeral rites because she was to exercise effective control of the government. It is not surprising, then, that laments by other wives and consorts do not appear. Similarly, for political reasons Jitō or others of her faction may have sought to suppress the voices of women associated with Kusakabe because of the potential power they (and their families) might have exercised in the succession. The politics of the act of anthologization is a topic that requires much more careful study.

The poem MYS 2: 170 is included in the *Man'yōshū* as a variant envoy to Hitomaro's *chōka* that we just examined. It reads:

aru hon no uta isshu	A poem from another book
Shima no miya	In the Garden Palace,
magari no ike no	in the Curved Pool,
hanachitori	the roaming water-birds
hitome ni koite	long for human eyes
ike ni kazukazu	and do not dive.[60]

The *Shima no miya*, here glossed as "the Garden Palace" by Levy, was Kusakabe's primary residence. It had originally been built by Soga no Kurayamada, Jitō's maternal grandfather. The water-birds are probably once again *katami* and considered as repositories of the spirit of the deceased crown prince, since birds were taken to be intermediaries between the realm of the living and that of the dead.[61] Like the courtiers, the birds are disconcerted by the crown prince's death. The set of *banka* continues with:

miko mo mikoto no miya no tonerira ka-	Twenty-three poems by the Servingmen at
nashibi itamite tsukuru uta ni-jū-sanshu	the Palace of the Crown Prince in their
	pain and sorrow
(171)	
takahikaru	O the Garden Palace
waga Hi no miko no	where our high-shining
yorozu yo ni	Prince of the Sun
kuni shirasamashi	was to rule the land
Shima no miya wa mo	for ten thousand generations!

In this painful cry, which reaches its peak with the pitiful sob, "O the Garden Palace," Kusakabe is identified with his father, the Emperor Temmu, through the designation *takahikaru Hi no miko*, "high-shining Prince of the Sun." The pain is a result of the frustrated expectation that Kusakabe would rule as emperor.

(172)

Shima no miya	O roaming water-birds
Ue no ike naru	in the Upper Pond of the Garden Palace
hanachitori	do not wing away
arabina yuki so	with wild fluttering,
kimi masazu tomo	even if our Lord is gone.

The spatial locus here remains the Shima no miya, although there is a slight shift from the Curved Pond of 170 to the Upper Pond here. This poem seems to belong to a *tama-shizume* ritual, an attempt to pacify the spirit of the deceased and to keep it resting in the water-birds at his former palace. The character *ara* in "*arabina yuki so*" recalls the *ara-tama* or "rough spirit" that had to be pacified. (The opposite is *nigi-tama*, "soft" or "gentle spirit.")

(173)

takahikaru	If you, our high-shining
waga Hi no miko no	Prince of the Sun
imashiseba	were here,
Shima no mikado wa	the Garden Palace gates
arezaramashi o	would not fall to ruin!

This lament seems to be spoken directly to the deceased. It is at once a true lament and a reproach directed at the deceased. The audience is led to imagine that not only will the palace fall to ruin, but the *toneri*'s future may also be in jeopardy, since it was not always easy to find a new patron in the aftermath of such a death. That is, in situations such as this, other princes would have already had their own contingents of loyal retainers and courtiers, who would not have necessarily welcomed Kusakabe's former retainers joining them, since these *toneri* would have been additional competitors for their prince's favor.

(174)

yoso ni mishi	Once viewed as of no consequence,
Mayumi no oka mo	Mayumi Hill
kimi maseba	with your presence, Lord,
tokotsu mikado to	is the site of eternal palace gates
tonoisuru ka mo	where we will stay and serve.

This pledge of loyalty to the crown prince even in his death must not have been without its own pathos as far as the living were concerned. As we saw earlier, there is some suggestion that those who served at the tombs of the imperial family were in some respects considered dead to the world of the living. If this was in fact true, then in this case we must hear the pitiful voice of servingmen who only recently had had visions of a glorious future in front of them now facing the prospect of a life of serving the dead. The phrase "eternal palace gates/ where we will stay and serve" must have weighed heavily on their hearts and minds as this verse was sung. The rhetorical strategy of claiming that the mere presence of the prince, even in death, transformed a formerly undistinguished site into one worthy of praise and attention is quite common in the *Man'yōshū*.

(175)

ime ni da ni	Not even in my dreams
mizarishi mono o	did I imagine this:
oboboshiku	with gloom, proceeding
miya ide mo suru ka	to your palace
sa-Hinokuma mi o	on the bending road by Hinokuma.

(176)

ametsuchi to	Thinking,
tomo ni owaemu to	"until the end
omoitsutsu	of heaven and earth,"
tsukaematsurishi	I served you.
kokoro tagainu	My heart has been betrayed!

These two *banka* clearly display the sense of anger and betrayal the *toneri* feel in the wake of their shattered dreams. Clearly such laments were addressed not only to the deceased but also to the living, to the assembled audience of mourners and other members of the court. In her study of contemporary Greek laments, Caraveli-Chaves found that many shared the same thematic structure, including a description of the plight of the mourner and an invitation to the audience to share in her pain and mourning. She noted that "far from being songs *about* the dead only, or even magical songs *to* the dead ... the thematic selection and organization in lament poetry bears the additional burden of serving the sense of identity of the living."[62] In these *banka* we may perhaps hear the voices of servingmen begging to have their own cruel fate, misfortune, and pain recognized, and thus somewhat assuaged. Even though each *banka* must have been presented by an individual, the shared offering of laments no doubt also served to create a bond among the *toneri*, united in their grief and anxiety.

(177)

asahi teru	Gathering
Sada no oka be ni	by Sada Hill
mureitsutsu	illumined by the rising sun
waga naku namida	the tears I cry
yamu toki mo nashi	know no ceasing.

(178)
mitatatshi no
Shima o miru toki
niwatazumi
nagururu namida
tomeso kanetsuru

When I looked
on the Garden where once you stood,
my tears streamed down
sudden showers
I could not stop.

(179)
Tachibana no
Shima no miya ni wa
akane kamo
Sada no oka be ni
tonoishi ni yuku

Although I do not tire
of the Garden Palace
at Tachibana,
I leave to serve
at the foot of Sada Hill.

Verse 177 refers to the gathering of the servingmen each morning at the *mogari no miya* to receive their commands just as they had done when Kusakabe was alive. During the period of the *mogari no miya* it seems that the daily routine and regimen of the palace was maintained to some extent. That this should have been the case is not surprising in light of the operative socio-political fiction that the deceased still reigned in his former capacity until the time of final burial. Song 179 also seems to allude to the requirement that the *toneri* gather at the *mogari no miya* on Sada Hill each morning before dawn. The singer protests—although only implicitly within a standard form of praise—that he never tires of looking on the former palace grounds of Kusakabe, yet he finds he must leave in the predawn hours for the temporary enshrinement palace.

(180)
mitatashi no
Shima o mo ie to
sumu tori mo
arabina yuki so
toshi kawaru made

O birds who make your home
in the very Garden where he stood,
do not wing away
with wild fluttering,
until the year has changed.

(181)
mitatashi
Shima no ariso o
ima mireba
haizarishi kusa
hai ni keru kama

When I now look
on the rough rocks
in the Garden where you stood,
are they not overgrown with grass
that did not grow before?

(182)
togura tate
kaishi kari no ko
su tachinaba
Mayumi no oka ni
tobikaeri kone

O gosslings we raised
in pens we built,
in nests we built,
fly back
to Mayumi Hill!

Verses 180 and 182 both concern birds as *katami* once again. The former is a *tama-shizume* verse; the latter also seeks to get the wandering birds to settle down. The intervening verse simply laments the condition of the empty palace grounds in the wake of Kusakabe's death while also alluding to the length of time that has passed. Part of its poignancy, though, comes from the irony that the crown prince's death should lead to life (the grass growing at the abandoned palace), but life that is finally useless in human social terms.

(183)

waga mi-kado	I, who had thought
chiyo tokotoba ni	our imperial halls
sakaemu to	would flourish eternally,
omoite arishi	for a thousand ages—
wareshi kanashi mo	how sad I am!

(184)

himukashi no	Though I await your summons
tagi no mi-kado ni	at the Imperial Gate
samoraedo	of the eastern waterfall,
kino mo kyō mo	you never call—
mesu koto mo nashi	not yesterday, not today.

(185)

mizu tsutau	Will I ever see again
iso no urami no	that path of azaleas
iwa tsutsuji	blooming full
moku saku michi o	over the stones
mata minamu kamo	where the stream bends?

Each of these songs expresses some regret and a sense of personal desolation. Verse 184 seems to indicate that the servingman realizes his faithful service during the period of temporary enshrinement will ultimately be for naught and that the rituals, too, may finally be futile. This is the same realization found earlier among the mourners in rural Greece even as they continue to sweep the grave site and bring food and flowers.

(186)

hitohi ni wa	The Great Eastern Gate
sen tabi mairishi	of the imperial palace
himukashi no	I passed through
ōki mi-kado o	a thousand times a day
irikatenu kamo	now I hesitate to enter.

(187)

tsure mo naki	If I return
Sada no okabe ni	to the foot of Sada Hill

kaerieba
Shima no mi-hashi ni
tare ka sumawamu

for no good reason
who will live
by the imperial bridge?

(188)
asa kumori
hi no irinureba
mi-tatashi no
Shima ni oriite
nakitsuru kamo

Morning overcast
the sun did not break through,
coming down
to the Garden where once you stood
how I wept!

(189)
asahi teru
Shima no mi-kado ni
oboboshiku
hito oto mo seneba
maura kanashi mo

By the imperial gates
illumined by the rising sun
not the slightest
rustle of men—
oh, the sadness in my heart!

These verses continue to express the sense of loss the *toneri* feel. Though they go through the same ritual motions as when the crown prince was alive (186), these motions no longer bring pleasure. Indeed, once again these *uta* seem to be, in part, expressions of resistance or protest, as in 187. The psychological sense of abandonment is stressed in 189 by drawing attention to the abandoned palace, once the center of bustling activity but now silent. The reason for this state has, of course, already been pointed to in 188—the sun (i.e., the crown prince, *Hi no miko*) no longer shines there. The remaining *banka* of this set read:

(190)
makihashira
futoki kokoro wa
arishi kado
kono waga kokoro
shizumekanetsu mo

Stout was my heart
like cyprus pillars,
but now
this heart of mine
cannot be pacified!

(191)
kekoromo o
haru fuyu makete
idemashishi
Uda no ōno wa
omōemu kamo

Will the great fields of Uda
be remembered,
where you went on imperial procession,
with stores of woolen clothes
for winter and for spring?

(192)
asahi teru
Sada no okabe ni
naku tori no
yo naki kaerau
kono toshi koro o

Like the birds that cry
on Sada's hillside
illumined by the rising sun,
I have cried each night
of this year!

(193)

hatakora ga	The path the farmers take
yoru-hiru to iwazu	each morning and night
yuku michi o	without being told
ware wa kotogoto	I'll take each day
miyaji ni zo suru	for my road to your palace!

migi, Nihonshoki ni iwaku, san-nen tsu-chinoto ushi no natsu shigatsu mizunoto hitsuji no tsuitachi no kinoto hitsuji ni ka-muagari-mashinu to ieri.	On the above, the Nihonshoki records the Crown Prince's death in summer, on the thirteenth day of the fourth month, in the third year of the reign [689].[63]

These poems bear our attention for several reasons. First, they are the only ex-tended set of *banka* exclusively by males. As such, they provide valuable hints con-cerning the type of public laments the servingmen and other low-ranking members of the court offered. Regrettably we have little information on the ritual context in which they would have been presented. Nevertheless, a few tentative conjectures can be made. It is probable that such laments were offered daily, probably at dawn and again at dusk. Internal evidence suggests, as we have seen, that the servingmen continued to assemble each morning before dawn to receive their orders from the crown prince, just as they had while he was alive. Known as *asa matsurigoto*, this was a typical blend of religious ritual with the daily administration of the government. The gates of the imperial palace, and those of the crown prince, were opened at dawn and closed after sunset. The *Nihonshoki* records the first attempt to inaugurate the *asa matsurigoto* in 636 in the reign of the Emperor Jomei:

Autumn, 7th month, 1st day. Prince Ōmata addressed Toyura no Ōmi, saying:—"The Min-isters and functionaries are remiss in their attendance at Court. Henceforth, let them attend at the beginning of the hour of the Hare [i.e., 5–7 A.M.] and withdraw after the hour of the Serpent [i.e., 9–11 A.M.]. Regulate this by means of a bell." The Ōmi, however, did not take this advice.[64]

All these laments are in the form of *tanka* rather than *chōka*. As we have seen, the *chōka* form was a vehicle for formal public laments. These, however, seem closer to the laments by women offered during the period of the temporary enshrinement of the Emperor Tenji. We do not know whether *chōka* similar to MYS 2: 167 were also offered daily. It is possible that shorter laments such as these by *toneri* were offered together with such *chōka*. Then again, the situation may have been similar to that which obtained in ancient Greece where large public ritual gatherings were distin-guished from smaller, more frequent lamentation sessions at the tomb.[65] Clearly the entire court could hardly afford to devote itself to mourning rituals each and every day for months and even years; on the other hand, if the records from Temmu's *mogari no miya* period are representative of the more general situation, then the evidence is equally clear that full-scale mourning rituals were held rather frequently. We are probably safe in assuming that the higher the rank of the deceased, the more extensive and intensive the mourning rituals would have been. The ability to bring together a great number of influential and powerful members of the court and the provincial clans in such ritual settings was itself a significant exercise and display of power. Thus, we may also surmise that the number of individuals, including *toneri*, assigned to full-time duty as mourners would vary according to the rank and status of the deceased. Although oral performative *banka* were no doubt found in each case, whether they were preserved in the *Nihonshoki* or in the *Man'yōshū* or not was probably often determined by political concerns rather than by strictly aesthetic considerations. The preservation of this large number of *banka* on the Crown Prince Kusakabe, for example, may be understood as a part of the historiographic project of the eighth-century Court, still in the hands of the Temmu–Jitō faction, to legitimate its power and position.

These laments should not be understood, however, as isolated expressions of grief later gathered together by the editors of the *Man'yōshū*. The manner in which these laments are now ordered and preserved is in considerable measure a consequence of the activity of the editors of the *Man'yōshū*; we can nevertheless still glean some useful information concerning the ritual context in which the *banka* must have been performed. To do this, however, requires a few working assumptions. First, these laments must be considered as coming out of a collective ritual, although the voice, unless otherwise indicated, should be thought of as first-person singular or plural, the standard for oral laments. In speaking about the Greek lament tradition, Alexiou points out that "The lament was always in some sense collective and never an exclusively solo performance. There is no example in Greek antiquity of a lament which has lost all traces of refrain."[66] Although there is no evidence that the audience in early Japan participated in the same way by joining in the refrain, it does seem that, whether it was in the female interior of the *mogari no miya* or in the surrounding space where the *toneri* lamented, there was usually a group of mourners gathered. Indeed, during the period of the seclusion of the women, we may assume that they could hear the laments of the servingmen outside and, thus, would have been part of the audience. Princess Nukata's poem "when the mourners withdrew from the Emperor's tomb and dispersed" (MYS 2: 155) seems to suggest as much.

We must, then, imagine *banka* such as these as having been *generated* in a collective ritual of mourning, with one lament perhaps evoking others that continue an earlier theme or expression.[67] A wide range of studies of different oral performative traditions has demonstrated how formulaic expressions can act as mental "triggers" of recall of related expressions, generating other songs. Phrases shared between and among the laments above include "water-birds" (*hanachitori*) in 170 and 172; "illuminated by the morning sun" (*asahi teru*) in 177, 189, and 192—significantly these are the only instances of this phrase in the *Man'yōshū*); "the Garden where once you stood" (*mi-tatashi no Shima*) in 178, 180, and 181; and "imperial halls" *mi-kado* in 183, 184, 186, and 189. Even where phrases are not shared, one can find thematic overlap as in 174 and 176, where service to the crown prince is emphasized.[68]

From the evidence obtained from the study of Greek oral laments we can make a few other tentative suggestions concerning the genesis and performance of such *banka*. To begin with, authorship is not a relevant category here, since these *uta* seem to be reworkings of earlier laments and even other types of songs, such as those of separation and longing. In Greece, laments are widely circulated and performed with the necessary adaptations and emendations to fit the specific case at hand. Even though these *banka* constitute the largest such group extant, they undoubtedly represent only a tiny percentage of the laments offered during the period of Kusakabe's temporary enshrinement. Moreover, it is likely that any given lament may have been performed repeatedly in either the same or slightly different form by either the same mourner or a number of different ones. The recognition of such multiple performances as a strong probability would help to explain the existence of identical or almost identical variants of some *banka* in the *Man'yōshū* ascribed in the editorial prose notes to different poets and/or to different loci. In this specific set of *banka* for Kusakabe, for example, we can now better appreciate the endnote to the *hanka* MYS 2: 168 and 169 and how these may indeed have also been performed (not written) by Hitomaro at the time of the temporary interment of a later crown prince. That is, if one thinks of these *banka* in oral performative terms, it is not necessary to choose between such notes by assuming that only one could be correct. To do so is to continue to operate out of a (perhaps unconscious) textual bias.

In Chapter Two we found that in the case of sovereigns the *mogari no miya* generally was built in the courtyard (often the southern courtyard) of the imperial palace. There is some suggestion from the *Nihonshoki* and the *Man'yōshū* that this was not the case following the death of a prince or princess. Then the *mogari no miya* seems to have been constructed on a hill some distance from the prince's or princess's palace. Internal evidence from the *banka* in this set indicates that the *toneri* traveled back and forth between the Garden Palace and Kusakabe's burial site on Mayumi or Sada Hill, several kilometers away.

Many scholars have argued that verse 170 belongs with the set of twenty-three *banka* by *toneri*. If it is included, one finds that poems 170–174 all focus on or are from Kusakabe's Garden Palace, whereas the next four laments, 174–177, are on Mayumi Hill, the site of the *mogari no miya*. The remaining poems seem to alternate between these two loci. What one is to make of this fact is a matter of some dispute, but it is clear that this alternating pattern is not fortuitous.[69] What is unclear, however, is whether these poems are so ordered because they were performed together, or whether they were only later arranged in this fashion by the *Man'yōshū* editors. Watase has gone so far as to argue that groups of four *toneri*, led by Hitomaro, produced these laments.[70] This is an intriguing suggestion, but one that, like so many others, ultimately cannot be proved. If one thinks about these *banka* in terms of oral generation and performance, though, it is difficult to believe they would have been recorded on the spot, as it were, by a scribe and passed down in that form.

In summation, then, the *banka* we have seen so far indicate that one can identify several distinct loci for the performance of laments. In the case of a deceased emperor the interior of the temporary enshrinement palace, constructed in the courtyard of the imperial palace, was an essentially female ritual space. The *banka* from this locus participated in both *tama-furi* and *tama-shizume* rituals. The evidence of a similar extensive female ritual complex in the case of a deceased prince is less sure, although an abbreviated version may be envisioned. The evidence from the *mogari no miya* of Crown Prince Kusakabe, though, suggests that the temporary burial site was at some remove from the prince's palace. This difference seems to have generated at least two distinct performative loci for male laments—the area outside the *mogari no miya* and the prince's former palace.

These sites themselves could function as *katami* or potential repositories of the *tama* of the deceased that, through *tama-furi* rituals, could be recalled to a place especially identified with the deceased and then kept or enshrined there through *tama-shizume* or pacification rituals. Then, too, other objects, both animate (birds and infants) and inanimate (*tamakazura* or wreaths, jewels, articles of clothing), could also serve as *katami*. The rituals involved not only certain actions—the waving of sleeves, encircling areas with special banners, and wearing special strings of jewels—but also the singing or recitation of laments that shared recognizable rhetorical patterns and subjects. Extended sessions or performances of laments might include elements of praise of the deceased, allusions to past shared sexual pleasures (including the sexual metaphors of undulating and tangled seaweed and the crossing of sleeves), the recollection of activities especially enjoyed by the deceased, the rehearsal of the pain and suffering the death has caused the survivors, expressions of disorientation as a result of the death, remonstrations against the deceased for having caused such pain or having abandoned loved ones and for apparently having ignored the loyalty and great expectations that had been placed on him, and so on.

There is a discernible difference in form between formal public *banka*, often *chōka* with envoys, and what most Japanese scholars have called private or personal laments, usually in *tanka* form. In addition, the forms of address used in speaking to the deceased are often clearly distinguished in terms of formality and familiarity or intimacy. It is not surprising that the death of a significant political figure in the imperial court should have occasioned laments of both types, since the lives and deaths of such figures had both public and private dimensions. Because these dimensions were never entirely discrete, one finds the funerary rites incorporating (and the term is entirely appropriate here) demonstrably political dimensions as well. Thus, in the public presentation of *chōka* extolling the deceased, individuals found the opportunity to identify themselves and their clans or branches with the deceased, to rehearse their history of loyal service and/or to make promises of continued loyalty and service, and to recount publicly (and, potentially at least, revise or augment) their clan genealogies.

When the extant *banka* are recontextualized in light of all these factors, it is clear they can no longer be read as simply mirroring individual human emotions. The complex religio-political situation surrounding the death of any member of the court meant that purely personal emotion could rarely if ever be expressed publicly. A large number of contingent factors would have constrained and channeled expressions of grief in public, just as they had expressions of love. Laments from the locus of the *mogari no miya* were in their genesis and performative contexts important vehicles of public expression in the politics of death in the court. At the same time, these *banka* came to be used as historical documents in the larger historiographic project giving narrative contour to the past.

The *mogari no miya* ritual complex was only one (and an occasional) expression of the ceremonial nature of the court, and as such, it must be understood as part of a much larger spectacle of public ritual in early Japan. In its oral performative context, ritual poetry provided a means of publicly and collectively ratifying the operative ideals of the community. At the same time it was a means of articulating responses to incongruities experienced by the community, including the death of the sovereign. In this way *uta* were dynamic agents in a larger historical moment of social and cultural definition. In reading these verses today, the roles of a variety of historical agents—poets, members of the court, editors of the extant texts, and others, all acting in terms of their own perceived self-interests—need to be considered and their probable intentions and motives recognized. Such poems do not simply record what happened in the court, nor as ritual poems do they express a static cultural ideology. In performance and in their textualization they at once mediated and were mediated by other cultural discourses (legal, economic, familial or genealogical, mythic, and ritual).

In generating powerful panegyrics, the oral court poets skillfully exploited the rhetorical possibilities available to them in the circulating body of myths, legends, and oral poetic devices. Mythic elements were often selectively (i.e., consciously) introduced for discernible rhetorical and political purposes. Public *banka* for politically powerful imperial family members, for instance, would often rhetorically invoke the myth of an unbroken line of imperial rule from the beginning of time in an effort to ameliorate or even deny the immediate discontinuity occasioned by death. At the same time, the *mogari no miya* rituals provided an important means for other families and clans to (re)establish relationships with the imperial family and to consolidate the positions of various factions within it. *Banka* and praise poems offered in such situations were elements of a complex process of achieving a consensus concerning the redistribution of power. Similarly, public poetry of praise of palaces and geographical sites, poems recording imperial excursions and hunts, and so on, all participated in the socio-political, religious, economic, and aesthetic life of the court. In the following chapter this complex mediation among different cultural discourses and between structure and history will be examined.

CHAPTER FIVE

Mythistory, Rhetoric, and the Politics of Marriage

The texts we have from early Japan are the products of complex negotiations among various cultural discourses. *Banka* and other examples of ritual poetry drew their cogency in part from their construction out of an available and readily recognized body of rhetorical forms, tropes, and *topoi*, which helped to link contemporary or recent historical occurrences with mythic paradigms or significant events from the past. Public rhetoric was an important resource used by individuals and factions in the court to promote their own interests.

Because the actions of every individual occupying strategic positions in relation to the succession were under close scrutiny during the period of temporary interment, any act was subject to being interpreted as a threat and could thus provoke an antagonistic or violent response. Consequently, individuals were extremely careful in their public statements and behavior and ever sensitive to the reactions of others.[1] An important, though little recognized, source of the danger in this situation was that no individual could control the significance placed on his or her actions, non-actions, or statements. That is, in the wake of the sovereign's death, individuals could be acted upon in such a way that rendered their own intention of little or no consequence in the transaction of meaning.

During the period of temporary interment, symbolic activity in the court was at its height. Drawing upon a culturally available fund of knowledge that included paradigmatic narratives, symbolic and ritual complexes, genealogies, and so on, historical agents framed or "mapped" the world based upon their understanding of the relative positions of other contingent agents within the socio-political web of the court. Saussure has taught us that the value of a sign is a function of its relations to other signs within the system. Hence, the same act performed by different persons occupying different positions within the court would not "mean" the same thing in every case. Thus, in attempting to understand the reports of events in the court following the death of a sovereign, we need to pay attention to the relational positions of the significant players and the (potentially conflicting) interpretive frames placed upon them. Insofar as historical actors were able to contextualize their own acts or those of other agents convincingly and authoritatively in ways that promoted their own perceived interests, they effectively exercised an important form of power—the power of signification. In this final chapter we will focus on a few instances of signifying-in-action and other instances of signifying in retrospect.

As we have already seen, oral performative poetry could be used to identify events and individuals in the court with mythic narratives and the relational positions of superiority and subordination found therein, but it could also be used to challenge or "stretch" the interpretive frames in a number of ways. This challenge was not only possible but inevitable, since the circumstances and relations in the court at any given time did not always match those in the paradigmatic narratives. Earlier I gave the example of Ninigi, the grandson of Amaterasu rather than her son, descending from the High Heavens and assuming power as probably a retrospective "rewriting" of the myth in order to legitimate the succession in the court in the wake of the death of the Crown Prince Kusakabe.

Such "framing" is not limited, however, to retrospective narrative. Ritual poetry, genealogies, and popular oral narratives were all used to shape the contours of a history in which the mythic past found expression in the present in the acts of the members of the imperial family. In this mythistory the radical disjunction in the socio-political life of the court occasioned by each imperial death was rhetorically transformed into an instance of replication on a higher level. The religio-political role of professional oral poets in the seventh century in declaiming this mythistory deserves more study.[2]

Let us turn to selected instances of the interplay of structure and history in the accounts of the imperial succession from the latter half of the sixth century to the end of the seventh century. Noting the strategic positions of individuals in the court, their marriage alliances, and their clan relationships will enable us to discover parallels—not lost on the early Japanese—with the relational positions of characters in several important myths. In 592 Soga no Umako, the powerful head of the Soga clan and Great Minister (Ōmi) of the Right, had the Emperor Sushun assassinated and then arranged to have one of his own granddaughters succeed as the Empress Suiko only a month later. The following set of praise poems preserved in the *Man'yōshū* is representative of the kind of formal exchanges found in the many ceremonial functions within the court. The rhetoric in such poetry serves the function of, in Levy's felicitous phrase, "crafting iconic images which 'prove' the divinity of the imperial family."[3]

20th year [612], Spring, 1st month, 7th day. A banquet, with saké, was given to all the high functionaries. On this day the Ōmi [Soga no Umako] proposed the health of the Empress, and sang a song, saying [*ōmi-sakazuki tatematsuriagarite utaite mosaku*]:—

yasumishishi	When we see
waga ōkimi no	our great sovereign

kakurimasu	who rules in peace
ama no yaso kage	emerge from the myriad clouds
idetatatsu	in the august sky
mi-sora o mireba	where you were hidden,
yorozu yo ni	how we pray
kakushimo ga mo	"May it be thus
chiyo ni mo	forever!
kakushimo ga mo	May it be thus
kashikomite	for a thousand ages
tsukaematsuramu	that in awe
orogamite	we might serve you,
tsakematsuramu	that reverently
utazuki matsuru	we might serve you!"
	We present tribute in song.

The Empress replied, saying:—

ma-Soga yo	O honorable Soga!
Soga no kora wa	The sons of the Soga
uma naraba	were they horses
Himuka no koma	would be steeds of Himuka;
tachi naraba	were they swords
Kure no ma-sai	would be the sacred swords of Kure!
ubeshi kamo	Right and proper it is
Soga no kora o	that the sons of the Soga
Ōkimi no	should be in the employ
tsukawasurashiki	of the sovereign.[4]

This type of praise poetry, no matter how hackneyed, played an important religio-political function in the court. In rhetorical form and content, it shares much with other oral performative *chōka* we have seen. It is a good example of the use of formal, stylized verse at an imperial banquet to praise the sovereign and to declare and reaffirm publicly the Soga clan's loyal service to the empress; at the same time, it functions to legitimate the Soga's high status. Soga no Umako's verse explicitly employs the mythology of Amaterasu as a subtext. In declaring that the empress emerges and reveals herself (literally "stands out"—*idetatatsu*) to the gathering of the members of the court, he recalls the figure of Amaterasu emerging from seclusion in the heavenly rock-grotto into the assembly of the myriad *kami*. In a manner similar to that in Prince Ikusa's boastful complaint, Umako rhetorically creates social distance between the empress and the other members of the court while simultaneously demonstrating a social proximity between the empress and himself, since he offers the verse directly to her and receives her praise in return. The empress's response confirms the Soga's relative status as subordinates in her employ while simultaneously elevating the Soga's status and prestige relative to all the other nobles and courtiers by using the honorific prefix *ma*, variously rendered as "true," "sacred," or "honorable," in conjunction with the clan name. These *uta*, then, display the symbionic relationship that existed in the court between the sovereign and the various powerful clans. This symbionic relationship must be borne in mind in reading each and every example of public performative poetry from the early Japanese court, including those that at first glance ostensibly have little or no political content.

The religio-political ideology of the imperial family's unique status demanded that the prestige of the Soga (or any other individual or clan) be expressed through this kind of rhetoric, which sketched the contours of the existent distribution of power within the frame of a mythistory.[5] Here the preeminence of the family of Soga no Umako within the court is declared right and proper. In order to appreciate why the special relationship between the clan of Soga no Umako and the Empress Suiko needed to be declared publicly in a ritual verse form and then later preserved in the *Nihonshoki*, one must understand the political machinations that brought Suiko to power. Turning back to the reign of the Emperor Kimmei (r. 539–571), we are able to see the Soga rise to preeminence through the skillful employ of the cultural discourses of genealogy and myth.

Kimmei is reported to have had five imperial consorts in addition to his empress-consort. The chart on the following page is based upon information provided by the *Nihonshoki*. Kimmei's empress-consort, Ishihime, was the daughter of his paternal half-brother and predecessor, the Emperor Senka, and thus his niece. His first two senior consorts were younger sisters of Ishihime, hence he married three sisters. His eldest son by the empress died during Kimmei's reign, so the mantle of successor fell on his second son, who eventually succeeded him as the Emperor Bidatsu. Thus far the succession is "normal," that is, predictable or immediately understandable. What needs to be examined is how the Senka–Kimmei–Bidatsu line ended and a Soga dynasty began with the Emperor Yōmei (r. 585–587), Soga no Umako's grandson. As the chart shows, Kitashi-hime, the daughter of Soga no Umako, was only the fourth wife of Kimmei and was thus in what would normally be a relatively weak position in terms of her children's prospects in the succession. And yet two of them did become sovereigns—Yōmei and Suiko.

Soga no Umako was first appointed as the Great Minister, a post he held until his death, by the Emperor Senka (r. 535–539). This strategic political position seems to have served as a counterweight to the genealogical superiority of the offspring of Kimmei's first three wives. When his eldest surviving son by Ishihime succeeded him as the Emperor Bidatsu (r. [572]–585), no Soga daughter was named an imperial consort. When Bidatsu's empress-consort, Hirohime, died in 11/575, however, Soga no Umako managed to have his granddaughter, Toyomike Kashikiya-hime, named

The Wives and Offspring of the Emperor Kimmei

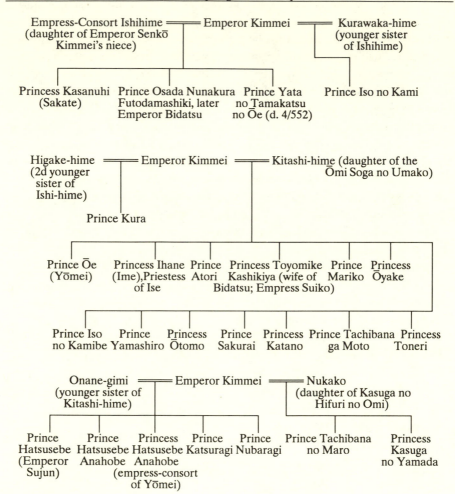

as the new empress-consort, effectively bypassing the other imperial consorts. The chart on the following page shows the wives of Bidatsu and their offspring.

The *Nihonshoki* entry for 3/5/578 notes that Princess Uji, Bidatsu's daughter by the Empress-Consort Hirohime, was appointed to serve as the imperial priestess of the Ise Shrine but was recalled when an "intrigue" with Prince Ikehe (*Ikehe no miko ni okasarenu*) was discovered. Unfortunately, this prince is not mentioned anywhere else, so his identity is unknown; nor do we know if another princess was named to the ritual post at Ise. One of the first acts of the Emperor Yōmei after the succession, however, was to appoint the Imperial Princess Sukate as the Ise Priestess, a post she held for the next thirty-seven years. This princess was his daughter by his third consort, Hiroko. Because of the silence of the text, it is impossible to reconstruct the political intrigue behind these developments, but we may recall that the position of the Ise Priestess was a strategically important one in mediating the succession. The fall from grace of Princess Uji can only have improved the positions of the Soga daughters.

The role of Soga marriage politics can be seen by noting that three of Bidatsu's daughters and his second empress-consort, Umako's granddaughter, were themselves married to strategically placed men—Princess Uji no Kaitako to Prince Shōtoku; Princess Owarida to Prince Hikohito, the son of Bidatsu and the former empress-consort; and Princess Tame to the prince who would succeed as the Emperor Jomei. Yōmei's own empress-consort, Anahobe no Hashibito, was his paternal half-sister as the daughter of Kimmei and Oane-gimi, the younger sister of Kitashi-hime. Thus, Yōmei's empress was a daughter of Soga no Umako, as was his second wife, Ishikina. After Yōmei's suspicious death in 587, his paternal half-brother and the brother of his empress-consort, Prince Hatsusebe, succeeded as the Emperor Sushun (r. 587–592). This prince did not receive the support of Soga no Umako, however, no doubt because he was the younger brother of Prince Anahobe, the candidate of the Monobe clan, who had tried to force his way into the *mogari no miya* after the death of the Emperor Bidatsu. Moreover, a daughter of Soga no Umako, Kawakami no Iratsume, had been appointed as a consort of the Emperor Sushun, but she was "stolen" by Yamato no Aya no Atai Koma, who had just assassinated Sushun on Umako's orders. When Umako learned of this act, which no doubt was itself a power play, he had Koma killed.

With his granddaughter in power as the Empress Suiko following Sushun's assassination, Soga no Umako had apparently realized his goal of ensuring Soga dominance. The *Nihonshoki* entry for 2/20/612, which immediately follows the verses of praise exchanged by Umako and Suiko cited above, reports that elaborate public rituals, involving the entire court, were held to mark the final burial of Kitashi-hime, the fertile Soga daughter who in many ways gave birth to the Soga dynasty. The

The Wives and Offspring of the Emperor Bidatsu

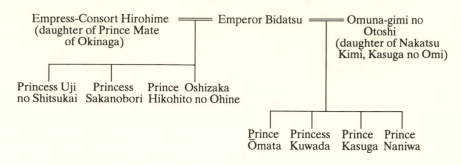

Empress-Consort Hirohime ══╤══ Emperor Bidatsu ══╤══ Omuna-gimi no
(daughter of Prince Mate   Otoshi
of Okinaga)   (daughter of Nakatsu
                                                   Kimi, Kasuga no Omi)

Princess Uji   Princess   Prince Oshizaka
no Shitsukai Sakanobori Hikohito no Ohine

Prince   Princess   Prince   Prince
Ōmata   Kuwada   Kasuga   Naniwa

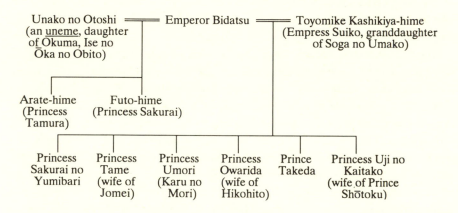

Unako no Otoshi ══╤══ Emperor Bidatsu ══╤══ Toyomike Kashikiya-hime
(an uneme, daughter   (Empress Suiko, granddaughter
of Okuma, Ise no   of Soga no Umako)
Ōka no Obito)

Arate-hime   Futo-hime
(Princess   (Princess Sakurai)
Tamura)

Princess   Princess   Princess   Princess   Prince   Princess Uji no
Sakurai no   Tame   Umori   Owarida   Takeda   Kaitako
Yumibari   (wife of (Karu no   (wife of   (wife of Prince
           Jomei)   Mori)   Hikohito)   Shōtoku)

central importance of marriage politics in the legitimating process is further indicated in the fact that Kitashi-hime is here styled *ōkisaki* or the empress-consort. Soga no Umako died on 5/20/626 and was given temporary burial; Suiko died the following spring. She was succeeded by the Emperor Jomei, the son of Prince Hikohito and Princess Arate-hime.

Jomei's succession was not a smooth one. After the Crown Prince Shōtoku died in 621, no successor was named before Suiko passed away in 628, indicating that no faction had been able to muster the support necessary to put up one of their candidates for this position. In the wake of Suiko's death, the final words of the empress were the central point of contention. Though of great importance, the complex and extended machinations in the court cannot be treated here. In a sense, though, Jomei's reign inaugurated a new dynastic branch of the imperial family. It is no accident, then, that the second poem in the *Man'yōshū*, the famous *kunimi uta* we saw earlier, is attributed to Jomei. From the perspective of the eighth century court, the figure of Jomei climbing Kagu-yama and surveying his realm in a *kunimi* ritual surely symbolized the success and power of his descendants who continued to rule the country and to find Yamato "a splendid land." What follows on the next page is a selective genealogical chart from the time of the Emperor Jomei (r. [629]–641).

Princess Takara, who later ruled the country on two separate occasions, first as the Empress Kōgyoku (r. [642]–645) and then as Saimei (r. [655]–661), was the maternal elder sister of Prince Karu. At the time of the death of Jomei in 641, Jomei's eldest son by this princess, Naka no Ōe (often rendered as Nakatsu Ōe), was only sixteen, so the empress-consort succeeded her husband. The Soga patriarch, Emishi, was then reappointed Ōmi or Great Minister, a position he had held under the Emperor Jomei; although the *Nihonshoki* reports that his son, Iruka, "took into his own hands the reins of government, and his power was greater than his father's."[6] Relations between Kōgyoku and the Soga seem to have quickly taken a turn for the worse. Within the year the Soga usurped a number of imperial prerogatives, brazenly building their own ancestral temple in Katsuragi without first obtaining the empress's permission, levying taxes, imposing forced labor on the people to build large tombs for Emishi and Iruka, and so on. The faction associated with the late Crown Prince Shōtoku seems to have taken special umbrage at these actions.

The *Nihonshoki* records an *uta* from this time attributed to Soga no Emishi and reports that he performed a *yatsura-mai*, a special dance involving sixty-four persons, eight each in eight circles, used in a ritual of raising an individual to the rank of heir apparent. This is an excellent example of the retrospective contextualized use of a popular song to criticize a member of the court.[7] Another entry, along with a popular *uta*, on the twelfth day of the tenth lunar month of the following year (643), reports that Soga no Iruka plotted to kill all the sons of Prince Shōtoku and then to place Prince Furuhito on the throne.[8] Iruka burned down Shōtoku's palace and pursued Prince Yamashiro, a son of the deceased crown prince, into the mountains. Realizing that they were about to be captured by troops loyal to Iruka, Prince Yamashiro, his entire family, and his consorts committed suicide in the Ikaruga Temple, effectively ending Shōtoku's line.

The Soga were not, however, without powerful enemies of their own in the court. On New Year's day of 644, Nakatomi no Kamatari (or Kamako), then thirty-one years of age, was appointed as the chief priest of the imperial *kami* cult (*kamu tsukasa no kami*). He moved quickly to block the Soga by forming an alliance with Prince Naka no Ōe, who was then nineteen or twenty. No passage in the *Nihonshoki* is more explicit concerning the crucial importance of marriage politics than the following from the Kōgyoku Chapter, detailing how Kamatari arranged to have the eldest daughter of Soga no Kurayamada married to Prince Naka no Ōe. (Her name is not given in the sources.) This entry follows another fascinating and lengthy one

The Emperor of Jomei (r. [629]-541) and his Main Offspring

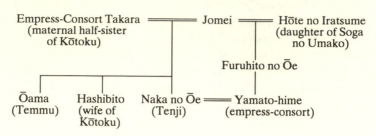

The Emperor Kōtoku and his Wives

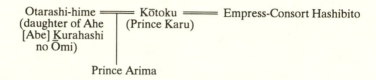

describing how Kamatari and Naka no Ōe gingerly sounded each other out before revealing their political intentions and ambitions to each other. The passage of immediate import reads:

Then Nakatomi no Kamako no Muraji counselled [Prince Naka no Ōe], saying:—"For him who cherishes great projects, nothing is so essential as support. I pray thee, therefore, to take to thee the eldest daughter of Soga no Kurayamada no Maro, and make her thy consort. When a friendly marriage relationship has been established, we can then unfold our desire to associate him with us in our plans. There is no shorter way to success than this." Now when Naka no Ōe heard this, he was much pleased, and acted in accordance with his advice in every particular. Nakatomi no Kamako no Muraji accordingly went himself, and as go-between conducted the marriage negotiations to a successful result. On the night, however, fixed upon for (the consummation of the marriage with) the eldest daughter, she was stolen away by a relation (his name was Musa no Omi).[9]

The *Nihonshoki* reports that Soga no Kurayamada was distraught over this sudden hitch in the plans until his younger daughter (Ochi no Iratsume?) offered herself as a substitute (see the chart that follows later in this chapter). Physical attraction or love was not involved in this or in similar marriage alliances. Like most marriages in the court, it was one of mutual political convenience for the families involved. The abduction of the eldest Soga daughter was also probably politically motivated. Musa no Omi, the individual who reportedly stole the Soga daughter from Naka no Ōe, was also known as Himuka no Omi. He is, thus, the same person who later betrayed Prince Furuhito to Naka no Ōe by reporting Furuhito's plans to seize power.

The marriage of Naka no Ōe and the second daughter of Soga no Kurayamada took place, giving Naka no Ōe an important ally. Meanwhile, Soga no Iruka continued to flaunt his power. The *Nihonshoki* details the various "offenses" of Emishi and Iruka in entries for the tenth and eleventh months or, in other words, in the season that was appropriate both ritually and according to narrative convention. The passage for 644 reads in part:

> Winter, 11th month. Emishi, Soga no Ōmi, and his son, Iruka no Omi, built two houses side-by-side on the Amakashi Hill. The Ōmi's house was called *Ue no Mikado* [The Upper Palace Gate]. Iruka's house was called *Hasama no Mikado* [The Valley Palace Gate]. Their sons and daughters were styled Princes and Princesses [*onokogo menokogo o yobite miko to iu*]. Outside the houses palisades were constructed, and an armoury was erected by the gate. . . . Stout fellows, armed with weapons, were constantly employed to guard the houses.
>
> The Ōmi made Naga no Atahi build the Hokonuki Temple on Mount Ōnihono. Moreover, he built a house on the east side of Mount Unebi and dug a pond, so as to make of it a castle. He erected an armoury, and provided a store of arrows. In his goings out and comings in he was always surrounded by an attendant company of fifty soldiers. . . . The people of the various *uji* came to his gate, and served him. He called himself their father, and them his children.[10]

Here the power of Soga no Emishi and his son are represented as such that many of the courtiers and clan heads served them and in their presence observed all the forms of etiquette and deference due a sovereign and crown prince. At the same time, this Soga faction was prepared for an armed confrontation. Naka no Ōe, Soga no Kurayamada, and Nakatomi no Kamatari, however, successfully plotted to do away with Iruka at a court function when tribute was being presented to the empress. In the immediate wake of Iruka's death, many of his troops from the eastern provinces, sensing a shift in the balance of power, abandoned the elderly Soga no Emishi. In the conflagration that enveloped Emishi's house after it came under attack, the earliest written imperial histories were totally or partially destroyed. Emishi was executed, and two days later the Empress Kōgyoku abdicated; Prince Karu assumed power as the Emperor Kōtoku. Public laments for both Iruka and Emishi, however, were permitted.

Once again, though, the succession was not a smooth one. The *Nihonshoki* says that Kōgyoku wished to turn her position over to her son by Jomei, Prince Naka no Ōe. Nakatomi no Kamatari, however, advised the prince that it would be awkward (and probably dangerous) if he were to succeed when his maternal uncle, Prince Karu, and his elder half-brother, Furuhito no Ōe, still enjoyed considerable support. Naka no Ōe took the hint and demurred to Prince Karu. Karu, however, was seemingly unsure of his own strength, for he in turn demurred to Furuhito no Ōe. Once again it seems that no one had clearly superior support, for Furuhito himself declined the kingship, declaring his wish to take the Buddhist tonsure and retire to Yoshino (as Temmu was to do twenty-five years later in 671). Only then did Prince Karu succeed as the Emperor Kōtoku. A daughter of the Emperor Jomei and Naka no Ōe's sister, Princess Hashibito, was appointed empress-consort. At the same time, Naka no Ōe was able to achieve a position of distinct strength through the appointment of Soga no Kurayamada, his father-in-law, as one of the two Great Ministers.

The precise details of the actions of Prince Furuhito thereafter are unclear. The *Nihonshoki*, however, reports that some sources referred to him as the Yoshino Heir Apparent, indicating that he continued to enjoy substantial support.[11] A series of entries in the first year of Kōtoku's reign report that a number of persons plotted with Furuhito to seize power; but a conspirator named Shidaru, Kibi no Kasa no Omi (i.e., Himuka Omi) informed Prince Naka no Ōe (or someone else, according to a variant) of the plans, and a preemptive attack was made on Furuhito and his troops. Furuhito and all his children died, and his consorts committed suicide by strangling themselves.[12] Kibi, the ancient name of the area around present day Okayama, was the name of the mother of both Kōgyoku and Kōtoku, as well as the area from which another consort of Jomei, Kaya no Uneme, had come, suggesting that Kibi no Kasa no Omi's ultimate loyalty in the succession dispute followed clan lines. Furuhito's elimination as a contender in the succession was, of course, to the advantage of both Kōtoku and Naka no Ōe.

Kōtoku's marriages mirrored the distribution of power at the top levels of the court. A glance at the last chart above will show that in addition to Princess Hashibito, the daughter of Kōgyoku and Jomei (and Naka no Ōe's sister), Kōtoku had two major consorts who were daughters of his Great Ministers. The senior consort was Otarashi-hime, a daughter of the Ōmi Ahe no Kurahashi no Maro (also called Ahe no Uchimaro), who had replaced Soga no Emishi; the junior consort was Chinu no Iratsume, a daughter of the other Great Minister, Soga no Kurayamada no Ishikawa. Thus, Kōtoku's empress-consort, his maternal niece, was a daughter of his two immediate predecessors, and his consorts were daughters of the two most powerful ministers in the court.

Kōtoku's position, though, was not as secure as it might appear at first glance, for Naka no Ōe, with the assistance of Nakatomi no Kamatari, seems to have outmaneuvered Kōtoku in the marriage politics. Kamatari displayed a flair for this sort of thing that was later to distinguish his clan (then known as the Fujiwara) throughout the Heian period.[13] First of all, Kōtoku's empress was a full sister of Naka no Ōe and thus had split loyalties. (One recalls here the story in the Suinin Chapter of the Empress-Consort Sao-bime and her elder brother, Prince Saohiko, where there are striking parallels.) Second, Kōtoku's senior consort was the daughter of a new Ōmi who may not yet have had the time to cultivate and strengthen all the necessary relationships with other clan heads and courtiers to wield significant power effectively. Finally, his junior consort was only the fourth daughter of Soga no Kurayamada, whereas Naka no Ōe was married to two older sisters. No offspring are reported from Kōtoku's marriage to Princess Hashibito, but a son, the tragic Prince Arima whose story we have already encountered, was born to Otarashi-hime.

The *Nihonshoki* reports that the Great Minister Ahe died on 3/17/649. Like the death of a sovereign, the death of one of the two Ōmi almost inevitably caused a serious rend in the socio-political fabric of the court and stimulated a flurry of political maneuvering.

3rd month, 17th day. Ahe no Ōmi died. The Emperor proceeded to the Shujaku-mon [The Southern Gate], where he raised up lamentations for him and showed much emotion. The Empress Dowager [Kōgyoku], the Prince Imperial [Naka no Ōe], and the other Princes, together with the Ministers of every rank, all, following his example, mourned and lamented.[14]

All the important members of the court gathered together for the mourning rituals, which were once again the occasion for political intrigues. The surviving Ōmi was from the Soga clan, but in the wake of the deaths of Soga no Emishi and Iruka there continued to be various competing factions within the larger clan. The very next line in the *Nihonshoki* reports that only a week after the death of the Ōmi Ahe no Kurahashi, another member of the Soga clan, Himuka, Soga no Omi informed Prince Naka no Ōe that his father-in-law, the Ōmi Soga no Kurayamada, was plotting to assassinate the crown prince. It is unclear why Naka no Ōe believed the accusations, but perhaps the fact that Himuka had earlier provided critical information concerning the alleged plot of Furuhito gave him credibility. Then again, Naka no Ōe may have feared that Soga no Kurayamada would use the power vacuum created by Ahe no Kurahashi's death to expand his own power base. Whatever the case, on Naka no Ōe's orders troops were gathered to attack Soga no Kurayamada, who, realizing he was in an impossible situation, assembled seven other members of his family in their estate temple, the Yamada-dera, where they committed suicide. A large number of attendants and supporters also took their own lives, and many others were subsequently executed or exiled. Naka no Ōe's ruthless nature and his outrage at the alleged plot against him may be discerned in the fact that the Ōmi's corpse was defiled by decapitation.

Shortly thereafter Naka no Ōe learned that the accusations against his father-in-law had in fact been false. Upon learning of her father's wrongful death, Naka no Ōe's wife, Miyatsuko-hime, is reported to have died of a broken heart. Most prob-

ably she too committed suicide. The *Nihonshoki* account of this bloody affair then
concludes by noting that Himuka no Omi was sent to Tsukushi (Kyūshū), which
some contemporaries took to be a form of exile. The two *banka* we saw earlier
offered to Naka no Ōe by a surrogate are then presented. These tragic events were
still very much a part of living memory a generation later when Hitomaro was active
as a poet and many of the persons in the court were directly related to Soga no
Kurayamada. In some ways over the following years, the descendants of Naka no Ōe
(Tenji) found themselves continually trying to expiate this terrible tragedy in their
family history.

On New Year's Day of the following year, 650, the era name was changed by
Kōtoku to Hakuchi, perhaps as a result of the unpleasant events of the preceding
year. A number of large public rituals were held to declare publicly that auspicious
omens had appeared in the land. Clearly Kōtoku was struggling to maintain his hold
on power at this point, having lost both of his great ministers in short order. That
his real power was limited, though, is suggested by the fact that Naka no Ōe was
not reprimanded in any way and remained the crown prince. There is something at
once pathetic yet instructive in a long passage that details a huge public gathering
in the court on the fifteenth of the second lunar month, only weeks after the New
Year's rituals, at which an albino pheasant was presented to the assembled throng
by the Emperor Kōtoku with great pomp and ceremony. The albino pheasant was
carried into the presence of the emperor on an elaborate litter borne by four high-
ranking courtiers as they passed through lines four deep of all the members of the
court. The occasion was used by Kōtoku to force Naka no Ōe to recognize publicly
his legitimacy by declaring that the omen was indeed a sign that the gods supported
his rule.

The Emperor straightaway called the Prince Imperial [Naka no Ōe], and they took [the
pheasant] and examined it together. The Prince Imperial having retired, made repeated obei-
sances, and caused the [newly appointed] Ōmi Kose to offer a congratulatory address, saying:—"The Ministers and functionaries offer their congratulations. Inasmuch as Your Majesty
governs the Empire with serene virtue, there is here a white pheasant, produced in the
western region. This is a sign that Your Majesty will continue for a thousand autumns and
ten thousand years peacefully to govern the Great-eight-islands of the four quarters. It is the
prayer of the Ministers, functionaries, and people that they may serve Your majesty with the
utmost zeal and fidelity." Having finished this congratulatory speech, he made repeated obei-
sances.[15]

In spite of these public declarations of loyalty, Kōtoku's support literally began
to slip away. Under the seventh month of 653, one finds the following entry:

This year the Prince Imperial [Naka no Ōe] petitioned the Emperor, saying:—"I wish the
Imperial residence were removed to the Yamato capital." The Emperor refused to grant his

request. Upon this the Prince Imperial took with him the Empress Dowager [Kōgyoku], the Empress Hashibito, and the younger Imperial princes, and went to live in the temporary Palace of Asuka no Kawara in Yamato. At this time the Ministers and Daibu, with the various functionaries, all followed and changed their residence. The Emperor resented this, and wishing to cast away the national Dignity [*kore ni yorite, sumeramikoto, uramite kuni o saritamawamu to omoshite*] had a palace built in Yamasaki. Then he sent a song to the Empress Hashibito, saying:—

kanaki tsuke	My pony
a ga kau koma wa	with a wooden yoke on
hiki desezu	I never led out.
a ga kau koma o	Has someone
hito mitsuramu ka	seen my pony?

5th year, Spring, 1st month, 1st day. In the night the rats migrated towards the Yamato capital.[16]

At this time Kōtoku was fifty-eight, Hashibito was approximately twenty-five, and Naka no Ōe twenty-eight. The precise meaning of this verse has been the subject of some dispute, but I agree with many commentators who have taken the pony (*koma*) here as a reference to Kōtoku's empress-consort, Hashibito. Yoshinaga Noboru has made a very interesting observation in noting that the last line of the verse is a double entendre, since the verb *miru*, "to see," includes a sexual nuance.[17] Assuming this to be the case, the expression is used in the same sense we do when we say two people are "seeing each other." If we tentatively adopt this reading, then the last line might be rendered as "Has someone been seeing my pony (i.e., wife)?" This someone would have been none other than Naka no Ōe. Once his empress and much of the court had physically abandoned him, Kōtoku was in an embarrassing and in many ways untenable situation—a leader without followers. *De jure* Kōtoku was still the emperor, but *de facto* Naka no Ōe had deposed him and effectively held the reins of power. Naka no Ōe's public departure from the capital is a striking instance of the immediate identity of symbol and reality. His possession of his mother and sister was an instance of "symbolic incest," but it also exposed Kōtoku's political impotence (itself symbolized by the lack of progeny by Hashibito).

Kōtoku reportedly died on 10/10 of the following year and was given final burial a scant two months later. We do not know if he died a natural death or not. From what we know of Naka no Ōe's ambitions, his ruthless nature, and his modus operandi, it is not inconceivable that Kōtoku was slain or forced to commit suicide. Somewhat surprisingly Naka no Ōe did not then succeed Kōtoku, even though he had been the crown prince. His main potential rival at this point, Prince Arima, Kōtoku's son, was only sixteen and thus not yet a serious contender. The empress dowager, however, returned to the throne again, now styled as the Empress Saimei.

Her reign witnessed, as we have seen, the alleged conspiracy of Prince Arima and Soga no Akae. When Arima was executed in late 658, Naka no Ōe's last major rival had been eliminated.

In the wake of the death of his father, Kōtoku, Arima found himself in a vulnerable and exposed position. Vulnerability was the antithesis of power in the court, for individuals situated in an exposed position frequently found allegations of treason and conspiracy brought against them. This was so for two related reasons: first, courtiers who recognized another's relatively weak position within the web of alliances and mutual need within the court often felt emboldened to make such accusations; second, in the wake of accusations against an exposed individual, few in the court were willing to risk their own positions by stepping forward to protect the accused, especially if the accuser was gauged to be in a more powerful or superior position. Earlier we saw that in a similar situation even Soga no Umako, finding himself outmaneuvered at one point, had to acquiesce to the execution of one of his own supporters. When he approached his majority in 658, Arima became a serious threat to the ambition of Naka no Ōe. In light of Arima's relatively weak position, however, it was almost a foregone conclusion that he would become another in a long line of tragic princes.

It is somewhat surprising to note that after Saimei passed away in 661, Naka no Ōe did not formally accede until either 1/3/668 or, according to another unnamed source, 3/667.[18] There has been much speculation as to why his formal installation was delayed for a period of six or more years. Some scholars have suggested that Kōtoku's empress, Hashibito, may have ruled during this period. Others, including Yoshinaga, have suggested that Naka no Ōe's "irregular" relationship with his full sister, Hashibito, may have mitigated against a formal accession. I find little solid evidence for the former hypothesis and the latter unconvincing. In early Japan an "irregular" relationship between a brother and a sister, whether actual or alleged, does not seem to have been enough in and of itself to disqualify one from succeeding as emperor. Rather, in both myths and the chronicles of earlier sovereigns a sexual brother–sister or similar relationship seems to have been an alternative means of appropriating the imperial charisma. In many societies the ability to break a major taboo publicly, such as sibling incest, and with impunity is itself a demonstration of power. It is impossible to know whether Naka no Ōe and Hashibito had a sexual relationship or not; in the final analysis, though, it is irrelevant whether the relationship was "real" or "symbolic." In the present instance it obscures the matter to separate symbolism from political "realities." The fact that Naka no Ōe was able to lead the Empress Hashibito—his sister and Kōtoku's wife—and all the others out of Kōtoku's capital simultaneously symbolized and realized Kōtoku's loss of the imperial charisma and its transference to Naka no Ōe. There is no need to appeal to some mystical symbolic power at work here; the symbolic act and the political reality are one and the same.

It is finally unclear whether Hashibito ever ruled or not, but evidence gleaned from the *Nihonshoki* chronology suggests that the length of time that elapsed before Naka no Ōe was ritually installed was probably due to the observance of a series of *mogari no miya* rituals, not to Hashibito's having occupied the throne or to some ritual pollution from which Naka no Ōe still suffered. First, Saimei died on 7/24/661 but was given temporary burial only on 11/7. The *Nihonshoki* reports that the temporary interment rites and collective public mourning lasted for nine days, with Prince Naka no Ōe presiding over the rituals. If the latter report is accurate, then one would expect Naka no Ōe to have also assumed control of the government. The *Nihonshoki*, indeed, goes on to attest to this development in a large number of entries, including extensive reports of how he met with official delegations from the Korean kingdoms. In sharp contrast, the Empress Dowager Hashibito is not mentioned at all until the following entries appear:

4th year [665], Spring, 2nd month, 25th day. The Empress Dowager Hashibito died.

3rd month, 1st day. For the sake of the Empress Dowager Hashibito, 330 persons entered religion.[19]

Hashibito's death during the period of Kōgyoku/Saimei's *mogari no miya* meant that Naka no Ōe was deprived of the presence of the two women who had been crucial supporters in his challenge to Kōtoku. In this situation it may have been to his advantage once again to sponsor large-scale *mogari no miya* rituals for Hashibito as well, for to do so would bring further prestige to his maternal lineage at the same time that it demonstrated his power to harness the efforts of large numbers of persons, allocate great amounts of monetary and other resources for these rituals, and extract declarations of loyalty from powerful courtiers and praise for his own family. Unlike the chaos that often characterized the liminal period following the death of a sovereign, there is no indication that Naka no Ōe was seriously challenged following either Saimei's death or that of Hashibito.

In addition to the deaths of Hashibito and Saimei, Naka no Ōe's grandmother passed away during this period (6/664). He was also in the midst of directing a military campaign on the Asian mainland. Saimei and Hashibito were both given final burial and interred together in the same tomb on the Hill of Ochi on 2/27/667, a respectful two years after Hashibito's death. Princess Ōta, the elder sister of Princess Uno (Jitō) and a wife of Prince Ōama (Temmu), was also buried on the same day in front of the other mausoleums. Considering the combination of all these factors, we need not assume that Hashibito reigned after Saimei's death. It seems likely that Naka no Ōe exercised control during this period as the heir apparent with the support of his sister and the prestige she brought in her person and status as empress dowager. Hashibito's own death prior to the final burial of Saimei, coupled with Naka no Ōe's vested interest in maintaining the prestige of Hashibito, meant that he could not formally succeed until after the completion of the final burial rites for her as well. Performing the final burial rites for Hashibito too soon could have been taken as a sign of disrespect. Thus, Naka no Ōe was formally installed as emperor only after both Hashibito and Saimei had been given final burial.

Poem of the Three Mountains: Legend and Political Allegory

If marriage and sexual relationships were factors in the creation and exercise of power in early Japan, then many so-called love poems from this period must be studied for possible socio-political meanings. The set of poems MYS 1: 13–15 is directly related to the events we have just examined. It may serve as an exemplar of how traditional narratives could be manipulated in order to comment on political history.

The poems are attributed to Naka no Ōe and are located under the reign of the Empress Saimei (r. 655–661). This attribution provides us with several pieces of information, as well as a few questions. First, although the author is purported to be Naka no Ōe, somewhat peculiarly the headnote does not refer to him as the crown prince or even as a prince. Nor is any other term of respect or rank used as is almost always done, even though an interlinear note goes on to identify him explicitly as "the Sovereign who ruled the realm under the heavens from the Ōmi Palace."[20] Why this should be so is unclear, but this anomaly cannot be a mere scribal error. The set is temporally located under Saimei's reign, which, based upon what we know about the way the imperial reigns were thought of by the compilers of the *Man'yōshū*, would mean it was believed to have come from the period between her formal accession in 655 to the time of her final burial on 2/27/667. Any further attempt to locate this set of poems temporally must be based upon either internal evidence or the relative location of the set among the other poems under Saimei's reign. Turning to the poems immediately preceding it, one finds that MYS 1: 8–9 are attributed to Princess Nukata, and verses 10–12 are ascribed to Princess Nakatsu "when she went on a procession to the hot springs of Ki." The name of this princess, Nakatsu, is of course the same as Nakatsu or Naka no Ōe. This correspondence has led a number of scholars to identify the princess as Hashibito after she had abandoned her husband, the Emperor Kōtoku, and went with her brother to Yamato. This probable identity heightens the necessity of rereading these poems, together with MYS 1: 13–15. A verse like MYS 1: 10, for instance, takes on an entirely different cast if one assumes Naka no Ōe to be the male alluded to. It reads:

Nakatsu sumeramikoto, Ki no ideyu ni idemashishi toki no mi-uta

Poem by the August Intermediate Sovereign Nakatsu when she went to the hot
springs of Ki

kimi ga yo mo
waga yo mo shiru ya
Iwashiro no
oka no kusane o
iza musubitena

The span of your life
and of my life too,
is determined by the grass
on Iwashiro Hill.
Come, let us bind it together.[21]

A few points are worthy of note here. First, Nakatsu is called *sumeramikoto*, a designation usually reserved for sovereigns, indicating that this princess held a special position of power. The *musubi* ritual referred to is the sort we saw earlier in conjunction with Prince Arima's death poem in which the intention was to bind in some object the *tama* of an individual to ensure that person's safe return, guarantee his fidelity, and so on. This poem may refer to a ritual pact made by Hashibito and her brother, Naka no Ōe. Whether sexual relations are implied or not is unclear. Although different Chinese characters are used in the text, orally the term *yo*, here rendered "span of life," is a homonym with *yo*, or "reign." Thus one could hear the verse to say "Your reign/ and my reign," giving it a distinctly political cast.

Further evidence that might help to locate these poems temporally, and thus MYS 1: 13–15 as well, must be sought in the *Nihonshoki*. There the Saimei Chapter records an imperial excursion to the hot springs of Ki in an entry dated 10/15/658, which includes "the songs of the dead" involving Prince Takeru, Saimei's grandson, and the son of Naka no Ōe and Ochi no Iratsume. On 11/9/658 there is another entry that reports that Prince Arima and others were sent to the hot springs of Ki where Naka no Ōe questioned him about an alleged plot against Saimei. Arima was executed two days later. Since the *Nihonshoki* does not report Saimei's return to the capital until 1/3/659, one may assume that during this entire period she was at the hot springs, along with a large entourage of imperial princes, princesses, and courtiers.

On the basis of these considerations, MYS 1: 13–15 may be presumed to be from this period or sometime thereafter, that is from 659 or later. Those verses read:

Nakatsu Ōe (Ōmi no miya ni ame no shita
shirashimeshishi   sumeramikoto)   no   mi-
yama no uta

Poem on the three mountains by Nakatsu
Ōe (the Sovereign who ruled the realm under the heavens from the Ōmi Palace)

Kagu-yama wa
Unebi o-oshi to
Miminashi to
ai arasoiki
kami yo yori

Kagu-yama
loved Unebi's masculinity
and struggled
with Miminashi.
From the age of the *kami*

kaku ni arurashi
inishie mo
shika ni are koso
utsusemi mo
tsuma o
arasōrashiki

that's how it was.
Thus it was too
in the distant past
and in the present world
people still
struggle over a mate.

hanka

Envoys

Kagu-yama to
Miminashi-yama to
aishi toki
tachite mi ni koshi
Inami kuni hara

This plain of Inami,
where the *kami*, rising,
came to watch
when Kagu-yama
and Miminashi-yama fought.

watatsumi no
toyohatakumo ni
irihi mishi
koyoi no tsukuyo
saya ni teri koso

This night,
when we have seen the sun plunge
through the banner of clouds
into the sea,
let the moon shine clear!

(migi isshu no uta, ima kamugauru ni hanka ni nizu. tadashi, furu hon kono uta o mochite hanka ni nosu. soe ni ima nao kono tsugite ni nosu. mata ki ni iwaku, Ame-Toyo-Takara-Ikashi-Hitarashi-hime no sumeramikoto no saki no yonnen ki-noto-mi ni sumeramikoto o tatete miko no mikoto to nasu to ieri.)

(The above poem on present consideration does not resemble an envoy. However, an old text includes it as an envoy. Thus we too have included it in that order. Then, too, the chronicle [i.e., *Nihonshoki*] says that the Sovereign was elevated to the rank of Crown Prince in the prior fourth year of the Empress Ame-Toyo-Takara-Ikashi-Hi-tarashi [i.e., Saimei], wood-junior, serpent.)[22]

The gender of the three mountains here has been a subject of considerable dispute among Japanese scholars. Without entering the fray here,[23] let me suggest that what we know of the political situation in the court at this time would suggest two men fighting over a woman. As a working hypothesis we may consider Kagu-yama to be female and the other two mountains to be male. (Alternatively, Kagu-yama and Miminashi-yama may both be male and Unebi-yama female. In this reading the character used for *o-oshi* would be read for its phonetic value only, not the semantic content, and thus could be translated as "beauty" or "loveliness" rather than "masculinity.") The opening long verse rehearses a legend that was already widely known at that time. But in the second half it links the central action of this legend, the struggle resulting from a love triangle, to the present, opening the way for the second envoy where one finds the legend used to frame recent events in the court.

The prose endnote directs us to an important point. The last verse does not really "fit" with the long opening verse if it is judged aesthetically in terms of what an envoy should be. It works quite well, though, if this set is read as a political allegory, perhaps suggesting the intention of the editors of the earlier texts. In order to determine the probable identities of the three mountains in this political reading, we need to look to the *Nihonshoki* for another man who competed with Naka no Ōe, the purported author of these verses, for the attention of a woman. There are at least two immediate possibilities: (1) Himuka no Omi, who "stole" the eldest daughter of Soga no Kurayamada the night before she was to be wed to Naka no Ōe; and (2) the Emperor Kōtoku, whose empress-consort, Hashibito, was "stolen" by Naka no Ōe and taken to Ōmi. Of these the latter is the more likely allusion here and would yield the following identifications: Kagu-yama = Hashibito; Unebi-yama = Naka no Ōe; and Miminashi-yama = Kōtoku.

If we accept these identifications as a working hypothesis, the envoys take on a heightened meaning along the following lines. The opening envoy alludes to the discord between the Emperor Kōtoku and his Empress-Consort Hashibito and her preference for her brother, Naka no Ōe. The suggestion that the *kami* viewed the struggle is a rhetorical attempt to legitimate the outcome, to say in effect that because the *kami* did not intervene, they have implicitly given their blessing to the political union (even if one chooses to deny any suggestion of a physical union) of Hashibito and Naka no Ōe. The second envoy seems to refer either to Kōtoku's death or to his having effectively been deposed. A possible hint pointing to the former is the first term, *watatsumi*, which is said to refer to the *kami* of the ocean and his power.[24] One of the locations of the land of the dead was believed to lie over the ocean and below the horizon, precisely where the sun in this verse is said to have plunged. Moreover, the death of a sovereign is often expressed in the *Man'yōshū* in terms of the sovereign being hidden in the clouds, again precisely the image conjured up by the envoy if one accepts the equation "sun" = the sovereign. The use of the sun and the moon to represent the sovereign and the crown prince respectively is found frequently in the *Man'yōshū*. The last envoy, then, is a boast of victory in the struggle for the female wife/sister, as well as in a larger power struggle. The phrase "let the moon shine clear!" may now be heard as an expression of hope that Naka no Ōe (the moon = the crown prince) might finally rule.

This type of political allegory is frequently used to make oblique (and sometimes not so oblique) comments about the political situation in the court. All the texts from early Japan employ popular legends at times to place both a narrative and an interpretive frame on a contemporary or recent situation in the court. The manipulation of traditional narrative materials in this way for historiographic purposes was a striking instrument of power.

Marriage Politics in the Seventh Century

One of the many cultural discourses found in the early Japanese court was that of kinship and genealogy. An important expression of this discourse was in marriage politics, the realization of strategic alliances between families through marriage. Marriage politics played a crucial role in Naka no Ōe's relentless, albeit patient, pursuit of power, as we have seen. The alliances he established were to be crucial in helping to determine the succession into the next century and down to the period in which the *Kojiki*, the *Nihonshoki*, and the *Man'yōshū* were compiled and committed to writing. Only by recognizing the strategic positions of central figures in the court and the interdependencies between and among them will we be able to appreciate the rational nature of the intentional acts of various individuals. Similarly the political dimensions of the process of the generation of texts and of anthologization in the *Man'yōshū* will emerge only if, among other factors, the role of marriage politics in the court is taken into account.

The chart on the following page focuses on the long-term consequences of the marriage alliance, established at the suggestion of Nakatomi no Kamatari, between Naka no Ōe and Soga no Kurayamada through the latter's daughters. As this chart shows, all the sovereigns from Tenji to Genshō (r. 715–724) were directly related to the house of Soga no Kurayamada no Ishikawa Maro through the marriage of two of his daughters to Tenji. In the second generation (i.e., the post-Tenji period) the Tenji–Miyatsuko branch emerged as dominant through the union of Tenji's brother, Prince Ōama (Temmu), and Princess Uno (Jitō), the child of Tenji and the second daughter of Soga no Kurayamada. The other major line from the house of Soga no Kurayamada associated with the imperial family was through his third daughter, Mei no Iratsume. Her union with Tenji produced two daughters, one of whom, Princess Ahe, was to accede in 707 as the Empress Gemmei. These two lines were eventually reunited through the marriage of Princess Ahe to Jitō's son, Prince Kusakabe. That union in turn produced two sovereigns—the Emperor Mommu (Prince Karu, r. 697–707) and the Empress Genshō (r. 715–724).

Tenji's empress, Yamato-hime, was a daughter not of Soga no Kurayamada but of Furuhito no Ōe. Yamato-hime must have already been married to Tenji (then Prince Naka no Ōe) when he had Furuhito slain in 645, since all of Furuhito's other children are reported to have died with him. Thus, Tenji eliminated both the father of his primary wife and Soga no Kurayamada, the father of his two major consorts. He seems to have used the support of these individuals to gain power but was unwilling to brook any perceived threat to his position from them. No offspring are reported from the Tenji–Yamato-hime union, but this may be an attempt by the

Soga Marriage Politics

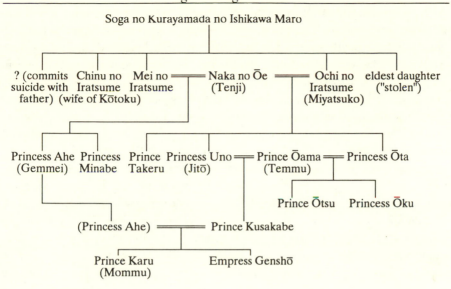

compilers of the *Nihonshoki* to deny the continuation of the Furuhito no Ōe line or at least any legitimacy in terms of the imperial succession.

Temmu married both of the female offspring of the Emperor Tenji and his senior consort, Miyatsuko, a daughter of Soga no Kurayamada no Ishikawa Maro. The male child from this union, Prince Takeru, is the young grandson whose death at about the age of eight so affected the Empress Saimei.

The chart above is limited to the Soga no Kurayamada line and, thus, does not present all the imperial consorts. It has the advantage, though, of enabling us to see at a glance the extent to which the assassinations in the court were intrafamilial and always a part of power politics. To appreciate why this was the case let us recall Foucault's suggestion that "power is not an institution, a structure, or a certain force with which certain people are endowed; it is the name given to a complex strategic situation in a given society."[25] Of course, power in early Japan was a function of one's strategic position within the total web of relations within the court. Yet, power did not permanently reside in any position, including that of sovereign, so that an individual merely had to occupy a given position in order to gain power. The case of the Emperor Kōtoku demonstrates this truism very well, since in the final months of his reign he was effectively powerless.

Power was realized only if one could achieve and maintain a consensus concerning the legitimacy of the relative distribution of position and prestige within the court. One way to improve one's relative status was, of course, to eliminate selected others who occupied crucial contiguous positions that might enable them to block one's own ambitions. A glance at the preceding chart, coupled with the knowledge of events in the court gleaned from the *Nihonshoki*, suggests that Tenji and Jitō well understood this political reality and had mastered the techniques of eliminating rivals while protecting themselves from recrimination. Naka no Ōe was quite prepared to do away with his fathers-in-law when he thought this act would be to his advantage. Similarly, Jitō had Prince Ōtsu, at once her nephew and a son of Temmu, executed when he came to be seen as a rival of her own son, Kusakabe, in the succession.

The *Nihonshoki* is in some ways a record of the vicissitudes of a large number of court families and clans. It contains the stories of the "winners" in the political struggles within the court to be sure, but also a large number of tales of those who were "losers." The opposite of power in the court was not manifested as a complete powerlessness; everyone had power to some extent over someone, and it could be measured and exercised only relative to that wielded by others. The distribution of power in the court, however, was in a constant state of flux, a situation greatly exacerbated by the deaths of significant figures. Power could not be assured or exercised through military might, marriage, or any other means alone; it was the result of the complex strategic situation that emerged out of the ongoing process of mediation among different groups. We have already seen how the seemingly most powerful persons in the country could be overthrown in very short order (e.g., Soga no Emishi and Soga no Kurayamada).

Shifts in the balance of power began with the rising perception of a person's vulnerability as a result of his or her inferior position in the fluctuating configuration of support in the court. Nakatomi no Kamatari's advice to Naka no Ōe bears on this point—no one could succeed in the undertaking of "great [political] projects" without the support of others who occupied critical administrative, genealogical, and symbolic positions in the court. The loss of such support by an individual manifested itself publicly in his being exposed to innuendo and attack (both verbal and physical).

The chart above also discloses a pattern of would-be sovereigns marrying not one daughter of a powerful minister but two in order to cement an important alliance. Both Tenji and Temmu do so, recalling, among others, the myth of Ninigi and the sisters Iwa-naga-hime and Ko-no-hana-no-sakuya-hime. In Temmu's case, it is striking that the elder sister, Princess Ōta, was ultimately "rejected," just as Iwa-naga-hime was, in that when Temmu appointed his empress, she was passed over in favor of her younger sister, Princess Uno. Moreover, both Iwa-naga-hime and Princess Ōta die shortly thereafter. The parallels were surely not lost on the early Japanese themselves. In the myth, as a result of the slight that Iwa-naga-hime suffered at the hands of Ninigi, the imperial family were cursed with mortality. In 689, the death of Jitō's own son, Kusakabe, just before he was to succeed his father must have seemed to some a bitter consequence of this mythistory. In order to appreciate why this was so, let us turn to the tragic tale of Prince Ōtsu, a son of the Emperor Temmu. This example will demonstrate the dialectical relationship between the operative religio-political symbol system on the one hand and real-life occurrences in historical time on the other.[26]

The Ōtsu no Miko Uta Monogatari

The case of Prince Ōtsu is instructive because it clearly demonstrates that mythic parallels provided interpretive frames for understanding acts and positional relations in the court as well as narrative strategies for presenting a reading of history. The tale of Yamato-takeru seems to have served as a paradigmatic narrative for "reading" (at the time and/or retrospectively) the real-life happenings in the seventh-century court surrounding the death of the Imperial Prince Ōtsu. Thus, the Yamato-takeru tale and a few poems scattered in the Man'yōshū can provide us with important clues concerning the historiographic process operative in retelling the death of Prince Ōtsu.

If the Nihonshoki account was given its present form in 720, then the account dates from approximately thirty years after the death of Prince Ōtsu. The events of the case may well still have been part of the living memory of some persons within the court and in the countryside. No scholar that I am aware of doubts the veracity of the two basic facts of this story: (1) the Emperor Temmu died on 9/9/686, and (2) three-and-a-half weeks later on 10/3 the Imperial Prince Ōtsu was executed on the orders of Jitō. These two deaths constituted two biological "facts" that had to be recognized, interpreted, and understood. The deaths and the contingent events and figures surrounding them had to be given meaningful narrative form. Since we are interested in the historical meaning given to these deaths, it is essential to recover what contemporaries or near-contemporaries of Prince Ōtsu made of his execution and the reasons for it. The Man'yōshū and the Nihonshoki show us the way(s) in which these events were given narrative and finally written form.

In Chapter Three, "The Liminal Period of Temporary Enshrinement," some of the Nihonshoki records concerning the massive and extended funeral and memorial rituals performed for Temmu were introduced. Temmu died, it will be recalled, on the ninth day of the ninth month of 686. Two days later laments began for him and, following Chinese form, construction of the mogari no miya was started in the South Courtyard. The Nihonshoki account of the events involving Prince Ōtsu immediately following the death of the emperor is cryptic:

24th day. The Emperor was temporarily interred in the South Court and mourning began. At this time the Imperial Prince Ōtsu conspired against the Imperial Prince (Kusakabe) [*sono toki ni atarite, Ōtsu no miko, Hitsugi no miko o katabukemu to su*].[27]

This brief entry gives narrative form to the crude facts of the two deaths, changing them into concrete events by supplying the scene (time and place), the main protagonists, and a causal explanation (and motive) for Ōtsu's execution. Within the court, in a now-familiar pattern, the death of the emperor led to an immediate flurry of political maneuvering for position and prestige. The following days were filled with ritual offerings, lamentations, and eulogies presented at the *mogari no miya*. These eulogies were offered by and for everyone in the court, from the Imperial Prince Kusakabe, the only son of Temmu and his empress (Jitō), and from the other imperial princes and princesses, to various palace officials, bureaucrats, clan representatives, and foreign emissaries. The *mogari no miya* rituals brought virtually everyone in the court and the power elites of the provinces together at the same site during an inherently unstable and volatile period. Precise details concerning everything that transpired in the capital at this time are lacking, but there are enough hints to allow one to make informed suppositions concerning the actions of a few central figures based upon the knowledge we have already gained concerning the liminal period of the *mogari no miya*.

The Jitō Chapter opens with the normal rehearsal of the lineage of the empress, records Prince Kusakabe to have been the only child of the Temmu–Jitō union, and recounts how Jitō had loyally followed her husband into the mountains of Yoshino at the time of the succession dispute following the death of Temmu's father, the Emperor Tenji. Then it announces Temmu's demise; this is followed immediately by an important series of entries providing the basic outline of the events that transpired within the next month or so:

In the first year of Akamitori, on the ninth day of the ninth month, the Emperor Ama no Nunahara oki no Mabito died. The Empress-consort presided over the Court and exercised control [*Kisaki, mi-kado matsurigoto kikoshimesu*].

Winter, 10th month, 2nd day. The Imperial Prince Ōtsu's treason was discovered. The Imperial Prince Ōtsu was arrested and there were arrested at the same time Otokashi, Yakuchi no asomi of Jiki-ko-shi rank, Hakatoko, Yuki no muraji of Lower Shōsen rank, and also the ōtoneri Omimaro, Nakatomi no asomi, Tayasu, Kose no asomi, a Silla priest named Kōjimu, with the toneri Toki no Michitsukuri and others, more than thirty persons in all, who had been led astray by the Imperial Prince Ōtsu.

3rd day. Death was bestowed on the Imperial Prince Ōtsu in his house at Osata. He was then twenty-four years of age. His consort, the Imperial Princess Yamanoe, hastened thither with her hair dishevelled and her feet bare, and joined him in death. All who witnessed sighed and sobbed.

The Imperial Prince Ōtsu was the third child of the Emperor Ama no nunahara oki no Mabito [i.e., Temmu]. His demeanour was noble and his language refined. He was beloved by the Emperor Ama mikoto Hirakasu-wake [i.e., Tenji, his grandfather]. When he grew to manhood he showed an eminent talent for learning, and was very fond of writing. The practice of composing Chinese verses had its origin with Ōtsu.

29th day. An Imperial decree was issued as follows:—"The Imperial Prince Ōtsu has been guilty of treason and has led astray officials and people, so that We, within the curtain, had no alternative. The Imperial Prince Ōtsu has now perished. His followers deserve the same sentence as the Prince, but We pardon them all. Toki no Michitsukuri is, however, banished to Izu." It was further decreed, saying:—"We cannot bring ourselves to inflict punishment on the Silla priest, Kōjimu, who was an accomplice in the Imperial Prince Ōtsu's treason. He is therefore exiled to the temple of the province of Hida."

11th month, 16th day. The Imperial Princess Ōku, who had been sent to attend at the Ise Shrine, returned to the capital.

17th day. There was an earthquake.[28]

The *Nihonshoki* references to Prince Ōtsu and his alleged conspiracy end here. In and of itself this brief episode in the imperial chronicle is unremarkable. And yet we may assume that the execution of an imperial prince was not a banal occurrence, either. The death of one of the ranking princes in the line of succession inevitably had consequences that would have reverberated throughout the court, negatively affecting the relative positions and prospects of some supporters while positively affecting still others. To be sure, this sort of political infighting and bloodshed was endemic to the court, but the question contemporaries must have asked themselves (and which we, too, must ask) is why was Ōtsu executed? What, if anything, did he do that would have provoked Jitō and her supporters to take such drastic action against him? And why were his alleged coconspirators punished only lightly, if at all?

The obvious answer to the first question, offered from the distance of 1300 years, is that Ōtsu was killed by the Jitō faction in a preemptive strike against a serious rival in the succession. What needs to be explored, though, is how this crass (and no doubt real) motive was handled in the narrative recountings of Ōtsu's execution. The *Nihonshoki* is characteristically vague in providing details of the purported plot. Indeed, we would be left wholly to our own imaginations were the *Nihonshoki* the only source of information about these events. Fortunately, a few poems germane to this situation survive in the *Man'yōshū*. The relevant poems include MYS 2: 105–106 and 163–166, and 3: 416. These poems deserve the attention of historians not so much for any "hard facts" they may contain as for the light they can cumulatively shed on the functioning of an underlying symbolic complex, widely shared by the early Japanese, which constituted a text-between-the-lines of the *Nihonshoki* account.

These *uta* and their prose headnotes may constitute the skeletal remains of an oral history of the events surrounding the death of this tragic prince that "made sense" precisely because its informing narrative strategy and interpretive frame were based upon well-known paradigmatic tales, including that of Yamato-takeru. The historical meaning for the early Japanese of Ōtsu's execution is to be found in the adopted and adapted tellings and retellings of the "fact" of his execution.

Before turning to the *Man'yōshū* poems, it will be useful to refresh our memory as to the blood relationships and relative social and political status of the major figures in this narrative. As was usually the case, there was no dearth of possible successors to the Emperor Temmu. He had only one son, Kusakabe, by his empress (Jitō) but a large number of sons by various consorts. Of these, the Imperial Princes Takechi, Ōtsu, Kawashima, Osakabe, Shiki, Naga, and Yuge bear mention, although the two major contenders for the throne seem to have been the half-brothers Ōtsu and Kusakabe. The mother of Prince Ōtsu was Princess Ōta, the elder sister of Jitō. A third child of Temmu who figures in the *Nihonshoki* passages on the execution of Ōtsu is the Princess Ōku, Ōtsu's younger sister. She had been appointed to the ritual position of the imperial priestess of the Ise Shrine in 673, the first year of Temmu's official reign. Thus, she occupied the same position Yamato-hime had in the Yamato-takeru tale, which was a locus of religio-political symbolic power. Lastly, according to the *Nihonshoki*, Princess Ōta, Ōtsu's mother, was given final burial on 2/27/667, so that for most of his life Ōtsu did not have his mother as a significant counterweight to Jitō. With Temmu's death, he was deprived of his last protector at the highest level of the court and, thus, suddenly found himself in a dangerously vulnerable position. Given the operative court rationality and the pressures it exerted upon those enmeshed in it, Ōtsu's downfall was almost predictable.

A number of entries in the Temmu Chapter suggest that Temmu himself hoped to avoid the kind of bloody succession dispute that he had lived through in the Jinshin War. That experience was burned into his mind and informed a number of steps he took. Through a variety of imperial edicts issued over the course of his reign, Temmu attempted to institute a court hierarchy in which bloodline was relatively devalued in some aspects while rank granted by imperial fiat garnered greater prestige, privilege, and power. The following decree from 679, in the middle of his reign, must be understood as a part of this larger project:

[1st month] 7th day. The Emperor issued a decree as follows:—"At the New Year let the Princes, Ministers, and public functionaries refrain from paying their respects to any persons except relatives of the grade of elder brothers or elder sisters and above, or to the senior members of the House. The Princes must not pay their respects even to their mothers, when the latter have not the title of Princess; nor must Ministers pay their respects to their mothers when the latter are of mean rank. Even on other ceremonial occasions than the New

Year the same rule is to be observed, and those who infringe it shall be punished according to circumstances.[29]

If observed and enforced, this decree would have had at least two related effects. First, it aimed to limit severely the number of individuals to whom courtiers and others could pay their respects on special ritual occasions in the court. The wider socio-political significance of this restriction is related to the fact that such ritual occasions were a critical time for publicly (and sometimes privately) forming and renewing political and family alliances. Moreover, they provided individuals and families the opportunity to display their relative power and prestige by having others come to them to offer greetings and perform other acts symbolic of the rank relationships between and among them. The converse action of visiting others could equally serve the same purpose, as members of the court no doubt took careful note of who deigned to pay their respects to whom, in what order, and so on. The second intended effect of the edict, closely related to the first, was to shift the loci of power away from clans and matrilineal bloodlines to a heightened emphasis on the sovereign as the *center* of the socio-political system. To understand how this shift could be achieved we must once again consider the situation in terms of the operative court rationality. Relying upon that rationality, this edict sought to establish a system that formally recognized only those court ranks granted by the emperor himself.

This edict, then, may be thought of as representing one element of a concerted political program intended to achieve a monopoly of sorts for the sovereign. Especially important in this regard is the attempt to limit the prestige and power of the women in the court—and, as a direct consequence, of the clans—by clearly implying that a person's rank, be it that of minister or even imperial prince, was a function solely of the pleasure and will of the sovereign. The emperor alone had the power to elevate any of his wives or concubines to the rank of princess or empress; conversely he would have the power to punish or constrain certain pressure groups by refusing to elevate them. It would be erroneous, however, to assume that the emperor was completely sovereign and immune to various socio-political constraints over his own actions. Nevertheless, by granting a son by a concubine of "mean rank" the rank of prince at an opportune time for his own purposes, for example, the emperor could "buy" the loyalty and gratitude of this son. He could do this, however, only if it was clear that the son's increased status was not due to the power of his mother's clan but to his continued good standing in the eyes of his father. Through the exercise of power of this sort, Temmu hoped to consolidate further his political control and ability to determine his successor.

Another decree issued five months later reports that a large imperial entourage journeyed to Yoshino, where Temmu had fled years earlier in the Jinshin period.

There in the place so immediately identified with his own destiny, he called together the empress-consort (Jitō) and six imperial princes to perform a remarkable ritual.[30] Almost certainly other members of the court were also present.

[679] 5th month, 5th day. The Emperor proceeded to the Palace of Yoshino.

6th day. The Emperor addressed the Empress Consort, the Imperial Prince Kusakabe, the Imperial Prince Ōtsu, the Imperial Prince Takechi, the Imperial Prince Kawashima, the Imperial Prince Osakabe, and the Imperial Prince Shiki, saying:—"We wish today to unite with you in making a vow to the Court, so that after a thousand years there may be no trouble. What think ye?" The Imperial princes answered together, saying:—"The reasonableness of this is manifest." Accordingly, His Highness the Imperial Prince Kusakabe stood forward first and made oath, saying:—"Ye gods of Heaven and Earth, and ye Emperors, bear witness! We, elder and younger brothers, young or mature of age, more than ten Princes in all, born each of different mothers, without respect of birth from the same or different mothers, together comply with the Emperor's behest, and will give each other mutual support and avoid contention. If, from this time forward, any of us should not keep this vow, may he himself perish and may his line become extinct! There will be no forgetfulness or failure."

The (other) five Imperial Princes took oath together in the above terms in order one after another, and thereupon the Emperor said:—"Ye, my sons, although each born of different mothers, are now in affection as if born of one mother." Accordingly, loosening out his collar, he took the six Imperial Princes to his bosom, and made oath, saying:—"If We contravene this oath, may Our body perish instantly!" The Empress-consort's oath was like that of the Emperor.

7th day. The Emperor's car returned to the Palace.

10th day. The six Imperial princes together paid their respects to the Emperor before the Great Hall.[31]

The purpose of this journey to Yoshino was to perform this ritual oath. The purpose of the oath is equally clear—to make the imperial princes "as if born of one mother." This one mother was, of course, Jitō, the only female mentioned in conjunction with this event and, most significantly, the natural mother of Kusakabe. Kusakabe comes out of this "adoption" ritual as the firstborn and only natural son. Even though the oath speaks of equality, in actuality it formally established the succession rank-order, with Kusakabe emerging as the heir apparent. Moreover, in this and other passages Kusakabe is always mentioned first. The rhetorically and ritually realized "fact" of Kusakabe's primacy among the imperial princes was to be confirmed formally a year and a half later in the second month of 681 in another public ritual in the imperial palace when he was installed as the crown prince and "was accordingly associated with the Emperor in the conduct of the myriad machinery of state."[32]

One might assume that Temmu and Jitō had skillfully managed to position Kusakabe to succeed his father, but this was not to be. The *Nihonshoki* gives no indication of what transpired in the court following the events described above, for neither Kusakabe nor Ōtsu is specifically mentioned in a long intervening period[33] until the following brief entry abruptly intrudes in the chronicle:

[683] 2nd month, 1st day. The Imperial Prince Ōtsu for the first time attended to matters of State [hajimete mi-kado no matsurigoto o kikoshimesu].[34]

Here we find Ōtsu exercising the powers formerly reserved to Kusakabe. It is unclear whether this development was the result of Kusakabe's having fallen seriously ill or whether Ōtsu had somehow maneuvered himself into a position of strength from which he was able to nudge Kusakabe aside. What this entry does indicate, however, is that already three years prior to Temmu's death, Ōtsu had emerged as a serious rival to Kusakabe.

In 685, Temmu was engaged once again in reshuffling the court system of ranks, including the rank order of the imperial princes, in his continued quest to consolidate his power further and to control the succession. Kusakabe reemerged as first in rank, with Ōtsu a close second, followed by Takechi, Kawashima, and Osakabe.[35] Of equal if not more import is the notice found in the Nihonshoki for the fifteenth day of the seventh lunar month of 686 when Temmu had fallen seriously ill: "The Emperor gave orders that all matters of the Empire, without distinction of great and small, should be referred to the Empress-Consort and the Prince Imperial [Kusakabe]."[36] Jitō was moving swiftly to reinforce her position and that of her son. Only a few months later Temmu died, and the first series of entries cited above concerning the alleged conspiracy of Prince Ōtsu appear.

It should be noted that Ōtsu and Kusakabe were apparently not only political rivals but rivals in love as well. The only information on this aspect of sexual politics in the court comes from the Man'yōshū, where we find the following intriguing poems (MYS 2: 107–110):

Ōtsu no miko, Ishikawa no Iratsume ni okuru mi-uta isshu	Poem sent by Prince Ōtsu to Lady Ishikawa
ashihiki no yama no shizuku ni imo matsu to ware tachinurenu yama no shizuku ni	Waiting for you, my love, in the trickling rain on the foothill-trailing mountain, I stand here drenched in that trickling mountain rain.
Ishikawa no Iratsume, kotae matsuru uta isshu	Poem presented by Lady Ishikawa in response
a o matsu to kimi ga nurekemu ashihiki no	You say, my Lord, you have been drenched waiting for me on the foot-trailing mountain.

yama no shizuku ni
naramashi mono o

O that I could be
that trickling rain!

Ōtsu no miko, hisoka ni Ishikawa no Iratsume ni au toki, Tsumori no Muraji Tōru
sono koto o ura e arawasu ni, miko no tsukurimashishi mi-uta isshu (imada tsubai-
ranarazu)

Poem by Prince Ōtsu when Tsumori Tōru
discovered through divination that the
Prince had secretly wed Lady Ishikawa
(The details are still unclear.)

ōbune no
Tsumori no ura ni
noramu to wa
masashi ni shirite
waga futari neshi

Knowing full well
that it would be told
in Tsumori's divination
(Tsumori of the great boat),
we two did sleep together.

Hinamishi no miko no mikoto, Ishikawa no
Iratsume ni okuritamau mi-uta isshu (Iratsume, asana o Ōnako to iu)

Poem sent by the Crown Prince Peer of
the Sun, to Lady Ishikawa
(The Lady's name was Ōnako.)

Ōnako o
ochi kata nobe ni
karu kaya no
tsuka no aida mo
ware wasureme ya

How could I ever forget
you, Ōnako,
even for the time
it takes to bundle a sheath
of grass cut on distant fields![37]

These poems provide an interesting perspective on the complex competition that existed between Ōtsu and Kusakabe. Here we find the suggestion that both these princes were involved with the same woman, Lady Ishikawa, one of the most intriguing figures found in the *Man'yōshū*. A Soga daughter and well-known poet in her own right, she seems to have been at the center of palace intrigue for several decades in the seventh century in a world where eros and power were deeply enmeshed. The prose headnote to MYS 2: 129 identifies her as "a lady-in-waiting at the palace of Prince Ōtsu" (*Ōtsu no miko no miya no makatachi*).[38] The fact that divination was involved in making the relationship of Prince Ōtsu and Lady Ishikawa public is of special interest, since it indicates the political dimensions of this form of religious practice. Note, too, the same phrase *hisoka ni*, "secretly," is used in the headnote to characterize this relationship and to imply its impropriety, even though such relationships were extremely common and usually not the subject of criticism.

If Ōtsu was indeed censured in some way for sleeping with Lady Ishikawa, then it is possible that Kusakabe had attempted to exercise his privilege of rank by bringing Lady Ishikawa into his own service. This would be a variant of the pattern we have seen of the emperor sending for a maiden or maidens only to have his messenger, in an act of insubordination fraught with political ambition, appropriate the women unto himself.[39] In this light the last poem may take on some ominous tones if the lines "the [brief] time/ it takes to bundle a sheath/ of grass cut on distant fields" allude to the summary execution of Prince Ōtsu.

In the light of similar cases that we have seen, it comes as no real surprise that the Temmu Chapter of the *Nihonshoki* locates the time of Ōtsu's "conspiracy" as the day of the ritual enshrinement of Temmu's corpse in the *mogari no miya*. This was the liminal period par excellence in the life of the court. In terms of both the socio-political structural realities of the period and the religio-political symbolic complex that found expression in myths, legends, and the funeral rituals themselves, political acts of a specific type were to be expected at this time. If we grant this, then what specifically are we to make of the charge leveled against Prince Ōtsu? The term used in the text is *katamu*, which Aston rendered as "conspired." Modern Japanese schol-ars, though, suggest that this is a very general legal term covering a wide range of acts. Thus, on the basis of the *Nihonshoki* alone, it appears impossible to determine precisely what constituted Ōtsu's conspiracy. Yet, it may be possible to make a few informed conjectures on this matter by using similar cases and tales we have already encountered. It is possible, for example, that Ōtsu somehow either slighted or ridi-culed Kusakabe during the *mogari no miya* rituals, as was found in the tale of Prince Anahobe. Or perhaps he usurped some small ritual prerogative of Jitō or Kusakabe. Then again, if Lady Ishikawa had once been sexually involved with Temmu, as the *Man'yōshū* suggests, she may have been secluded in his *mogari no miya*. What if the "secret union" of Ōtsu and Lady Ishikawa, referred to in MYS 2: 109, occurred at this time?

There is some suggestion that this possibility might have been the case, or at least that it was considered to have been so at the time the *Man'yōshū* was compiled and edited. The poems on Ōtsu's "secret" sexual union with Lady Ishikawa are placed after verses 105 and 106, which concern Ōtsu's "secret" visit to the Ise Shrine. The general organizational principle followed by the editors of the *Shoku-Man'yōshū* was to arrange the poems in chronological order under the respective reigns from which they were presumed to have come. The order in which these verses are found in the manuscripts, then, suggests that the events involved, including the divination by Tsumori, were considered to have come after the visit to the Ise Shrine. Thus, Ōtsu's sexual union with Lady Ishikawa is located in the liminal period of the emperor's *mogari no miya*. During this period such an act would have been subject to interpre-tations ascribing political intention to it or ritual impurity if sexual abstinence was supposed to be observed. Whatever the case, the characterization of both acts—the journey to Ise and the union with Lady Ishikawa—as "secret" links them together as part of a larger conspiracy on Ōtsu's part.

All these possibilities are, then, only conjectures that finally cannot be proved or disproved. Moreover, we must also entertain the possibility that Ōtsu did nothing at all. His relative position within the court in the wake of the emperor's death, coupled with the structural and performative dynamics informing the mythic and ritual complex surrounding the period of the *mogari, no miya*, may have sufficed to generate the forces leading to his execution. That is, we need not even assume that he committed some offense, since it is entirely possible the charges were trumped up by Jitō or others in order to eliminate a major competitor. In admitting this possibility, we face the paradox that the most important texts that have survived to tell us about the death of Ōtsu stand as almost impenetrable barriers to finding out "what really happened." And yet, knowing as we do that the *Nihonshoki* was written by members of the Temmu–Jitō faction, even if it had provided an explicit account of the seditious acts of Ōtsu, we might well be wary of accepting that account at face value.

It is at this point that the other poems related to these events preserved in the *Man'yōshū* may serve as important historical documents, though of a special sort. Although they cannot provide us with any evidence that is beyond challenge, these verses can shed light on the way the early Japanese themselves made sense of the occurrences within the period framed by the two biological "facts" of the deaths of Temmu and Prince Ōtsu. The *Nihonshoki* account itself can generate a number of possibilities as we have seen, but it is only in the *Man'yōshū* poems that we find the early Japanese making a choice among them. These poems and their prose headnotes represent a startling example of what Sahlins has called the "structure of conjuncture," which he defines as "the practical realization of the cultural categories in a specific historical context, as expressed in the interested action of the historic agents, including the microsociology of their interaction."[40] The poems MYS 2: 105–106 are especially crucial here.

Ōtsu no miko, hisoka ni Ise no Jingu ni orite agari komashishi toki no Ōku no hi-memiko no mi-uta nishu

Two poems by Princess Ōku when her brother Prince Ōtsu left to return to the capital after a secret visit to the Shrine at Ise

waga seko o
Yamato e yaru to
sa-yo fukete
akatoki tsuyu ni
waga tachi nureshi

Sending my brother
off to Yamato,
I stand
in the deepening night
till drenched with the dew of dawn.[41]

futari yukedo
yuki sugi kataki
aki yama o
ika ni ka kimi ga
hitori koyuramu

The autumn mountains
are hard to pass through
even when two go together.
How, my Lord, will you
cross over them alone?[42]

The province of these *uta* is not indicated. Nonetheless, several points of interest emerge from a careful consideration of them. First, since they are chronologically located under the reign of the Empress Jitō, these poems are implicitly emplotted in the period after the death of Temmu but before Ōtsu's execution. Thus, Ōtsu's secret visit to the Ise Shrine is posited as falling between 9/9 and 10/2/686 when Ōtsu was arrested. Wada Shigeki, among others, has argued persuasively that the timing can be narrowed even further to sometime between 9/24, the date of the temporary interment of Temmu's corpse, a ritual at which Ōtsu certainly had to be in attendance, and 10/2.[43] Since the Temmu Chapter locates the alleged conspiracy at the time of this ritual, it may well be that Ōtsu left for the Ise Shrine shortly after its conclusion.

If this timing is assumed, whether as fact or simply as narrative time, in stating that Prince Ōtsu "*secretly* journeyed to the Ise Shrine" (*hisoka ni Ise no Jingu ni orite*) the prose headnote draws a clear connection between the journey to Ise and a plot to seize power. Why this should be so is not difficult to see. In terms of the operative *tama*-related belief system and the attendant symbolic and ritual complex, the imperial *tama* had departed from Temmu's body at the time of his death. Rituals would have been performed in the *mogari no miya* to attract the *tama* back. But the crucial point is that this was not the only site where rituals to call down the imperial *tama* were held. The Ise Shrine was another. Sahlins has suggested that "a given society will have certain strategic sites of historical action, evenementially hot areas, and other areas relatively closed."[44] Our study has demonstrated that the *mogari no miya* and the Ise Shrine were both such strategic sites in the wake of the death of an important political figure. If one takes the scenario found in the tale of Yamato-takeru as a readily available interpretive frame that could be superimposed on the situation in the court following Temmu's demise, then Ōtsu's journey to the imperial priestess of Ise was a symbolic religio-political act undertaken with the intention of gaining legitimacy in the succession through the performance of a *tama-furi* ritual to attract back and appropriate the imperial *tama* unto himself. This appropriation was to be realized through the assistance of his sister, the Ise Priestess, and her magico-religious powers.

Verse 105 contains a few hints of the political dimension of Ōtsu's visit to the Ise Shrine. First, Princess Ōku uses the term *seko*, a familiar form of address used for a husband or younger brother, in referring to Ōtsu. This verse also intimates that the Ise Priestess stayed up in an all-night vigil while her brother returned to the capital. The situation is to be understood as more than a sign of her worry and concern for Ōtsu; instead, it is the same type of ritual act we encountered earlier in the set (MYS 2: 85–89) of "four poems [plus a variant] by the Empress Iwanohime, thinking of the Emperor." Princess Ōku's vigil is intended magically to ensure Ōtsu's safety. At the same time, the compilers of the *Man'yōshū* create a thematic correspondence between verses 105–106, where the verb *tachinureshi*, "stand drenched" (in the dew), is related to Princess Ōku, and verses 107–108, where it is Prince Ōtsu who stands drenched (*tachinurenu*) in the rain. The suggestion of sexual intimacy in the latter set is conjoined with the former through the shared verb.

Earlier it was suggested that the Yamato-takeru tale may have provided a readily available interpretive frame for the conspiratorial "reading" of Ōtsu's motives. Since the *Kojiki* itself was committed to writing only in 712, however, approximately a generation after the Ōtsu incident, the precise lines of influence between the Yamato-takeru tale and the Ōtsu narrative are anything but sure. It seems likely, though, that in its general outline the Yamato-takeru tale, which contains many more folkloric elements, predated the Ōtsu incident and would have circulated orally. What is clear are the areas of confluence, the shared elements and patterns in these tales, that provide an important glimpse into the world of meaning created and sustained by the Japanese in the seventh and eighth centuries. If nothing else, it is apparent that these two tales belong to the same structural type. The main protagonist in both is an imperial prince who fails to succeed his father, and both include the critical narrative elements of a secret journey to a close female relative serving as the imperial priestess of the Ise Shrine and a problematic sexual relationship. They preserve, I would argue, the living memory of competing loci of political legitimacy and power, centering on the women in the *mogari no miya* and the Ise Shrine.

The extant texts suggest that the operative religio-political symbol system contributed to the generation of a number of tales of the same structural type, which sought to explain (and in some cases to explain away) certain acts of human agents in the court in the unstable succession process. The structural relations of the figures in the myths and other paradigmatic narratives frequently mirror those found in the socio-political order of the court. This is not to imply that every tale was based on an actual historical situation (i.e., represents a form of euhemerism). Rather, in their tellings such tales were (re)cast in terms of readily recognizable social relationships. Where the correspondence between the structural relations of major figures in a given situation in the court and that found in a paradigmatic narrative or set was very close, the known narrative structures could influence the ways in which human agents acted and reacted to the movements of others. That is, one might see instances of mytho-praxis or "social dramas" (Victor Turner) played out in the court.

But even though the paradigmatic narratives could be adopted and adapted to one's immediate needs, this alone would not guarantee success. The same narrative might be used to different effect by other parties to impose a certain interpretive frame on a given situation that another party normally would not passively accept.

Individuals or factions could deny that a given paradigmatic narrative was relevant to their immediate situation and, thus, attempt to thwart its power to channel actions and the subsequent interpretations placed on them.

In the case of Prince Ōtsu, we have perhaps an instance of an individual who, finding himself in a vulnerable position, sought to appropriate the symbolic and legitimating power offered by a paradigmatic narrative and its informing symbolic complex through adapting his actions in clearly recognizable ways. Jitō seems to have recognized this strategy and moved swiftly to negate its potential symbolic power by eliminating Ōtsu. At the same time the Yamato-takeru tale was turned to her own advantage by serving as the interpretive frame for the conspiratorial charges brought against Ōtsu. Jitō's swift and ruthless response in executing Ōtsu is an instance of the actions of a historical agent effectively canceling certain anticipated scenes in the performance of a social drama. She brought down the curtain, as it were, by rewriting the "script" so that the main actor was removed from the stage.

If Jitō's summary execution of Ōtsu effectively blocked the immediate historical realization of a symbolic scenario that promised the appropriation of the imperial charisma or *tama* onto the person of Ōtsu, the power of the informing symbolic complex was not to be easily denied in the long run. There are a few other *uta* scattered in the *Man'yōshū* that, combined with those already introduced, result in a fuller *uta monogatari* about Prince Ōtsu. Though little more than a skeletal outline, it is possible to reconstruct "The Ōtsu no miko uta monogatari." This narrative version of events may have circulated in the late seventh and eighth centuries alongside those of Yamato-takeru and other tragic princes. As such it would represent a popular version of the incident that was repressed in various ways in the official written histories of the eighth-century court.

The poem MYS 3: 416 is categorized as a *banka*. It is popularly known as Prince Ōtsu's death verse. Along with the attached prose editorial notes, it reads:

Ōtsu no miko, mimakarashime rayuru toki, Iware no ike no tsutsumi ni shite namida o nagashite tsukurimashishi mi-uta isshu

Poem by Prince Ōtsu, weeping on the banks of the Iware Pond when he was about to be put to death

momozutau
Iware no ike ni
naku kamo o
kyō nomi mite ya
kumo gakurinamu

The duck that cries
on Iware Pond,
where the vines crawl on the rocks:
will I see it just today
and then be hidden in the clouds?

(migi, Fujiwara no miya no Akamitori gan-nen fuyu jū gatsu nari)

(The above incident occurred in winter, the tenth month, of the first year of Akamitori [686], during the period of the Fujiwara Palace.)[45]

The prose headnote attributes this poem to Prince Ōtsu immediately after he was arrested, since he was summarily executed the following day. Ōtsu is acknowledged in the *Nihonshoki* to have been an accomplished poet, especially of Chinese verse, and indeed a death poem in Chinese attributed to him also is extant.[46] Yet we need not accept the attribution of authorship of MYS 3: 416 without reservation. This verse may have been created by someone else and only retrospectively ascribed to Ōtsu. In order to accept the attribution of authorship of these two *uta*, one must assume that Ōtsu had not only the presence of mind in the face of impending execution to compose them but also the freedom and the supplies to do so. Moreover, one must assume that the poems were somehow smuggled out of his place of detention. The term *kumo gakurinamu*, "be hidden in the clouds," was used in the *Man'yōshū* to refer to the death of sovereigns or crown princes. Its presence here may represent an oblique claim that Ōtsu was the rightful heir, similar to the case found in the *Kojiki* where after Yamato-takeru's visit to the Ise Shrine, there is a sudden shift to terms used in relation to him that were normally reserved for sovereigns.

In addition to this verse there are four other *uta* classified as *banka* in the *Man'yōshū* that are related to the death of Prince Ōtsu. The poems MYS 2: 163–166 are all located under the reign of the Empress Jitō and ascribed to Princess Ōku. With the attached editorial notes they read:

Ōtsu no miko kamuagarimashishi ato, Ōku no hime miko Ise no Itsuki no miya yori miyako ni agaru toki no mi-uta nishu

Two poems by Princess Ōku when, after the death of Prince Ōtsu, she came up from the Shrine of our offerings at Ise to the capital

kamukaze no
Ise no kuni ni mo
aramashi o
nani shika kokemu
kimi mo aranaku ni

For what have I come
when I might have stayed
in the land of Ise,
of the divine wind,
now that you are no longer?

mimaku hori
waga suru kimi mo
aranaku ni
nani shika kokemu
uma tsukaruru ni

For what have I come
when you,
whom I prayed to see,
are no longer?
I have only tired my horse.

Ōtsu no miko no kabane o Kazuraki no Fu-takami-yama ni utsushi haburu toki, Ōku no hime miko no awashibi itamu mi-uta nishu

Two poems by Princess Ōku in sorrow when they removed and reburied the remains of Prince Ōtsu on Futakami Mountain in Katsuragi

utsusomi no
hito ni aru ware ya
ashita yori wa

O, I who am among
the living
from tomorrow will

Futakami-yama o
irose to waga mimu

iso no ue ni
ouru ashibi o
ta oramedo
misubeki kimi ga
ari to iwanaku ni

migi isshu, ima kamugauru ni, utsushi haburu uta ni nizu. kedashi utagawaku wa,
Ise no kamu miya yori miyatsuko ni kaeru
toki, michi no e ni hana o mite kanshō
aietsu shite kono uta o tsukuru ka

look on Futakami Mountain
as you, my brother.

I would pluck
the andromeda that grows
on the beach,
but no one says that you
who should see it are here.

The above poem does not seem to be about
the removal of the Prince's remains. Might
it have been made by the Princess when
sorrow overcame her upon viewing the
flowers by the road when she returned to
the capital from the Ise Shrine?[47]

The first two *banka*, 163 and 164, appear to be the type of remonstration by a mourner directed at the deceased that we encountered earlier in the oral lament tradition of rural Greece. Princess Ōku was removed from her position as the Ise Priestess within a matter of weeks after Ōtsu's execution. If the prose headnote is accurate, these oral laments would have been offered at the temporary interment site, whereas the latter two come from the time of the disinterment of the corpse and its removal for final burial in the mountains. It is impossible to determine if the *uta* actually came out of these performative loci or whether they are only narratively emplotted there. The *Nihonshoki* contains no entries concerning either the temporary or the final burial rites for Ōtsu; though in light of the circumstances, the period of temporary burial was probably kept brief by Jitō in order to forestall any possible maneuvers involving Ōtsu's supporters. We must not forget that such funeral rites had the potential to turn into venues for dramatic political action and violence, a situation still found today.

The editorial endnote cited above suggests that the compilers of the *Man'yōshū* had little or no personal acquaintance with the oral lament tradition, for they seem to assume that the flowers (*ashibi*) must have been present before the grieving princess's eyes at the time this verse was created. Such an assumption may indicate how quickly the oral *banka* tradition died in the court after the performative locus of the *mogari no miya* rituals disappeared. At the same time, one senses the presence of a literate or graphic mentality informing this endnote. It expresses reservations about the attribution of the occasion of the last *uta* because of its semantic content, yet we have seen other examples of poems in which the content ostensibly has little or nothing to do with death and funeral rituals and yet they were used as oral laments at the grave site.

In MYS 2: 105–110 and 163–166 and 3: 416 we have, I think, the skeletal remains of a tale of the tragic Prince Ōtsu. Although broken up and scattered in three different locations within the *Shoki-Man'yōshū*, the tale can readily be reconstructed. The poems follow the pattern found in the Yamato-takeru tale of using such *uta* to heighten the dramatic effect and the pathos of the prince's death. The figure of Ōtsu, once regarded as a real-life political threat to the dynastic ambitions of Jitō, has been transformed into a literary figure. Ironically, although Ōtsu was denied power in the seventh-century court, through the "*Ōtsu no miko uta monogatari*," the prose and poetic tale of Prince Ōtsu, his specter has had the power to haunt the imagination of the Japanese over the centuries.

Ritual Poetry and the Succession After Temmu's Death

There are surprisingly few *banka* extant from the *mogari no miya* of Temmu, although there must have been hundreds performed, since the *Nihonshoki* reports extensive mourning and memorial rituals until the time of final burial. We will confine our focus to a few additional poems related to the succession: MYS 2: 159–161, 2: 167–169, and 1: 45–49. The set in MYS 2: 159–161 read:

sumeramikoto kamuagarimashishi toki no
ōkisaki no mi-uta isshu

Poem by the Empress when the Sovereign
passed away

yasumishishi	Our Lord, sovereign
wago ōkimi no	of the earth's eight quarters,
yūsareba	when evening falls
mishi tamaurashi	surely you must gaze on,
ake kureba	when morning comes
toitamaurashi	surely you must go to view
Kamu oka no	the yellow leaves
yama no momichi o	on the mountain slopes of Kamu-oka.
kyō mo kamo	Today perhaps
toitamawamashi	you go to view them,
ashita mo kamo	tomorrow, too, perhaps
meshi tamawamashi	you will gaze on them.
sono yama o	Looking back on
furisakemitsutsu	that mountain,
yūsareba	when evening falls
aya ni kanashibi	how sad I am!
ake kureba	when morning comes
urasabi kurashi	how desolate my day!
aratae no	The sleeves
koromo no sode wa	of my mourning robes
furu toki mo nashi	are never dry.

(issho ni iwaku, sumeramikoto kamuagarimashishi toki no ōki-sumeramikoto no
ōmi-uta nishu)

(One source says, "Two verses by the Empress Dowager at the time of the Sovereign's having passed away.")

moyuru hi mo
torite tsutsumite
fukuro ni wa
iru to iwazu ya
omo shiranaku mo

Do they not say
you can take a burning fire
and hold it in a sack?
Yet I cannot
meet you!

kita yama ni
tanabiku kumo no
aogumo no
hoshi sakari yuki
tsuki o sakarite

On the northern mountain
the trailing clouds,
the blue clouds,
break off and leave the stars,
break off from the moon.[48]

Although attributed to Jitō, it is quite possible that this poem was performed in her stead by a surrogate oral poet. The *chōka* shares many elements we have already seen in other public ritual poems, beginning with the opening "Our Lord, sovereign of the earth's eight quarters." The elements of parallelism and the use of the image of the yellow leaves again are common. At the same time, this *banka* is reminiscent in some ways of the female laments from rural Greece that we saw earlier. It opens by referring to the activities of the deceased, then introduces a sharp contrast and veiled protest, heightened by the echoed parallelism of "when evening falls . . . when morning comes," of the situation of the widow who finds her husband's death has left her nights lonely and her days desolate. The first envoy also seems to call into doubt a bit of popular wisdom in an especially powerful image, since the "fire" (*hi*), which according to a popular saying one can catch and keep, is at the same time the "sun" (*hi*), that is, the emperor. When we recall that the *tama-furi* and *tama-musubi* rituals were designed to effect a similar end, capturing and "tying up" the *tama* or spirit of the dead, the image is even more apposite. It is unfortunate that we do not have any detailed information on the occasion and locus of the genesis and performance of this lament, although they were undoubtedly related to one of the rituals of the *mogari no miya*.

In the previous chapter we looked at some of the *banka* from the *mogari no miya* of Kusakabe. His death seems to have led to the inclusion of more *banka* in the *Man'yōshū* than did Temmu's because the succession was once again somewhat in doubt. In MYS 2: 167–169, Hitomaro's *chōka* and two envoys "at the time of the Crown Prince Hinamishi's *mogari no miya*," the *banka* opens by recalling the cosmogony and the descent of the grandson of Amaterasu, Ninigi, then links the imperial succession to Kusakabe and the expectation of the people that he would succeed his father and rule as his ancestors had. As we have seen, only *banka* for deceased individuals who had occupied positions of importance in the line of succession rehearse the mythic origins of the imperial family. Those for others further down the line tend to concentrate on the desolation and sense of loss felt by the surviving spouse. Although the *chōka* suggests that in the wake of Kusakabe's death "the Prince's courtiers/ do not know which way to turn," the final envoy, MYS 2: 169, ends on a note of despair mixed with a touch of renewed expectation:

akanesasu	The crimson-shining sun
hi wa teraseredo	still shines,
nubatama no	but that the moon is hidden
yo wataru tsuki no	in the pitch-black night it crosses—
kakaraku oshi mo	alas!

This verse, like all public *banka*, is not merely a personal lament; it also expresses a collective emotion and desire that the imperial succession continue unbroken. Moreover, the verse was meant no doubt to reassure the assembled crowd that though the crown prince had died, the imperial line continued and everything was under control. The attached editorial endnote suggests that this was probably a standard public statement following the death of a crown prince. It says: "In one book, the latter poems are together with a verse from the time of the *araki no miya* of a later Crown Prince."[49]

Bearing this envoy in mind, let us turn to MYS 1: 45–49, a ritual sequence used in an accession ceremony.[50] Mythic elements are once again employed because of the immediate relationship of the generative and performative occasion of the verses to the question of the succession.

Karu no miko no Aki no no ni tadorima-shishi toki, Kakinomoto no Asomi no Hi-tomaro no tsukuru uta	Verse by Kakinomoto no Asomi no Hito-maro on the occasion of Prince Karu's night-sojourn on the Aki plain

yasumishishi	Our Lord
wago ōkimi	who rules the land in peace,
takaterasu	child
hi no miko	of the high-shining sun,
kamunagara	a very god,
kamusabisesu to	manifests his divine will
futoshikasu	and departs
miyako o okite	the firmly-pillared capital,
komoriku no	and up the mountain slopes
Hatsuse no yama wa	of Hatsuse,
maki tatsu	the hidden land,
ara yama michi o	on rough mountain trails,
iwagane	where bristling timber stands,
saeki oshinabe	pushes through

sakatori no	the rooted rocks and tangled trees,
asa koemashite	like a soaring bird
tamakagiru	in morning clears the crest;
yū sarikureba	when twilight comes
mi-yuki furu	faintly like a jewel's soft gleam
Aki no ōno ni	on the pure snow-fallen
hatasusuki	vast fields of Aki,
shino o oshinabe	he bends down the bannergrass
kusamakura	and small bamboo
tabiyadori sesu	and grass for pillow
inishie omoite	sojourns the night,
	recalling the past.
Aki no no ni	The traveler sojourning
yadoru tabibito	on the fields of Aki
uchinabiki	stretches out,
i mo nurame ya mo	yet cannot sleep,
inishie omou ni	recalling the past.
ma-kusa karu	Although it is a wild field
arano ni wa aredo	where they cut the splendid grass,
momichiba no	as the *katami* of our Lord,
suginishi kimi ga	gone like the yellow leaves,
katami to so koshi	we have come.
himukashi no	On the eastern fields
no ni kagiroi no	the flames appear
tatsu miete	and rise;
kaerimi sureba	looking back
tsuki katabukinu	the moon is sinking.
Hinamishi no	The hour when
miko no mikoto no	the Crown Prince, Peer of the Sun,
uma namete	would line his steeds
mi-kari tatashishi	and set out on the royal hunt
toki wa kimukau	comes to meet us.[51]

Prince Karu, the traveler in this verse, was the son of the Crown Prince Kusakabe and Princess Ahe. Kusakabe appears here under his honorary name Hinamishi, Peer of the Sun. The *Nihonshoki* reports that Kusakabe led the mourning rituals for Temmu and oversaw the construction of his tomb. It was expected that he would succeed his father, and preparations to that end appear to have been well underway. The following entries just prior to final burial two years after Temmu's death are indicative of this:

[688] Winter, 11th month, 4th day. The Prince Imperial, accompanied by the Ministers and public functionaries, as well as by the guests from the frontier lands, went to the *mogari no*

miya and made lamentation. On this occasion offerings of food were made, and the tata-fushi dance performed. The Ministers each advanced in turn and pronounced a eulogy, setting forth the services rendered by their ancestors.

5th day. More than 190 Emishi brought tribute on their backs, and in this fashion pronounced a eulogy.

11th day. Minushi, Fuse no Asomi, and Miyuki, Ōtomo no Sukune, pronounced eulogies alternately. Chitoko, Tagima no Mahito, of Jiki-kwō-shi rank, in a eulogy recited the succession to the throne of the Imperial ancestors. When this ceremony was finished, the Emperor was buried in the Ōchi *misazagi* [mausoleum].[52]

One would have expected Kusakabe to have succeeded to the throne at the start of the New Year, but this did not happen. It is unclear what intervened, but Kusakabe may have fallen seriously ill. He is not mentioned at all until the entry that announces his death on 4/13/689. An entry for 3/24, however, announces that a general amnesty was proclaimed in the country, an action sometimes taken in order to earn merit that could be used to cure a seriously ill member of the imperial family. Whatever the case, Kusakabe's death must have come as a great shock to Jitō, since he was her only child by Temmu. Her grandson, Prince Karu, was only about eight years old at the time, so as a stopgap measure Jitō formally acceded to power at the start of the following New Year.

With this in mind, it is possible to date MYS 1: 45–49 fairly precisely by using internal evidence and noting its relative position in the *Man'yōshū*. First, the poem is located under the reign of Jitō, which allows us to locate it between her formal accession on 1/1/690 and her abdication in 697. More specifically, the verse is located between MYS 1: 40–44, a series of poems on an imperial excursion to Ise, an event the *Nihonshoki* reports occurred in the spring of the sixth year of Akamitori (692), and MYS 1: 50, a verse with the headnote, "Poem of the builders of the Fujiwara Palace." Again the *Nihonshoki* reports that this palace was completed in the spring of 694. Finally, since internally the *chōka* speaks about the snow-covered fields of Aki, we can assume the occasion to have been in the winter. This allows us to say that the sequence on the journey to the Aki plain is set in the winter of 692 or 693. In addition, there is strong circumstantial evidence that the night in question was in fact that of the winter solstice, an important ritual time.

If the generative and performative temporal locus of this sequence above is correct, Prince Karu would have been only ten (or eleven by the Eastern count) at this time. This fact would seemingly militate against the purpose of the journey to Aki having been simply to hunt. Instead, the purpose seems to have been a ritual one immediately related to the question of the succession. A major piece of evidence for this interpretation is found in the second envoy, where we are told that the fields of Aki are the deceased crown prince's *katami*. This fact has not gone unnoticed by

Edwin Cranston, one of the few Western scholars to treat this sequence at any length, although he misses its full import. Cranston perceptively describes the movement of the *chōka*: "The exposition of forward movement is in irresistible stages. There is a sense of speed, of some dreadful urgency. The poem is one long narrative sentence, with a reversed-syntax last line whose incomplete grammar gives a receding feeling, a penetration into the mind. Now the action is over, and the examination of feeling begins."[53]

Cranston takes the *chōka* to be Hitomaro's description of the journey to the fields of Aki. This is the "action" section of the sequence; the envoys present subjective feeling. Of verses 46 and 47 he comments: "Here there is something deeper—a feeling that the scene matches death. . . . The wild fields are the dead man's *katami*, the thing by which to remember him. The dead always have their *katami*—a palace, a river, an orphaned child. There is a trace of this searching-for-the-dead here too, though the implication is that time has passed."[54] What Cranston does not notice is that the rush of motion as Prince Karu is rhetorically pictured going up the mountain slopes echoes earlier mythic narratives. Although here it is an ascent rather than a descent, the description of the departure of the grandson of the Empress Jitō recalls that of another grandson, Ninigi no mikoto, as he left the Heavenly Rockseat (*iwakura*), descended from the High Heavens to the earth, pushing through the myriad clouds to establish the imperial rule. Prince Karu, as a living *kami*, is described pushing through the rooted rocks and tangled trees—"child/ of the high-shining sun/ a very god/ manifests his divine will/ and departs" (*takaterasu/ hi no miko/ kamunagara/ kamusabisesu to/ . . . miyako o okite*). He is portrayed as soaring up the mountains like a bird, reaching the fields of Aki in the morning.

When twilight comes, he prepares a bed of grass to lie on. The characters used to write the phrase *tamakagiru* lead one to translate it as something like "faint as jewel's gleam," but orally this could also be heard as "faintly the *tama* (spirit)" comes at twilight. Twilight and dawn are, of course, precisely the time between darkness and light. As such, these liminal periods have been believed to be especially efficacious times to establish communication with the spirit world or the world of the dead. The *chōka* ends with the site defined only by the past of the deceased crown prince. There is nothing about the hunt itself; instead the focus is on the pause in the journey and the sleepless night the young prince spent on the fields of Aki, his father's *katami*. Although Cranston asserts that the action has stopped, in fact the ritual action continues.

In early Japan, journeying into the mountains was, as we have already seen, sometimes part of a ritual of inviting the spirit of a dead person to return (*tamagoi*), as in MYS 2: 85, the poem of longing for the deceased Emperor Nintoku attributed to Iwanohime. The fact that the fields of Aki are Kusakabe's *katami* strongly suggests that this excursion was associated with such a ritual purpose. Furthermore, if the journey had been only a sentimental one, it would not have required the *chōka* form. The *chōka* ends with *kusamakura/ tabiyadori sesu/ inishie omoite*, three elements—grass for pillow, stopping overnight on a journey, and thinking of the past—that constitute a single complex found elsewhere in the Japanese religio-aesthetic tradition.

The first envoy, verse 46, informs us that the traveler stopping on the plain of Aki lies down, but thinking of the past he cannot sleep. The next verse refers to the "rough" or "wild fields" (*arano*) but also attaches the honorific prefix *ma-* to "grass" (*kusa*), no doubt because the site is Kusakabe's *katami*. It is his presence, albeit in noncorporal form, that transforms this place into a sacred site, or as Shirakawa Shizuka has called it, "a foreign enchanted land where spirits of the dead reside."[55] This implicit rhetorical claim is at one with those used whenever a sovereign moves the capital, builds a new palace, or goes on an imperial excursion. The geographical site in and of itself would not draw the young prince and his entourage; it is only its ritual association with the deceased crown prince that does so.

Verse 48, the penultimate envoy, carries the time from evening to the crack of dawn as the first streaks of sunlight break on the eastern horizon and the moon sinks in the west. Cranston has written of this and the following verse:

We are here in the realm of time and symbol as well as of place. The travelers have spent the night in the open, and now the first flicker of dawn comes. The full moon goes down in the west, and there is an ineffable moment when silence and light reign over both horizons. The sinking moon is too obviously a symbol of death to reject—and yet Kusakabe was called Hinamishi—Peer of the Sun. Hitomaro the ironist is evident again. . . . In a way, 49 is the reading or commentary for the symbolism of 48. Verse 48 establishes the circularity of time—the movement of moon and sun, and we know that both moon and sun somehow stand for the fallen prince. That prince is at last named in the first line of 49. *Fi-namisi*, "sun-peer," following *tuki Katabukinu*, "the moon has sunken." Verse 48 has brought the dawning hour when the prince once set out on the hunt, and his hunting is now evoked in all its royal dignity. So much we can see in the first four lines of 49. But in the last line we are specifically told that "the hour comes to meet us" (*toki Fa kimukaFu*). I think the circularity of this expression is significant. The rising sun comes over the horizon, a new day begins. It is the day which in the past would have seen Hinamishi off on the hunt. But now only the hour comes. The prince will never come again. At best his son ("sun") may stand in his place. The dead prince and his horses vanish into the dreams of the night as day breaks over the fields.[56]

Cranston comes close to understanding the deep ritual meaning of this poem, but he backs away from it and gives us a "modern" reading instead. Recently, a revisionist reading, offered by scholars such as Mori Asao, Shirakawa Shizuka, Nagafuji Yasushi, and Kikuchi Takeo,[57] suggests that this is at base a ritual or magico-religious verse. According to Cranston, the passage of time is the main theme of this sequence: time has passed since Kusakabe's death, and although he may be remembered, "now only the hour comes. The prince will never come again." He argues that although Hitomaro may suggest rhetorically that time is circular, death is final and belies this claim. Cranston's reading, however, is at once too modern and Western, ignoring the early Japanese understanding of death. If we recall that a period of mourning of over two years was held for Temmu, and we posit the same length of time for Kusakabe, then Prince Karu's journey to the Aki plain would have taken place at approximately the same interval.

Mori Asao has provided an invaluable clue to interpreting the sequence by asserting that "the basic reason for Hitomaro's poem centering on Karunomiko's appearance at this mysterious time is deeply related to the ritual temporal structure of the *daijō-sai* as enthronement ceremony." Moreover, "The core of the *daijō-sai* ritual takes place during the hour of the hare (5–7 A.M.)."[58] This is precisely the time period found in verse 48. Mori argues that the mountain plain of Aki was the site of an accession ritual, probably transferring the mantle of crown prince or heir apparent to Prince Karu. The scene is in the mountains in an open field in winter, a hunting ground that is the late Crown Prince Kusakabe's *katami*. In some ways the description of the site of the young prince's all-night vigil recalls the role of *shiki* or open-air ceremonial grounds in ancient Japan. According to Ellwood: "In the earliest period there were no shrine buildings. Probably the clan *kami* was worshipped in a *shiki* or field spread with white stones set outside the community. It would be across a stream, and the crossing would be an act of purification. It would probably be on high ground, even far up a mountain. . . . The *shiki* would be marked off by the emblems of a sacred place, evergreen branches (*sakaki*) or stripes of white cloth."[59]

This description does not seem far from the actions and scene of the *chōka*, which record the ritual procession to the mountain fields of Aki and the clearing and smoothing of the ground. The *hatasusuki* (*hata* = "banner," *susuki* = "pampas grass") recalls the banners surrounding certain sacred sites. Ellwood notes that in the *daijō-sai*, the imperial successor must remain awake all night, with the crucial ritual event occurring at the crack of dawn when the emperor-to-be communes with his ancestral spirits and is filled with the imperial *tama*. Not only that, the most auspicious time for such a ritual of transition was the winter solstice, a liminal point of transition in the solar year. When MYS 1: 46–49, the four envoys, are read as a sequence rather than as separate lyrical expressions, they sketch a similar scenario.

Verse 46 portrays the young prince lying awake, recalling the past. The phrase *inishie omou ni*, "recalling the past," should also be understood as a ritual invocation calling back the *tama* of the deceased Crown Prince Kusakabe. Verse 47 picks up this theme, noting that the site is the deceased's *katami*, the place where his specter is most easily contacted. Verse 48 takes us to the crack of dawn. Long recognized as one of Hitomaro's finest verses, these lines are more than a description of the natural scene. Here we are not in "the realm of symbol," as Cranston would have it, but of ritual time and space. In ritual, profane time can be overcome, as the distinctions of past and present meld together and disappear in an emotive movement of the participants' minds and hearts.

The introduction of the sun and the moon at this point in the sequence is crucial to our understanding of the ritual meaning of what happened on the fields of Aki almost thirteen centuries ago. "The sinking moon is too obviously a symbol of death to reject—and yet Kusakabe was called Hinamishi—Peer of the Sun. Hitomaro the ironist is evident again," Cranston writes. But Hitomaro is not the ironist here; he is a ritual specialist of the sacred operating out of the central worldview of early Japan and more especially of the imperial religio-political ideology. Kusakabe is at once the sunken moon and the rising sun precisely because of the belief in the existence of only one imperial *tama* that is ritually transferred from one generation of rulers to the next, from the time of Amaterasu down to the present. The rhetorical identity of sun and moon here is in that sense little different from the conceptual understanding informing the English expression "The king is dead! Long live the king!"

In Hitomaro's *banka* at the time of the temporary enshrinement of Kusakabe or Hinamishi, MYS 2: 167, we find the crown prince explicitly identified with the full moon:

wago ōkimi	If our Lord,
miko no mikoto no	the Crown Prince,
ame no shita	had lived to follow him [i.e., Temmu]
shirashimeshiseba	and rule the realm under heaven,
harubana no	how like the spring blossoms,
tōtokaramu to	he would have been noble,
mochizuki no	how like the full moon,
tatawashikemu to	he would have waxed great.

Moreover, in verse 169, an envoy to the *chōka* from which this passage was taken, Hitomaro had already prepared the way or set the scene for the climactic verses in the *Aki no no* sequence:

akanesasu	The crimson-shining sun
hi wa teraseredo	still shines,
nubatama no	but that the moon is hidden
yo wataru tsuki no	in the pitch-black night it crosses—
kakaraku oshi mo	alas!

In verse 49 the full moon is seen to rest on the western horizon while the sun is about to appear in the east. In contradistinction to Cranston's comment on this verse that "now only the hour comes. The [deceased] prince will never come back," the verse clearly suggests that it was precisely the return of the deceased crown prince's spirit that was awaited in great expectation by the party accompanying Prince Karu. Hitomaro is not indulging in some flight of poetic imagination, momentarily confusing the young Prince Karu with Kusakabe. Here the past is ritually recovered and experienced in the present in the accession ritual in which Karu becomes the crown prince. The renewal of nature and society is accomplished through the ritually realized identity of Kusakabe/Karu in the imperial lineage, as the succession is publicly performed and affirmed. What we have here is not a lament on the passage of time and the irreversibility of death, but just the opposite—a ritual for renewal, for calling back the dead crown prince, who returns and participates in the accession ritual of his son. The poetic sequence cannot be understood in modern symbolic terms. Just as MYS 2: 159–161, treated above, must be understood to say that the deceased Emperor Temmu does return to gaze on the colored leaves of autumn, we must understand this sequence in terms of the religio-political worldview that characterized the time of its genesis and performance.

One can almost hear a collective sigh of relief between the lines of this sequence as Prince Karu is to be confirmed ritually as heir apparent. The final verse brilliantly maintains the sense of high drama and tension that characterized the moment by using the present tense of the verb—*kimukau*. Cranston captured this drama in his commentary by noting that "we are specifically told that 'the hour comes to meet us,'" but in his formal translation he shifts without any warrant to the present perfect. Hitomaro's use of the present tense, though, skillfully captures the agitated expectation both of Karu no miko's imminent transformation into the crown prince and, further in the future, of his accession to the throne as emperor, continuing the line of Temmu—an event that was to be realized five years later in 697.

The verses in MYS 1: 45–49, then, are examples of poetry used in a religio-political ceremony. As in the other ritual poems we have seen, the rhetorical linkage established between the death of a member of the imperial family and the natural seasonal cycle ("gone like the yellow leaves," "like the blossoms of spring"), as well as regular changes in celestial phenomena (the waxing and waning moon, the moon or stars hidden by clouds), functions to translate an individual death into replication in a higher level of mythistory. The *tama*-based belief system allowed the early Japanese to deny the finality of death by asserting that the imperial *tama* continued to live as it is passed into the next sovereign or heir apparent. Death inevitably claimed everyone, occasioning great grief and often turmoil in the court; but public *banka* served as important vehicles for declaiming the message that "the crimson-shining sun still shines." The MYS 1: 45–49 sequence appears in the *Man'yōshū* as it does because it is an important record of the ritual legitimation of the succession. As such, it was part of the larger historiographic project of the eighth-century Court, even as it is great poetry.

Much of the public performative poetry of the court poets employs rhetorical devices to identify the imperial family with the mythic origins of the nation. The acts of the imperial family—setting out on a procession, viewing the land, building a palace, or even dying—are presented as the "great deeds" of *kami*, consonant with those recounted in the imperial myths. The mythic paradigms figure especially in *banka* and other ritual verses for individuals close to the succession. The mythistory these public performative pieces helped to create and promulgate was soon to be committed to writing. In textual form this factional mythistory assumed a permanence unknown in its oral stage and was to become a national mythology. Even in this fixed form, however, this mythistory has remained a cultural resource on which the Japanese have drawn over the centuries in numerous ways and for various purposes, national and factional, down to the present. In studies of the *Kojiki*, the *Nihonshoki*, and the *Man'yōshū*, one must be sensitive to the conditions of their production and to their impact and reception over time. The meaning of these texts remained and remains open to negotiation within the received possibilities of significance.

Imagining History

By now the accuracy of Huntington and Metcalf's statement, cited at the beginning of this study, that "events surrounding the death of the king reveal most strikingly the nature of [the] polity and the structure of its political competition" should be apparent. The death of the sovereign or crown prince in early Japan threw the socio-political hierarchy of the court into immediate disarray, but it also generated the politics of death—the process of reestablishing a new order. This was a dynamic dialectical process involving both inherited symbolic dimensions and contingent his-torical conditions. As such, it is an instance of a more general cultural historical process Sahlins has called the "symbolic dialogue of history—dialogue between the received categories and the perceived contexts."[1]

Our exploration of the liminal period of temporary enshrinement and the events reported to have occurred then has disclosed a number of heretofore unrecognized aspects of early Japanese culture: (1) the nature of the early Japanese polity and the forms of competition for power, position, and prestige found in the court, especially during this time; (2) the multiple social and ritual functions of oral performative verse in the court; and (3) the historiographic project of the eighth-century Court as evinced in the extant texts. All these aspects bear review, for they not only are relevant for our understanding of early Japan but perhaps also possess broader meth-odological implications for a number of fields.

This is the first study in either Japanese or English to have looked systematically at the politics of death in early Japan. Although Japanese historians and *Man'yōshū* scholars have begun to explore the double burial practices, they have not linked these ritual practices to the larger issues of narrative (oral and written) strategy, the symbolic imagination, and cultural ideology. To have any legitimacy, the new socio-political order following the death of a sovereign had to be imagined (symbolically and ritually) before it could be realized. To put this another way, the cultural order that was threatened by the sovereign's death had to be restored by organizing the newly emergent situation in terms of a privileged past. The politics of death entailed the transactional creation of meaning and order (narrative and socio-political) in the wake of death. Whereas death is "a given" of the human condition (even for divine rulers), the meaning of any individual death is not; this meaning is socially negotiated. The symbolic universe of early Japan ("the received categories") provided the site for this special form of socio-political competition, as well as the terms in which the competition was played out in history; but the outcome was not predetermined. In their application (or performance), cultural structures of meaning (symbolic, mythic, ritual, legal, aesthetic) are continually subjected to practical re-valuations. They are not static or timeless but are continually mediating and being mediated by other symbolic structures. As we have seen, the same received categories can be used to quite different effect through a skillful manipulation of their perception and context. This point is something that has largely escaped the interest of both Western and Japanese scholars. Most studies continue to present a static picture of early Japan and to suggest that rituals serve the essentially conservative function of maintaining the existing power structure and order or preserving a timeless Japanese religiosity. No one, to my knowledge, has studied the ways in which these early rituals were used to challenge and offer alternatives to the status quo. Although ritual was (and is) a cultural resource employed in the creation and maintenance of symbolic worlds of meaning, it was (and is) also used as a political tool in the competition for and the control of the seat of power.[2]

The extant texts do not reveal a "primitive" or "prelogical mentality" in early Japan but rather an operative court rationality that, if Elias is correct, is similar to that found in all court societies. This rationality was one of the central principles that organized the perceptions of all members of the society, and it pervaded the public rhetoric and the thoroughgoing ritual nature of the daily life of the court. Few of the narratives found in the *Kojiki* or the *Nihonshoki*, or many of the poems in the *Man'yōshū*, can be understood without recognizing its influence. All future studies of these texts must consider the significance not only of the modes of textual production in early Japan but also of the textual practices of the court itself.

In this study we have noted the ways in which the early Japanese "imagined" the biological "fact" of death and in doing so (re)created their world of meaning. It is important to retain the plural here—"the *ways* in which the early Japanese imagined death"—because any given death could be understood variously by different individuals and groups, both at the time and retrospectively. Although the *tama*-based belief system was generally shared, it could be used to generate a variety of interpretations of the context in which a specific death occurred and its significance. Historical agents were not, as we have seen, constrained to employ conventional cultural concepts or interpretive frames in a single prescribed way, or to play prescribed or tightly "scripted" roles in an intractable social drama. On the other hand, in a strategic ploy to realize their own or factional goals in the socio-political competition in the court following the death of the sovereign, individuals could consciously assume recognizable paradigmatic roles and perform symbolically "loaded" acts. Yet the acknowledgment of a symbolic logic and reason informing these actions is not to say (as some symbolic anthropologists or "Levi-Straussian" structuralists do) that this internal symbolic logic in some way inexorably "drives" human actions and expressions in history.

Although I have sought to meet Bourdieu's challenge (quoted in the Introduction) in attempting to understand the double burial ritual in its practical context, the results of my inquiry have indicated that "the conditions in which [the ritual] functions, and the means it uses to attain them," to quote Bourdieu, are not firmly established but are themselves continually in the process of being (re)defined. Consequently, the significance and functions that historical agents confer on a determinate practice are themselves fluid. Here I find myself in closer agreement with Sahlins's position to the effect that when received cultural categories and narrative interpretive frames are put into play in history, they are also put at risk by being subject to re-valuation and manipulation. This leads Sahlins to speak in terms of structure, event, and finally, between these two, the "structure of conjuncture." ("An event is not simply a phenomenal happening . . . apart from any given symbolic scheme. An event becomes such as it is interpreted. Only as it is appropriated in and through the cultural scheme does it acquire an historical *significance*.") By the "structure of conjuncture" he means, "the practical realization of the cultural categories in a specific historical context, as expressed in the interested action of the historic agents, including the microsociology of their interaction."[3] Although Sahlins's terminology has not been adopted in my work, his general argument has helped to inform it. Any inquiry into the "microsociology" of the interaction of historical agents in early Japan must include the operation of the court rationality and the available symbolic schemes and paradigmatic narratives. But the inquiry must also include an awareness that in any specific instance these factors were mediated by other cultural discourses—genealogical, aesthetic, legal—that helped to create the context in which specific human interactions were imagined, realized, and then interpreted and transformed into events.

For instance, we have seen that because of his position in the socio-political constellation of the court and the genealogical relations relevant to the succession, a Prince Ōtsu might find himself suddenly vulnerable in the wake of the sovereign's death. In such a case, the identities of others occupying symbolically powerful positions (Jitō as empress-consort, Kusakabe as crown prince, Princess Ōku as the Ise Priestess, the Great Ministers, and so on) and their specific relationships to Ōtsu and to each other (aunt/stepmother, only son, half-brother, sister, father-in-law) become immediately relevant. Furthermore, they are critical in the determination of an individual's strategy in the sequential unfolding of the politics of death in history. In addition to eliciting all this information, the student of the extant texts needs to determine the interrelationships of the religio-political positions these individuals occupied within the overall symbolic universe and the resultant balance of power.

When all these elements are factored together in the case of Prince Ōtsu, it appears that the Ise Shrine, where Ōtsu's sister was the chief priestess, may have been one of the few, if not the only, symbolically strategic and "evenementially hot" loci in the determination of the succession that was available to Ōtsu. If this was so, then both his secret journey there and Jitō's interpretation of its political intention were dictated by the specific historical conjunction of unique circumstances and a limited number of available symbolic possibilities.

Recurring throughout this work has been the reminder that the site of the events under study—the double burial practices, assassinations, incidents of "incest"—is finally to be located in the scene of writing itself. Thus, while drawing on Huntington and Metcalf in selecting the events following the death of sovereigns as a focus of study, I have not assumed that the "events" recounted in the texts are objective accounts and, thus, unproblematic. Rather, I have argued that the recounted events are themselves already interpretations or constructs realized through some form of retrospective narrative ordering.[4]

This retrospective ordering was not limited to casting activities in the court in terms of paradigmatic narratives or myths, though this was common enough (e.g., the patterned accounts relating the death of a sovereign or would-be ruler with the niiname-sai), for the narratives were themselves subject to manipulation and change. If and when an unexpected order or social formation came into being in the court that did not "match" readily available paradigms of a normal succession, then this "reality" might be retrospectively projected onto an available myth and (re)imagined or inscribed therein. (For example, when the Crown Prince Kusakabe suddenly died shortly before he was to be ritually installed as the emperor, the narrative told of Amaterasu's son suddenly turning back midway in his descent from the High Heavens to take up his rule on earth and the substitution of his son, Ninigi.) One of the significant findings of this study has been that myth, too, was a cultural resource that could be used for a variety of purposes, including conflicting ones. Myth was not static but subject to alteration in order better to reflect existing situations. For this reason it may often be better to speak of "mythistory" rather than "myth," insofar as in popular usage the latter term frequently carries the connotation of an unchanging or timeless paradigmatic narrative.

To turn to some of the significant disclosures in this study of the forms of political competition in early Japan, we have found that the practice of double burial and its associated tama-based symbolic and ritual complexes involved two distinct loci of female power in determining the succession—the interior of the mogari no miya and the Ise Shrine. Whereas the significance of the Ise Shrine in the imperial ideology and as the locus of the daijō-sai has been recognized, the role of the Ise Priestess as a fulcrum of religio-political power during the period of temporary enshrinement of a sovereign has not been widely acknowledged. This study has demonstrated that the Ise Shrine and more especially the person of the Ise Priestess played strategic roles in the politics of death at this time. The early Japanese belief that death was the result of the *tama*'s having left the corporal body, coupled with the ideological concept of a single imperial *tama* that had been ritually transferred from one sovereign to the next in an unbroken line since the time of Amaterasu, contributed to the importance of these two loci. Underlying this importance is the fact that women performed rituals (*tama-furi*, *tama-shizume*, *tama-musubi*) there that were specifically designed to regain control of the imperial *tama*.

A number of myths—Izanagi–Izanami, Amaterasu–Susano-o, and Yamato-takeru—as well as narratives in the *Kojiki* and entries in the *Nihonshoki* have been shown to be related to the *tama*-based symbolic and ritual complex. Prince Ōtsu's secret journey to his sister, the Ise Priestess, was an act based on his and his audience's (i.e., the court's) shared understanding of the operative symbolic universe. It was, then, a culturally meaningful act. Similarly, viewed within the field of the operative religio-political symbol system, Prince Anahobe's attempt to break into the *mogari no miya* in order to possess the widowed empress now can be recognized as a symbolically meaningful and rational act performed in an effort to appropriate the imperial charisma unto (or into) himself. These two cases represent different strategies in the politics of death, both involving (explicitly or implicitly) a mixture of death, irregular sexual relations, and power. For a number of reasons, the symbolic complex of "incest" and its relation to the politics of death evinced in our texts has been virtually ignored in the Japanese scholarship. But this is a topic that will require more study. The process by which female loci of religio-political power were abolished also needs to be explored. I have suggested that the adoption of the practice of cremation may have been intended as a way of curtailing female power by abolishing the performative locus of the crucial female ritual role in the *mogari no miya* complex. Even if this intention was not present, the real results were the same.

This study is also the first to have taken seriously the oral nature of much of the public life of the court in early Japan. Because of this, an effort has been made to reconstruct the oral performative contexts of selected *uta* in order to restore their "voice" and their social and ritual functions. This work is only a preliminary and in many ways exploratory essay, but perhaps it has demonstrated the need to reconsider many of the *uta* in the *Man'yōshū* and the *Kiki kayōshū* in oral performative terms. This would itself mark a significant shift in the field of Japanese literary studies. The use of examples of Greek oral laments and fieldwork studies of this tradition in rural Greece suggests that careful comparative studies can disclose heretofore unrecognized dimensions of the extant texts. An important point that emerged was that in the performance of oral laments, the deceased is often given a voice, so that the same mourner carries on a dialogue, as it were, with the dead individual by performing both roles. The recognition of the voice of the dead led to the retranslation of a number of *banka*; it also implies the need to rethink many examples of this genre and to listen for other voices in the texts.

Introducing the oral performative context of *chōka*, including the boastful complaint of Prince Ikusa (MYS 2: 5–6), demonstrated the ways in which such public rhetorical forms participated in the social process of marking out social distance and intimacy in the hierarchical court society. At the same time, it became clear that a simple content analysis of the *uta* was insufficient; one needed to draw on audience-oriented criticism as well. Although only a very limited number of *uta* could be treated here, the results perhaps illustrate the advantage of adopting these approaches while factoring in the court rationality, which structured both the generation of the various forms of public rhetoric and their reception. To say this, however, is not to imply that the courtiers were hopelessly trapped in "the prisonhouse of language" unique to their society. I have argued that public expressions of pure personal emotion were largely curtailed and all expressions were highly stylized. Yet we also found that the poetry of early Japan *is* accessible to the modern reader, whether in the treatment of Prince Ikusa's boastful complaint in the context of a hierarchically organized social structure, or in the study of *banka* that enabled us to "hear" the human voice in the grieving process embedded in these texts.

At the same time, this inquiry has also brought to the fore a number of important problems related to the shift in early Japan from an oral to a literate culture. Among other things, the usefulness of the concept of authorship in relation to much of the early poetry has been called into question, as have inflated claims of individual originality. A critical subject for further study would be the ideological and political dimensions of the uses of literacy and the acts of writing, editing, and anthologization. Future studies of the texts from early Japan might, for instance, consider the question of why certain poems and narratives have been included as they are and where they are while others have apparently been repressed or broken up and scattered (e.g., "The Ōtsu no miko uta monogatari").

Any study of early Japan must use the extant texts as the basic sources, but we need to study not only the texts themselves as the New Critics would, but also— and more important—the cultural and historical practice of the texts. The *Kojiki*, *Nihonshoki*, and *Man'yōshū* represent a rich site for the study of the ways in which the eighth-century court appropriated, adopted, adapted, and disseminated the symbolic possibilities available to it in its retrospective ordering of the past. At the same time, these texts are the site of "negative graphic space"—of textual repressions, erasures, elisions, and forms of camouflage that beg for further study. Although the topic could be treated in only a limited way in the last chapter, these texts invite serious investigation of the manner in which textual production, both oral and written, mediated and was mediated by other forms of discourse. To recall only one example, we found that the types of *banka* depended upon the relational position of the deceased in terms of the succession. If the deceased had occupied a strategic position (e.g., crown prince or high-ranking imperial prince) and the *banka* was offered for an imperial patron, then the lament would rehearse the mythistory of the imperial line and the great deeds of the deceased. If, however, the *banka* were offered by low-ranking courtiers (e.g., the twenty-three *banka* by *toneri* on the death of Kusakabe), then the laments stressed their sense of disorientation and abandonment in the wake of the death. On the other hand, if the deceased had not had a position in the succession, then even when commissoned by and offered for a member of the imperial family, the *banka* would stress the sense of longing and abandonment felt by the surviving spouse. Then, too, the *banka* preserved in the *Man'yōshū* tend to be for individuals in the Temmu–Jitō line of descent, indicating that the politics of anthologization also requires study.

The present interdisciplinary work has been necessarily preliminary in nature and in the conclusions it draws. Yet it was undertaken in the belief that interdisciplinary studies are essential in the effort to explore the cultural histories of the relations between and among different orders of knowledge—their methods and the practical consequences of their application, their underlying determinations and necessity at given times and in given situations, the modes of their mediating and mediation by others, their re-valuations in historical praxis, and so on. Our subject has been and is the human imagination in history and the ramifications of the forms of its sociocultural realization. In his study of the theater state of nineteenth-century Bali, Geertz has remarked that "The real is as imagined as the imaginary."[5] One might add that the present is as imagined as the past. And both have a shared history that one enters into through an act of creative imagination. The modern historical consciousness is not, of course, the same as that which yielded the mythistory of early Japan, yet the exercise of the creative imagination, albeit in different ways and to different ends, is shared with Hitomaro in the seventh century. A master at stimulating anamnesis through the rhetorical use of mythic themes, he could himself enter it at specific emplotted sites through the cry of a plover. This cry still echoes for the modern historian and the reader through their encounter with texts.

Ōmi no umi	The Ōmi sea—
yūnami chidori	when plover skimming
na ga nakeba	the evening waves cry,
kokoro mo shino ni	my heart like dwarf bamboo
inishie omōyu	bends back in thought to the past.

(MYS 3: 266)

Glossary of Japanese Terms

Ame no uke-hashi	the Heavenly Floating Bridge connecting heaven and earth
aratama	the "rough spirit" of a *kami* or deceased individual
asa matsurigoto	the daily morning ritual at imperial palaces where courtiers and others lined up to receive their day's orders
asobibe	a guild of ritual functionaries in the court whose primary duties included the death rituals
banka	literally "coffin-pullings songs," laments for the dead
chinkon-sai	a ritual to pacify the spirit (*tama*) of the dead
chōka	a long poem. Most early examples were public oral pieces.
daijō-sai	the imperial accession ritual
fudoki	provincial records, compiled on the orders of the Empress Gemmei in 713, dealing with geography, local and regional customs, and myths and legends. Only five are extant and only one, the *Izumo fudoki*, survives in full.
hanka	a short envoy, usually in the thirty-one syllabic form of *tanka*, added to a *chōka* ("long poem")
hi (ho)	fire
imo	a term of endearment used for one's wife or lover, also younger sister
inaki	a granary
kami	a Japanese divinity (divinities)
kami no yo	"The Age of the Gods," the mythological period prior to the time of the first human emperor, Jimmu
katami	a place, object, or person that serves as a repository for the spirit of a deceased individual
kataribe	ritual reciters of myths, clan genealogies, and so on
Kiki kayō	the modern term for the verses preserved in the *Kojiki* and the *Nihonshoki*

273

kofun	burial mounds in the form of artificial hills, often in the shape of keyholes
kotoage	to offer sacred words, to take an oath
kotodama	the spirit power of words, the magical efficacy of sacred words
kotodama shinko	the belief in *kotodama*
Kujiki	a historical chronicle in ten books covering the mythological "Age of the Gods" to the reign of the Empress Suiko (r. 592–628). The extant manuscript of this text dates from the Heian period and its date of composition remains in dispute. It may be the history reportedly ordered by Soga no Umako in 620 that was partly destroyed in a fire set during a succession dispute.
kunimi	ritual land viewing
maga-tama	crescent-shaped stones or beads believed to have sacred powers; one of the three imperial regalia
maki	"scroll," a book of the *Man'yōshū*
mi	an honorific prefix added to nouns associated with the imperial family (e.g., *miya*, imperial "house" or "palace"; *mitama* = imperial "spirit")
miko	a female shaman
miru	to see
mogari no miya (*araki no miya*, *mogari-ya*)	the palace of temporary interment or temporary enshrinement
mono	spirit or thing
muro	a windowless wooden structure
musubi-matsu	the ritual of tying the branches of a pine tree (*matsu*) together to ensure the safe return of an individual or group
musubu (musubi)	to tie or bind something or someone
nakime	ritual female mourners
nigitama	the gentle or benevolent spirit of a *kami* or deceased person
niiname-sai	the First Fruits or Harvest Festival, usually held in the eleventh lunar month
norito	Shinto ritual prayers and invocations
ochi-mizu	a purification rite performed in the Yoshino mountains and believed to ensure longevity

ōfusuma (matoko ōfusuma)	"coverlet spread on the true couch," a ritually woven sacred silk coverlet or shawl used in the *daijō-sai*, the imperial accession ritual. In the myth of the descent of Ninigi, the grandson of Amaterasu, Ninigi is wrapped in the *ōfusuma* as an act legitimating his sovereignty.
sakahagi	the reverse, and thus ritually inauspicious, skinning of the pony in the Amaterasu–Susano-o mythic sequence
shinobikoto	a eulogy
Shoki-Man'yōshū	the first two books of the *Man'yōshū*, in which the poems are arranged chronologically according to imperial reign. These books are generally considered to have been compiled earlier than the rest.
sokui-rei	a simple civil accession ceremony
sōmon (sōmonka)	dialogue poems. One of three categories of poems, along with *banka* and *zōka*, recognized by the compilers of the *Man'yōshū*. One verse is a response to another.
sumeramikoto	the sovereign. The modern reading is *tennō*.
tama	spirit or soul
tama-furi	rituals performed to call back the spirit of the deceased, including the action of waving one's kimono sleeves
tamakazura	a wreath that served as a *katami*, a temporary repository for the spirit of the deceased
tama-musubi	ritual actions intended to "bind" the spirit of the deceased to a specific site or object
tama-shizume	ritual actions to pacify the spirit of the deceased
tanka	a poem of thirty-one syllables, usually in 5-7-5-7-7 form
toneri	low-ranking servingmen, guards, and courtiers
uji	clan(s)
ukei	a magical oath
uranai	divination
uta	song or verse
utaibito	oral performers of *uta*
uta monogatari	prose and verse narratives (e.g., the Yamato-takeru *uta monogatari*)

wazauta	popular songs frequently used for purposes of satirical political comment
yatsura-mai	a special dance involving sixty-four persons performed as part of the accession ritual complex
yokikoto (yogoto)	special forms of address and praise to be used in association with the imperial family
Yomi no kuni (ne no kuni)	the underworld and land of the dead
zōka	miscellaneous verses. One of three categories of poetry recognized in the *Man'yōshū*

Notes

Mythistory, Ritual, and Poetry in Early Japan

1. Peter L. Berger and Thomas Luckmann, *The Social Construction of Reality: A Treatise in the Sociology of Knowledge* (Garden City, N.Y.: Doubleday and Co., 1966), p. 103.

2. Richard Huntington and Peter Metcalf, *Celebrations of Death: The Anthropology of Mortuary Ritual* (Cambridge and New York: Cambridge University Press, 1979), p. 2.

3. But see now François Mace, *La mort et les Funerailles dans la Japon Ancien*, Bibliotheque Japonaise (Paris Publications Orientalistes de France, 1986). The only English-language piece I know of is Mogami Takayoshi, "The Double-Grave System" in *Studies in Japanese Folklore*, ed. Richard M. Dorson (New York: Arno Press, 1980), pp. 167–180, but this deals with contemporary practices in a few isolated areas of the country. J. Edward Kidder mentions "the Shrine of temporary interment" in passing, but he does not indicate its significance; see *Japan Before Buddhism*, rev. ed. (New York: Frederick A. Praeger, 1966), p. 152. For popular cultural surveys, see George B. Sansom, *Japan: A Short Cultural History* (Stanford: Stanford University Press, 1931), pp. 12–14; and Paul Varley, *Japanese Culture*, 3d ed. (Honolulu: University of Hawaii Press, 1984), pp. 12–15. On *kofun*, see Akamatsu Ken, "The Significance of the Formation and Distribution of *Kofun*," *Acta Asiatica* 31 (1977): 24–50.

4. For an important study of the politics of regulating funerary rituals in another time and place, see Pascal Hintermeyer, *Politiques de la mort: tirées du Concours de l'Institut, Germinal au VIII Vendemiaire au IX* (Paris: Payôt, 1981).

5. NKBT 68: 294–295; W. G. Aston, trans., *Nihongi: Chronicles of Japan from the Earliest Times to A.D. 697*, 2 vols. in one (Rutland, Vt., and Tokyo: Charles E. Tuttle Co., 1972), 2: 219. The complete entry concerning the regulation of funeral practices may be found in NKBT 68: 292–295 and Aston, ibid., pp. 217–220.

6. Pierre Bourdieu, *Outline of a Theory of Practice*, Cambridge Studies in Social Anthropology, no. 16 (Cambridge: Cambridge University Press, 1977), p. 114.

7. My major criticism of Ian Hideo Levy's work on the *Man'yōshū* is that he uncritically assumes that myth and ritual function exclusively as social cohesive forces. He is not alone in this, of course, and the situation is due no doubt to the failure of historians of religions to present the dynamic nature of ritual in culture. In an otherwise exemplary study, R. Howard Bloch, a scholar of medieval French literature, makes the same unfortunate as-

sumption about religious ritual. See his *Etymologies and Genealogies: A Literary Anthropology of the French Middle Ages* (Chicago: University of Chicago Press, 1983), p. 15.

8. My colleague, Marilyn Waldman, has deeply influenced my thinking in this and related areas. See her important article, "Tradition as a Modality of Change: Islamic Examples," *History of Religions* 25 (May 1986): 318–340.

9. For a translation and study of one *fudoki*, see Michiko Yamaguchi Aoki, *Izumo Fudoki* (Tokyo: Sophia University, 1971).

10. The *Norito* are available in NKBT 1; an English translation is Donald L. Philippi, *Norito: A New Translation of the Ancient Japanese Ritual Prayers* (Tokyo: Sophia University, 1973).

11. For a partial translation, see Felicia G. Bock, *Engi-shiki: Procedures of the Engi Era* (Tokyo: Sophia University, 1972).

12. Donald L. Philippi, trans., *Kojiki* (Tokyo: University of Tokyo Press, 1968), p. 41; NKBT 1: 44–47.

13. On this subject in English, see Konishi Jin'ichi, *A History of Japanese Literature*, vol. 1: *The Archaic and Ancient Ages*, trans. Aileen Gatten and Nicholas Teele (Princeton: Princeton University Press, 1984), pp. 160–163, 365–373, passim.

14. For a study of Ōtomo Yakamochi, see Paula Doe, *A Warbler's Song in the Dusk: The Life and Work of Ōtomo Yakamochi (718–785)* (Berkeley: University of California Press, 1982).

15. The latter translation is that found, for instance, in Earl Miner, Hiroko Odagiri, and Robert E. Morrell, *The Princeton Companion to Classical Japanese Literature* (Princeton: Princeton University Press, 1985), p. 299.

16. For an introduction to this topic in English, see R. E. Teele, "Speculations on the Critical Principles Underlying the Editing of the *Man'yōshū*," *Tamkang Review* 7 (October 1976): 1–16.

17. Ian Hideo Levy, *Hitomaro and the Birth of Japanese Lyricism* (Princeton: Princeton University Press, 1984), p.7. Levy suggests that with Hitomaro, poetry "unmistakably comes to serve the deliberate iconic establishment of imperial divinity, a task which would have been redundant in archaic ceremony" (p. 9).

18. H. Byron Earhart, *Japanese Religion: Unity and Diversity*, 3d ed. (Belmont, Calif.: Wadsworth Publishing Co., 1982), p. 31. This text remains the most balanced introduction in English to the subject.

19. Robert Weimann, *Structure and Society in Literary History*, expanded ed. (Baltimore: Johns Hopkins University Press, 1984), p. 48.

20. Hayden White, *Metahistory: The Historical Imagination in Nineteenth-Century Europe* (Baltimore: Johns Hopkins University Press, 1973), p. 2.

21. This felicitous phrase is borrowed from Bloch, *Etymologies and Genealogies*, p. 14, where it is used in another cultural context.

22. Yoshinaga Noboru, *Man'yō—bungaku to rekishi no aida* (Osaka: Sōgensha, 1967).

23. Marshall Sahlins, *Islands of History* (Chicago: University of Chicago Press, 1985), p. vii.

CHAPTER ONE
Ritual Poetry in the Court

1. Parry's work may best be appreciated by consulting Albert B. Lord's *The Singer of Tales* (Cambridge, Mass.: Harvard University Press, 1960). A useful introduction to the field of orality is Walter J. Ong, *Orality and Literacy: The Technologizing of the Word* (London and New York: Methuen, 1982), which contains a very helpful bibliography.

2. Cf. Tsuchihashi Yutaka, *Kodai kayō to girei no kenkyū* (Tokyo: Iwanami Shoten, 1965); "Jōdai no saishiki to uta no jutō," *Kokubungaku: kaishaku to kanshō* 29, no. 1 (January 1964): 26–34; "Kunimi uta no Man'yō ni okeru tenkai," *Kokugo kokubun* 27, no. 10 (October 1958): 24–37.

3. Cf. Konishi, *A History of Japanese Literature*, 1: 20–52, 83–99, passim.

4. Cf. M. C. Haguenauer, "La danse rituelle dans la cérémonie du chinkonsai," *Journal Asiatique* (April-June 1930): 300–350; Harmut O. Rotermund, "Quelques aspects de la magie verbale dans les croyances populaires du Japan," in *Mélanges Offerts à M. Charles Haguenauer*, ed. Bernard Frank (Paris: Collège de France, 1980), pp. 425–442; Gary L. Ebersole, "The Buddhist Ritual Use of Linked Poetry in Medieval Japan," *The Eastern Buddhist* n.s., 16, no. 2 (Autumn 1983): 50–71, and "The Religio-Aesthetic Complex in *Manyōshū* Poetry with Special Emphasis on Hitomaro's *Aki no no* Sequence," *History of Religions* 23 (August 1983): 18–36.

5. *Kokinshū: A Collection of Poems Ancient and Modern*, trans. and annotated by Laurel Rasplica Rodd with Mary Catherine Henkenius (Princeton: Princeton University Press, 1984), p. 35.

6. Cf. "Such songs came into being when heaven and earth first appeared. However, legend has it that in the broad heavens they began with Princess Shitateru and on earth with the song of Susano-o no mikoto." Ibid.

7. Itō Haku, "Man'yōjin to kotodama," in *Man'yōshū kōza*, ed. Hisamatsu Senichi, vol. 3: *Gengo to hyōgen* (Tokyo: Yuseidō, 1973), pp. 46–63. Konishi Jin'ichi has recently asserted that "The word [*kotodama*] itself does not appear before the age of the *Man'yōshū*, but the concept definitely existed in the Archaic Age" (*A History of Japanese Literature*, 1: 103).

8. Itō, ibid., pp. 56ff.

9. For an instance of an oral culture that has consciously (and so far successfully) attempted to keep literacy at bay—and done so by incorporating the written word and even tape recorders into their mythology in a negatively valued way—see David M. Guss, "Keeping It Oral: A Yekuana Ethnology," *American Ethnologist* 13 (August 1986): 413–429.

10. Konishi, *A History of Japanese Literature*, 1: 204. See chap. 3, "The Character of the Ancient Age," in this work for Konishi's full argument. He seems unaware of the work of Ong, Jack Goody, and others on orality and literacy.

11. NKBT 6: 188–189. My translation.

12. An editorial note in the manuscript gives the two variants, presented here in brackets. Levy does not translate them. (See note 13.)

13. NKBT 5: 102–103; Ian Hideo Levy, *The Ten Thousand Leaves*, vol. 1 (Princeton: Princeton University Press, 1981), pp. 390–392. A prose note attached to this sequence allows this poem to be precisely dated. It reads: "On the third month, first day, of the fifth year of Tempyō [734], you visited me at my home. I present you this on the third. From Yamanoue Okura, with humility To His Excellency the Ambassador to China" (p. 392).

14. A similar poem from the *Man'yōshū* (13: 3254) also praises the land as a land of *kotodama*:

shikishima no	The Land of Yamato
Yamato no kuni wa	Of girded islands
kotodama no	Is a land succored by
tasukuru kuni zo	The kotodama: then
masakiku ari koso	May our future be happy.

(Trans. Konishi, *A History of Japanese Literature*, 1: 103)

15. NKBT 67: 129. A partial translation may be found in Konishi, *A History of Japanese Literature*, 1: 100. Aston, *Nihongi*, 1: 60, does not take note of the special significance of *kotoage* and simply translates it as "he spake, and said."

16. NKBT 67: 94–95; Aston, *Nihongi*, 1: 26.

17. NKBT 1: 218–219; Philippi, *Kojiki*, p. 246. An editorial note in the *Kojiki* explicitly says that Yamato-takeru was dazed by a hailstorm raised by the mountain *kami* because he had uttered *kotoage*.

18. Konishi, *A History of Japanese Literature*, 1: 101–107, gives other examples.

19. See NKBT 7: 162–167. A translation of MYS 16: 3885–3886 may be found in The Nippon Gakujutsu Shinkōkai translation of *The Manyōshū* (New York: Columbia University Press, 1964), pp. 275–277.

20. See NKBT 68: 497–499; Aston, *Nihongi*, 2: 392.

21. There are a large number of works that deal with *kunimi*. Cf. Tsuchihashi, *Kodai kayō to girei no kenkyū*, pp. 265–378, and his "Kunimi uta no Man'yō ni okeru tenkai," pp. 24–37; Takasaki Masahide, *Man'yōshū sōkō*, vol. 3 of *Takasaki Masahide chosakushū* (Tokyo: Ōfusha, 1971), pp. 514–540; Sakurai Mitsuru, *Man'yōbito no dōkei: minzoku to bungei no ronri* (Tokyo: Ōfusha, 1977), pp. 89–123; Shirakawa Shizuka, *Shoki Man'yō-ron* (Tokyo: Chūō Kōronsha, 1979), pp. 113–178. As is often the case, Origuchi Shinobu was one of the first to deal with this topic. Cf. his explication of MYS 1:2 in *Origuchi Shinobu zenshū*, vol. 9 (Tokyo: Chūō Kōronsha, 1965), pp. 161–192.

22. Levy, *The Ten Thousand Leaves*, p. 38.

23. See Alicia Matsunaga, "The Land of Natural Affirmation: Pre-Buddhist Japan," *Monumenta Nipponica* 21, (August-November 1966): 203–209; and Levy's *Hitomaro*, pp. 25–28. Matsunaga's reading is especially problematic, arguing for a "prelogical mentality" in early Japan and suggesting that the poem demonstrates that the early Japanese had a natural, spontaneous, and unmediated appreciation of nature.

24. Levy, *Hitomaro*, p. 28.

25. Cf. "(An) animistic sensibility . . . lies behind the patterned, ritual evocations of the land in early poetry. *Here are statements of an unchanging and essentially religious truth that exists in the collective mind of the clan*" (Levy, *The Ten Thousand Leaves*, p. 7, emphasis added); and "For the purposes of literary history . . . there are two aspects of ritual that seem essential, its particular qualities of voice and time. The ritual voice is the collective one, rather than the individual, and it sings not of a unique moment in an individual's life but of an eternal, ceremonial moment in the life of the clan. Any moment captured in a ritual poem is one in an infinite series of essentially identical moments, and the speaker or actor in such a poem performs in this moment with the measured, predetermined gestures and speech evolved from its repetition through time down to his own turn on the ritual stage" (Levy, *Hitomaro*, p. 24).

26. This point is made abundantly clear in the work of Berger and Luckmann, Victor Turner, and others. Note, for example, the title of a collection of essays presented at a recent annual meeting of the American Ethnological Society—*Text, Play, and Story: The Construction and Reconstruction of Self and Society*, ed. Edward M. Bruner (Washington, D.C.: The American Ethnological Society, 1985). See especially the introduction by Bruner.

27. Aston, *Nihongi*, 1: 119; NKBT 67: 198–199.

28. Aston, *Nihongi*, 1: 135; NKBT 67: 214–215. Romanization of the place name has been altered from Aston's rendering to conform to that of the NKBT edition. In general, I will silently follow this procedure whenever doing so will not cause undue confusion to the reader consulting only Aston.

29. See NKBT 67: 82–83 and 214–215. The Genesis account of creation includes a similar element of verbal praise: after each day's creation, Yahweh pronounces it good.

30. On the ritual expression of this celebration at the Ise Shrine, see Robert S. Ellwood, "Harvest and Renewal at the Grand Shrine of Ise," *Numen* 15 (November 1968): 165–190.

31. Aston, *Nihongi*, 1: 257; NKBT 67: 365. Translation of the *uta* is from Donald L. Philippi, *This Wine of Peace, This Wine of Laughter* (New York: Mushina Books, Grossman Publishers, 1968), p. 79. The *Kojiki* version of this can be found in Philippi, *Kojiki*, p. 276 and in NKBT 53: 241–243.

32. Aston, *Nihongi*, 1: 346; NKBT 67: 471–473. The translation of the *uta* is from Philippi, *This Wine of Peace*, p. 82.

33. Cf. Tsuchihashi, *Kodai kayō to girei no kenkyū*, pp. 13ff. Yoshida Yoshitaka had earlier argued that the land-viewing ritual originated in the court. See his "Omoi kuni uta no tenkai," *Bungaku* 16, no. 7 (July 1948): 1–8.

34. NKBT 4: 188–189; Levy, *The Ten Thousand Leaves*, pp. 200–201.

35. For a translation of this verse see Levy, *The Ten Thousand Leaves*, pp. 181–182.

36. On the Ritsuryō system, see Alan L. Miller, "Ritsuryō Japan: The State as Liturgical Community," *History of Religions* 11 (August 1971): 98–124; Joseph M. Kitagawa, "The Japanese *Kokutai* (National Community): History and Myth," *History of Religions* 13 (February 1974): 209–226; and Inoue Mitsusada, "The *Ritsuryō* System in Japan," *Acta Asiatica* 31 (1977): 83–112.

37. The *Kojiki*, *Nihonshoki*, and *Man'yōshū* do not contain any clear indication that performance of the *kunimi* ritual was restricted to the sovereign or to her/his representatives at this time. At least one entry in the *Nihonshoki*, though, suggests that ascending a hill and reciting sacred words was not confined to the *kunimi* but was a more general practice. More important, it demonstrates that ritual could be used as a form of political protest in early Japan. The entry from the fourth year of the reign of the Emperor Temmu (675 C.E.) is enigmatic and probably purposely vague:

11th month, 3rd day. A certain man [*hito arite*] ascended the hill east of the Palace, and having uttered words of evil omen [*oyozure koto shite*], cut his throat and died. Those who were on duty on that night received everyone a step in rank. There was a great earthquake in this month (Aston, *Nihongi*, 2: 330; NKBT 68: 420–421).

38. See especially "*Man'yōshū* no 'mi'," chap. 1 of Morishige Satoshi, *Buntai no ronri* (Tokyo: Kazama Shobō, 1967).

39. On the aspect of pacification found in *mi*, see especially Tsuchihashi Yutaka, " 'Miru' koto no tama-furi-teki ishiki," *Man'yō* 39 (April 1961).

40. NKBT 4: 66–67; Levy, *The Ten Thousand Leaves*, p. 84. Levy's translation transforms the intimate noun *imo* into the neutral "your." Levy fails to translate two variants noted in the *Man'yōshū*. For these see NKBT 4: 66.

41. NKBT 1: 95–97; Philippi, *Kojiki*, p. 98.

42. These poems have been treated at length by Levy in his *Hitomaro*, pp. 96–102.

43. NKBT 4: 28–31; Levy, *The Ten Thousand Leaves*, pp. 56–58.

44. Levy, *Hitomaro*, p. 100.

45. The imperial excursions to Yoshino recorded in our three basic texts include:

Reign	Year	Dates	Reign	Year	Dates	Reign	Year	Dates
Jimmu	663 B.C.E.	8/2 +		691	1/16-22		695	2/8-15
Ōjin	288 C.E.	10/1	(cont.)		4/16-22	(cont.)		3/11-14
Yūryaku	458	10/3-6			7/3-12			6/18-26
	460	8/18			10/13-20			8/24-30
Saimei	659	3/1		692	5/12-16			12/5-13
Tenji	671	10/19			7/9-28		696	2/3-13
		(Prince Ōama)			10/12-19			4/28-5/4
(Kōbun)	672	"		693	3/6-13			6/18-26
Temmu	679	5/5-7			5/1-7		697	4/7-14
Jitō	689	1/18-21			7/7-16	Mommu	701	2/20-27
		8/4			8/17-21			6/29-7/10
	690	2/17			11/5-10		702	7/11
		5/3		694	1/24	Genshō	723	5/9-13
		8/4			4/7-14	Shōmu	724	3/1-5
		10/5			9/4		725	?
		12/12-14					736	6/27-7/13

Takiguchi Yasuki ["*Man'yōshū* maki ichi Yoshino sanka no keifu," *Kodai bungaku* 19 (1980): 77–89] suggests that only the entries from Saimei on are reliable, thus indicating even further the extent to which the emergence of Yoshino as a sacred ritual site was related to the Temmu–Jitō reigns.

46. See NKBT 68: 404–405; Aston, *Nihongi*, 2: 317–318.

47. See NKBT 68: 349–350; Aston, *Nihongi*, 2: 310.

48. Ohama Itsuhiko, "Jitō tennō wa naze Yoshino e itta ka?" *Kokubungaku: kaishaku to kanshō* 34, no. 2 (February 1969): 63.

49. NKBT 4: 24–25; my translation. For Levy's translation, see *The Ten Thousand Leaves*, pp. 51–52. There is an editorial note in the *Man'yōshū* following the last poem that says, "The *Nihonshoki* says that an imperial procession to the Yoshino Palace was made on the fifth day of the fifth month in the eighth year of the reign." Levy mistakenly gives this as 680 rather than 679.

50. See, for example, Yamamoto Kenkichi, *Kakinomoto no Hitomaro* (Tokyo: Kōdansha, 1968), pp. 105ff., and Shirakawa, *Shoki-Man'yō-ron*, pp. 114–127.

51. NKBT 4: 22–23; my translation. For Levy's rendering, see *The Ten Thousand Leaves*, pp. 49–50.

52. See NKBT 4: 22 n. 22; Yamamoto, *Kakinomoto no Hitomaro*.

53. NKBT 4: 146–149; Levy, *The Ten Thousand Leaves*, p. 154.

54. NKBT 4: 168–169; Levy, *The Ten Thousand Leaves*, p. 177, slightly adapted.

55. The adjectival phrase *aratae*, here rendered "of the rough wisteria cloth" following Levy, also refers to the rough hemp cloth used for mourning robes. An example of the latter is found in MYS 2: 159 (see below in the text).

56. NKBT 4: 36–39; Levy, *The Ten Thousand Leaves*, pp. 64 and 66–67, adapted.

57. Morishige, *Buntai no ronri*, p. 93.

58. Morishige claims to have distinguished four distinct changes in the meaning and usage of *mi* evinced in the poetry collected in the *Man'yōshū*. His four stages are (1) the *mi* of the mythic stage found in poems such as MYS 1: 13–15, (2) that of the public *chōka* of Hitomaro epitomized by the phrase *yasumishishi waga ōkimi*, (3) the *mi* of the literary poets like Akabito where the world is experienced as out there in terms of *yo no naka*, and (4) the bifurcated *mi* found in Iemochi's poetry. One of Morishige's most important arguments is for the necessity of distinguishing oral poetry, including Hitomaro's *chōka*, from written poetry. He suggests that the introduction of writing altered human consciousness and, if he is correct, the early Japanese experienced ("saw") the world differently. I am not sure that the extant texts are sufficient in number to make the fine distinctions Morishige makes, but the general direction of his thought is suggestive. For my purposes a more general distinction between oral and written poetry will suffice, although one must also remember that in the transitional period, oral texts were written down and later performed from the written texts. The *norito* and the *Heike monogatari* would be examples of this phenomenon. One of the first attempts to consider the effects of the introduction of the Chinese script and literacy on the oral culture of Japan is David Pollack, *The Fracture of Meaning: Japan's Synthesis of China from the Eighth through the Eighteenth Centuries*, chap. 1 (Princeton: Princeton University Press, 1986).

59. The phrase "the geographicization of space" is from Karl Luckert, *The Navaho Rainbow Bridge Religion* (Flagstaff: Museum of Northern Arizona, 1977). There is at this time no single generally accepted term to refer to the "emplotment of the scene" (Kenneth Burke), even though the historical phenomenon is universal.

60. For a useful introduction to the universal process, both collective and individual, of creating a sense of "place" out of "space," see Yi-Fu Tuan, *Space and Place: The Perspective of Experience* (Minneapolis: University of Minnesota Press, 1977).

61. The term "peripheral" is taken from Edward Shils. See especially his *Center and Periphery* (Chicago: University of Chicago Press, 1967). Hitomaro's poetry is poetry of the "center" insofar as he was employed by the imperial family as a court poet.

62. Clifford Geertz, "Centers, Kings, and Charisma: Some Reflections on the Symbolics of Power," in his *Local Knowledge: Further Essays in Interpretive Anthropology* (New York: Basic Books, 1983), p. 125.

63. Ibid., p. 124.

64. See NKBT 4: 146–149; Levy, *The Ten Thousand Leaves*, p. 154.

65. This point is clearly made in MYS 3: 312:

Poem by the Minister of Ceremonies, Lord Fujiwara Umakai, at the time when, under imperial orders, he built the new palace at Naniwa.

In the old days they called it
rustic Naniwa [*Naniwa inaka to iwarekeme*]. But now
that we have moved our palace here,
how like a capital it's become!

(Levy, *The Ten Thousand Leaves*, p. 176; see NKBT 4: 166–167)

66. NKBT 4: 144–145; Levy, *The Ten Thousand Leaves*, p. 151. In giving the translation of the prose headnote I have dropped the word "written" (i.e., "poem written by") from Levy's translation, since it is misleading. I am not sure that Hitomaro *wrote* his ritual poetry. Indeed, the style seems more oral than not. In other cases, I have silently substituted "poem made by" or "poem by" for Levy's "written by," since this is still faithful to the original "*tsukuru*" but does not prejudice the question.

67. NKBT 4: 146–147; Levy, *The Ten Thousand Leaves*, pp. 152–153. See also Levy, *Hitomaro*, pp. 90–93. I have adapted Levy's translation of the headnote but have otherwise maintained his translation here. As will become clear, though, I prefer to consider verses such as this as having been orally performed in the presence of the imperial family member mentioned. Thus, the pronouns "he," "Him" and so on in Levy's translation may be replaced by "you," "your," and so on, as appropriate.

68. NKBT 1: 126–127; Philippi, *Kojiki*, p. 140.

69. NKBT 4: 10–13; Levy, *The Ten Thousand Leaves*, pp. 39–40.

70. Cf. "*Man'yōshū* no koi uta," *Origuchi Shinobu zenshū*, 9: 366–420, 8: 241–259, passim.

71. It is significant that the eighth-century editors of the *Man'yōshū* themselves were uncertain of the historical accuracy of the headnote and raised serious questions in an accompanying lengthy editorial note, which, if it ultimately does not resolve the problem, indicates the level of historical consciousness at this time in the court. See Levy, *The Ten Thousand Leaves*, pp. 40–41.

For my immediate purposes, it is finally unimportant whether this poem was recited during the excursion of the twelfth lunar month of 640 or on some other journey not noted in the *Nihonshoki*. The crux of my argument is based on the assumption that this and similar poems were publicly recited and were not privately written pieces. If they were public performative poems, they necessarily had the socio-political dimensions I have suggested.

Were they private works, there would be no need for the honorifics used or the declamatory praise. Levy has given a reading of MYS 1: 5–6 that differs significantly from my own (see *Hitomaro*, pp. 117–119).

72. Norbert Elias, *The Court Society*, trans. Edmund Jephcott (Oxford: Basil Blackwell, 1983), p. 111. Elias is speaking specifically of the *ancien regime* in France but with the stated intention of developing models for the comparative studies of court societies. Among other structural regularities, he finds that:

Of every fairly stable elite group, caste or social stratum that is exposed to pressure from below and often from above as well, it can be said—and will be stated explicitly here as a structural *regularity* of such units—that, to the people comprising it, their mere existence as members of an elite social unit is, partly or absolutely, a value and end in itself. The maintenance of distance thus becomes a decisive motor or matrix of their behaviour. The value of this existence needs no justification for the people involved, above all no utilitarian explanation. They do not seek a wider meaning transcending this existence. And wherever elitist tendencies are present in a society, the same phenomenon manifests itself. (p. 102)

73. I refrain from using the term "authorial intention," since there is evidence that some of the poems were commissioned from professional poets by members of the nobility. Saying this is not to deny, however, that many nobles and members of the imperial family could and did compose poetry themselves.

74. Such "boastful complaints" are, of course, found in everyday life today, too, wherever individuals are conscious of their position within a hierarchical structure and complain in such a way that boasts of their status (e.g., feeling pressured to meet a publisher's deadline or burdened by the appointment to another committee by the dean). My point, of course, is that we should not read the public "complaints" in the *Man'yōshū* any differently. In context, all such boastful complaints are the speakers' implicit claims of importance, of occupying a higher status than others in the institutional hierarchy.

75. We do not know how many other princes were included in the emperor's retinue, but the large number of children from the emperor's wives and consorts generally required the distinction of mere princes from imperial princes and of ranking within these divisions as well. Unfortunately, nothing is known of Prince Ikusa. The *Man'yōshū* preserves an instructive example of a poem of complaint and longing presented by a wife who had been left behind while her husband accompanied the emperor on a procession. See MYS 4: 543–545 in NKBT 4: 260–261; Levy, *The Ten Thousand Leaves*, pp. 265–267. Note that a surrogate generates and performs these songs of longing, standing in for the woman left behind. Nevertheless, they are in the first-person form.

76. Nippon Gakujutsu Shinkōkai, trans., *The Manyōshū*, p. xiv.

77. Cf. Levy, *Hitomaro*, p. 148.

78. Levy, *The Ten Thousand Leaves*, p. 133. For the original, see NKBT 4: 114–115.

79. Levy, *Hitomaro*, pp. 66ff.

80. See ibid., p. 162, where Levy is speaking specifically about MYS 2: 207–212.

81. On this point see especially Watase Masatada, *Shima no miya no bungaku*, vol. 3 of *Kakinomoto Hitomaro kenkyū* (Tokyo: Ōfusha, 1976).

82. One manuscript has the variant mountain name "Murokami-yama" here. See NKBT 4: 82–83. Levy does not provide this information.

83. NKBT 4: 82–83; Levy, *The Ten Thousand Leaves*, pp. 100–101, slightly adapted. Levy does not give the variants. I have not given one variant line found in an interlinear note to the second envoy—*hitotsu ni iu, chiri na magaiso*—since it does not change the meaning.

84. NKBT 4: 152–153; Levy, *The Ten Thousand Leaves*, pp. 160–161, adapted. I have taken the poem to be addressed directly to Prince Niitabe and, thus, have substituted second-person singular pronouns for Levy's third-person pronouns.

85. Levy, *Hitomaro*, pp. 94–95. Levy treats this poem on pp. 93–96. He finds in this verse a "convincing subjective voice" presenting a "psychological rather than iconic focus, emphasizing the courtier's own subjective emotions of fealty." In order to make this argument, though, Levy has to strain the syntactical content of the poem to its limits in arguing that "Hitomaro's exclamatory 'delight' ('tanoshi mo') is an expression of anticipation by an individual about to join the ritual but, at the moment when he expresses this, still perceiving it from outside. When he reaches the palace and dismounts, his individuality will be submerged in the ritual, but here as he rides, it is his personal voice that speaks to us" (pp. 94–95). This verse, then, is assumed to have been composed (and recited?) on horseback! Even within the ritual, however, the subjective experience would not disappear, since the experience of the morning ritual of receiving one's orders would be one thing for a courtier in favor but quite another for one who had fallen from favor.

86. Aston, *Nihongi*, 2: 330; NKBT 68: 420–421.

87. Cf. Sasaya Ryōzō, "Musubi-gami no shinkō," *Kokugakuin zasshi* 64, nos. 8–9 (August-September 1963): 83–111.

88. NKBT 4: 80–81; Levy, *The Ten Thousand Leaves*, p. 99. Poems 134 and 139 are variants of this. See NKBT 4: 80–81; Levy, ibid., p. 99; and NKBT 4: 84–85; Levy, ibid., p. 103.

89. NKBT 4: 114–117; Levy, *The Ten Thousand Leaves*, pp. 134–135. A variant has *na nomi kikite/ ari ineba*.

90. Cf. Hashimoto Tatsuo, "Me oto no naki: Man'yō tobu uta to Hitomaro," *Kokubungaku: kaishaku to kanshō* 35, no. 7 (July 1970): 65–72; Kobayashi Yukio, Ikeda Yasaburo, and Kadokawa Gen'yoshi, eds., *Kami to kami o matsuru mono*, vol. 1 of *Nihon bungaku no rekishi* (Tokyo: Kadokawa Shoten, 1967), pp. 262–266; Yoshii Iwao, *Yamato-takeru* (Tokyo: Gakuseisha, 1977), pp. 202ff.; Mori Asao, "Ama kudaru Temmu," *Kokubungaku kenkyū* 67 (March 1979): 10–18.

91. NKBT 4: 90–91; Levy, *The Ten Thousand Leaves*, pp. 108 and 109.

92. Bearing these points in mind, one may be better able to appreciate the controversial argument of Umehara Takeshi in his *Kakusareta jūjika* that Hōryūji was built not so much to enshrine the spirit of a minister wrongly accused of treason in a benign sense as to *constrain* or imprison it.

93. J. H. Kamstra, *Encounter or Syncretism: The Initial Growth of Japanese Buddhism* (Leiden: E. J. Brill, 1967), p. 106. See also pp. 105–109 and 354ff.

94. Aston, *Nihongi*, 2: 255; NKBT 68: 334–335. Compare the manner in which the courtier Soga no Akae insinuates his dissatisfaction to the prince with the following from Saint-Simon, reporting a conversation he had with the second dauphin, a grandson of Louis XIV, in whom Saint-Simon had placed his hopes and planted his ideas and schemes:

I thought it right to sound out the Dauphin in the first days of his new glory. . . . I took care to say a word about our standing. . . . I told him how right he was not to lose sight of the least part of his legitimate rights, and I seized the favourable moment to tell him that if he, who was so great and whose position was so secure, had reason to watch over it, how much more had we whose rank was often disputed and sometimes even withdrawn almost without our daring to complain. . . .

Finally the conversation turned to the king. The Dauphin spoke of him with great tenderness and gratitude; I immediately expressed the same feelings, except that affection and gratitude should not become a dangerous admiration. I hinted that the king did not know of many things and had unfortunately placed himself in a position where he could not know of them, although with his kindness he certainly would not be insensitive to them if he knew.

This string, gently plucked, immediately produced a full resonance. The prince admitted the truth of what I said and immediately began to attack the ministers. He spoke at length on the limitless authority they had usurped over the king, on the dangerous use they might make of it, the impossibility of anything reaching the king or coming from him without their interference. He did not name anyone, but clearly indicated that this form of government was entirely against his taste and his maxims.

Then he came back to the king, lamented the bad education he had had and the ruinous hands into which he had successively fallen. In this way, since, on the pretext of policy and authority, all power and advantages existed only for the ministers, his heart, by nature kind and just, had been constantly deflected from the right path without his noticing.

I took the opportunity to draw his attention to the arrogance of the ministers towards the duke and those of even higher rank. He was indignant." (*Memoires*, vol. 18, chap. 106, pp. 5ff., cited in Elias, *The Court Society*, pp. 202–203)

The similarities to the situation in the early Japanese court are striking and suggestive. Many passages in the *Nihonshoki* take on a new meaning when they are read bearing the court rationality that motivated the actions of the ministers, courtiers, and the sovereigns as well.

95. Levy does not translate this note. One source attributes the poem to Hitomaro; see NKBT 4: 87 n. 5.

96. NKBT 4: 86–89. My translations. See also Levy, *The Ten Thousand Leaves*, pp. 104–106.

97. Cf. Mircea Eliade, "The 'God Who Binds' and the Symbolism of Knots," in his *Images and Symbols: Studies in Religious Symbolism* (New York: Sheed and Ward, 1969), pp. 92–124.

98. For a brief introduction to one such example in medieval Japan, see Ebersole, "The Buddhist Ritual Use of Linked Poetry."

99. NKBT 4: 122–125; Levy, *The Ten Thousand Leaves*, pp. 141–143.

100. Cf. Itō Haku, *Man'yōshū no kajin to sakuhin* (Tokyo: Hanawa Shobō, 1975), 1: 226–229. A very different reading of this poem, which takes no cognizance of any ritual meaning or intention, may be found in Robert H. Brower and Earl Miner, *Japanese Court Poetry* (Stanford: Stanford University Press, 1961), pp. 97–99.

101. NKBT 4: 124–125. For a different translation, see Levy, *The Ten Thousand Leaves*, p. 143. A strikingly similar image of sleeping on rocks for a pillow is found in an oral funeral lament recorded in rural Greece, describing a man who had died near the ocean far from his home: "He had seaweed for a blanket and white foam for a sheet,/ and a mound of little beach pebbles as a pillow for his head." Cited in Loring M. Danforth, *The Death Rituals of Rural Greece* (Princeton: Princeton University Press, 1982), p. 103.

102. NKBT 4: 198–199. Levy does not translate all of the editorial note. See *The Ten Thousand Leaves*, p. 212.

103. Ibid.

104. I follow Cranston here in rendering the *makurakotoba* or pillow word for Unebi, *tamatasuki*, as "of the jeweled sleeve cords" rather than Levy's "where the maidens/ wear cords of jewels." See Edwin A. Cranston, "The Ramifying Vein: An Impression of Leaves—A Review of Levy's Translation of the *Man'yōshū*," *Journal of Japanese Studies* 9 (Winter 1983): 120.

105. A variant noted in the *Nishi Honganji bon* manuscript used for the NKBT edition has been omitted in the translation here, since it does not change the meaning and would unnecessarily break the flow of the translation. I have included it in the *romaji* transliteration. See NKBT 4: 26–27.

106. Hira is the name of a town in present-day Shiga Prefecture located north of Ōtsu-shi.

107. NKBT 4: 26–27; Levy, *The Ten Thousand Leaves*, pp. 53–55, adapted slightly. The translations of the envoys are my own.

108. Levy treats MYS 2: 29–31 in *Hitomaro*, pp. 111–116. According to Levy, this set "was apparently composed, not as Hitomaro accompanied an imperial procession, but on a private journey." He cites no authority for this statement or for the claim that this is "a private elegy for that public site by the Ōmi Sea which was once 'firmly pillared' with Tenji's palace" (p. 111).

109. Among the sources I have drawn on are Yamamoto, *Kakinomoto no Hitomaro*, pp. 44–77; Sakurai Mitsuru, *Kakinomoto Hitomaro-ron* (Tokyo: Ōfusha, 1980), pp. 119–129; Itō, *Man'yōshū no kajin to sakuhin*, 1: 205–239; Watase, *Kakinomoto Hitomaro kenkyū*, 3: 268–273.

110. See Yamamoto, *Kakinomoto no Hitomaro*, pp. 44–51.

111. See, for example, Sakurai, *Kakinomoto Hitomaro-ron*, pp. 126ff.

112. Here I agree wholeheartedly with Sakurai. See ibid., p. 127.

113. Aston *Nihongi*, 2: 286; NKBT 68: 366–367.

114. The *Nihonshoki* does, however, preserve a few examples of *wazauta* that are critical of Ōtomo (Kōbun). See NKBT 68: 380–381; Aston, *Nihongi*, 2: 299; and Philippi, *This Wine of Peace*, pp. 129, 135, and 149. The fact that the compilers of the *Nihonshoki* would incorporate *wazauta* critical of Ōtomo but not of Tenji is indicative of how they could be selective at times in order to further the interests of their own faction. *Wazauta* are often included in the *Nihonshoki* as foreshadowing the downfall of an individual or family. For an introduction to this topic, see Nishimura Sey, "Retrospective Comprehension: Japanese Foretelling Songs," *Asian Folklore Studies* 45, no. 1 (1986): 45–66.

115. See the entries for 11/23 and 11/29/671 in NKBT 68: 379–381; Aston, *Nihongi*, 2: 298–299.

116. Levy, *Hitomaro*, p. 114.

117. Yamamoto, *Kakinomoto no Hitomaro*, pp. 56–58. For Princess Kage's lament, see NKBT 68: 10–13; Aston, *Nihongi*, 1: 402.

118. Cf. Margaret Alexiou, *The Ritual Lament in Greek Tradition* (London: Cambridge University Press, 1974), pp. 83–101.

119. NKBT 4: 104–107; Levy, *The Ten Thousand Leaves*, pp. 124–126, adapted.

120. Misaki Hisashi, "Asuka no himemiko no araki no miya shiron," *Bungaku*, *gogaku* 93 (1982): 18. See also Misaki's "Asuka no miko banka shiron," *Man'yō* 90 (December 1975): 48–62.

121. Note the following examples of recriminations against the deceased by close relatives from laments recorded in Greece. The first is by a mother and mother-in-law of a young woman who died shortly after marriage and childless:

—Wretched girl, think again! Have pity on your mother.
—If you do not return, if you do not appear,
   they will insult you, and go and take the dowry
   from your husband's house, because you left no child!

(Cited by Alexiou, *Ritual Lament*, p. 46)

The next example is from the fourth century C.E.:

Ammia, wise daughter, how is it you died so soon?
Why did you hasten to die, or which of the Fates overtook you?
Before we decked you for the bridal garland in the marriage chamber
you left your home and your grieving parents.
Your father, and all the country, and your mother lamented
for your most untimely and unwedded youth.

(Ibid., pp. 106–107)

122. NKBT 4: 112–113. The poem itself reads:

Nakisawa no	At the Nakisawa Shrine
mori ni mi-wa suru	I offer sacred wine
inore domo	and pray, but
wago ōkimi wa	you, my Lord,
takahi shirashinu	now rule the high heavens.

123. On this point, see Misaki, "Asuka no himemiko no araki no miya shiron," pp. 19ff.

124. See Aoki Takako, *Man'yō banka-ron* (Tokyo: Hanawa Shobō, 1984), pp. 131–143.

125. See Levy, *The Ten Thousand Leaves*, pp. 127–131. He has analyzed these verses in *Hitomaro*, pp. 137–146.

126. NKBT 68: 502–503; Aston, *Nihongi*, 2: 398.

127. NKBT 68: 530–531; Aston, *Nihongi*, 2: 420.

128. For more detailed background on this period in relation to these verses, see Yoshinaga, *Man'yō—bungaku to rekishi no aida*, pp. 96ff.; and Takagi Hiroshi, *Man'yō kyūtei no aikan* (Tokyo: Tokyodō Shuppan, 1977), pp. 298–337.

129. NKBT 4: 108–109; Levy, *The Ten Thousand Leaves*, p. 127.

130. For a detailed study of this myth, see Yanai Kyūsaku, *Ama no iwato shinwa no kenkyū* (Tokyo: Ōfusha, 1977).

131. Levy, *The Ten Thousand Leaves*, pp. 127–128. See NKBT 4: 108–109 for the original Japanese, plus variants that Levy does not acknowledge, including the use of the verb *harau*, "to sweep up" or "to clean up."

132. NKBT 4: 110–111; Levy, *The Ten Thousand Leaves*, pp. 128–129.

133. Ibid.

CHAPTER TWO
The Mythology of Death and the *Niiname-sai*

1. Sahlins, *Islands of History*, p. vii.

2. Clifford Geertz, "Religion as a Cultural System," in his *The Interpretation of Cultures* (New York: Basic Books, 1973), p. 93.

3. See, for example, Frank E. Reynolds and Earle Waugh, eds., *Religious Encounters with Death* (University Park: Pennsylvania State University Press, 1976); Huntington and Metcalf, *Celebrations of Death*; Maurice Bloch and Jonathan Parry, eds., *Death and the Regeneration of Life*

(Cambridge: Cambridge University Press, 1982). For an influential study of the changing concept and experience of death in Europe, see Philippe Aries, *The Hour of Our Death* (New York: Alfred A. Knopf, 1981). For recent studies of the changing concept of death in Japanese history, see Tamura Yoshirō and Minamoto Ryōen, eds., *Nihon ni okeru sei to shi no shisō* (Tokyo: Yūhikaku, 1977), and in Japanese Buddhism, Kasahara Kazuo and Oguri Junko, eds., *Iki-zama, shini-zama—Nihon minshū shinkōshi*, vol. 178 of the *Rekishi Shinsho* (Tokyo: Kyōikusha, 1979).

4. These and subsequent translations in this section are from Levy, *The Ten Thousand Leaves*, pp. 229 and 124 respectively.

5. Ibid., pp. 115 and 132.

6. Ibid., p. 214, adapted.

7. Ibid., pp. 132, 127, and 231.

8. Ibid., pp. 143 and 212, adapted.

9. Joseph Kitagawa's arguments may be found in "Reality and Illusion: Some Characteristics of the Early Japanese World of Meaning," *Journal of the Oriental Society of Australia* 11 (1976): 3–18, and in "A Past of Things Present: Notes on Major Motifs in Early Japanese Religions," *History of Religions* 20 (August–November 1980): 27–42.

10. Cf. Geertz, *The Interpretation of Cultures*, pp. 90ff., where he suggests "a religion is: (1) a system of symbols which acts to (2) establish powerful, pervasive, and long-lasting moods and motivations in men by (3) formulating conceptions of a general order of existence and (4) clothing these conceptions with such an aura of factuality that (5) the moods and motivations seem uniquely realistic."

11. Cf. Hori Ichiro, *Folk Religion in Japan* (Chicago: University of Chicago Press, 1968) and "Mysterious Visitors from the Harvest to the New Year," in *Studies in Japanese Folklore*, ed. Dorson, pp. 76–106.

12. Levy, *The Ten Thousand Leaves*, pp. 108–109; NKBT 4: 90–91.

13. Cf. Yukawa Hisamitsu, "Tenji banka-gun no ron," *Kodai bungaku* 20 (1981): 89–102; Aoki Takako, *Man'yō banka-ron*, p. 282; Itō, *Man'yōshū no kajin to sakuhin*, 1: 12.

14. This belief survived into the medieval period, when the cry of birds, often the *hototogisu*, was a common element in poetry. *Kokinshū* 9: 412, the lament of a woman for her recently deceased husband, is one such example:

kita e yuku	How they cry
kari zo naku naru	As they wing off to the north!
tsurete koshi	It seems the geese
kazu wa tarade zo	Have lost one from the number
kaeru bera naru	Which flew here with them in the fall.

(Trans. Brower and Miner, *Japanese Court Poetry*, p. 212)

In *Goshūishū* 20: 1164, Izumi Shikibu (d. c. 1030) speaks of her "soul" (*tama*) as a firefly, flying off to an unfaithful lover.

mono omoeba	As I fall in sadness
sawa no hotaru mo	At his neglect, the firefly of the marsh
waga mi yori	Seems to be my soul
akugareizuru	Departing from my very flesh
tama ka to zo miru	And wandering in anguish off to him.

(Ibid., p. 222)

This belief is also found in *Shinkokinshū* 11: 1034 attributed to Princess Shokushi (d. 1201). Brower and Miner rightly note of the poem that "It plays upon the notion that while a person was still alive, his spirit might leave his body and go visit the object of his feeling—of love or hate—trailing an invisible, weightless cord that attached spirit and body. If this cord were broken, the person would die."

tama no o yo	O cord of life!
taenaba	Threading through the jewel of my soul,
nagaraeba	If you will break, break now:
shinoburu koto zo	I shall weaken if this life continues,
yowari mo zo suru	Unable to bear such fearful strain.

(Ibid., p. 301)

15. NKBT 4: 62–63; Levy, *The Ten Thousand Leaves*, p. 81.

16. Cf. Hori, *Folk Religion in Japan*, esp. chap. 4, "Mountains and Their Importance for the Idea of the Other World," pp. 141–179; and Nelly Naumann, "Yama no kami—die japanische Bergottheit," *Folklore Studies* 22 (1963): 133–366.

17. Huntington and Metcalf, *Celebrations of Death*, p. 2.

18. But see the annotations and notes in NKBT 1: 52ff. and Philippi, *Kojiki*, pp. 53ff.

19. Philippi, *Kojiki*, pp. 57–58; NKBT 1: 60–61.

20. The same theme and pattern are repeated in the Susano-o narrative in the *Kojiki* where a female *kami*, Ō-ge-tsu-hime, and grain and other foodstuffs are created. Other variants are found in the *Nihonshoki* involving different *kami*. See Aston, *Nihongi*, 1: 32–33.

21. Philippi, *Kojiki*, p. 58 n. 18.

22. See Aston, *Nihongi*, 1: 21.

23. Philippi, *Kojiki*, p. 61.

24. Ibid., p. 68.

25. *Muraji* is one of the hereditary titles or *kabane* granted by the sovereign to powerful families in early and medieval Japan. On this, see Richard J. Miller, *Ancient Japanese Nobility: The Kabane Ranking System* (Berkeley and Los Angeles: University of California Press, 1974).

Many of the myths in the *Kojiki*, the *Nihonshoki*, and the *fudoki* were intended to justify retrospectively the status of various clans, families, and guilds by locating their origins in the mythic past.

26. For an interesting discussion of this phrase in a later passage of the myth, see Alan L. Miller, "*Ame No Miso-Ori Me* (The Heavenly Weaving Maiden): The Cosmic Weaver in Early Shinto Myth and Ritual," *History of Religions* 24 (August 1984): 27–48.

27. Philippi, *Kojiki*, pp. 71–73.

28. Ibid., p. 73.

29. Aston, *Nihongi*, 1: 33–34.

30. Philippi, *Kojiki*, p. 71 n. 1 [citing *Hirata Atsutane zenshū*, vol. 1 (Tokyo: Itchido Shoten, 1911), p. 365].

31. Ibid., p. 74.

32. Alan Miller, "*Ame No Miso-Ori Me*," p. 47.

33. The *Nihonshoki* presents several variants of this episode. The first largely follows the *Kojiki* version (see Aston, *Nihongi*, 1: 34–36); in the second version, Amaterasu produces offspring from her own swords, and Susano-o does the same from his own beads (pp. 36–37); the third version is of interest in that another *kami*, Ha-akaru kami, gives Susano-o *maga-tama*, which Susano-o then exchanges with Amaterasu for her sword, after which they both produce offspring (pp. 37–38); the fourth version is similar to the second (pp. 39–40).

34. The suggestion of divine or royal incest here was sufficiently strong so that in the Tokugawa period neo-Confucianists attacked the Shinto establishment on this point. See Philippi, *Kojiki*, p. 76 n. 1.

35. Ibid., pp. 79–80; NKBT 1: 78–81.

36. Nelly Naumann, "*Sakahagi*: The 'Reverse Flaying' of the Heavenly Piebald Horse," *Asian Folklore Studies* 41, no. 1 (1982): 7–38.

37. Matsumae writes that "we can conclude that Amaterasu's entering of the cave and her reappearance represent her death and resurrection" ["The Heavenly Rock-Grotto Myth and the Chinkon Ceremony," *Asian Folklore Studies* 39, no. 2 (1980): 10]. This article remains the best treatment of this episode available in a Western language.

38. Tsuda Sōkichi, for example, argued that it was the mythic description of a solar eclipse [cf. *Jindaishi no kenkyū* (Tokyo: Iwanami Shoten, 1924), pp. 191–192], as did Ōbayashi Taryo at one point [cf. *Nihon shinwa no kigen* (Tokyo: Kadokawa Shoten, 1961), pp. 132ff.]. Naumann, "*Sakahagi*," also tends to read this myth in broad and general terms: Susano-o represents the powers of death, Amaterasu those of life, and so forth.

39. Matsumae, "The Heavenly Rock-Grotto Myth," p. 14.

40. Philippi, *Kojiki*, pp. 85–86; NKBT 1: 82–83.

41. Philippi, *Kojiki*, p. 86 n. 25.

42. Aston, *Nihongi*, 1: 29; NKBT 67: 98–99.

43. On double burial in general, see the seminal essay by Robert Hertz, "Contribution à une étude sur la réprésentation collective de la mort," *Année sociologique* 10 (1907): 48–137; an English translation may be found in *Death and the Right Hand*, trans. Rodney and C. Needham (New York: Free Press, 1960). More recently, Huntington and Metcalf's *Celebrations of Death* builds on Hertz's work. For Greek culture, see among others: Danforth, *The Death Rituals of Rural Greece*; Alexiou, *The Ritual Lament in Greek Tradition*; Anna Caraveli-Chaves, "Bridge Between Worlds: The Greek Women's Lament as Communicative Event," *Journal of American Folklore* 93, no. 368 (April-June 1980): 129–157. For Central Asia, I. Lopatin, *The Cult of the Dead Among the Natives of the Amur Basin* (The Hague: Mouton, 1960); for South America, J. C. Crocker, "The Mirrored Self: Identity and Ritual Inversion Among the Eastern Bororo," *Ethnology* 16, no. 2 (1977): 129–145; for Judaism, E. Meyers, *Jewish Ossuaries: Reburial and Rebirth*, Biblica et Orientalis No. 24 (Rome: Biblical Institute Press., 1971); for Melanesia, Roy Wagner, *Habu: The Innovation of Meaning in Daribi Religion* (Chicago: University of Chicago Press, 1972), and D. Tuzin, "The Breath of a Ghost: Dreams and the Fear of the Dead," *Ethos* 3 (1975): 559–578.

44. For the complete myth and variants, see Philippi, *Kojiki*, pp. 137–147; NKBT 1: 124–139; and Aston, *Nihongi*, 1: 64ff.; NKBT 67: 134ff.

45. Aston, *Nihongi*, 1: 84.

46. Ibid.

47. Ibid., pp. 84–85.

48. Ibid., p. 85.

49. Ibid., pp. 85–86.

50. Ibid., p. 83.

51. On this question, however, one may consult the conclusions Robert Ellwood reached in his excellent monograph, *The Feast of Kingship: Accession Ceremonies in Ancient Japan* (Tokyo: Sophia University Press, 1973), esp. pp. 73–77.

52. For recent examples, see the many works of Mircea Eliade, including *Cosmos and History: The Myth of the Eternal Return* (New York: Harper and Row, 1959), *Birth and Rebirth* (New York: Harper and Row, 1958), and *Images and Symbols: Studies in Religious Symbolism* (New York: Sheed and Ward, 1969); Victor Turner, *The Ritual Process* (Chicago: Aldine, 1969); and especially Bloch and Parry, eds., *Death and the Regeneration of Life*, a sustained study of this relationship expressed in various cultures.

53. Cf. Ōno Sokyō, "Nihon shinwa to niiname no matsuri," *Shintōgaku* 8 (August 1956): 31–41; Kikuchi Takeo, "Hinkyū girei to niiname," *Kokubungaku kenkyū* 73, no. 3 (March 1981): 12–21; Naoki Kōjiro, "Niiname to daijō no yomi to imi," *Man'yō* 65 (October 1967): 15–24; and Origuchi, "Daijō-sai no hongi," in *Origuchi Shinobu zenshū*, 3: 174–240.

54. Obayashi Taryo, "Niiname ni shutsugen suru ōja—korosareru ōja," *Bungaku* 48, no. 5 (May 1980): 160–169.

55. Ellwood, *The Feast of Kingship*, p. 48.

56. See Philippi, trans., *Norito*, pp. 72–75; NKBT 1: 452–457.

57. Aston, *Nihongi*, 1: 64; NKBT 67: 134–135.

58. Alan Miller, "*Ame No Miso-Ori Me*," pp. 29 and 31. Miller treats this passage at length on pp. 29–32.

59. Philippi, *Kojiki*, p. 123; NKBT 1: 112–113.

60. See Aston, *Nihongi*, 1: 64–65; NKBT 67: 134–135.

61. In his *Kojiki-den*, Motoori Norinaga suggested that the characters for the name of the pheasant (*na-naki-me*) should be understood as meaning "Name-calling Woman." The editors of NKBT 1 dismiss this (see NKBT 1: 114–115 n. 3). Aston (*Nihongi*, 1: 65 n. 5) seemed willing to follow Chamberlin, who had accepted Motoori's reading. I would suggest that these questions are of interest and import insofar as one wants to study the effect of the introduction of writing on Japanese culture and thought. Insofar as one accepts the *Kojiki* (and to a much lesser extent the *Nihonshoki*), however, as preserving (whether in whole or in part, in the original or in altered form) previously oral myths, *uta*, and so on, all the possible oral meanings could have—and at some point probably would have—come to mind. According to Jack Goody and Ian Watt, in oral societies "the meaning of each word is ratified in a succession of concrete situations, accompanied by vocal inflexions and physical gestures, all of which combine to particularize both its specific denotation and its accepted connotative usage" ["The Consequences of Literacy," *Comparative Studies in Society and History* 5 (1962–1963): 306]. The oral nature of this myth, as well as one of its didactic functions, is suggested by the fact that the *Kojiki* includes two *kotowaza*, popular sayings, associated with it. Any usage of either of these sayings in everyday conversation would have recalled the underlying myth to the early Japanese.

62. Little is known about Ama-no-sagume. The poem MYS 3: 292, however, alludes to a no-longer-extant myth of her descent from heaven in a boat of stone:

hisakata no	The boat of stone
Ama no sagume ga	in which rode [Ama-no-]Sagume,
iwafune no	goddess from the far firmament,
hateshi Taka-tsu wa	found anchorage in Taka Harbor;
ase ni keru kamo	now it has turned shallow.

(NKBT 4: 160–161; Levy, *The Ten Thousand Leaves*, p. 170)

63. Philippi, *Kojiki*, p. 125; NKBT 1: 114–117.

64. Aston, *Nihongi*, 1: 65–66; NKBT 67: 136–137.

65. See Philippi, *Kojiki*, p. 125 n. 11 and p. 75 n. 8.

66. See Ellwood, *The Feast of Kingship*, pp. 70–72. In a private communication (December 19, 1985) Ellwood writes that he continues to believe the *niiname* to have been "a time of testing of both imperial and marital legitimacy (or both in the case of heirs) which involved banging on doors, entering the residence of a *hime*, and reclining on a couch—from which one might arise with a bride and a throne, or dead or at least expelled like Susano-o if one does not do something right."

67. See Alan Miller, "*Ame No Miso-Ori Me*," p. 31; Ellwood, *The Feast of Kingship*, pp. 59ff., 70–71, 134–135, passim; and Saigō Nobutsuna, "Nadoko-ōfusuma to ama-no-hagoromo," in *Shi no hassei: bungaku ni okeru genshikodai no imi* (Tokyo: Miraisha, 1974).

68. See Philippi, *Kojiki*, pp. 183–185; NKBT 1: 164–167.

69. Aston, *Nihongi*, 1: 138–140; NKBT 67: 218–221.

70. Ellwood, *The Feast of Kingship*, p. 42.

71. Philippi, *Kojiki*, p. 324; NKBT 1: 282–285.

72. See NKBT 67: 418–421; Aston, *Nihongi*, 1: 300ff.

73. For the *Nihonshoki* entry, see NKBT 68: 170–171; Aston, *Nihongi*, 2: 119. For the *Kojiki* version, see NKBT 1: 343; Philippi, *Kojiki*, p. 393.

74. See Obayashi Taryo, "Niiname ni shutsugen suru ōja—Korosareru ōja."

75. For an interesting discussion of Frazer's creation of the "myth" of Nemi, see Jonathan Z. Smith, "When the Bough Breaks," *History of Religions* 12 (May 1973): 342–371 [rpt. in *Map Is Not Territory: Studies in the History of Religions* (Leiden: E. J. Brill, 1978), pp. 208–239].

76. Philippi, *Kojiki*, p. 213; NKBT 1: 188–189.

77. NKBT 67: 502–503; Aston, *Nihongi*, 1: 373–374.

78. Ellwood, *The Feast of Kingship*, p. 42.

79. This motif is strikingly similar to that found in the Indian epic, the *Mahabharata*, involving the Pandava brothers.

80. Aston, *Nihongi*, 1: 375–376; NKBT 67: 506–507.

81. Ellwood, *The Feast of Kingship*, p. 45.

82. Aston, *Nihongi*, 1: 379–380; NKBT 67: 510–511.

83. Ibid.

84. Aston's translation here (see Aston, *Nihongi*, 1: 381 n. 2) is unfounded and has not received support from modern Japanese scholars.

85. The translation of this verse is Philippi's, *This Wine of Peace*, p. 70. For the standard interpretation of the meaning of this verse, see NKBT 67: 513–514 n. 6.

86. The term *soso chihara* is a combination of an onomatopoeic word, *soso*, "the rustling sound of reeds," and a place name, *chihara*. *Chihara* can also be read *ashihara* or "Land of Reed Plains," another name for Yamato. *Asachihara*, then, is "Shallow Land of Reed Plains."

87. Here one finds a clear suggestion that Prince Oshiwa had ruled as the *de facto* sovereign during the period of temporary enshrinement until he was murdered, even though he never formally acceded and is not recognized in the official list of emperors and empresses. At least this implicit claim is permitted to be voiced here.

88. Aston, *Nihongi*, 1: 379–383; NKBT 67: 512–515.

89. See Philippi, *Kojiki*, pp. 370–383, esp. pp. 370–372. Philippi has also translated the relevant passage from the *Harima fudoki*. See "Additional Note 28," pp. 424–425.

CHAPTER THREE
The Liminal Period of Temporary Enshrinement

1. An important exception to this statement is Wada Shigeki, "Mogari no kiso-teki kō-satsu," *Shirin* 52, no. 5 (September 1969): 32–90. Wada argues that a proper understanding of the practice of double burial in early Japan is essential in order to appreciate the cultural and political history of the period. This piece was one of the first to alert me to the significance of this topic.

2. Philippi, *Kojiki*, pp. 126–129; NKBT 1: 117–119.

3. See, for instance, Katsura Yoshihisa, *Mizu to hi no denshō* (Tokyo: Miyoi Shobō, 1978), pp. 1ff., where he treats this episode.

4. Aston, *Nihongi*, 1: 66; NKBT 67: 136–137.

5. This "explanation" does not ring true. Although it is only a hypothesis, one can imagine another version of this myth in which Aji-shiki-taka-hiko-ne took on the mantle of Ame-no-waka-hiko.

6. In English, see for example Ivan Morris's *The Nobility of Failure: Tragic Heroes in the History of Japan* (New York: Meridian, 1975). In Japanese, see Yoshii, *Yamato-takeru*.

7. Philippi, *Kojiki*, pp. 250–252; NKBT 1: 222–225.

8. See the following entries:

[192] Winter, 11th month, 1st day. The Emperor [Chūai] commanded his Ministers, saying:—"The Prince, Our father, died before We reached the status of a youth. His divine spirit became changed into a white bird and ascended to Heaven. Our longing regard for him knows not a day's intermission. Therefore it is Our wish to procure white birds and to keep them in the pond within the precincts of the *misazagi*, so that, looking on these birds, we may comfort our feelings of longing." Orders were therefore sent to the various provinces to send tribute of white birds.

Intercalary 11th month, 4th day. The province of Koshi sent tribute of four white birds. Now the messengers who were sent with the birds stayed for the night on the bank of the river Uji. Then Prince Kama-mi-wake, of Ashikami, seeing the white birds, made inquiry, saying:—"Whither are you taking these white birds?" The men of Koshi answered and said:—"The Emperor, out of his longing [*koi tamawashite*] for the Prince, his father, intends to keep them as pets. Therefore do we bring them as tribute." Prince Kama-mi-wake spake to the men of Koshi, saying:—"These may be white birds, but when they are roasted they will become black birds." So he forcibly seized the white birds and carried them away. Hereupon the men of Koshi came and reported to the Emperor, who was indignant at the affront offered by Prince Kama-mi-wake to the late prince, and sending troops, put him to death. Prince Kama-mi-wake was the younger brother of the Emperor [Chūai] by a different mother. (Aston, *Nihongi*, 1: 217–218; see also NKBT 67: 320–323)

In this entry we can see that the white birds functioned as a type of *katami*, an object used to recall to mind a deceased individual. In addition, we once again see how contention for power following the death of a sovereign often led to fratricide. Whether Kama-mi-wake actually performed the actions attributed to him, the story as narrated in the *Nihonshoki* functions to discredit him by explicitly stating that his acts constituted an affront to his deceased father, thus portraying him as unfilial. The *Nihonshoki* notice of this incident concludes with a Sinified sentence: "The people of that time said:—'A father is Heaven, an elder brother is a Lord; how can he escape execution who is wanting in respect to Heaven, and who thwarts his Lord?' " (ibid). When the editors of the *Nihonshoki* wanted to make a point, especially a factional one, they were seldom subtle.

9. See Edwin A. Cranston, "Water Plant Images in the *Man'yōshū*," *Harvard Journal of Asiatic Studies* 31 (1971): 137–178.

10. Kure Tetsuo, "Mogari no miya no genkei," *Kodai Bungaku* 18 (1979): 48–54, has looked at this question. For those sovereigns for which a location for the *mogari no miya* is given, we find the following:

Sovereign	Location of mogari no miya
Empress Suiko	in "the Southern Court" (Aston, *Nihongi*, 2: 155)
Emperor Jomei	"north of the palace" (Ibid., 2: 170)
Emperor Kōtoku	in "the southern courtyard" (Ibid., 2: 247)
Empress Saimei	"at Asuka-gahara" (Ibid., 2: 272)
Emperor Tenji	"in the New Palace" [*shin-miya*] (Ibid., 2: 290)
Emperor Temmu	"in the South Court" (Ibid., 2: 380)

Though hardly conclusive, the evidence seems to suggest that the South Courtyard was the favored location.

11. Aston, *Nihongi*, 1: 388; NKBT 67: 520–521. In a note, Aston recognized the significance of this entry by noting that the families assigned to the *misazagi* became something of an outcaste group because they were no longer considered among the living. He suggests they may have become part of the *eta* or *hinin* (literally "not human") outcaste group, which included leather workers, renderers, executioners, and so on. On the official census register see NKBT 68: 553 n. 19–4.

12. Readers may well ask how the dates incorporated in the table can be of any use, since the chronology of much of the *Nihonshoki* has long been suspect and a source of great debate among scholars. I am aware of the extent and the complexity of the problems, yet if consulted carefully and with common sense the *Nihonshoki* can be of immense use to historians. It can be used, for example, by limiting one's attention to the later chapters, but it can also be used as is and *in toto* to study the narrative patterns and structures that informed early Japanese historiography. In this study I will draw on both approaches to this most basic of texts for the study of early Japan.

13. Robert Ellwood, "Patriarchal Revolution in Ancient Japan: Episodes from the *Nihonshoki* Sujin Chronicle" (Paper delivered at the Annual Meeting of the American Academy of Religion, Anaheim, California, November 24, 1985).

14. Aston, *Nihongi*, 2: 26; NKBT 68: 48–49.

15. Kikuchi, "Hinkyū girei to niiname," pp. 12–21. This article is of central importance to the argument of this section.

16. Aston, *Nihongi*, 2: 170; NKBT 68: 234–235.

17. Aston, *Nihongi*, 2: 171; NKBT 68: 236–237.

18. Kikuchi, "Hinkyū girei to niiname," p. 19.

19. All regnal dates here are the traditional dates following the *Nihonshoki*. Those from the sixth century on are generally considered to be reliable, whereas earlier dates are suspect. As will become evident for my purposes here, however, the historicity of these dates is not of immediate importance.

20. See Aston, *Nihongi*, 1: 221–223; NKBT 67: 326–329.

21. See Aston, *Nihongi*, 1: 317–318; NKBT 67: 438–441.

22. See Aston, *Nihongi*, 2: 89; NKBT 68: 130–131.

23. Aston, *Nihongi*, 2: 104–105; NKBT 68: 152–153.

24. See Aston, *Nihongi*, 2: 102–104; NKBT 68: 148–153.

25. See Arnold Van Gennep, *The Rites of Passage* (Chicago: University of Chicago Press, 1960). Two modern studies of systems of double burial that draw on Van Gennep's model are Danforth, *The Death Rituals of Rural Greece*, and Huntington and Metcalf, *Celebrations of*

Death. Bloch and Parry in their introductory essay in *Death and the Regeneration of Life* play down Van Gennep's contributions and rely more on the slightly earlier seminal book by Robert Hertz, *Death and the Right Hand*.

26. Sir George Sansom, *A History of Japan to 1334* (Stanford: Stanford University Press, 1958), p. 93.

27. Aston, *Nihongi*, 2: 106; NKBT 68: 154–155.

28. Aston, *Nihongi*, 2: 106–107; NKBT 68: 154–155.

29. Aston, *Nihongi*, 2: 107–108; NKBT 68: 156–157.

30. I almost want to say "reading," but since the period in question here would still have been in the oral stage of Japanese culture, this expression would be inappropriate.

31. Aston, *Nihongi*, 2: 109; NKBT 68: 158–159.

32. Ibid.

33. Aston, *Nihongi*, 2: 109–110; NKBT 68: 158–161.

34. This Prince Hikohito is another figure about whom very little is known. The only other reference to him is in the Bidatsu Chapter, where he is listed as the only son of Bidatsu and his first empress, Hiro-hime, who died in the same year (in the eleventh lunar month!); she was elevated to the rank of empress-consort. Hikohito was later married to his half-sister, a child of Bidatsu and Kashikiya-hime, the Soga daughter who later became the Empress Suiko.

35. Aston, *Nihongi*, 2: 111; NKBT 68: 160–161.

36. Aston, *Nihongi*, 2: 112; NKBT 68: 160–161.

37. Aston, *Nihongi*, 2: 107 n. 8.

38. See the classic study by Yanagita Kunio, "*Imoto no chikara*" ("The Power of the Younger Sister/Wife"), available in the *Teihon Yanagita Kunio shū*, 36 vols. (Tokyo: Chikūma Shobō, 1972–1974, 1977–1979).

39. See Aston, *Nihongi*, 1: 54. There he is called Onamushi no kami, one of his many names. The *Nihonshoki* myths concerning O-kuni-nushi are very abbreviated, indicating no doubt that the Court wished to repress the Izumo mythic/historical tradition.

40. The *Kojiki* version of the O-kuni-nushi myth may be found in Philippi, *Kojiki*, pp. 92–136; NKBT 1: 91–124.

41. Philippi suggests this may be "an underground grotto or tomb" (*Kojiki*, p. 98 n. 6).

42. Ibid., p. 99; NKBT 1: 96–97.

43. Philippi, *Kojiki*, pp. 407–408.

44. Ibid., p. 408.

45. There is, however, an interesting inversion of the Ame-no-waka-hiko myth. Here the arrow is returned to its owner by emerging along with O-kuni-nushi *up* out of the hole. In the Ame-no-waka-hiko myth, the would-be ruler of the land shoots a sacred arrow through the pheasant messenger up to the High Heavens. From there it is thrust back *down* through the hole, striking Ame-no-waka-hiko dead and exposing his claim to the throne as spurious.

46. Philippi, *Kojiki*, pp. 102–103; NKBT 1: 98–99.

47. Ibid., p. 123; NKBT 1: 112–113.

48. Aston, *Nihongi*, 1: 74; NKBT 67: 144–145.

49. Aston, *Nihongi*, 2: 120; NKBT 68: 171.

50. Aston, *Nihongi*, 2: 143; NKBT 68: 196–197. Aston mistakenly gives the date as the twenty-eighth rather than the twentieth. Kitashi-hime was the empress-consort of Kimmei and the mother of both the Emperor Yōmei and the Empress Suiko.

51. For these records see Aston, *Nihongi*, 2: 157–164; NKBT 68: 216–227.

52. See Aston, *Nihongi*, 2: 162; NKBT 68: 224–225.

53. See Aston, *Nihongi*, 2: 177; NKBT 68: 244–245.

54. Levy, *The Ten Thousand Leaves*, p. 123; NKBT 4: 102–103.

55. See Aston, *Nihongi*, 2: 217–220; NKBT 68: 292–295.

56. Aston, *Nihongi*, 2: 220; NKBT 68: 294–295.

57. Aston, *Nihongi*, 2: 219; NKBT 68: 294–295.

58. This fact belies the assertion in the opening passage of the Kōtoku Chapter that this emperor "made not distinction of noble and mean" (*tōtoki iyashiki toerabazu*; Aston, *Nihongi*, 2: 195; NKBT 68: 268–269). Such opening characterizations of the sovereign, found in every chapter of the *Nihonshoki*, are highly stylized and Sinified and need have little in common with the actual idiosyncrasies and personality traits of the individuals in question.

59. See Aston, *Nihongi*, 2: 178; NKBT 68: 244–245.

60. Most notably, mention might be made of Hintermeyer, *Politiques de la mort*, and Alexiou, *The Ritual Lament in Greek Tradition*. The former deals with the attempts to regulate funerary practices following the French Revolution. Alexiou makes some important comments on how the regulation of funeral practices and specifically the banning of female laments in Greek antiquity were designed to take out of the widow's (i.e., female) hands the power to determine the inheritance. On the politics of funeral rituals in the French court, see R. E. Giesey, *The Royal Funeral Ceremony in Renaissance France* (Geneva: Librairie E. Droz, 1960).

61. Aston, *Nihongi*, 2: 232; NKBT 68: 306–307.

62. Aston, *Nihongi*, 2: 274; NKBT 68: 352–353. White mourning garments are also mentioned in MYS 2: 230, a poem dated in 715. See NKBT 4: 28–29; Levy, *The Ten Thousand Leaves*, p. 146.

63. Translation of the verse is from Philippi, *This Wine of Peace*, p. 112; NKBT 68: 350–351.

64. See, for example, the opening pages of the Tenji Chapter in which the majority of entries concern Japan's relationships with the various Korean kingdoms.

65. Aston, *Nihongi*, 2: 371; NKBT 68: 472–473.

66. For this narrative, see Philippi, *Kojiki*, pp. 226–227, and Aston, *Nihongi*, 1: 186–187. The story is also referred to in MYS 18: 4111–4112, a set composed by Ōtomo Yakamochi on, according to the prose endnote, the twenty-third of the fifth lunar month of 749. See NKBT 7: 290–293; for a translation see Nippon Gakujutsu Shinkokai, *The Manyōshū*, pp. 156–157.

67. Aston, *Nihongi*, 2: 373; NKBT 68: 472–473. Aston's translation does not include the date.

68. Cited in Aston, *Nihongi*, 2: 373 n. 2. For a full translation into French, see Hagenauer, "La danse rituelle dans la cérémonie du chinkonsai," pp. 327–328. For more on this ritual, see also Matsumae Takeshi, "The Heavenly Rock-Grotto Myth and the Chinkonsai Ceremony."

69. Ban Nobutomo, *Ban Nobutomo zenshū*, 5 vols. (Tokyo: Kokusho Kankōkai, 1907–1909), 2: 651.

70. See Alan Miller, "*Ame No Miso-Ori Me* (The Heavenly Weaving Maiden)."

71. Aston, *Nihongi*, 1: 133; NKBT 67: 214–215.

72. Aston, *Nihongi*, 2: 376; NKBT 68: 476–477.

73. On Yakushi, see M. W. De Visser, *Ancient Buddhism in Japan*, vol. 1 (Leiden: E. J. Brill, 1935), pp. 18–21, 293–294, passim. Also on Asia in general, see Raoul Birnbaum, *The Healing Buddha* (Boulder, Colo.: Shambhala, 1979).

74. Aston, *Nihongi*, 2: 377; NKBT 68: 478–479.

75. Ibid.

76. Aston, *Nihongi*, 2: 380–381; NKBT 68: 480–483.

77. See Watase Masatada, "Hitomaro hinkyū banka no tōjō: sono uta no ba o megutte," *Kokubungaku: kaishaku to kanshō* 35, no. 7 (July 1970): 32–41, and his *Kakinomoto Hitomaro kenkyū*.

78. Aston, *Nihongi*, 2: 387; NKBT 68: 491–492.

79. Aston, *Nihongi*, 2: 384; NKBT 68: 488–489.

80. Aston, *Nihongi*, 2: 385; NKBT 68: 488–489.

81. Levy, *The Ten Thousand Leaves*, p. 107; NKBT 4: 88–89. I have altered the translation of the headnote to reflect more closely the sense of the original. Levy has "upon the death of the Emperor," which might be taken to suggest the poem immediately followed Temmu's demise. In fact, if the scholarly consensus is correct, the ritual offering was made some six months after the death. In addition, I have translated the poem as if Jitō's words were addressed directly to the spirit of the deceased rather than to an audience of living individuals. Levy's translation of the poem represents a significant step in the right direction, as he graphically represents the words as direct speech. He does not realize, however, that during the period of the *mogari no miya* it was believed that communication with the deceased was possible. Evidence from comparable situations in other cultures that practice double burial demonstrates conclusively that oral laments are often, if indeed not usually, addressed directly to the deceased. In the next chapter we will have occasion to look at several examples of this direct address from contemporary female funeral laments.

82. Cf. Aston, *Nihongi*, 2: 389ff.; NKBT 68: 494ff.

83. Aston, *Nihongi*, 2: 387; NKBT 68: 490–491.

84. Aston, *Nihongi*, 2: 388; NKBT 68: 492–493.

85. Aston, *Nihongi*, 2: 386; NKBT 68: 490–491.

86. The translation is from Levy, *The Ten Thousand Leaves*, p. 112; NKBT 4: 94–95. Levy mistakenly gives the year as 694 rather than 693. The headnote clearly says eight years after Temmu's death, not the eighth year of Jitō's reign. See NKBT 4: 94 n. 1.

87. Aston, *Nihongi*, 2: 413; NKBT 68: 522–523.

88. Aston, *Nihongi*, 2: 386; NKBT 68: 490–491.

89. Aston, *Nihongi*, 2: 388; NKBT 68: 492–493.

90. Aston, *Nihongi*, 2: 391–392; NKBT 68: 496–497.

CHAPTER FOUR

The Poetry of the *Mogari no Miya*

1. The literature suggesting that women in early Japan played certain shamanic roles is voluminous, dating from the huge corpus of Origuchi Shinobu. See the following among many: Hori Ichiro, *Hori Ichiro Chosakushū*, vol. 8 (Tokyo: Miraisha, 1982), pp. 330–343, 367–

413, passim; Kobayashi Yukio et al., eds., *Kami to kami o matsuru mono*; Sakurai Mitsuru, *Man'yōshū no fūdo* (Tokyo: Kodansha, 1977); and especially Yamakami Izumo, *Miko no rekishi* (Tokyo: Yuzankaku Shuppan, 1973).

2. Among the many treatments of MYS 2: 147–155, I have found the following especially useful: Shirakawa, *Shoki Man'yō-ron*, pp. 189–197; Wada, "Mogari no kiso-teki kōsatsu," esp. pp. 46ff.; Yoshinaga, *Man'yō—bungaku to rekishi no aida*, pp. 125ff.; Yukawa, "Tenji banka-gun no ron"; Sakashita Keihachi, "Banka no hōhō: Yamato no ōkisaki no tennō banka," *Kokubungaku: kaishaku to kyōzai no kenkyū* 28, no. 7 (May 1983): 112–116; Itō, *Man'yōshū no kajin to sakuhin*, 1: 12–21; Itō Haku and Hashimoto Tatsuo, eds., *Man'yōshū monogatari* (Tokyo: Yuhikaku Bukkusu, 1977), pp. 57–64; Origuchi, "Nukada-jō," in *Origuchi Shinobu zenshū*, 9: 444–460; and Aoki Takako, *Man'yō banka-ron*, pp. 31–37, 291–293, passim.

3. NKBT 4: 88–89; Levy, *The Ten Thousand Leaves*, p. 106.

4. See NKBT 4: 88–89 n. 5.

5. See Levy, *The Ten Thousand Leaves*, p. 107, where he translates the prose note as, "One book has the *following* poem, presented by the Empress when the Emperor's illness suddenly took a turn for the worse" (emphasis added). The original note does not explicitly indicate that the note refers to the following poem, but I prefer this reading.

6. NKBT 4: 88–89; Levy, ibid.

7. Yukawa, "Tenji banka-gun no ron," p. 90, has pointed out that the entire set has been so ordered that from one verse to the next, time unfolds in a linear sequential progression.

8. NKBT 4: 88–89. I have adapted Levy's translation (*The Ten Thousand Leaves*, p. 107) to approximate more nearly what I take to be the meaning and ritual intention of the verse. I assume it is addressed to the deceased.

9. NKBT 68: 488–489.

10. See NKBT 67: 452–453.

11. NKBT 67: 492–493.

12. NKBT 4: 88–91; Levy, *The Ten Thousand Leaves*, pp. 107–108.

13. Levy, *Hitomaro*, p. 58. The use of this type of hypothetical statement ("If you were a jewel" and "if you were a robe") is not antithetical to a ritual setting, as witness the following lament recorded in rural Greece in the 1970s:

How can a ribbon rot? How can an amulet get covered with cobwebs?
How can a precious carnation from Venice wither and die?
My child, where can I put the *ponos* [pain] I feel for you?
If I toss it by the roadside, those who pass by will take it.
If I throw it in a tree the little birds will take it.
I will place it in my heart so that it will take root there,
so that it will cause me *ponos* as I walk, so that it will kill me as I stand,

I will go to a goldsmith to have it gold-plated.
I will have it made into a golden cross, into a silver amulet,
so that I can worship the cross and kiss the amulet.

Commenting on this lament, Loring Danforth notes: "Here the bereaved mother expresses the view that she must not allow the *ponos* she feels at the death of her child to dissipate. She must nourish her pain, her grief, her sorrow, as long as possible. She must cherish these emotions dearly because it is through them alone that she is able to keep alive the memory of her child" (*The Death Rituals of Rural Greece*, p. 143). The poem MYS 2: 150 must be understood along these lines. The grieving concubine, too, suggests that she must grieve continuously for the deceased emperor, for only then can she hold onto his presence. For more information on *ponos*, see n. 49 below.

14. Sakashita Keihachi, for instance, has argued this point. See his "Banka no hōhō," p. 151.

15. NKBT 4: 90–91; Levy, *The Ten Thousand Leaves*, p. 108. Levy does not include the attributions given for these poems. The reading of the name here is uncertain, so I have followed the suggestion of the NKBT editors. This name appears only one other time in the *Man'yōshū* after MYS 4: 492. Because Levy again ignores the attribution of the verse to this woman, in his presentation it is not clear that this poem was by a woman, presumably the wife or lover of Tabe Ichihiko.

16. NKBT 4: 90–91; Levy, *The Ten Thousand Leaves*, pp. 108–109.

17. Cf. Levy, *Hitomaro*, pp. 60–61.

18. "Introduction: Secular Ritual," in *Secular Ritual*, ed. Sally F. Moore and Barbara G. Myerhoff (Assen/Amsterdam: Van Gorcum, 1977), p. 5.

19. Claude Lévi-Strauss, *Tristes Tropiques* (New York: Atheneum, 1970), p. 231.

20. NKBT 4: 90–91; Levy, *The Ten Thousand Leaves*, p. 109.

21. Ibid.

22. See especially Yoshinaga, "Kentai banka mogari no miya de utawareta mono de nai," chap. 7 of his *Man'yō*, pp. 111–128.

23. NKBT 68: 331–333; Aston, *Nihongi*, 2: 252–253. The purported age of Prince Takeru found in the *Nihonshoki* is not without serious problems, as Itō Haku has pointed out. Takeru's mother was Soga no Miyatsuko-hime, and his father was Naka no Ōe. The *Nihonshoki* reports that Princess Miyatsuko died in 648 of a broken heart after her father was wrongly executed. If Prince Takeru was eight when he died in 658, then the entry concerning Takeru's death would have him dying two years before his birth! Miyatsuko was also the mother of Princess Ōta and the future Empress Jitō. (See Itō, *Man'yōshū no kajin to sakuhin*, 1: 18.)

The empress's implied statement here that she never thought of her eight-year-old grandson as young is not as difficult to appreciate as one might think, if one understands how the pain experienced after the death of a loved one can affect a person. Observing a comparable situation in rural Greece, Danforth notes that *ponos* ("pain" or "grief")

prevents the full acceptance of death and leads those in mourning to believe that a return from the world of the dead is possible. Because of this complex of emotions a situation devoid of hope is transformed into a situation with hope. People are led to take literally, for a time at least, the metaphors of death as marriage and death as *xenitia* ["exile"]. *Ponos* makes one treat the deceased as if he were still alive. If a woman feels *ponos* and *kamoudhia*, then she will deny that the time and money she spends caring for the grave of the deceased are in vain. By creating hope, these emotions also change one's perceptions of the world. For example, people repeatedly told a woman who had spent a great deal of money on a very elaborate funeral for her eighty-year-old father that since he had been so old she should not have spent so much money. Invariably she replied: "He may have seemed old to you, but to me, because of the *ponos* I feel, he was not old." (*The Death Rituals of Rural Greece*, p. 142)

Might one not plausibly imagine this lament by the grieving empress as a retort to those in the court who told her that her grief was excessive for such a young prince? We know that others felt free to criticize her for presumed excesses on other scores. (See, for instance, the entry for 11/3/658 in NKBT 68: 334; Aston, *Nihongi*, 2: 225.)

24. NKBT 68: 333–335; Aston, *Nihongi*, 2: 255. I have slightly altered Aston's translation of the poems and have followed the NKBT editors in separating the second and third songs.

25. See NKBT 68: 330–331; Aston, *Nihongi*, 2: 251. There are several poems in the *Man'yōshū* that some scholars, on the basis of the prose headnotes, have suggested come from this imperial journey to the hot springs of Ki. See MYS 1: 9–12 and 9: 1665–1666. If this supposition is correct, these poems would be by members of the imperial entourage. Takagi Hiroshi says that the strong sense of this journey having been a pleasure outing indicates that no one in the court was aware of the events that would lead to the execution of Prince Arima within a week or so. See his *Man'yō kyūtei no aikan*, esp. pp. 158–184 on Prince Arima.

26. Cf. Akima Toshio, "Shisa no uta: Saimei tennō no kayō to asobi-be," *Bungaku* 40, no. 3 (March 1972): 97–112, and "Songs of the Dead: Poetry, Drama, and Ancient Death Rituals of Japan," *Journal of Asian Studies* 41 (May 1982): 485–509.

27. Akima, "Songs of the Dead," pp. 485 and 486.

28. See "Greek Funeral Laments and *Banka*" in the text.

29. Akima has also arrived at this conclusion, writing: "I am now convinced . . . that the words *wakaki ko* (young child) were, as part of the original songs of the dead, an adaptable element that could be altered as the case demanded, changed, for instance, to *hashizume* (my love)." Akima, "Songs of the Dead," p. 490.

30. Ibid.

31. Ibid., p. 489.

32. For Philippi's translation of these poems, see *This Wine of Peace*, pp. 109–110.

33. Danforth, *The Death Rituals of Rural Greece*, p. 86.

34. The study of different forms of conversations with absent others has only recently received serious scholarly attention. Cf. Mary M. Watkins, *Invisible Guests: The Development of Imaginal Dialogues* (Hillsdale, N.J.: Analytic Press, 1986), where some of the therapeutic aspects of imaginal dialogues are studied.

Conversations with the dead are quite common in oral laments in various cultures. Note, for example, the following oral lament from the Kaluli, a New Guinea tribe, and the comments on it by an anthropologist who did extensive fieldwork among them.

hill at Tolɔ creek
my father
O

hill at Tolɔ creek
my father
E

Father, where are you going?
Father, where are you going?

I'm going to the hill at Tolɔ creek,
I'm going to the fruited *odag* tree there
O

I'm going to the hill at Tolɔ creek,
I'm going to the fruited *odag* tree there,
E

[The ethnographer who recorded this lament comments:] Kaluli always assume that a song is constructed in the first person as a personal statement referring to the thoughts and feelings of the singer or of a spirit. . . . Here the singer laments the loss of his father by suggesting that he has gone to the hill at Tolɔ creek. The singer assumes that if he names the hill above Tolɔ creek, listeners will know that this local hill is the site of an *odag* tree. It is "inside the words" that the father, as a bird, is in the *odag* tree. From this impregnated phrase, the singer shifts to rhetorical questioning of the father. . . . Then . . . the singer shifts from his own first-person stating and questioning and supplies the response of the father. The line is in the first-person present ("I'm going to. . . ."), but it is now the spirit who is speaking and not the singer. [Steven Feld, *Sound and Sentiment: Birds, Weeping, Poetics, and Song in Kaluli Expression* (Philadelphia: University of Pennsylvania Press, 1982), pp. 141–142]

35. NKBT 68: 310–311; Aston, *Nihongi*, 2: 235. The translations of the poems are mine.

36. There does not seem to have been anything like these communal ossuaries in early Japan, although the *Nihonshoki* contains several references to individuals being given final burial together, including the case of the Empress Saimei and her grandson that we saw earlier. J. Edward Kidder has noted the great variety of burial practices found in the Jomon, Yayoi, and Tumulus periods, including interment of corpses in urns, burial jars, hollowed-out logs, cists, and tumuli. See his *Japan Before Buddhism*, pp. 104–110, 149ff., passim.

37. Caraveli-Chaves, "Bridge Between Worlds," p. 143. Danforth suggests that "laments constitute a public language, a cultural code, for the expression of grief. They provide the bereaved with a set of shared symbols, what Lévi-Strauss has called a social myth, which

enables them not only to organize their experience of death in a culturally meaningful way but also to articulate it in a socially approved manner. Women singing laments are communicating in a symbolic language and in the context of a public performance" (*The Death Rituals of Rural Greece*, pp. 73–74).

38. Caraveli-Chaves, "Bridge Between Worlds," p. 147.

39. Geertz, "Religion as a Cultural System," in his *The Interpretation of Cultures*, p. 119.

40. Danforth, *The Death Rituals of Rural Greece*, pp. 140–141.

41. Ibid., p. 140.

42. NKBT 4: 114–117. I have slightly adapted Levy's translation (*The Ten Thousand Leaves*, pp. 133–135) in several places. For the sake of consistency I have changed "catalpa twig" (*tamazusa*) in line 19 of the translation to "catalpa staff," as the term is rendered by Levy in the second envoy; similarly I have corrected "scarlet leaves" (*momichi*) in line 34 to "yellow leaves," as correctly suggested by Levy in the envoy. In addition, I have included the editorial notes on variants that Levy does not acknowledge either in his translation or in footnotes.

A translator faces something of a dilemma in rendering terms such as *imo* and *wagimoko* here. [Cf. the comments of Eric Rutledge on this point and problems with Levy's attempts in "The *Man'yōshū* in English," *Harvard Journal for Asiatic Studies* 43 (June 1983): 284; and Cranston, "A Ramifying Vein" p. 137.] As employed here, these terms are obviously terms of endearment and intimacy. Levy's "my girl" (line 26) is hardly appropriate, and the phrase "my wife," which he employs elsewhere, is perhaps too impersonal and emotionally distanced. Something like "you, my love" is preferable here. Once again I have understood these *banka* as spoken to the absent partner.

For some reason Levy finds the opening epithet, *ama tobu ya*, untranslatable (see Levy, ibid., p. 133 n. 5). This set phrase, however, seems to me to add significantly to the lament by supplying an implicit bitter irony. First, as Levy notes, there is a pun on the place name, Karu—"light" or "buoyant"—but this *makurakotoba* also recalls the emotional state of the young Hitomaro as he used to travel the Karu road to meet his lover. The bitter irony is that after the death of his wife, when this *banka* was sung, everything had changed. On the same road his heart was now heavy and "tears of blood fell," an inversion of both his earlier emotions and the superficial semantic content of the *makurakotoba* of the place. The irony of the situation, though, immediately parallels the case of Yamato-takeru reported in the *Kojiki* where he, too, dreamed of flying through the sky and returning to a lover, only to find himself fatally wounded instead and merely able to drag himself along on weak legs.

Although I have retained Levy's translation in the main text, I am not entirely satisfied with it, nor do I believe it is the only reading possible. I would translate the lines after the first grammatical caesura based on the assumption that the voice of the deceased was conveyed through the medium of the catalpa bow. Another *banka* (MYS 2: 217) attributed to Hitomaro on "the death of the *uneme* [maiden] of Kibi in Tsu" includes the following lines, which may also refer to a failed ritual attempt to call the spirit of the dead back:

azusayumi	even I who hear the sound
oto kiku ware mo	of the catalpa bow
obo ni mishi	saw her but faintly—
koto kuyashi o	what a lamentable fact!

43. NKBT 4: 118–119; Levy, *The Ten Thousand Leaves*, pp. 136–137, adapted.

44. Levy, *Hitomaro*, p. 165.

45. NKBT 4: 120–121; Levy, *The Ten Thousand Leaves*, p. 138.

46. Danforth, *The Death Rituals of Rural Greece*, p. 65.

47. Levy, *Hitomaro*, p. 164.

48. Ibid., p. 165.

49. Once again fieldwork studies provide invaluable insight into the emotional reasons and forces behind the offering of laments. Danforth's presentation of the full existential meaning of *ponos* is especially apropos here:

In order to understand the manner in which the original social reality of the bereaved [with the deceased] is maintained, and the process by which a new reality is constructed and death finally accepted, it is necessary to consider why women in mourning engage so intensely and for so long in their social relationships with the dead. The answer given most frequently by the bereaved women of Potamia as to why they visit the graveyard every day for five years is, "The pain pulls me" [*Me travai o ponos*]. The concept of *ponos* (plural, *poni*), which can be glossed as pain, grief, suffering, or sorrow, is essential to an appreciation of the emotional experience of women in mourning in rural Greece. All the care and attention that women devote to their dead relatives is motivated by *ponos*, or *kamoudhia*, another term used in this context, which is a local variant of the standard term *kaimos*, meaning anguish, sorrow, yearning, or pained longing. Women go to the graveyard because they have *ponos*, because they have *kamoudhia*. Without these emotions, they say, they would not go anywhere. Even if the women do not really want to go to the graveyard, the *ponos* they feel for the dead forces them to go. (*The Death Rituals of Rural Greece*, p. 141)

Ponos and *kamoudhia*, then, appear to be very close equivalents of the Man'yō term *koi*, love and longing. One recalls Hitomaro's explanation of why he found himself in the marketplace his deceased wife used to frequent: "I did not know what to say/ what to do/ but simply could not listen/ and so, perhaps to solace/ a single thousandth/ of my thousand-fold longing/ I stood at the Karu market/ where often you, love, had gone/ . . . I could do nothing/ but call your name." As one ponders the close similarities of the Man'yō *banka* and the Greek laments, the following passage from Danforth is important:

It is the *ponos* one feels at a person's death that makes one deny the finality of death and cling to the hope that death is, like the departure at marriage or the departure for *xenitia* [foreign or distant lands], a departure from which a return is possible. . . . It is this *ponos*, then, that maintains the religious perspective toward death and enables the conversation with the deceased to continue. . . . *Ponos* makes one treat the deceased as if he were still alive. (Ibid., p. 142)

50. My interpretation of these and the following poems by the *toneri* are based on reading *Man'yōshū* scholarship in Japanese over the past few years. As far as I know, only Levy has

treated any of these poems in English. See his *Hitomaro*, pp. 161–165. Among the Japanese sources mention might be made of Aoki Takako, *Man'yō banka-ron*, pp. 101–108; Yoshii Iwao, "Toneri no naki," *Kokubungaku: kaishaku to kanshō* 35, no. 7 (July 1970): 57–65; Yoshinaga, *Man'yō*, pp. 85–95; Sakurai, *Kakinomoto Hitomaro-ron*, pp. 44–50; Watase, "Hitomaro hinkyū banka no tōjō," pp. 32–41, and *Kakinomoto Hitomaro kenkyū*, 3: 117–134; Takagi Hiroshi, *Man'yō kyūtei no aikan*, pp. 250–255; Toyama Ichiro, "Hinamishi mikoto banka ni okeru Tenji tennō no keishō," *Kokugo kokubun* 55, no. 5 (May 1986): 36–51; and Hirayakata Hideko, "Shima no miya no tonerira banka no kōsei," *Man'yō* 116 (December 1983): 31–45.

51. *Sasutake no*, "luxuriant" or "lushly growing bamboo," is a *makurakotoba* that suggests that the prince brought prosperity to the land.

52. NKBT 4: 96–99. I have adapted Levy's translation here. See *The Ten Thousand Leaves*, pp. 114–116. I have once again translated the *chōka* as spoken directly to the deceased. The envoys, however, seem to express collective emotions, leading me to change Levy's "I's" to "we" in each case. He does not acknowledge any of the variants.

53. See Watase, *Kakinomoto Hitomaro kenkyū*, 3: 115ff.

54. See Yamamoto, *Kakinomoto no Hitomaro*, pp. 208–225.

55. Levy's translation of this *chōka* seems to go astray as a result of confusion caused by the ambiguous referents here. In his rendering, all the actions in the opening section are taken to be performed by the myriad *kami*—they push apart the eightfold clouds—something that clearly runs counter to both the underlying myth and the grammar of the Japanese. Once he has begun in this vein, though, Levy is led into some forced and awkward translations such as "sent down to us" for *kamukudari* rather than "descended god-like." Levy's initial decisions meant that he could not accommodate the subject, *kami no mikoto*, and so it seems he ignored it.

56. Yamamoto, *Kakinomoto no Hitomaro*, p. 214.

57. See MYS 1: 29, 2: 162, 3: 443, and so forth.

58. The following example was recorded by Danforth: "Nikos, what pain you have caused us. You poisoned our hearts" (*The Death Rituals of Rural Greece*, p. 12).

59. Aston, *Nihongi*, 2: 391; NKBT 68: 495.

60. NKBT 4: 98–99; Levy, *The Ten Thousand Leaves*, p. 116, slightly adapted.

61. Birds frequently function as intermediaries in this way in Greek laments as well. See, for instance, Danforth, *The Death Rituals of Rural Greece*, pp. 112–115, passim, and Michael Herzfeld, "Ritual and Textual Structures: The Advent of Spring in Rural Greece," in *Text and Context: The Social Anthropology of Tradition*, ed. Ravindra Jain. Association of Social Anthropologists Essays in Social Anthropology, vol. 2 (Philadelphia: Institute for the Study of Human Issues, 1977), pp. 29–50, for the symbol of the swallow in rites of transition and exorcism, for example.

62. See Caraveli-Chaves, "Bridge Between Worlds."

63. NKBT 4: 98–103. For Levy's translations from which these are adapted, see *The Ten Thousand Leaves*, pp. 116–122.

64. NKBT 68: 230–231; Aston, *Nihongi*, 2: 167.

65. Alexiou reports that "The *próthesis* [wake] was a formal affair, with a large number of people grouped around the bier in more or less set positions. Lamentation at the tomb on the other hand was at once more restricted and more personal, involving the direct communication between the relatives and the dead" (*The Ritual Lament in Greek Tradition*, p. 8).

66. Ibid., p. 134.

67. Caraveli-Chaves, for example, notes: "Successful couplets or entire songs composed [more properly "orally generated"] by various village people, some dead now, are remembered and circulated orally in one or several villages. Even individual lines, considered particularly successful because of their poetic merit, are singled out, discussed, sung, and at times consciously used for new compositions" ("Bridge Between Worlds," p. 131).

68. The internal structure of this set of *banka* has occasioned considerable discussion and controversy over the years. I cannot enter into this subject here, but for two of the more recent examples, see Watase, *Kakinomoto Hitomaro kenkyū*, 3: 154–182; and Hirayakata, "Shima no miya no tonerira banka no kōsei," pp. 31–45. Watase's three-volume work is the most detailed study, with the most sustained argument, of Hitomaro's corpus that I know. His views are forcefully presented and cogently argued, challenging many of the standard interpretations that have long held sway in Man'yō studies. As might be expected, they have not been universally accepted. For one reaction, see the review by Nakagawa Yukihiro, "Butsuzō to busshiki saikai to: Watase Masatada-shi *Kakinomoto Hitomaro kenkyū: Shima no miya no bungaku o yomu*," *Man'yō* 101 (July 1979): 37–46.

69. This pattern is also not the only discernible one. For another possibility, see Hirayakata, "Shima no miya no tonerira banka no kōsei," p. 43, for a chart outlining an alternative structural pattern.

70. Watase, *Kakinomoto Hitomaro kenkyū*, pp. 90ff.

CHAPTER FIVE
Mythistory, Rhetoric, and the Politics of Marriage

1. It is in this light that many passages in the *Nihonshoki* must be read. Cf. the entries following the death of the Emperor Tenji; NKBT 68: 382ff.; Aston, *Nihongi*, 2: 300ff.

2. A useful introduction to this topic is Inoue Tatsuo, *Kodai ōken to kataribe* (Tokyo: Kyōikusha, 1979).

3. Levy, *Hitomaro*, p. 14.

4. NKBT 68: 196–197; Aston, *Nihongi*, 2: 142–143. See also Philippi, *This Wine of Peace*, p. 76. The translation of these verses is my own, adapted from those above.

5. Similar forms of rhetorical praise proclaiming a "mythistory" are found in other hierarchical societies as well. For a few examples out of many one might cite, see Donald Lawrence Brenneis and Fred R. Myers, eds., *Dangerous Words: Language and Politics in the Pacific* (New York: New York University Press, 1984); Maurice Bloch, ed., *Political Language and Oratory in Traditional Society* (New York: Academic Press, 1975); Sabine G. MacCormack, *Art and Ceremony in Late Antiquity* (Berkeley: University of California Press, 1981); and John Charlot, *The Hawaiian Poetry of Religion and Politics: Some Religio-Political Concepts in Postcontact Literature*, Institute for Polynesian Studies Monograph No. 5 (Laie: University of Hawaii Press, 1985).

6. NKBT 68: 236–237; Aston, *Nihongi*, 2: 171.

7. See NKBT 68: 244–245; Philippi, *This Wine of Peace*, p. 175. For Aston's translation, see Aston, *Nihongi*, 2: 178. For more background on this period and this ritual dance, see Takagi Hiroshi, *Man'yō kyūtei no aikan*, pp. 57ff.

8. NKBT 68: 294; Aston, *Nihongi*, 2: 181.

9. NKBT 68: 254–255; Aston, *Nihongi*, 2: 185.

10. NKBT 68: 259–261; Aston, *Nihongi*, 2: 189–190, adapted. The names of the two houses on the Amakashi Hill suggest the hierarchical relationship of the father and son, but they may also allude to Taoist *ying-yang* theory concerning political rule with the conjunction of high and low, peak and valley.

11. See NKBT 68: 278–279; Aston, *Nihongi*, 2: 204.

12. NKBT 68: 277–279; Aston, *Nihongi*, 2: 204.

13. For more on the Fujiwara, see Joseph M. Kitagawa, "The Shadow of the Sun: A Glimpse of the Fujiwara and the Imperial Families in Japan," in his *On Understanding Japanese Religion* (Princeton: Princeton University Press, 1987), pp. 98–116.

14. NKBT 68: 306–307; Aston, *Nihongi*, 2: 232.

15. NKBT 68: 314–315; Aston, *Nihongi*, 2: 238.

16. NKBT 68: 320–321; Aston, *Nihongi*, 2: 245, adapted.

17. Yoshinaga, *Man'yō—bungaku to rekishi no aida*, p. 8.

18. See NKBT 68: 367; Aston, *Nihongi*, 2: 287.

19. NKBT 68: 362–363; Aston, *Nihongi*, 2: 283.

20. NKBT 4: 16–17; Levy, *The Ten Thousand Leaves*, p. 44. The absence of any title of rank may be the result of scribal oversight, but that hardly seems likely. A more intriguing possibility, which I have seen no one address, may be that Naka no Ōe temporarily fell out of imperial favor at some point. The *Nihonshoki* insinuates that the Empress Kōgyoku was caught by surprise when Naka no Ōe had Soga no Iruka murdered in her presence, which would indicate that he did not always confide in her. Then, too, the compilers of the *Man'yōshū* may have been embarrassed by the suggestion of an incestuous relation and thus tried to put a little distance between the Temmu-Jitō line and Tenji.

21. NKBT 4: 16–17; Levy, *The Ten Thousand Leaves*, p. 43, headnote slightly adapted. Kitagawa rightly notes that various "imperial consorts of early Japan were given the title *na-katsu-sumera-mikoto*, which could mean either 'the one who carries on the imperial duty between the death of her husband and the accession of the next emperor' or 'the august medium who transmits the *mikoto* (divine word) of the heavenly *kami*' " [*Religion in Japanese History* (New York: Columbia University Press, 1966), p. 22; see also *On Understanding Japanese Religion*, p. 101]. He notes that "Both interpretations of this title are plausible, and one and the same woman can combine both functions" (*Religion in Japanese History*, p. 22 n. 45). The original Chinese characters or *man'yogana* used in MYS 1: 10 are visually suggestive of additional encoded meaning. For instance, the character for "mother" is used for the phonetic value "mo" of the opening phrase, perhaps alluding to Naka no Oe's maternal line. The characters used in the place name "Iwashiro" literally mean something like "rock of ages" or "reign (as long as) the rocks," and thus contain the wished-for goal of the political machinations of Naka no Oe and Hashibito. Finally, the two characters read as "iza" in the last line have as their semantic meaning "the past and the future." Thus, the last part of this verse may be visually appropriated to mean "May the past and the future be bound together (as we bind this grass)." A growing number of Japanese scholars have argued that greater attention needs to be paid to the specific characters employed in many such instances in the *Man'yōshū*. Although I have not been able to do so here, it is clear that future studies would profit from adopting this focus. It would open up yet other fascinating aspects of the interplay of orality and literacy, the ideological dimensions of writing/reading, and the transactional creation of meaning therein.

22. NKBT 4: 16–19. The translation is adapted from Levy, *The Ten Thousand Leaves*, pp. 44–45, but as will become clear, my reading differs significantly from his. For a brief critique of Levy's rendering, see Cranston, "The Ramifying Vein," pp. 116–119. Cranston's reading is very much along the lines I am suggesting.

23. See Omodaka Hisakata, *Man'yōshū chūshaku*, vol. 1 (Tokyo: Chūō Kōronsha, 1957), pp. 138–148, for an overview of the different arguments. Among the many modern pieces that address this set, I have used the following: Yoshinaga, *Man'yō—bungaku to rekishi no aida*; Itō, *Man'yōshū no kajin to sakuhin*, 1: 184–190; Takagi Hiroshi, *Man'yō kyūtei no aikan*; and Sakurai, *Man'yōshū no fūdo*. The *Nihon koten bungaku taikei* does not acknowledge any possible political allegories here, but the other major modern annotated collection of classical Japa-

nese literature, Akiyama Ken et al., eds., *Nihon koten bungaku zenshū* (NKBZ) (Tokyo: Shōga-kukan, 1973–1976), does, as do almost all modern secondary studies. See NKBZ 1: 71.

24. Cf. NKBT 4: 17 n. 15.

25. Michel Foucault, *La volonté de savoir* (London: Lane, 1978), p. 123. This idea is very similar to Pierre Bourdieu's understanding of power. At one place Bourdieu writes that "This means that symbolic power does not lie in 'symbol systems' in the form of an 'illocutionary force' but that it is defined in and by a determinate relationship between those who exercise power and those who undergo it, i.e., in the very structure of the field within which belief is produced and reproduced" ["Symbolic Power," *Critique of Anthropology* 4, nos. 3–4 (Summer 1979): 83].

26. The textual references to Prince Ōtsu have occasioned a large number of studies in Japanese. I have consulted Aoki Takako, *Man'yō banka-ron*, pp. 336–340, passim; Kamihori Shinobu, "Ōku no himemiko to Ōtsu no mikoto," *Man'yō* 54 (January 1965): 13–29; Naoki Kojiro, *Jitō tennō* (Tokyo: Yoshikawa Kōbunkan, 1960); Sakurai, *Man'yōshū no fūdo*, pp. 61–74; Takagi Hiroshi, *Man'yō kyūtei no aikan*, pp. 186ff.; and Yoshida Yoshitaka, "Ōtsu ōji-ron—Temmu-chō no seisō to *kudeta* ni kanren shite," *Bungaku* 40, no. 9 (September 1972): 19–40.

27. NKBT 68: 480–481; Aston, *Nihongi*, 2: 380.

28. NKBT 68: 486–487; Aston, *Nihongi*, 2: 383–384.

29. Other related edicts that indicate the extent to which the emperor sought to control everything in the court from style, color of dress, and hair styles to funeral practices and the etiquette of daily social intercourse include the entries for 10/13/679, 3/25/680, 4/3/681, 5/11/681, 9/9/681, 3/28/682, 8/22/682, 9/2/682, and 12/3/682. Such elements are not "minor details" or mere curiosities, however, but rather the expressions of what in another, yet similar, connection Elias described as "a type of [socio-political] organization by which each act received a prestige-character symbolizing the distribution of power at the time" (*The Court Society*, p. 84). The entry for 4/3/681, for instance, reads:

3rd day. A prohibitory law in 92 articles was established, and was accordingly promulgated with the following words:—"The costumes of all from the princes of the Blood down to the common people, and the wearing of gold and silver, pearls and jewels, purple, brocade, embroidery, fine silks, together with woolen carpets, head-dresses and girdles, as well as all kinds of coloured stuffs, are regulated according to a scale the details of which are given in the written edict." (NKBT 68: 446–447; Aston, *Nihongi*, 2: 350)

That for 5/11 of the same year reads:

Worship was paid to the august spirit [*mi-tama*] of the imperial ancestors. On this day the Emperor issued a decree, saying:—"The deference paid by public functionaries to the [female] Palace officials is far too great. Sometimes they go to their doors and address their plaints to them, sometimes they pay court to their houses [*ie*] by offerings of presents. If there should be any such cases in future, the offenders will be punished according to circumstances." (NKBT 68: 446–447; Aston, *Nihongi*, 2: 351, adapted)

What the emperor could not abide was the fact that others within the palace besides himself were seen as—and thus, no doubt, were—competing loci of power and the dispensation of prestige and favor. Once again it is specifically the women who are singled out for criticism.

30. For an interpretation of the spatio-temporal significance of Yoshino in the Temmu–Jitō period, see Iwashita Takehiko, "Hitomaro no Yoshino sanka shiron," *Kokugo to kokubungaku* 59, no. 11 (November 1982): 42–51; Ōhama, "Jitō tennō wa naze Yoshino e itta ka?" pp. 60–64; Ueno Satoshi, "Hitomaro no Yoshino sanka no kōsō to hyōgen," *Kokubungaku kenkyū* 74 (June 1981): 1–12; Yoshida Yoshitaka, "Yoshino sanka to Jitō chō," *Kokubungaku: kaishaku to kyozai no kenkyū* 28, no. 7 (May 1983): 122–127; and Shirakawa, *Shoki Man'yō-ron*, pp. 113ff.

31. NKBT 68: 434–437; Aston, *Nihongi*, 2: 341–342.

32. Aston erroneously has this entry under the first month. See NKBT 68: 444–445; Aston, *Nihongi*, 2: 349–350.

33. The only exception to this statement is the entry for 11/16/680 where it is mentioned that Crown Prince Kusakabe was sent to make a ceremonial call on a Buddhist priest who had fallen seriously ill.

34. NKBT 68: 457; Aston, *Nihongi*, 2: 359.

35. See the entry for 1/21/685 in NKBT 68: 467–469; Aston, *Nihongi*, 2: 368.

36. NKBT 68: 479; Aston, *Nihongi*, 2: 378.

37. NKBT 4: 70–73; Levy, *The Ten Thousand Leaves*, pp. 89–90, adapted. It seems to me that Levy has especially misunderstood the last poem.

38. NKBT 4: 78–79; Levy, *The Ten Thousand Leaves*, p. 97. Lady Ishikawa apparently entered the service of the imperial family as a child of about thirteen, following the system whereby families and clans were required to provide daughters for such purposes. Such women often served as concubines, although they commonly had multiple liaisons. If the *Man'yōshū* is any guide to these matters, in her life Lady Ishikawa had relations with two Emperors (Tenji and Temmu), several princes (Ōtsu, Kusakabe, and Yuge), several high-ranking Buddhist priests, and a number of high-ranking courtiers. Such women were also the centers of literary salons and seem to have generated and preserved many *uta monogatari*. The socio-political and literary world of the women in the early Japanese court deserves much more study by Western scholars.

39. MYS 2: 126 presents the picture of Lady Ishikawa taking the lead in attempting to seduce a young courtier. See NKBT 4: 76–79; Levy, *The Ten Thousand Leaves*, pp. 95–96. The prose endnote is so stylized that it is difficult to accept its contextualization as historical fact. Lady Ishikawa herself seems to have become a figure in *uta monogatari*.

40. Sahlins, *Islands of History*, p. xiv.

41. NKBT 4: 70–71. Levy's translation, *The Ten Thousand Leaves*, p. 89, mistakenly gives "twilight" rather than "dawn" for *akatoki*. Consequently his translation misses the fact that the poem refers to an all-night ritual vigil of the sort found in the "Four poems by the Empress Iwanohime, thinking of the Emperor [Nintoku]" (MYS 2: 85–89). Earlier I argued that these *uta* should be understood as *banka*.

42. Ibid.

43. Wada Shigeki, "Mogari no kiso-teki kōsatsu."

44. Sahlins, *Islands of History*, p. xiii.

45. NKBT 4: 198–201; Levy, *The Ten Thousand Leaves*, p. 212, slightly adapted.

46. The poem (*shih*) in Chinese on this occasion survives in the *Kaifūsō*, compiled in 751. As rendered by Burton Watson, it reads:

The Golden crow lights on the western huts;
evening drums beat out the shortness of life.
There are no inns on the road to the grave—
whose is the house I go to tonight?

        [*Japanese Literature in Chinese*, vol. 1 (New York: Columbia University Press, 1975), p. 18]

Watson notes that "the golden crow" is a conventional term for the sun. Here the symbol of the sun setting suggests the approaching end of Ōtsu's dynastic hopes.

47. NKBT 4: 94–97; Levy, *The Ten Thousand Leaves*, pp. 113–114, adapted.

48. NKBT 4: 92–95; my translation. See also Levy, *The Ten Thousand Leaves*, p. 111. Levy mistranslates this verse because of his failure to understand that this *banka*, like most, is spoken directly to the dead who is experienced as present in spirit. On this point, see Rutledge, "The *Man'yōshū* in English," pp. 281–282.

49. NKBT 4: 98–99.

50. This section is adapted from an earlier article in which I treated this sequence. See "The Religio-Aesthetic Complex in *Manyōshū* Poetry."

51. NKBT 4: 32–35; my translation adapted from Levy, *The Ten Thousand Leaves*, pp. 61–62, and from Edwin Cranston's, in "Five Poetic Sequences from the *Man'yōshū*," *Journal of the Association of Teachers of Japanese* 13 (1978): 5–40. I take the poems to refer specifically to Karu no miko, not to the others in attendance on him. In the *daijō-sai*, it is the soon-to-be sovereign who must remain awake all night. This interpretation militates against acceptance of Cranston's pluralizing of the subject, "*tabibito*," in verse 46.

52. NKBT 68: 492–493; Aston, *Nihongi*, 2: 388–389.

53. Cranston, "Five Poetic Sequences from the *Man'yōshū*," p. 29.

54. Ibid., p. 30.

55. See Shirakawa, *Shoku Man'yō-ron*, pp. 69–112.

56. Cranston, "Five Poetic Sequences from the *Man'yōshū*," pp. 31–32.

57. See Mori Asao, "Kakinomoto Hitomaro no jikan to saishiki—Aki no jūryō uta o megutte," in *Kanshō Nihon koten bungaku*, ed. Nakanishi Susumu, vol. 3: *Man'yōshū* (Tokyo: Kadokawa Shoten, 1976), pp. 357–365; Shirakawa, *Shoki Man'yō-ron*; Nagafuji Yasushi, *Kodai Nihon bungaku to jikan-ishiki* (Tokyo: Miraisha, 1980), pp. 82–93; and Kikuchi Takeo, "Banka to shinwa: Aki no no no uta o megutte," *Kokubungaku kenkyū* 85, no. 3 (March 1985): 20–28.

58. Mori, "Kakinomoto Hitomaro no jikan to saishiki," p. 361.

59. Ellwood, *The Feast of Kingship*, p. 43.

CONCLUSION
Imagining History

1. Sahlins, *Islands of History*, p. 144.

2. For a recent overview of this subject nexus, see David I. Kertzer, *Ritual, Politics, and Power* (New Haven: Yale University Press, 1988).

3. Sahlins, *Islands of History*, p. xiv.

4. Sahlins notes in a wry phrase that "there is no such thing as an immaculate perception" (ibid., p. 146).

5. Clifford Geertz, *Negara: The Theatre State of Nineteenth-Century Bali* (Princeton: Princeton University Press, 1980), p. 136.

Bibliography

Akamatsu Ken. "The Significance of the Formation and Distribution of Kofun." *Acta Asiatica* 31 (1977): 24–50.

Akima Toshio, "Shisa no uta: Saimei tennō no kayō to asobi-be." *Bungaku* 40, no. 3 (March 1972): 97–112.

———. "Songs of the Dead: Poetry, Drama, and Ancient Death Rituals of Japan." *Journal of Asian Studies* 41 (May 1982): 485–509.

Akiyama Ken et al., eds. *Nihon koten bungaku zenshū.* 51 vols. Tokyo: Shōgakukan, 1973–1976.

Alexiou, Margaret. *The Ritual Lament in Greek Tradition.* London: Cambridge University Press, 1974.

Ando Nobuhiro. "Chinkon no sōbō." *Nihon bungaku* 31, no. 4 (April 1982): 48–49.

Anzu Sunahiko. "Kami to mikoto." *Kokugakuin zasshi* 59, nos. 10–11 (October–November 1958): 8–18.

Aoki, Michiko Yamaguchi, trans. *Izumo Fudoki.* Tokyo: Sophia University, 1971.

Aoki Takako. "Banka no jitsuyōsei to bungakusei." *Kokubungaku: kaishaku to kanshō* 35, no. 7 (July 1970): 84–91.

———. *Man'yō banka-ron.* Tokyo: Hanawa Shobō, 1984.

Aston, W. G., trans. *Nihongi: Chronicles of Japan from the Earliest Times to A.D. 697.* Rutland, Vt., and Tokyo: Charles E. Tuttle Co., 1972.

Ban Nobutomo. *Ban Nobutomo zenshū.* 5 vols. Tokyo: Kokusho Kankōkai, 1907–1909.

Barthes, Roland. "Historical Discourse." In *Introduction to Structuralism*, edited by Michael Lane. New York: Basic Books, 1970.

Basso, Keith H. " 'Stalking with Stories': Names, Places, and Moral Narratives among the Western Appache." In *Text, Play, and Story: The Construction and Reconstruction of Self and Society*, edited by Edward M. Bruner. Washington, D.C.: American Ethnological Society, 1985.

Bauman, Richard. *Verbal Art as Performance.* Rowley, Mass.: Newbury House Publishers, 1977.

Beasley, W. G., and E. G. Pulleyblank, eds. *Historians of China and Japan.* London: Oxford University Press, 1961.

Beidelman, T. O. "Myth, Legend and Oral History." *Anthropos* 65 (1970): 74–97.

Bender, Ross. "The Hachiman Cult and the Dōkyō Incident." *Monumenta Nipponica* 34, no. 1 (Spring 1979): 125–153.

Berger, Peter L., and Thomas Luckmann. *The Social Construction of Reality: A Treatise in the Sociology of Knowledge.* Garden City, N.Y.: Doubleday and Co., 1966.

319

Bloch, Maurice, ed. *Political Language and Oratory in Traditional Society*. New York: Academic Press, 1975.

————, and Jonathan Parry, eds. *Death and the Regeneration of Life*. Cambridge: Cambridge University Press, 1982.

Bloch, R. Howard, *Etymologies and Genealogies: A Literary Anthropology of the French Middle Ages*. Chicago: University of Chicago Press, 1983.

Bock, Felicia G. "The Rites of Renewal at Ise." *Monumenta Nipponica* 29, no. 1 (1974): 55–68.

————, trans. *Engi-shiki: Procedures of the Engi Era*. Tokyo: Sophia University, 1972.

Bourdieu, Pierre. *Outline of a Theory of Practice*. Cambridge Studies in Social Anthropology, no. 16. Cambridge: Cambridge University Press, 1977.

————. "Symbolic Power." *Critique of Anthropology* 4, nos. 3–4 (Summer 1979): 77–85.

Brenneis, Donald Lawrence, and Fred R. Myers, eds. *Dangerous Words: Language and Politics in the Pacific*. New York: New York University Press, 1984.

Brower, Robert H. and Earl Miner. *Japanese Court Poetry*. Stanford: Stanford University Press, 1961.

Bruner, Edward M., ed. *Text, Play, and Story: The Construction and Reconstruction of Self and Society*. Washington, D.C.: The American Ethnological Society, 1985.

Bynum, David E. *The Daemon in the Woods: A Study of Oral Narrative Patterns*. Center for the Study of Oral Literature. Cambridge, Mass.: Harvard University Press, 1978.

Canary, Robert H., and Henry Kozicki, eds. *The Writing of History: Literary Form and Historical Understanding*. Madison: University of Wisconsin Press, 1978.

Caraveli, Anna. "The Song Beyond the Song: Aesthetics and Social Interaction in Greek Folksong." *Journal of American Folklore* 95, no. 376 (April–June 1982): 129–158.

————. "The Bitter Wounding: The Lament as Social Protest in Rural Greece." In *Gender and Power in Rural Greece*, edited by Jill Dubisch, pp. 169–194. Princeton: Princeton University Press, 1986.

Caraveli-Chaves, Anna. "Bridge Between Worlds: The Greek Women's Lament as Communicative Event." *Journal of American Folklore* 93, no. 368 (April–June 1980): 129–157.

Charlot, John. *The Hawaiian Poetry of Religion and Politics: Some Religio-Political Concepts in Postcontact Literature*. Institute for Polynesian Studies Monograph No. 5. Laie: University of Hawaii Press, 1985.

Cranston, Edwin A. "Water Plant Images in the *Man'yōshū*." *Harvard Journal of Asiatic Studies* 31 (1971): 137–178.

————. "Five Poetic Sequences from the *Man'yōshū*." *Journal of the Association of Teachers of Japanese* 13 (1978): 5–40.

————. "The Ramifying Vein: An Impression of Leaves—A Review of Levy's Translation of the *Man'yōshū*." *Journal of Japanese Studies* 9 (Winter 1983): 97–138.

Crocker, J. C. "The Mirrored Self: Identity and Ritual Inversion Among the Eastern Bororo." *Ethnology* 16, no. 2 (1977): 129–145.

Danforth, Loring M. *The Death Rituals of Rural Greece*. Princeton: Princeton University Press, 1982.

Doe, Paula. *A Warbler's Song in the Dusk: The Life and Work of Ōtomo Yakamochi (718–785)*. Berkeley: University of California Press, 1982.

Doi Kōchi. *Kodai densetsu to bungaku*. Vol. 2 of *Doi Kōchi chosakushū*. Tokyo: Iwanami Shoten, 1977.

Dorson, Richard M., ed. *Studies in Japanese Folklore*. New York: Arno Press, 1980.

Earhart, H. Byron. *Japanese Religion: Unity and Diversity*. 3d ed. Belmont, Calif.: Wadsworth Publishing Co., 1982.

Ebersole, Gary L. "The Religio-Aesthetic Complex in *Manyōshū* Poetry with Special Emphasis on Hitomaro's *Aki no no* Sequence." *History of Religions* 23 (August 1983): 18–36.

————. "The Buddhist Ritual Use of Linked Poetry in Medieval Japan." *The Eastern Buddhist* n.s. 16, no. 2 (Autumn 1983): 50–71.

Eco, Umberto. *The Role of the Reader: Explorations in the Semiotics of Texts*. Bloomington: Indiana University Press, 1979.

Eliade, Mircea. *Shamanism: Archaic Techniques of Ecstasy*. Princeton: Princeton University Press, 1964.

————. "The 'God Who Binds' and the Symbolism of Knots." In his *Images and Symbols: Studies in Religious Symbolism*, pp. 92–124. New York: Sheed and Ward, 1969.

Elias, Norbert. *The Court Society*. Trans. Edmund Jephcott. Oxford: Basil Blackwell, 1983.

Ellwood, Robert S. "The Saigū: Princess and Priestess." *History of Religions* 7 (August 1967): 35–60.

————. "Harvest and Renewal at the Grand Shrine of Ise." *Numen* 15 (November 1968): 165–190.

————. *The Feast of Kingship: Accession Ceremonies in Ancient Japan*. Tokyo: Sophia University Press, 1973.

————. "A Cargo Cult in Seventh-Century Japan." *History of Religions* 23 (February 1984): 222–239.

————. "Patriarchal Revolution in Ancient Japan: Episodes from the *Nihonshoki* Sujin Chronicle." Paper delivered at the Annual Meeting of the American Academy of Religion, Anaheim, California, November 24, 1985.

Fardon, Richard, ed. *Power and Knowledge: Anthropological and Sociological Approaches*. Edinburgh: Scottish Academic Press, 1985.

Feld, Steven. *Sound and Sentiment: Birds, Weeping, Poetics, and Song in Kaluli Expression*. Philadelphia: University of Pennsylvania Press, 1982.

Finnegan, Ruth. *Oral Literature in Africa*. Oxford: Clarendon Press, 1970.

————. *Oral Poetry: Its Nature, Significance, and Social Context*. Cambridge: Cambridge University Press, 1977.

Foucault, Michel. *La volonté de savoir*. London: Lane, 1978.

————. *Power/Knowledge: Selected Interviews and Other Writings, 1972–1977*. Translated and edited by Colin Gordon. Brighton, Sussex: Harvester Press, 1980.

Frank, Bernard, ed. *Mélanges Offerts à M. Charles Haguenauer*. Paris: Collège de France, 1980.

Furuhashi Nobutaka. "Man'yō tanka no hyōgen kōzo—kōro shinin uta no baai." *Kokugo to kokubungaku* 59, no. 9 (September 1982): 13–29.

Gearhart, Suzanne. *The Open Boundary of History and Fiction: A Critical Approach to the French Enlightenment*. Princeton: Princeton University Press, 1984.

Geertz, Clifford. *The Interpretation of Cultures*. New York: Basic Books, 1973.

———. *Negara: The Theatre State of Nineteenth-Century Bali*. Princeton: Princeton University Press, 1980.

———. *Local Knowledge: Further Essays in Interpretive Anthropology*. New York: Basic Books, 1983.

Giesey, R. E. *The Royal Funeral Ceremony in Renaissance France*. Geneva: Librairie E. Droz, 1960.

Goffman, Irving. *Frame Analysis: An Essay on the Organization of Experience*. Boston: Northeastern University Press, 1986. (Originally published by Harper and Row, 1974)

Goody, Jack. *The Domestication of the Savage Mind*. Cambridge: Cambridge University Press, 1977.

———. *The Interface Between the Written and the Oral*. Cambridge: Cambridge University Press, 1987.

———, and Ian P. Watt. "The Consequences of Literacy." *Comparative Studies in Society and History* 5 (1962–1963): 304–345.

Guss, David M. "Keeping It Oral: A Yekuana Ethnology." *American Ethnologist* 13 (August 1986): 413–429.

Haguenauer, M. C. "La danse rituelle dans la cérémonie du chinkonsai." *Journal Asiatique* (April–June 1930): 300–350.

Handelman, Don. "Rites of the Living, Transformations of the Dead." *Reviews in Anthropology* 12 (Summer 1985): 220–231.

Hashimoto Tatsuo. "Hitomaro saku 'Hatsusebe no himemiko Osakabe no miko uta' no kō." *Man'yō* 64 (July 1967): 11–20.

———. "Me oto no naki: Man'yō tobu uta to Hitomaro." *Kokubungaku: kaishaku to kanshō* 35, no. 7 (July 1970): 65–72.

Hertz, Robert. *Death and the Right Hand*. Trans. Rodney and C. Needham. New York: Free Press, 1960.

Herzfeld, Michael. "Performative Categories and Symbols of Passage in Rural Greece." *Journal of American Folklore* 94, no. 371 (January–March 1981): 44–57.

Hintermeyer, Pascal. *Politiques de la mort: tirées du Concours de l'Institut, Germinal au VIII Vendemiaire au IX*. Paris: Payôt, 1981.

Hirayakata Hideko. "Shima no miya no tonerira banka no kōsei." *Man'yō* 116 (December 1983): 31–45.

Hisamatsu Sen'ichi. *Kodai shiika ni okeru kami no gainen* ["Concepts of 'Kami' in Japanese Ancient Songs and Poems"]. Tokyo: Daiichi Shōbō, 1967.

Honko, Lauri. "Balto-Finnic Lament Poetry." *Studia Fennica* 17 (1974): 9–61.

Hori Ichiro. "Mysterious Visitors from the Harvest to the New Year." In *Studies in Japanese Folklore*, edited by Richard M. Dorson, pp. 76–106. New York: Arno Press, 1980.

———. "*Man'yōshū* ni awareta sōsei to takai-kan reikon-kan ni tsuite." *Nihon shūkyō-shi kenkyū* 2 (1963): 49–93.

———. *Folk Religion in Japan*. Chicago: University of Chicago Press, 1968.

————. *Hori Ichiro chosakushū*. Vol. 8. Tokyo: Miraisha, 1982.

Huntington, Richard, and Peter Metcalf. *Celebrations of Death: The Anthropology of Mortuary Ritual*. Cambridge and New York: Cambridge University Press, 1979.

Imura Tetsuo. "Oyako, kyōdai no naki." *Kokubungaku: kaishaku to kanshō* 35, no. 7 (July 1970): 72–77.

Inaoka Kōji. "Hitomaro no hyōgen ito: Kawashima banka to Kibi no Tsu uneme banka." *Bungaku, gogaku* 93 (1982): 1–13.

Inoue Mitsusada. *Shinwa kara rekishi e*. Vol. 1 of *Nihon no rekishi*. Tokyo: Chūō Kōronsha, 1965.

————. "The *Ritsuryō* System in Japan." *Acta Asiatica* 31 (1977): 83–112.

Inoue Tatsuo. *Kodai ōken to kataribe*. Tokyo: Kyōikusha, 1979.

Isogai Masayoshi. "Uneme to miko." In *Nihon josei no rekishi*, edited by Tsubota Itsuo. Vol. 1. Tokyo: Atatsuki kyōiku tosho, 1977.

Itō Haku. "Hensha no ito: *Man'yōshū* maki ichi no baai." *Kokugo kokubun* 27, no. 10 (October 1958): 63–74.

————. "Man'yōjin to kotodama." In *Man'yōshū kōza*, edited by Hisamatsu Senichi. Vol. 3: *Gengo to hyōgen*, pp. 46–63. Tokyo: Yuseidō, 1973.

————. "Banka no sekai." *Kokubungaku: kaishaku to kanshō* 35, no. 7 (July 1975): 10–25.

————. *Man'yōshū no kajin to sakuhin*. 2 vols. (*Kodai wakashi kenkyū*, vols. 3 and 4.) Tokyo: Hanawa Shobō, 1975.

———— and Hashimoto Tatsuo, eds. *Man'yōshū monogatari*. Tokyo: Yuhikaku Bukkusu, 1977.

Iwahashi Koyata. "Temmu tennō to *Kojiki*." *Kokugakuin zasshi* 63, no. 9 (September 1962): 50ff.

Iwashita Takehiko. "Hitomaro no Yoshino sanka shiron." *Kokugo to kokubungaku* 59, no. 11 (November 1982): 42–51.

Jain, Ravindra, ed. *Text and Context: The Social Anthropology of Tradition*. Association of Social Anthropologists Essays in Social Anthropology, vol. 2. Philadelphia: Institute for the Study of Human Issues, 1977.

Jauss, Hans Robert. *Towards an Aesthetic of Reception*. Minneapolis: University of Minnesota Press, 1982.

Kamihori Shinobu. "Ōku no himemiko to Ōtsu no mikoto." *Man'yō* 54 (January 1965): 13–29.

Kamstra, J. H. *Encounter or Syncretism: The Initial Growth of Japanese Buddhism*. Leiden: E. J. Brill, 1967.

Kantorowicz, Ernst. *The King's Two Bodies: A Study in Medieval Political Theory*. Princeton: Princeton University Press, 1957.

Kasahara Kazuo and Ogiri Junko, eds. *Iki-zama, shini-zama—Nihon minshū shinkōshi*. Vol. 178 of the *Rekishi Shinsho*. Tokyo: Kyōikusha, 1979.

Katsura Yoshihisa. *Mizu to hi no denshō*. Tokyo: Miyoi Shobō, 1978.

Kawakami Tomiyoshi. *Man'yō kajin no kenkyū*. Tokyo: Ōfusha, 1983.

Kawashima Jiro. "Kibi no Tsu no uneme banka dokukai no hitotsu no kokoromi." *Man'yō* 114 (July 1983): 16–34.

Keene, Donald. "The *Kojiki* as Literature." *Transactions of the Asiatic Society of Japan*, 3d series, 18 (July 1983): 99–132.

Kelsey, W. Michael. "The Raging Deity in Japanese Mythology." *Asian Folklore Studies* 40, no. 2 (1981): 213–236.

Kertzer, David I. *Ritual, Politics, and Power*. New Haven: Yale University Press, 1988.

Kidder, J. Edward, Jr. *Japan Before Buddhism*. Rev. ed. New York: Frederick A. Praeger, 1966. (Originally published 1959)

————. *Early Buddhist Japan*. New York: Praeger Publishers, 1972.

Kikuchi Takeo. "Banka-ron." Parts 3 and 4. *Kokubungaku kenkyū* 57, no. 10 (October 1975): 1–9; 64, no. 2 (February 1978): 12–21.

————. "Hinkyū girei to niiname." *Kokubungaku kenkyū* 73, no. 3 (March 1981): 12–21.

————. "Banka to shinwa: Aki no no no uta o megutte." *Kokubungaku kenkyū* 85, no. 3 (March 1985): 20–28.

Kimura Ryūshi. *Kiki ronkō*. Tokyo: Kasama Shoin, 1977.

Kishi Toshio. "Man'yō uta no rekishi-teki haikei." *Bungaku* 39, no. 9 (September 1971): 74–87.

Kitagawa, Joseph M. *Religion in Japanese History*. New York: Columbia University Press, 1966.

————. "The Japanese *Kokutai* (National Community): History and Myth." *History of Religions* 13 (February 1974): 209–226.

————. "Reality and Illusion: Some Characteristics of the Early Japanese World of Meaning." *Journal of the Oriental Society of Australia* 11 (1976): 3–18.

————. "A Past of Things Present: Notes on Major Motifs in Early Japanese Religions." *History of Religions* 20 (August–November 1980): 27–42. (Reprinted in *On Understanding Japanese Religion*, pp. 43–58.)

————. *On Understanding Japanese Religion*. Princeton: Princeton University Press, 1987.

Kobayashi Shigemi. "Kagosaka, Oshikuma ōkimi monogatari: 'kuma' no geinō to 'kazuku tori' no geiyō." *Nihon kayō kenkyū*, no. 5 (October 1967): 6–13.

Kobayashi Yoshinori. "The *Kun* Readings of the *Kojiki*." *Acta Asiatica* 46 (1984): 62–84.

Kobayashi Yukio, Ikeda Yasaburo, and Kadokawa Gen'yoshi, eds. *Kami to kami o matsuru mono*. Vol. 1 of *Nihon bungaku no rekishi*. Tokyo: Kadokawa Shoten, 1967.

Konishi Jin'ichi. *A History of Japanese Literature*. Vol. 1: *The Archaic and Ancient Ages*. Translated by Aileen Gatten and Nicholas Teele. Princeton: Princeton University Press, 1984.

Kume Tsunetami. "Man'yō kajin no shi." *Kokubungaku: kaishaku to kanshō* 35, no. 7 (July 1970): 92–98.

Kuramori Seiji. "*Man'yōshū* to girei bunka." *Kokugakuin zasshi* 17, no. 11 (November 1967): 61–72.

Kurano Kenji. "Kataribe to *Kojiki*, fudoki." *Kokubungaku: kaishaku to kanshō* 29, no. 1 (January 1964): 45–50.

———— and Takeda Yūkichi, eds. *Kojiki, Norito* (NKBT, Vol. 1). Tokyo: Iwanami Shoten, 1958.

Kuratsuka Akiko. *Fujo no bunka*. Tokyo: Heibonsha, 1979.

Kure Tetsuo. "Mogari no miya no genkei." *Kodai bungaku* 18 (1979): 48–54.

Kuroda Toshio. *New Light on Early and Medieval Japanese Historiography*. Translated by John A.

Harrison. University of Florida Monographs, Social Sciences, no. 4. Gainesville: University of Florida Press, 1959.

Kurtz, D. C., and J. Broadman. *Greek Burial Customs*. London: Thames and Hudson, 1971.

Ledyard, Gari. "Galloping Along with the Horseriders: Looking for the Founders of Japan." *Journal of Japanese Studies* 1 (1974): 217–254.

Lévi-Strauss, Claude. *Tristes Tropiques*. New York: Atheneum, 1970.

Levy, Ian Hideo, trans. *The Ten Thousand Leaves*. Vol. 1. Princeton: Princeton University Press, 1981.

————. *Hitomaro and the Birth of Japanese Lyricism*. Princeton: Princeton University Press, 1984.

Lewis, I. M., ed. *Symbols and Sentiments: Cross-cultural Studies in Symbolism*. London: Academic Press, 1977.

Lopatin, I. *The Cult of the Dead Among the Natives of the Amur Basin*. The Hague: Mouton, 1960.

Lord, Albert B. *The Singer of Tales*. Cambridge, Mass.: Harvard University Press, 1960.

Luckert, Karl. *The Navaho Rainbow Bridge Religion*. Flagstaff: Museum of Northern Arizona, 1977.

MacCormack, Sabine G. *Art and Ceremony in Late Antiquity*. Berkeley: University of California Press, 1981.

Maruyama Masao. "Rekishi ishiki no kiso." In his *Rekishi shisōshū* Tokyo: Chikuma Shobō, 1972.

Masuda Katsumi. "Bungakushi jō no *Kojiki*." *Bungaku* 48, no. 5 (May 1980): 1–9.

Masuda Seiichi. *Hanawa to kodaishi*. Tokyo: Shinchōsha, 1976.

Matsudaira Narimitsu. "The Concept of 'Tamashii' in Japan." In *Studies in Japanese Folklore*, edited by Richard M. Dorson, pp. 181–197. New York: Arno Press, 1980.

Matsumae Takeshi. "Taiyō no fune to tokoyo-shinkō." *Kokugakuin zasshi* 62, nos. 2–3 (February–March 1961): 23–43.

————. "Amaterasu-mi-tama no kami kō." *Kokugakuin zasshi* 62, no. 10 (October 1961): 49–55.

————. "The Heavenly Rock-Grotto Myth and the Chinkonsai Ceremony." *Asian Folklore Studies* 39, no. 2 (1980): 9–22.

————, ed. *Tenchi kaibyaku to kuni umi shinwa no kōzō*. Vol. 3 of *Kōza Nihon no shinwa*. Tokyo: Yūseidō, 1976.

Matsunaga, Alicia. "The Land of Natural Affirmation: Pre-Buddhist Japan." *Monumenta Nipponica* 21, nos. 1–2 (August–November 1966): 203–209.

Matsunaga, R., and Alicia Matsunaga. *The Buddhist Philosophy of Assimilation*. Tokyo: Sophia University Press, 1967.

Miller, Alan L. "Ritsuryō Japan: The State as Liturgical Community." *History of Religions* 11 (August 1971): 98–124.

————. "*Ame No Miso-Ori Me* (The Heavenly Weaving Maiden): The Cosmic Weaver in Early Shinto Myth and Ritual." *History of Religions* 24 (August 1984): 27–48.

Miller, Richard J. *Ancient Japanese Nobility: The Kabane Ranking System*. Berkeley and Los Angeles: University of California Press, 1974.

Miller, Roy Andrew. "The 'Spirit' of the Japanese Language." *Journal of Japanese Studies* 3 (Summer 1977): 251–298.

Miner, Earl, ed. *Principles of Classical Japanese Literature*. Princeton: Princeton University Press, 1985.

Miner, Earl, Hiroko Odagiri, and Robert E. Morrell. *The Princeton Companion to Classical Japanese Literature*. Princeton: Princeton University Press, 1985.

Misaki Hisashi. "Asuka no miko banka shiron." *Man'yō* 90 (December 1975): 48–62.

———. "Asuka no himemiko no araki no miya shiron." *Bungaku, gogaku* 93 (1982): 14–27.

———. "Kibi no Tsu no Uneme banka shiron—Hitomaro banka to hanashimono." *Kokugo to kokubungaku* 59, no. 11 (November 1982): 52–62.

Mogami Takayoshi. "The Double-Grave System." In *Studies in Japanese Folklore*, edited by Richard M. Dorson, pp. 167–180. New York: Arno Press, 1980.

Moore, Sally F., and Barbara G. Myerhoff, eds. *Secular Ritual*. Assen/Amsterdam: Van Gorcum, 1977.

Mori Asao. "Kakinomoto Hitomaro no jikan to saishiki—Aki no jūryō uta o megutte." In *Kanshō Nihon koten bungaku*, edited by Nakanishi Susumu. Vol. 3: *Man'yōshū*, pp. 357–365. Tokyo: Kadokawa Shoten, 1976.

———. "Ama kudaru Temmu." *Kokubungaku kenkyū* 67 (March 1979): 10–18.

Morishige Satoshi. *Buntai no ronri*. Tokyo: Kazama Shobō, 1967.

Morris, Ivan. *The Nobility of Failure: Tragic Heroes in the History of Japan*. New York: Meridian, 1975.

Nagafuji Yasushi. *Kodai Nihon bungaku to jikan-ishiki*. Tokyo: Miraisha, 1980.

Nakagawa Yukihiro. "Butsuzō to busshiki saikai to: Watase Masatada-shi *Kakinomoto Hitomaro kenkyū: Shima no miya no bungaku* o yomu." *Man'yō* 101 (July 1979): 37–46.

Nakanishi Susumu. "Kodai bungaku to mujō-kan." *Kokubungaku: kaishaku to kanshō* 35, no. 7 (July 1970): 105–110.

———. *Man'yō no shi to shijin*. Tokyo: Toyoi Shobō, 1972.

———. *Man'yō no sekai*. Tokyo: Chūō Kōronsha, 1973.

———. "The Spatial Structure of Japanese Myth: The Contact Point Between Life and Death." In *Principles of Classical Japanese Literature*, edited by Earl Miner, pp. 106–129. Princeton: Princeton University Press, 1985.

Naoki Kōjiro. *Jitō tennō*. Tokyo: Yoshikawa Kōbunkan, 1960.

———. "Niiname to daijō no yomi to imi." *Man'yō* 65 (October 1967): 15–24.

Naumann, Nelly. "Yama no kami—die japanische Bergottheit." *Folklore Studies* 22 (1963): 133–366.

———. "*Sakahagi*: The 'Reverse Flaying' of the Heavenly Piebald Horse." *Asian Folklore Studies* 41, no. 1 (1982): 7–38.

Nippon Gakujutsu Shinkōkai, trans. *The Manyōshū*. New York: Columbia University Press, 1964.

Nishimura Sey. "Retrospective Comprehension: Japanese Foretelling Songs." *Asian Folklore Studies* 45, no. 1 (1986): 45–66.

Nishitsunoi Masayoshi. "Geinō no shūkyō-teki igi." *Shūkyō kenkyū* 36, no. 2 (December 1962): 1–24.

————. *Kodai saishi to bungaku*. Tokyo: Chūō Kōronsha, 1966.

Obayashi Taryo. *Nihon shinwa no kigen*. Tokyo: Kadokawa Shoten, 1961.

————. "The Origins of Japanese Mythology." *Acta Asiatica* 31 (1977): 1–23.

————. "The Structure of the Pantheon and the Concept of Sin in Ancient Japan." *Diogenes* 98 (Summer 1977): 117–132.

————. "Niiname ni shutsugen suru ōja—korosareru ōja." *Bungaku* 48, no. 5 (May 1980): 160–169.

Ōguma Kiichirō. *Kodai bungaku no genryū*. Tokyo: Ōfusha, 1977.

————. *Kodai bungaku no dentō*. Tokyo: Kasama Shoin, 1978.

Ohama Itsuhiko. "Jitō tennō wa naze Yoshino e itta ka?" *Kokubungaku: kaishaku to kanshō* 34, no. 2 (February 1969): 60–64.

————. "Chinkon no fumi: Man'yō shiron." *Bungaku* 39, no. 9 (September 1971): 1–11.

Ohata Kiyoshi. *Man'yōbito no shūkyō*. Tokyo: Yamamoto Shoten, 1979.

Okada Hidehiro. *Wakoku no jidai*. Tokyo: Bungei Shunjū, 1976.

Ong, Walter J. *Interfaces of the Word*. Ithaca: Cornell University Press, 1977.

————. *Orality and Literacy: The Technologizing of the Word*. London and New York: Methuen, 1982.

Ōno Sokyō. "Nihon shinwa to niiname no matsuri." *Shintōgaku* 8 (August 1956): 31–41.

Opland, Jeffrey. "*Imbongi Nezibong*: The Xhosa Tribal Poet and the Contemporary Poetic Tradition." *PMLA* 90 (1975): 185–208.

Origuchi Shinobu. *Origuchi Shinobu zenshū*. Vols. 2, 3, 8, 9, 24. Tokyo: Chūō Kōronsha, 1965.

Ozaki Chōō. "Kodai bungaku to jisatsu." *Kokubungaku: kaishaku to kanshō* 35, no. 7 (July 1970): 98–104.

Philippi, Donald L., trans. *Kojiki*. Tokyo: University of Tokyo Press, 1968.

————. *This Wine of Peace, This Wine of Laughter*. New York: Mushina Books, Grossman Publishers, 1968.

————. *Norito: A New Translation of the Ancient Japanese Ritual Prayers*. Tokyo: Sophia University, 1973.

Pollack, David. *The Fracture of Meaning: Japan's Synthesis of China from the Eighth through the Eighteenth Centuries*. Princeton: Princeton University Press, 1986.

Reynolds, Frank E., and Earle Waugh, eds. *Religious Encounters with Death*. University Park: Pennsylvania State University Press, 1976.

Rodd, Laurel Rasplica, trans., with Mary Catherine Henkenius. *Kokinshū: A Collection of Poems Ancient and Modern*. Princeton: Princeton University Press, 1984.

Rutledge, Eric. "The *Man'yōshū* in English." *Harvard Journal of Asiatic Studies* 43 (June 1983): 263–290.

Sahlins, Marshall. *Historical Metaphors and Mythical Realities: Structure in the Early History of the Sandwich Islands Kingdom*. Association for Social Anthropology in Oceania Special Publications, no. 1. Ann Arbor: University of Michigan Press, 1981.

————. *Islands of History*. Chicago: University of Chicago Press, 1985.

Saigō Nobutsuna. "Yomi no kuni to ne no kuni—chika no sekai ni tsuite." *Bungaku* 39, no. 11 (November 1971): 19–35.

———. *Shinwa to kokka: kodai ronshū*. Tokyo: Heibonsha, 1977.

Saito Yasuki. "Kunimi no genryū." *Nihon bungei kenkyū* 37, no. 3 (October 1985): 20–33.

Sakamoto Kazuko. "Nihon shinwa ni okeru sōsō girei." In *Tenchi kaibyaku to kuni umi shinwa no kōzō*, edited by Matsumae Takeshi, pp. 163–183. Vol. 3 of *Kōza Nihon no shinwa*. Tokyo: Yūseidō, 1976.

Sakamoto Tarō, Ienaga Saburō, Inoue Mitsusada, and Ōno Susumu, eds. *Nihonshoki* (NKBT, Vols. 67 and 68). Tokyo: Iwanami Shoten, 1965, 1967.

Sakashita Keihachi. "Banka no hōhō: Yamato no ōkisaki no tennō banka." *Kokubungaku: kaishaku to kyōzai no kenkyū* 28, no. 7 (May 1983): 112–116.

Sakurai Mitsuru. "Kōro shijin uta to jōshi aishō uta no nagare." *Kokubungaku: kaishaku to kanshō* 35, no. 7 (July 1970): 42–49.

———. *Man'yōbito no dōkei: minzoku to bungei no ronri*. Tokyo: Ōfusha, 1977.

———. *Man'yōshū no fūdo*. Tokyo: Kodansha, 1977.

———. *Kakinomoto Hitomaro-ron*. Tokyo: Ōfusha, 1980.

Sansom, Sir George B. *Japan: A Short Cultural History*. Stanford: Stanford University Press, 1931.

———. *A History of Japan to 1334*. Stanford: Stanford University Press, 1958.

Sarbin, Theodore R., ed. *Narrative Psychology: The Storied Nature of Human Conduct*. New York: Praeger Publishers, 1986.

Sasaya Ryōzō. "Musubi-gami no shinkō." *Kokugakuin zasshi* 64, nos. 8–9 (August–September 1963): 83–111.

Shils, Edward. *Center and Periphery*. Chicago: University of Chicago Press, 1967.

Shiraishi Mitsukuni. *Norito no kenkyū*. Tokyo: Shibundō, 1941.

Shirakawa Shizuka. *Shoki Man'yō-ron*. Tokyo: Chūō Kōronsha, 1979.

Smith, Jonathan Z. *Map Is Not Territory: Studies in the History of Religions*. Leiden: E. J. Brill, 1978.

Snellen, J. B., trans. "Shoku Nihongi, Chronicles of Japan, Continued from 687–791 A.D." *Transactions of the Asiatic Society of Japan*, 2d series, 11 (1934): 151–239; 14 (1937): 209–278.

Spear, Thomas T. "Oral Traditions: Whose History?" *History in Africa* 8 (1981): 165–181.

Starkey, David. "Representation through Intimacy: A Study in the Symbolism of Monarchy and Court Office in Early-Modern England." In *Symbols and Sentiments: Cross-cultural Studies in Symbolism*, edited by I. M. Lewis. London: Academic Press, 1977.

Sugano Masao. "Tokoyo-yuku shinwa no keisei." *Kokugakuin zasshi* 62, no. 10 (October 1962): 42–48.

Takagi Hiroshi. *Man'yō kyūtei no aikan*. Tokyo: Tokyodō Shuppan, 1977.

Takagi Ichinosuke. *Takagi Ichinsuke zenshū*. Vol. 1. Tokyo: Kōdansha, 1976.

———. Gomi Tomohide, and Ōno Susumu, eds. *Man'yōshū* (NKBT, Vols. 4–7). Tokyo: Iwanami Shoten, 1957–1965.

Takasaki Masahide. "Kojiki-den shoron." *Kokugakuin zasshi* 63, no. 9 (September 1962): 4–22.

————. *Man'yōshū sōkō*. Vol. 3 of *Takasaki Masahide chosakushū*. Tokyo: Ōfusha, 1971.

Takiguchi Yasuki. "*Man'yōshū* maki ichi Yoshino sanka no keifu." *Kodai bungaku* 19 (1980): 77–89.

Tamura Yoshirō and Minamoto Ryōen, eds. *Nihon ni okeru sei to shi no shisō*. Tokyo: Yūhikaku, 1977.

Teele, R. E. "Speculations on the Critical Principles Underlying the Editing of the *Man'yōshū*." *Tamkang Review* 7 (October 1976): 1–16.

Terada Junko. "Nukata-ō 'Miwa yama' no uta o megutte." *Kokubungaku kenkyū*, no. 67 (March 1979): 1–9.

Toyama Ichiro. "Hinamishi mikoto banka ni okeru Tenji tennō no keishō." *Kokugo kokubun* 55, no. 5 (May 1986): 36–51.

Tsuchihashi Yutaka. "Kunimi uta no *Man'yō* ni okeru tenkai." *Kokugo kokubun* 27, no. 10 (October 1958): 24–37.

————. " 'Miru' koto no tama-furi-teki ishiki." *Man'yō* 39 (April 1961).

————. "Jōdai no saishiki to uta no jutō." *Kokubungaku: kaishaku to kanshō* 29, no. 1 (January 1964): 26–34.

————. *Kodai kayō to girei no kenkyū*. Tokyo: Iwanami Shoten, 1965.

————. *Kodai kayō zenchushaku—Nihonshoki-hen*. Tokyo: Kadokawa Shoten, 1976.

————. *Kodai kayō zenchushaku—Kojiki-hen*. Tokyo: Kadokawa Shoten, 1983.

————. "Hitomaro to Iwanohime no ōkisaki no uta." *Bungaku* 52, no. 8 (August 1984): 1–11.

————, and Konishi Jin'ichi, eds. *Kodai kayō shū* (NKBT, Vol. 3). Tokyo: Iwanami Shoten, 1957.

Tsuda Sōkichi. *Jindaishi no kenkyū*. Tokyo: Iwanami Shoten, 1924.

Tsunoda Ryusaku, trans. *Japan in Chinese Dynastic Histories*. South Pasadena: Perkins, 1951.

Tsunoji Naoichi. "Banka shō." *Kokubungaku: kaishaku to kanshō* 35, no. 7 (July 1970): 117–131.

Tuan, Yi-Fu. *Space and Place: The Perspective of Experience*. Minneapolis: University of Minnesota Press, 1977.

Turner, Terence. "Narrative Structure and Mythopoesis: A Critique and Reformulation of the Structuralist Concepts of Myth, Narrative, and Poetics." *Arethusa* 10 (1977): 103–163.

Turner, Victor. *The Ritual Process*. Chicago: Aldine, 1969.

————. *Dramas, Fields, and Metaphors: Symbolic Action in Human Society*. Ithaca: Cornell University Press, 1974.

Ueda Masaaki. "Sōsō girei to sekai kanrin." *Kokubungaku: kaishaku to kanshō* 35, no. 7 (July 1970): 111–116.

Uegaki Setsuya. "Shi ni yuku hitobito no naki." *Kokubungaku: kaishaku to kanshō* 35, no. 7 (July 1970): 51–56.

Ueno Satoshi. "Hitomaro no Yoshino sanka no kōsō to hyōgen." *Kokubungaku kenkyū* 74 (June 1981): 1–12.

————. "Takechi ōji banka no hōhō." *Kokubungaku kenkyū* 80 (June 1983): 1–11.

Umehara Takeshi. "Suitei no uta." *Subaru* 12 (1973): 270–324.

————. *Koten bungaku no naka no joryū kajin.* Tokyo: Kyōiku Shuppan Senta, 1977.

————. *Umehara Takeshi zen taiwa.* Tokyo: Shueisha, 1977.

Van Gennep, Arnold. *The Rites of Passage.* Chicago: University of Chicago Press, 1960.

Varley, Paul. *Japanese Culture.* 3d ed. Honolulu: University of Hawaii Press, 1984.

Wada Shigeki. "Mogari no kiso-teki kōsatsu." *Shirin* 52, no. 5 (September 1969): 32–90.

Wakamori Taro et al. *Jimbutsu Nihon no rekishi.* Vol. 1: *Asuka no hika.* Tokyo: Shōgakukan, 1974.

Waldman, Marilyn Robinson. "Tradition as a Modality of Change: Islamic Examples." *History of Religions* 25 (May 1986): 318–340.

Watase Masatada. "Hitomaro hinkyū banka no tōjō: sono uta no ba o megutte." *Kokubungaku: kaishaku to kanshō* 35, no. 7 (July 1970): 32–41.

————. *Kakinomoto Hitomaro kenkyū.* 3 vols. Tokyo: Ōfusha, 1976.

Watkins, Mary M. *Invisible Guests: The Development of Imaginal Dialogues.* Hillsdale, N.J.: Analytic Press, 1986.

Watson, Burton, trans. *Japanese Literature in Chinese.* Vol. 1. New York: Columbia University Press, 1975.

Wechsler, Howard J. *Offerings of Jade and Silk: Ritual and Symbol in the Legitimation of the T'ang Dynasty.* New Haven: Yale University Press, 1985.

Weimann, Robert. *Structure and Society in Literary History.* Expanded ed. Baltimore: Johns Hopkins University Press, 1984. (Originally published 1976)

White, Hayden. *Metahistory: The Historical Imagination in Nineteenth-Century Europe.* Baltimore: Johns Hopkins University Press, 1973.

Yamaji Heishiro. "Tenji jū-nen jūni-gatsu no dōyō ni tsuite." In *Wakabungaku no sekai*, edited by Wakabungaku Kenkyūkai. Tokyo: Kasama Shoin, 1973.

Yamakami Izumo. "Wazauta no seiritsu to keishō." *Geinōshi kenkyū* (April 1965): 17–45.

————. *Miko no rekishi.* Tokyo: Yuzankaku Shuppan, 1973.

Yamamoto Kenkichi. *Kakinomoto no Hitomaro.* Tokyo: Kōdansha, 1968.

Yanagita Kunio. *Teihon Yanagita Kunio shū.* 36 vols. Tokyo: Chikūma Shobō, 1972–1974, 1977–1979.

Yanai Kyūsaku. *Ama no iwato shinwa no kenkyū.* Tokyo: Ōfusha, 1977.

Yokoi Hiroshi. "Banka no hassō to hyōgen." *Kokubungaku: kaishaku to kanshō* 35, no. 7 (July 1970): 78–84.

Yoshida Yoshitaka. "Omoi kuni uta no tenkai." *Bungaku* 16, no. 7 (July 1948): 1–8.

————. "Takechi banka-ron." *Man'yō* 51 (April 1964): 1–12.

————. "Temmu hinkyū no bungakushi-teki igi." *Kokugo to kokubungaku* 488 (November 1964): 13–24.

————. "Kiki sōka to Man'yō banka no aida." *Kokubungaku: kaishaku to kanshō* 35, no. 7 (July 1970): 26–32.

————. "Ōtsu ōji-ron—Temmu chō no seisō to *kudeta* ni kanren shite." *Bungaku* 40, no. 9 (September 1972): 19–40.

————. "Kakinomoto Hitomaro ni okeru Jitō chō josetsu." *Bungaku* 50, no. 9 (September 1982): 79–99.

————. "Yoshino sanka to Jitō chō." *Kokubungaku: kaishaku to kyozai no kenkyū* 28, no. 7 (May 1983): 122–127.

Yoshii Iwao. "Yamato-takeru no mikoto monogatari to juka—sono sōka ni tsuite no ichi kasetsu." *Kokugo kokubun* 27, no. 10 (October 1958): 52–62.

————. "Hi-chū shussan narabi ni Umi-sachi, Yama-sachi shinwa no tennō shinwa e no kyūshu ni tsuite." *Man'yō* 61 (October 1966): 33–55.

————. "Toneri no naki." *Kokubungaku: kaishaku to kanshō* 35, no. 7 (July 1970): 57–65.

————. *Yamato-takeru.* Tokyo: Gakuseisha, 1977.

Yoshinaga Noboru. *Man'yō—bungaku to rekishi no aida.* Osaka: Sōgensha, 1967.

Yukawa Hisamitsu. "Tenji banka-gun no ron." *Kodai bungaku* 20 (1981): 89–102.

Index of
Man'yōshū Poems Cited

Index